THE HISTORY OF
HIGHER EDUCATION

THE HISTORY OF HIGHER EDUCATION

Major Themes in Education

Edited by
Roy Lowe

Volume II
The nature of the university

Routledge
Taylor & Francis Group

LONDON AND NEW YORK

First published 2009
by Routledge
2 Park Square, Milton Park, Abingdon, Oxon, OX14 4RN, UK

Simultaneously published in the USA and Canada
by Routledge
270 Madison Avenue, New York, NY 10016

Routledge is an imprint of the Taylor & Francis Group, an informa business

Typeset in 10/12pt Times NR MT by Graphicraft Limited, Hong Kong
Printed and bound in Great Britain by
MPG Books Ltd., Bodmin, Cornwall

British Library Cataloguing in Publication Data
A catalogue record for this book is available from the British Library

Library of Congress Cataloging-in-Publication Data
The history of higher education : major themes in education / edited by Roy Lowe.
p. cm.
Includes bibliographical references and index.
ISBN 978-0-415-37854-3 (set) – ISBN 978-0-415-38469-8 (vol. 1, hardback) –
ISBN 978-0-415-38470-4 (vol. 2, hardback) – ISBN 978-0-415-38471-1
(vol. 3, hardback) – ISBN 978-0-415-38472-8 (vol. 4, hardback) –
ISBN 978-0-415-38473-5 (vol. 5, hardback)   1. Education, Higher--History.
I. Lowe, Roy.
LA173.H584 2008
378.09–dc22
2008008884

ISBN10: 0-415-37854-0 (Set)
ISBN10: 0-415-38470-2 (Volume II)

ISBN13: 978-0-415-37854-3 (Set)
ISBN13: 978-0-415-38470-4 (Volume II)

Publisher's Note

References within each chapter are as they appear in the original
complete work.

CONTENTS

CONTENTS

ACKNOWLEDGEMENTS

The publishers would like to thank the following for permission to reprint their material:

Taylor & Francis for permission to reprint A. B. Cobban, 'Concept of a University', from *The Medieval Universities: Their Development and Organization*, A. B. Cobban, Copyright © 1975 Methuen, London. Reproduced by permission of Taylor & Francis Books UK.

Oxford University Press for permission to reprint Hastings Rashdall, 'What is a University?', in Hastings Rashdall, *The Universities of Europe in the Middle Ages*, ed. F. M. Powicke and A. B. Emden, Oxford University Press, 1936, pp. 1–24. Rashdall's original publication date was 1893.

Sheldon Rothblatt for permission to reprint Sheldon Rothblatt, 'Loss and Gain: John Henry Newman in 2005', in Ann Lavan (ed.), *The University and Society: From Newman to the Market*, Conference proceedings, UCD College of Human Sciences, University College Dublin, 2006, pp. 15–29.

Blackwell Publishing for permission to reprint Cyril Bibby, 'T. H. Huxley's Idea of a University', *Universities Quarterly* (now *Higher Education Quarterly*), Vol. X, 1955–56, Turnstile Press, London, pp. 377–390.

Oxford University Press for permission to reprint Abraham Flexner, 'The Idea of a Modern University', in Abraham Flexner, *Universities: American, English and German*, Oxford University Press, London, 1930, pp. 3–36.

Blackwell Publishing for permission to reprint R. H. Tawney, 'An Experiment in Democratic Education', *The Political Quarterly*, May 1914, pp. 62–84.

SCM-Canterbury Press for permission to reprint Walter Moberley, 'Changing Conceptions of the University's Task', in Sir Walter Moberley, *The Crisis in the University*, SCM Press Ltd, London, 1949, pp. 30–49.

Cambridge University Press and Sheldon Rothblatt for permission to reprint Sheldon Rothblatt, 'The Idea of the Idea of a University and its Antithesis', in Sheldon Rothblatt, *The Modern University and its Discontents*, Cambridge University Press, Cambridge, 1997, pp. 1–49.

Oxford University Press for permission to reprint A. H. Halsey and M. A. Trow, 'The Changing Functions of Universities', in A. H. Halsey and M. A. Trow, *The British Academics*, Faber and Faber, London, 1971, PP. 31–37.

Sheldon Rothblatt and John Donald Publishers (an imprint of Birlinn Ltd.) for permission to reprint Sheldon Rothblatt, 'Federal Universities and multi-campus systems: Britain and the United States since the nineteenth century in J. J. Carter and D. J. Withrington, eds., *Scottish Universities: Distinctiveness and Diversity*, John Donald Publishers, Edinburgh, 1992, pp. 164–187.

'The Idea of a Multiversity', reprinted by permission of the publisher from *The Uses of the University*, fifth edition, by Clark Kerr, pp. 1–34, Cambridge, Mass.: Harvard University Press, Copyright © 1963, 1972, 1982, 1995, 2001 by the President and Fellows of Harvard College.

Oxford University Press for permission to reprint A. H. Halsey, 'Ideas of the University', in A. H. Halsey, *Decline of Donnish Dominion: The British Academic Profession in the Twentieth Century*, Clarendon Press, Oxford, 1995, pp. 23–57 and 369–375.

Taylor & Francis for permission to reprint Harold Silver, 'Pressures and Silences', from *Higher Education and Opinion Making in Twentieth Century England*, Harold Silver, Copyright © 2003 Harold Silver, Reproduced by permission of Taylor & Francis Books UK.

Disclaimer

INTRODUCTION

This second volume brings together well-known and significant statements on the nature of the university, its changing aims and purposes. Questions around the central functions of the universities have been contested over time. The essays assembled here reflect the ways in which the arguments have changed and illustrate the enduring tension between concepts of a university education which see it as being in one sense or another removed from day-to-day concerns and, on the other hand, as being central to technological and scientific advancement.

The collection begins with two essays focused on the medieval antecedents of the modern European universities. First, in Chapter 29 A. B. Cobban explores the question of exactly what was meant by a studium generale, the term most frequently used to define what went on within the late medieval foundations, and this is also a central concern of the second extract. Chapter 30 is taken from the pioneering work by Hastings Rashdall, who places great stress on the examples of Paris, Bologna and Salerno as prototypical universities.

Another of the great voices of the nineteenth century in this field was John Henry Newman, and the extract selected from his *The Idea of a University* is the chapter in which he argues memorably for knowledge to be its own end, for the universities to pursue learning for its own sake (Chapter 31). This proved to be an argument that had massive reverberations during the following century, attracting sympathisers and critics in equal measure. At a notable conference in Dublin in 2005, Sheldon Rothblatt reflected on the more recent resonances of Newman, relating his thinking to recent developments across Europe and in North America and ranging over contemporary discussions of the nature of the university. It seemed very appropriate, therefore, to include this essay as Chapter 32 in this volume. T. H. Huxley was another notable contributor to the nineteenth-century debate on the nature of the university. In a famous lecture, given at Aberdeen in 1976, Huxley spelt out his vision of the ideal university (Chapter 33). This is complemented by a thoughtful essay by Cyril Bibby (Chapter 34), first published in the *Universities Quarterly*, 1955–6, which has been selected to illustrate the ways in which Huxley's thinking evolved over time and how he related to other contemporary commentators.

Chapter 35 is Abraham Flexner's account of 'the idea of a modern university', extracted from his influential book on German, English and American universities, published in 1930, and also widely influential. It stands as an interesting testament to the tensions surrounding the debate on the universities during the interwar years. On the one hand Flexner called for a sensitivity to the ever-increasing demands of science, but he also made clear his aversion to the concept of the university as a home for technological or vocational studies. Almost paradoxically, he did find a role within the academy for medicine and law.

Two essays reflect the increasing involvement of Oxford and Cambridge universities with the wider community during the early twentieth century, and both were written by eminent participants who took time to reflect on what they were about. Albert Mansbridge, who was, of course, the founder of the Workers' Educational Association, had been closely involved in the development of university extension work and in the extract reproduced here from his 1923 book (Chapter 36), he makes the case for a university with a social conscience. R. H. Tawney was the pioneer tutor of the two first university tutorial classes at Rochdale and Longton, and therefore a close collaborator with Mansbridge. His article, taken from the *Political Quarterly*, 1914, is an authoritative account of the first years of this new enterprise and a powerful advocacy of this nascent movement (Chapter 37).

No account of attempts to reform English universities during the twentieth century would be complete without reference to Bruce Truscott and Walter Moberley. Bruce Truscot (the pseudonym of A. E. Peers, a professor of Modern Languages in one of the so-called civic universities) published his book *Red Brick University* in 1943 to generate debate on the role and purposes of these civic universities. The extract reproduced here (Chapter 38) reflects on the ways in which these relatively new urban foundations could, and even should, enshrine the ideals of the ancient universities and whether the constraints of time and place meant that other ends were more appropriate. Similarly, in Chapter 39 Walter Moberley, writing at the end of the 1940s, reflects on the extent to which the ideals of a university education can be preserved in an age of democratisation and collectivisation. Linked with them is the account by H. C. Dent (Chapter 40) of the evolution of the idea of a university from the medieval up to the modern period. This essay reflects thoughtfully on other work done on this theme during the mid-twentieth century.

The extract from Sheldon Rothblatt's *The Modern University and its Discontents* (Chapter 41) has been chosen because it ranges widely over the evolution of the idea of a university, throwing light on the ways in which justifications took on differing forms in Germany, in America and elsewhere and how they were modified over time. Briefer and more succinct, but similarly wide ranging, the opening chapter of Halsey and Trow's exhaustive survey of the British academic profession (Chapter 42), which appeared in 1971, also reflects on the evolution of an ideal. A. H. Halsey, at Oxford, and Martin Trow, at Berkeley, were two of the most astute commentators on academia for many years, and their collaboration and their joint ability to draw on a rich vein of sociological research in both continents resulted in a memorable publication.

Lionel Robbins was one of the architects of the systematisation of higher education in Britain in the decades following the Second World War, and the seminal 1963 Report which famously bears his name is quoted elsewhere in this collection. In 1966 he lectured at the Conference des Recteurs Europeens (whose origins were identified in Chapter 17 by John Blake in Volume I). He used this address (Chapter 43) to reflect on the ways in which pressure of numbers allied to an ever-increasing rate of scientific and technological change were obliging those within the universities to rethink their mission. He argued that increases in scale, resulting in much larger institutions and a reworking of the nature of specialisation were inevitable corollaries of these changes.

Another potent commentator on the postwar university scene was Eric Ashby. The two extracts selected from his work deal, first, with the idea of a university, and, second, with the emergence of mass higher education. In Chapter 44 he reflects on the survival of a particular view of the role of the universities and the ways it had been threatened by recent social change. For him it was essential that the universities retained the power to control, to some degree at least, their redefinition. His second essay (Chapter 45) reflects that of Robbins, predicating a massive increase in the scale of the university as well as a democratisation of the system.

More recently, two of the most insightful commentators on the academy have been Sheldon Rothblatt and Clark Kerr. It is only appropriate that their work is well-represented towards the end of this volume. The emergence of federal universities has been a long-term interest of Rothblatt and in an address to an international audience at Aberdeen in 1992 (Chapter 46) he reflected on the viability of this model and the likely role of multi-campus universities at the end of the twentieth century. In similar vein, Kerr speculated, at roughly the same time, about the emergence of a pluralistic university to serve a pluralistic society (Chapter 47). A second extract from his work, reproduced here as Chapter 48, reflects on the emergence of the multiversity at the end of the twentieth century.

The British counterpoint to Rothblatt's and Kerr's thinking came from A. H. Halsey and Harold Silver. Accordingly, the penultimate extract is taken from Halsey's 1995 book *Decline of Donnish Dominion* (Chapter 49) and represents his thinking on the evolution of the ideal of a university. In conclusion, Chapter 50, the extract from Silver's work, reflects, ominously, that the external voices which drove change in the universities for the first three-quarters of the twentieth century have been silenced by the combined weight of government and bureacratisation. His essay carries the uncomfortable message that the contexts within which discussion of the evolution of higher education take place, and, indeed, the very nature of such discussions, can only be very different in the century which has just begun.

29

CONCEPT OF A UNIVERSITY

A. B. Cobban

Source: A. B. Cobban, *The Medieval Universities: Their Development and Organization*, London: Methuen, 1975, pp. 21–36.

The medieval university was essentially an indigenous product of western Europe. Classical civilization did not produce the equivalent of these privileged corporate associations of masters and students with their statutes, seals and administrative machinery, their fixed curricula and degree procedures.[1] Centres of higher education such as the philosophical schools of Athens, dating from the fourth century B.C.,[2] the law school of Beirut which flourished between the early third and mid-sixth century,[3] or the imperial university of Constantinople, founded in 425 and functioning intermittently until 1453,[4] may have anticipated the medieval universities in some respects, for example in terms of embryonic organization and the emergence of regular courses of study.[5] But collectively the distinguishing features of the medieval university seem to have been nowhere reproduced in previous institutional form; and there does not appear to be any organic continuity between the universities which evolved towards the end of the twelfth century and Greek, Graeco–Roman, Byzantine or Arabic schools. However much the universities may have owed to the impulse of Greek, Roman or Arabic intellectual life their institutional crystallization was a new departure born of the need to enlarge the scope of professional education in an increasingly urbanized society.

Although there may have been no real physical continuity between the universities and the schools of the ancient world, a fictional link was generated in the form of the *translatio studii* whereby the centre of learning was deemed to have passed from Athens to Rome, from Rome to Byzantium and hence to Paris.[6] This notion of the *translatio studii*, which appeared in the Carolingian age, acquired a popular currency with the emergence of the universities which were then seen as the embodiment of the *studium* and, as such, ranking alongside the other two great powers by which Christian society was directed, the spiritual (*Sacerdotium*) and the temporal (*Imperium*).[7]

4

The ideological thesis that the universities were the lineal successors to the Greek, Graeco–Roman and Byzantine schools with respect to the *translatio studii* may be historically unsound, but it probably helped provide propagandist support for the universities in their struggle to establish themselves, in their first period of life, as a quasi-independent order in the community free from undue ecclesiastical or secular control.[8]

The terminology relating to medieval universities and the problems of contemporary definition are still among the more intractable matters surrounding the origins of the universities. The word 'university' has nothing to do with the universality of learning, and it is only by accident that the Latin term *universitas* has given rise to the established nomenclature.[9] For *universitas* was a general word of wide application in the twelfth, thirteenth and fourteenth centuries and was used to denote any kind of aggregate or body of persons with common interests and independent legal status: it indicated a defined group whether a craft guild or a municipal corporation.[10] When employed in an academic context the term referred not to the university as an abstraction, as a complete entity in itself, but to the body of masters and students or of masters and students combined depending upon the organizational type of the particular university. It was not, it seems, until the late fourteenth and fifteenth centuries that *universitas* came into use as a convenient shorthand label applied especially to academic corporations,[11] just as terms like *collegium*, *congregatio* or *corpus* came to acquire similar association with specific groupings in society.

The medieval term which most closely corresponds to our concept of a university is *studium generale*.[12] For most of the thirteenth century this designation appears to have had no precise technical or legal signification. Initially, *studium generale* may have been an entirely descriptive phrase, the *studium* part indicating a school where there were organized facilities for study and *generale* referring neither to the general or universal nature of the subjects taught nor to the number of students involved, but to the ability of the school to attract students from beyond the local region. The extent of the range of attraction which a thirteenth-century school had to exhibit before it would be classified as 'general' is, however, a vexed question to which there is no easy solution. Was it necessary for the school with claims to be 'general' to draw students from another country, or simply from different parts of the same country, or even from a more limited area? Moreover, the term *studium generale* is not much found in the first half of the thirteenth century. The earliest documentary evidence for the use of the term appears to be with reference to the University of Vercelli in 1237.[13] And the first papal enactment which employs *studium generale* seems to be that of Innocent IV of 1244 or 1245 establishing the University of the Court of Rome.[14] In the second half of the thirteenth century the usage is more common, but it is not until the fourteenth century that it acquired a precise juristic meaning and became the normal term to express the abstraction of a fully-fledged university. Throughout the thirteenth century several terms were used with apparently much the same connotation as the currently imprecise *studium generale*, for example *studium universale*,[15] *studium commune*[16] and *studium solempne* (or *solemne, solenne*).[17] But perhaps the alternative term to *studium generale* which was most frequently employed in the thirteenth century was simply *studium*. It was used in the first half of the thirteenth century in both papal and non-papal sources in relation to such centres as Bologna, Paris, Oxford, Palencia, Vercelli, Padua, Naples, Valencia and Toulouse.[18] And *studium* continued to be common throughout the remainder of the century and even beyond.[19] In view of the alternating nature of the terminology it is improbable that there is much distinction to be drawn between *studium* and *studium generale* as used in the thirteenth century, that is to say, before the latter assumed a strict legal meaning.

The *Siete Partidas* (1256–63), the legislative code of Alfonso X of Castile, provides one of the earliest commentaries on the nature of the *studium generale*. Title XXXI,[20] given over to the universities, deals with such matters as the payment of teachers and teaching methods, university discipline, the organization of student life, examinations and the granting of the licence, and jurisdictional affairs. Two basic requirements are here stipulated for *studium generale* status: the school must have masters for each of the seven arts and also for canon and civil law; and a *studium generale* could only be erected by authority of the pope, the emperor, or the king.[21] This attempted definition lacks reference to theology and medicine as superior faculty studies; and the right of a king to confer *studium generale* status in the full ecumenical sense was not to be generally accepted, and was doubtless prompted by the actions of Spanish rulers in founding *studia generalia* without papal or imperial assistance.[22] Later juristic thought classified such foundations as *studia generalia respectu regni* on the grounds that privileges granted to a *studium* by a local ruler had no validity beyond the confines of the kingdom.[23] Although the section on *studium generale* in the *Siete Partidas* is historically important because it is a *rara avis* at this juncture in the thirteenth century and is an early example of secular legislative activity for universities, it furnishes only a partial and presumably Spanish view of *studia generalia* which is not in any way definitive. As one of the few contemporary accounts of the *studium generale* before the late thirteenth and fourteenth centuries the *Siete Partidas* is somewhat disappointing.

Clearly, the conception of *studium generale* was a vague one for most of the thirteenth century, and only towards the end of it was it beginning to achieve a precise legality. Originally, the expression meant no more than a celebrated school which attracted students from a wide area and which could provide teaching, not only in arts, but in at least one of what became the superior faculties in the universities, law (civil and canon), theology or medicine. Facilities of this nature presuppose that the school was capable of maintaining an adequate teaching staff from year to year. In *c*. 1200 only centres such as Bologna, Paris, Oxford and Salerno could sustain teaching in the higher disciplines and, consequently, only these few would have been customarily regarded as 'general'. But with the multiplication of *studia* in Italy and France, moulded on the archetypal universities of Bologna and Paris, it was natural that some of these centres should claim for themselves the status of *studium generale*. It seems that any school could assume 'general' standing, but whether it came to be accepted as such would, in all probability, be decided by the force of custom. Before legal precision was evolved, the final arbiter of whether a school was *generale* as opposed to *particulare* was informed educated opinion.

A wholly new dimension came into being when papal and imperial authority arrogated the right to establish *studia generalia* by specific enactment. The first imperial university, and indeed the first university of all to be erected by a definite act, was founded at Naples in 1224 by the Emperor Frederick II: the earliest papal university was that of Toulouse created by Gregory IX in 1229; and in 1244 or 1245 Innocent IV established a *studium generale* in the papal curia at Rome.[24] These foundations seem to have given birth to the idea that the power to erect *studia generalia* was vested in papal or imperial prerogative.[25] This notion gathered momentum and was accepted doctrine by the fourteenth century. The consequence of this was that the *generale* constituent of the expression *studium generale* was radically transformed. Whereas *generale* had formerly been no more than a descriptive adjunct pointing to the drawing capacity of the school, it had now acquired an ecumenical character conferred by papal or imperial endowment, and especially by the former. If *studia generalia* were to be created artificially and were to derive a universal nature from papal or imperial authority, it became necessary to define more closely the privileges which stemmed from this enhanced but delimited academic situation. And here there was little that was innovatory. As part of their organic growth the earliest universities had evolved a number of *de facto* special privileges, and the most important of these were incorporated as essential ingredients of the status of *studium generale* as defined by fourteenth-century Italian juristic thought from which much of the medieval commentary on university terminology is derived.

In the course of the thirteenth century there were two privileged concepts which, above all, came to be associated with the expression *studium generale*. The more concrete of the two was the right of beneficed clergy to receive the fruits of their benefices while non-resident at a *studium generale* for the purposes of study. Dispensation of ecclesiastics from residence for study in the schools had been granted by the papacy and individual bishops from the twelfth century. In 1207 Innocent III had attempted to limit this privilege to schools of a reputable standard, but did not specify these as *studia generalia*.[26] The bull of Honorius III of 1219, *Super Speculam*, granted non-residence with revenues for five years to holders of prebends and benefices engaged as teachers or students of theology in theological schools.[27] This privilege was not confined to Paris or any other *studium generale*, and presumably applied to all *studia* or *scholae* where theology was taught at a satisfactory level. But in the mid-thirteenth century the canonist Hostiensis (Cardinal Henry of Susa), in his *Summa* on the Decretals, interpreted the non-residence provisions of *Super Speculam* to apply exclusively to a *studium generale* and not to a *studium specialis*,[28] which seems to be synonymous with *studium particulare*. Doubtless the opinion of Hostiensis was coming to reflect a general canonistic view that non-residence with revenues ought to be confined to *studia generalia* as the best safeguard both for the maintenance of theological standards and for the prevention of misuse of ecclesiastical incomes.[29] Cases from the middle years of the thirteenth century indicate that dispensation from residence was, in practice, being closely related to the status of *studium generale*. Innocent IV, in his foundation bull for the university of the papal curia at Rome (1244–5), specifically granted the privilege of non-residence to beneficed clerks.[30] And in 1246 Innocent IV issued a bull granting regents non-residence in the *studium* which the king of Aragon proposed to found at Valencia;[31] while in 1260 Alexander IV recognized as a *studium generale* the school founded at Seville by Alfonso the Wise for the study of Latin and Arabic, and conferred the privilege of non-residence on the students.[32] The schools of Narbonne provide an interesting commentary on this matter of non-residence. In 1247 Innocent IV, petitioned by the archbishop of Narbonne, granted to the teachers and students at Narbonne the same privilege of non-residence enjoyed by 'scolares in studiis generalibus commorantes'.[33] Narbonne was not then a *studium generale*; consequently, the award illustrates both that dispensation from residence was a recognized prerogative of a *studium generale* and that this privilege might be exceptionally conferred on a reputable *studium* even if it were not 'general'. By the fourteenth century the privilege of dispensation from residence for beneficed clergy had become a salient feature of the privileged nature of a *studium generale*.

The second and more theoretical privilege which came to be exclusively associated with the status of *studium generale* was that of the *ius ubique docendi*:[34] that is to say, the right of the holder of a degree from a *studium generale* to teach in any other university without undergoing further examination. This power claimed by a *studium generale* to endow its masters with a teaching licence of universal validity would have established the untrammelled mobility of university teachers, would have made possible a European-wide academic commonwealth which transcended race and provincialism in the collective pursuit and dissemination of learning. Although the concept of the *ius ubique docendi* was perhaps the most important legal attribute of a *studium generale* from the late thirteenth century, and was normally included in the foundation charters of new fourteenth-century universities,[35] the reality was very different, and it is doubtful if it acted as much of a binding force on Europe's medieval universities.

The origin of the *ius ubique docendi* is to be sought ultimately in the monopoly power to grant the teaching licence (*licentia docendi*) which the heads of cathedral schools had exercised within their defined jurisdictional areas from the twelfth century.[36] But the emergence of the universities with their degree-awarding procedures helped to advance the idea that the possessor of a master's or doctor's degree from a *studium generale* carried with it a teaching licence of general application. In the case of the earliest universities this evolved as a prescriptive right: it was a *de facto* privilege which centres such as Bologna and Paris enjoyed because graduates of these celebrated schools were deemed to have a natural superiority over products of lesser *studia*. But when, in 1233, Pope Gregory IX conferred the *ius ubique docendi* on the graduates of the papally-founded University of Toulouse with all the privileges exercised by the Parisian masters,[37] two grades of *ius ubique docendi* were thereby thrown into relief: the customary type of Paris and Bologna and this newly-born artificially-endowed licence of ecumenical validity. In the course of time, a third category appeared, namely the officially conferred *ius ubique docendi* whose application was general but with the exception of named universities; for example, in 1255 Alexander IV awarded the graduates of the *studium generale* at Salamanca the right to teach in all *studia generalia* except Bologna and Paris;[38] and in 1332 John XXII excepted Paris from the terms of the *ius ubique docendi* conferred upon the University of Cahors.[39] From such instances it is clear that the status of *studium generale* was considered to be compatible with a limited right of *ius ubique docendi*.

When the university system came within the orbit of papal and imperial authority there was pressure to place the status of *studium generale* and the *ius ubique docendi* on a more rational basis. This affected the position of *studia generalia* with only customary (*ex consuetudine*) as opposed to documentary claims to 'general' recognition and to the universal teaching licence. In 1289 Pope Nicholas IV formally recognized as a *studium generale* the University of Montpellier which had long been treated as 'general' by custom, and conferred upon its doctors the *ius ubique docendi*.[40] And in 1291–2 two bulls were issued by Nicholas IV which officially bestowed the *ius ubique docendi* upon the old-established universities of Paris and Bologna.[41] In 1306, by a bull of Clement V, Orléans, which had been recognized as a *studium generale* before the mid-thirteenth century (i.e. *ex consuetudine*), was granted all the privileges of the *studium generale* of Toulouse which included the *ius ubique docendi*.[42] In the case of Padua, a confirmation of all its privileges as a *studium generale* was obtained by a bull of Clement VI in 1346.[43] However, this process of rationalization was not entirely complete and not without its anomalies. For example, Oxford seems never to have procured officially the *ius ubique docendi*, although both Edward I and Edward II unsuccessfully petitioned the papacy to have the privilege granted.[44] Likewise, the University of Angers appears to have had no express papal recognition of the *ius ubique docendi* even when, in the fourteenth century, it was widely acknowledged to be a *studium generale*.[45] While these cases point to the inconsistencies in the more centralized university system that was emerging under distant papal and imperial tutelage, it is nevertheless true that by the fourteenth century the *ius ubique docendi* had become one of the cardinal legal hallmarks of the status of *studium generale*, and a school lacking this capacity to confer degrees carrying a teaching licence of wide application was distinguished as a *studium particulare*.[46] It is probable that there were such 'particular' schools in France and Italy employing university graduates to teach beyond an elementary arts level. Some may even have tried to institute graduation machinery, but unless they could base a claim to 'general' standing either upon established custom or on a papally or imperially awarded teaching licence these *studia* would have been classified as 'particular' by fourteenth-century juristic opinion.

It would be misleading to imagine that the *ius ubique docendi* provides a realistic model for the operation of the medieval university system. The ideal of a university commonwealth of teachers moving freely from one position to another among Europe's *studia generalia* is one that was scarcely realized. Although much needs to be discovered about the professional careers of university teachers, there is sufficient evidence to indicate that university particularism tended to prevail against the supranational implications of the *ius ubique docendi*. Here one must remember that the *ius ubique docendi* was an artificially forced concept imposed upon the university world by papal or imperial decree. As such, it was an attempt to circumvent the natural inequalities of *studia generalia* with respect to institutional maturity and degree of community recognition. It was a mechanical contrivance designed to reduce the *studia generalia* to a fictive common denominator. Not surprisingly, the old-established universities were unwilling to implement a system which detracted from their achieved position in the van of higher education. After granting the privileges of Paris, including the *ius ubique docendi*, upon the University of Toulouse in 1233, Gregory IX had to mollify the Parisian masters with the assurance that no interference with their own privileges was intended.[47] The sensitivity of the Paris masters was not misplaced as the Toulouse settlement prefigured the progressive dilution of the monopolistic powers of the earliest universities which inevitably ensued from the multiplication of *studia generalia* invested with the teaching licence of ecumenical validity. Although the old-established universities were pressurized into theoretical conformity by seeking confirmation of the status of *studium generale* and the acquisition of the *ius ubique docendi*, they gave only limited effective support to the projected international academic order.

The principle of the mutual recognition of degrees and the teaching licence broke down even in the case of major universities like Paris and Oxford. In the early fourteenth century something akin to an academic tarriff war raged between these *studia generalia*, each refusing to accept and licence the graduates of the other without fresh examination.[48] And the conflict between Paris and Oxford is only a striking instance of what appears to have been a fairly common phenomenon. Many universities continued to impose examination on graduates from elsewhere before allowing them to teach their own students; for example, Montpellier, Angers and Orléans insisted in the most explicit terms that all potential regent masters from other universities should be subject to examination.[49] As there was no written system of examination at medieval universities, degrees being normally awarded on the twin bases of physical completion of course requirements and a series of private and public oral examinations and exercises of presumably varying severity, there existed few stable criteria by which one university could evaluate the standard attained by a graduate of another without carrying out its own investigation. The *ius ubique docendi* might theoretically impose a uniformity of standard, but this was unreal and appears to have been treated as such. Moreover, as was stressed at the University of Orléans in 1321, the unrestricted immigration of 'foreign' doctors into a university might lead to vitriolic disputes among the teaching masters for the custom of the available students and to the situation whereby some teachers had only a handful of students or none at all.[50] More specifically, financial considerations militated against the implementation of the universal teaching licence on any scale. The growth of salaried lectureships, which date from the thirteenth century in the universities of southern Europe and later spread to those of the north,[51] had two main effects for the operation of the *ius ubique docendi*. Academic mobility tended to be curbed as there was increased financial inducement for teachers to remain for several years in one position: and secondly, when the salaried system became more entrenched, teaching posts were inevitably limited to a minority of graduates. Consequently, the *ius ubique docendi* implications of the mastership or doctorate came for many to be no more than a titular honour. Generally speaking, it may be said that the way in which the universities developed did not set up the conditions for the realization of the *ius ubique docendi*. The university system did not encourage a wandering scholar population *per se*; individuals moved from centre to centre for a definite purpose and not as part of an army in restless quest for knowledge. Indeed, the concept of *ius ubique docendi* is something of a red herring for university history.[52] Although a crucial legal attribute of the rank of *studium generale* from the late thirteenth century, it received only a minimal observance. For circumstances dictated a pattern of academic protectionism rather than free intercourse, and this was the path trodden by the university system of medieval Europe. The relative failure of papal and imperial authority to make the universities prisoners of ecumenical conformity is eloquent testimony of the boisterous individuality that is so marked a feature of university growth in the middle ages.

There was probably no final contemporary agreement as to what exactly constituted a *studium generale*. It was no easy matter to formulate a legal definition which would encompass all the possible permutations involved in this thorny problem. The terminology had emerged piecemeal in the first half of the thirteenth century, had crystallized by 1300, and was given more rigorous legal form in the fourteenth century. Although it would not be possible to present a definitive view of a *studium generale*, even in the fourteenth century, one can underline features which seem to be common to most. In essence, a *studium generale* was a guild organization of masters or students or of masters and students combined, having a high degree of juridical autonomy, the right to elect its own officers, statutory making powers, and a communal seal. It had the drawing strength to attract students from a wide area and, in addition to arts, offered instruction in at least one of the superior faculties of law, theology, or medicine, maintaining a nucleus of regent masters to meet diverse teaching requirements. From the late thirteenth century it seems to have been necessary for a *studium* to have papal or imperial endorsement of its 'general' standing. It may be that occasionally a municipality or ruler purported to found a *studium generale ab initio*, without reference to pope or emperor;[53] but unless, in the fourteenth century, papal or imperial recognition were subsequently obtained, the *studium* would not be received as 'general'. Associated with the status of *studium generale* were a number of privileges, the two most important of which were that of dispensation from residence for beneficed clerks studying or teaching at a *studium generale*, and the theoretical concept of the *ius ubique docendi*, which endowed the university with a prestigious aura but not with much in the way of practical benefit. A *studium generale* might exhibit further privileges, but a clear distinction has to be drawn between those rights which were common to *studia generalia* and those which were additional privileges not vested in the status of *studium generale* itself. Rights common to *studia generalia* cannot by definition embrace their particular relationships with external authorities. The relationships of European *studia* with external bodies, whether episcopal, archiepiscopal, civic, regal or imperial were clearly so diverse that they could not be reduced to a simple formula, and could not be deduced from the general title of *studium generale*. For example, freedom from episcopal or archiepiscopal authority was not a right inherent in the fourteenth-century concept of a *studium generale*; for this, a university required an express papal award.[54]

The documentation arising from the process of rationalization which overtook Europe's universities in the late thirteenth and fourteenth centuries gives an insight into the variety of situations with which the papal and imperial powers had to grapple. If one examines the matter through papal legislation, it is found that papal letters or formal bulls for the erection of *studia generalia* fall into one of at least four categories.[55] They may erect a new *studium generale* where none has existed before;[56] they may found a *studium* on the basis of an older one which has since declined or even disappeared;[57] they may seem to erect a new *studium* without reference to a former

12

one, though it is known that an existing *studium* was flourishing at the time of the papal letter;[58] or lastly, the existence of a *studium generale* is admitted in the preamble of the document which then, on request of the ruler to strengthen it, proceeds to confirm the institution.[59] It is possible that several schools, which had some claim to be regarded as *studia generalia ex consuetudine* in the thirteenth century found themselves victims of selective rationalization and were denied the legal standing of *studium generale*. The schools at Lyons and Rheims may have come within this category.[60] It is difficult to explain their arrested development, but it is well to consider that a number of small schools in France and Italy had been thought of as *studia generalia* either implicitly or explicitly but which, through decline or some other cause, were not regarded later as proper candidates for fully-fledged university status. The existence of such schools must make one wary of thinking of the *studia generalia* of the thirteenth century as embracing only those which ultimately received official standing.

The concept of *studium particulare* was essentially a negative one used normally in contradistinction to *studium generale*. It seems therefore not to be found before the expression *studium generale* gained currency in the third and fourth decades of the thirteenth century: and even in the remainder of the century it is not used with any frequency. The *Siete Partidas* of Alfonso X of Castile (1256–63) stated that an *estudio particular* could be established by any municipal council or bishop whereas an *estudio general* must be founded by a pope, emperor, or king.[61] Beyond this, it is not further defined, although the commentary on the *estudio general* suggests by contrast that an *estudio particular* would not have a guild organization of masters and students and would provide far fewer teaching facilities than a 'general' school: indeed, if very small, it may have only a single teaching master.[62] It does not appear that the term *studium particulare* refers to any one kind of school, but to a variety of types ranging from an elementary school to one of relatively advanced educational form. By definition, the drawing power of the *studium particulare* would not be extensive and most 'particular' schools served the needs of a town or a limited region. Many of them appear to have been engaged in the education of the clergy locally as an end in itself, but some were probably geared to the university system. For example, in the Italian universities it was common for students to enrol for a law degree without undergoing the arts course, having already acquired a good proficiency in arts prior to entering the university.[63] A competent arts training, with perhaps elements of legal instruction, could certainly be obtained in some of the town or municipal *studia particularia* of the more advanced type; and it is likely that several of them came to be regarded as feeder schools for the universities. But the view that *studia particularia* had their being only as subordinate institutions dependent on the universities would do violence to the numerous schools which were rooted in local education and fulfilled a self-contained purpose.

The term *studium particulare* was not much favoured by the founders of thirteenth-century *studia*. It is not easy to discover instances in which the title is expressly used when establishing a school: instead, founders, whether municipal authorities or cathedral chapters, tend to use *studium* by itself or else they describe the school with reference to the specific functions for which it was founded, for example, *scolae grammaticales or scolae artibus*: sometimes the school is not conceptualized as a definite entity and the foundation is simply announced through the employment of teachers for required disciplines.[64] The impression gained is that the founders of lesser *studia* were disinclined to avail themselves of the title *studium particulare* either because the term had inferior connotations or because it was not naturally current outside juristic circles.

The terminology governing the medieval universities is hedged around with anomalies which presumably reflects an incomplete policy of rationalization superimposed by legal authority on a spontaneous, haphazard movement. In the earliest phase of their existence, the universities were guild organizations without permanent buildings or any of the trappings and encumbrances which are allegedly necessary for their twentieth-century successors. But stripped of all the adjuncts which have cumulated over the centuries, the inflated administrative machinery, the financial, building and other concerns which so detract from the primary academic purpose, the modern university is, in essence, the lineal descendant of the medieval *studium generale*. For the most part, teachers and students still function in group associations, the acquisition of a degree is still the practical end product of a competitive system whose criteria and standards are those of the teaching guild, and the ceremonial and terminology are strongly evocative of the medieval past. Whatever the differences in scale and technology, there is a hard core of perennial problems which have taxed the minds and ingenuity of university legislators from the thirteenth century to the present day. Matters of organizational form and democratic procedures, the housing and disciplining of the academic population, curricular, teaching and degree arrangements, the acceptable extent of student participation in university affairs, university-community relations and the eternal struggle to preserve university independence vis-à-vis external authorities, these are just some of the issues which reveal the strands of continuity linking the medieval *studia generalia* and the universities of the modern world. Beyond the superstructural layers of the twentieth-century university one arrives ultimately at a derivative from a medieval archetypal form.

Notes

1 See the comments of S. Stelling-Michaud, 'L'histoire des universités au moyen âge et à la renaissance au cours des vingt-cinq dernières années', *XIe Congrès*

International des Sciences Historiques, Rapports, i (Stockholm, 1960), p. 98; also C. H. Haskins, *The Rise of Universities* (New York, 1923), pp. 3–4.

2 On the philosophical schools of Athens see Clarke, *Higher Education in the Ancient World*, cit., ch. 3, pp. 55 ff.

3 Ibid., pp. 116–17, 136.

4 Ibid., pp. 130 ff.

5 E.g. the Beirut law school had a regular academic course of five years with definite curricular arrangements (ibid., pp. 116–17). The University of Constantinople combined, in one centre, teachers of grammar, rhetoric, philosophy and law (ibid., p. 130); also S. S. Laurie, *Lectures on the Rise and Early Constitution of Universities* (London, 1886), pp. 15–16.

6 Stelling-Michaud, art. cit., pp. 98–9; H. Rashdall, *The Universities of Europe in the Middle Ages*, 3 vols., ed. F. M. Powicke and A. B. Emden (Oxford, 1936), i, pp. 2, 23. See also C. Morris, *The Discovery of the Individual 1050–1200*, cit., p. 50 and note.

7 E.g. the statement of Alexander of Roes *c.* 1281: 'Hiis siquidem tribus, scilicet sacerdotio imperio et studio, tamquam tribus virtutibus, videlicet vitali naturali et animali, sancta ecclesia catholica spiritualiter vivificatur augmentatur et regitur' quoted in Rashdall, op. cit., ed. cit., i, pp. 2, n. 1, 23; trans. in G. Leff, *Paris and Oxford Universities in the Thirteenth and Fourteenth Centuries* (New York, 1968), p. 3. See also H. Grundmann, 'Sacerdotium, Regnum, Studium,' *Archiv für Kulturgeschichte*, 34 (1952), pp. 5 ff.

8 As late as the fifteenth century Paris University still claimed to be the inheritor of the *studium* as transmitted from ancient Egypt to Paris via Athens and Rome: see *Chartularium Universitatis Parisiensis*, 4 vols., ed. H. Denifle and E. Chatelain (Paris, 1889–97), v, no. 2120.

9 On *universitas* see H. Denifle, *Die Entstehung der Universitäten des Mittelalters bis 1400* (Berlin, 1885), pp. 29 ff.; Rashdall, op. cit., i, pp. 4 ff., 15; Leff, op. cit., pp. 16–17.

10 See e.g. the detailed exposition by P. Michaud-Quantin, *Universitas: expressions du mouvement communautaire dans le moyen âge latin* (L'Eglise et l'Etat au Moyen Age, 13, Paris, 1970), passim and Michaud-Quantin, 'Collectivités médiévales et institutions antiques' in *Miscellanea Mediaevalia*, i, ed. P. Wilpert (Berlin, 1962), pp. 239 ff.

11 Denifle, op. cit., esp. pp. 34 ff.; Rashdall, op. cit., i, pp. 16–17.

12 On the concept of *studium generale* see Denifle, op. cit., ch. 1, pp. 1 ff., and Rashdall, op. cit., i, pp. 6 ff.; ii, pp. 2–3. See also Stelling-Michaud, 'L'histoire des universités . . .', art. cit., pp. 99–100 and G. Ermini, 'Concetto di "Studium Generale"', *Archivio Giuridico*, cxxvii (1942), where the divergent views of H. Denifle, C. Meiners, F. C. von Savigny, A. Pertile, F. Schupfer and G. Kaufmann on the essential features of *studia generalia* are conveniently summarized.

13 Denifle, op. cit., p. 2 and n. 2.

14 Ibid., p. 3 and n. 11.

15 One of the earliest occurrences of *studium universale* is to be found in documentation for 1229–30 relating to the University of Toulouse (ibid., p. 2).

16 An early instance of the expression is in connection with the nascent University of Oxford in *c.* 1190 (Rashdall, *Universities*, i, p. 6, n. 2; iii, p. 31 and n. 2.)

17 Used e.g. by Pope Alexander IV in 1256 with reference to Montpellier (Denifle, op. cit., p. 3 and n. 10; see also Rashdall, op. cit., i, p. 6, n. 2).

18 Denifle, op. cit., pp. 5–6.

19 Ibid., pp. 6–7.

20 *Las Siete Partidas des rey don Alfonso el Sabio*, 3 vols., ed. por la real academia de la historia (Madrid, 1807), ii, titulo xxxi, pp. 339–46.

21 Titulo xxxi, ley 1 (p. 340).

22 The main features of the Spanish universities are summarized by Rashdall, op. cit., ii, pp. 64–5; also H. Wieruszowski, *The Medieval University: Masters, Students, Learning* (New York, 1966), pp. 91–4.

23 Rashdall, op. cit., i, p. 11; ii, p. 79.

24 For these three foundations see ibid., i, p. 8.

25 Ibid., i, pp. 8–9; Leff, *Paris and Oxford Universities* . . . , cit., p. 18.

26 Rashdall, op. cit., i, p. 9, n. 2.

27 The bull is printed in *Chartularium Universitatis Parisiensis*, cit., i, no. 32.

28 See the quote from Hostiensis in Denifle, *Die Entstehung* . . . , cit., p. 19, n. 94.

29 The financing of clergy to study in sub-standard schools was considered tantamount to fraudulent misuse of ecclesiastical revenues.

30 Extracts from the papal award are given by Denifle, op. cit., p. 302, n. 326, and by Rashdall, op. cit., ii, p. 28, n. 3.

31 Rashdall, op. cit., ii, p. 107.

32 Ibid., ii, p. 91. Little is known about the school in the thirteenth century.

33 *Les régistres d'Innocent IV* (ed. E. Berger), i (Paris, 1884), no. 2717.

34 On the *ius ubique docendi* see Rashdall, op. cit., i, pp. 9–15; also Stelling-Michaud, 'L'histoire des universités . . .', art. cit., p. 100.

35 See Rashdall, op. cit., i, pp. 9–10; Leff, op. cit., p. 18.

36 On this subject see P. Delhaye, 'L'organisation scolaire au xiie siècle', *Traditio*, v (1947), pp. 211 ff., esp. pp. 253 ff. (Ecoles des maîtres agrégés).

37 The bull is printed in M. Fournier, *Les Statuts et Privilèges des Universités françaises depuis leur fondation jusqu'en 1789* (Paris, 1890–2), i, no. 506. The *ius ubique docendi* provision is thus expressed: 'Et ut quicumque magister ibi examinatus et approbatus fuerit in qualibet facultate, ubique sine alia examinacione regendi liberam habeat potestatem'.

38 See the bull of Alexander IV in *Archiv für Literatur- und Kirchengeschichte*, v (ed. H. Denifle and F. Ehrle, Freiburg im Breisgau, 1889), pp. 170–2. The restrictions with respect to Bologna and Paris were removed in 1333: Rashdall, op. cit., ii, p. 78.

39 See the bull of John XXII in Fournier, op. cit., ii, no. 1425.

40 See ibid., ii, no. 903.

41 The bull for Paris is printed in C. E. Bulaeus, *Historia Universitatis Parisiensis*, iii (Paris, 1666), pp. 449–50 and in *Chartularium Universitatis Parisiensis*, cit., ii, no. 578; and for Bologna in M. Sarti, *De Claris Archigymnasii Bononiensis Professoribus a saeculo xi usque ad saeculum xiv* (Bologna, 1769–72) I, i, p. 59.

42 See Fournier, op. cit., i, no. 19.

43 For this bull see A. Riccobonus, *De Gymnasio Patavino* (Padua, 1722), fos. 4, 5.

44 See e.g. Leff, *Paris and Oxford Universities* . . . , cit., pp. 94–5. Edward II's letter of 26 December 1317 to the pope requesting that the *ius ubique docendi* be formally conferred on the University of Oxford is printed in *Chartularium Universitatis Parisiensis*, ii, no. 756. See also G. L. Haskins, 'The University of Oxford and the "ius ubique docendi" ', *E.H.R.*, lvi (1941), pp. 281 ff.

45 Rashdall, *Universities*, ii, pp. 154–5.

46 On *studium particulare* see below, pp. 34 ff.

47 *Chartularium Universitatis Parisiensis*, i, no. 101. Examining of Toulouse graduates was to continue at Paris in spite of the award of the *ius ubique docendi* to the University of Toulouse. See also C. E. S. Smith, *The University of Toulouse in the Middle Ages* (Wisconsin, 1958), p. 58.

48 See *Statuta Antiqua Universitatis Oxoniensis*, ed. S. Gibson (Oxford, 1931), *De resumentibus* (before 1313: revised dating of G. Pollard) pp. 53–4: '. . . quia ex mutua vicissitudine obligamur ad antidota, eos qui Oxonienses receperunt ad determinandum et ipsi Oxonie ad determinandum admitti poterunt, et qui Parisius vel alibi ubi Oxonienses a resumpcione maliciose excluduntur, nec ipsi Oxonie admittantur'.

49 See the statutes of the Montpellier university of medicine, 1220, in Fournier, *Statuts*, ii, no. 1194; for Angers see Rashdall, op. cit., i, p. 14, n. 3; and for Orléans see the statute of 20 June 1321 in Fournier, i, no. 78.

50 Fournier, i, no. 78.

51 On the growth of salaried lectureships see A. B. Cobban 'Medieval Student Power', *Past and Present*, no. 53 (1971), pp. 28 ff. at pp. 47–8 (with notes).

52 P. Delhaye in his otherwise excellent and scholarly article does not question the universal validity of the teaching licence; see 'L'organisation scolaire . . .', *Traditio*, v (1947), p. 268.

53 See Rashdall's discussion in op. cit., i, p. 11, n. 1 (cont. on p. 12).

54 On particular and common privileges of *studia generalia* see the comments of A. B. Cobban, *The King's Hall within the University of Cambridge in the later Middle Ages*, Cambridge Studies in Medieval Life and Thought, 3rd. series, vol. 1 (Cambridge, 1969), p. 107.

55 See Cobban, 'Edward II, Pope John XXII and the University of Cambridge', *B.J.R.L.*, xlvii (1964), pp. 49 ff. at p. 70, and the same author's *The King's Hall*, cit., pp. 35–6.

56 E.g. see the foundation-bull for Prague (1347–8) printed in *Monumenta Historica Universitatis Praguensis*, ii (ed. Dittrich and Spirk, Prague, 1834), pp. 219–22; also Rashdall, op. cit., ii, p. 215.

57 See e.g. the foundation-bull for Perpignan (1379) printed in Fournier, *Statuts*, ii, no. 1438, in conjunction with the earlier history of the *studium* given by Rashdall, op. cit., ii, pp. 96–7.

58 E.g. see the bull of Nicholas IV for Montpellier (1289) in Fournier, op. cit., ii, no. 903, together with the past history of the university outlined in Rashdall, op. cit., ii, pp. 119 ff., esp. at p. 130.

59 See e.g. the bull of Alexander IV for Salamanca (1255) in *Archiv für Literatur- und Kirchengeschichte*, cit., v, pp. 168–9; also the remarks of Rashdall, op. cit., ii, p. 77.

60 Rashdall, op. cit., i, pp. 8, n. 1, 13 and n. 1; ii, pp. 4, 331 ff.

61 *Las Siete Partidas . . .* , ed. cit., ii, titulo xxxi, ley 1 (p. 340).

62 Loc. cit.

63 E.g. see S. Stelling-Michaud, *L'Université de Bologne et la pénétration des droits romain et canonique en Suisse aux xiiie et xive siècles*, Travaux d'Humanism et Renaissance, xvii (Geneva, 1955), p. 81.

64 I am indebted to my research student Miss S. Winterbottom for useful information about thirteenth-century 'particular' schools in Aragon and Valencia.

30

WHAT IS A UNIVERSITY?

Hastings Rashdall

Source: H. Rashdall, *The Universities of Europe in the Middle Ages*, ed. F. M. Powicke and A. B. Emden, Oxford: Oxford University Press, 1936, pp. 1–24. Originally published 1893.

Of the older works on universities in general the most important are—CONRINGIUS, *De Antiquitatibus Academicis Dissertationes Septem* (ed. Heumannus, with HEUMANNI, *Bibliotheca Historica Academica*, Göttingen, 1739; and *Opera*, Brunswick, 1730, vol. v); MIDDENDORPIUS, *Academiarum Orbis Christiani Libri duo*, Cologne, 1567 (*Libri iv*, 1594; *Libri viii*, 1602); LAUNOIUS, *De Scholis Celebrioribus*, Paris, 1672.

The following may also be mentioned: HAGELGANS, *Orbis Literatus Academicus Germano-Europaeus*, Frankfurt, 1737; ITTERUS, *De Honoribus Academicis Liber*, Frankfurt, 1685.

MEINERS, *Geschichte der Entstehung und Entwickelung der hohen Schulen* (Göttingen, 1802–5), long remained the only modern work on this subject as a whole, and that a completely uncritical one. SAVIGNY began the scientific investigation of the subject, in his *Geschichte des römischen Rechts im Mittelalter* (Heidelberg, 2. Aufl. 1834, &c.); but he is only valuable for the Italian universities and the legal faculties. MALDEN, *On the Origin of Universities* (London, 1835), is full of blunders; more valuable contributions to university history were made by Sir William HAMILTON in his polemical articles in the *Edinburgh Review* (1831–4), reprinted in *Discussions on Philosophy and Literature, Education, and University Reform* (London, 1852). VALLET DE VIRIVILLE, *Histoire de l'instruction publique en Europe* (Paris, 1849), hardly pretends to be a serious history of the universities. The subject has naturally been the theme of many academical addresses, pamphlets, &c., but it will be enough to mention DÖLLINGER, *Die Universitäten sonst und jetzt* (Munich, 1867; *Universities Past and Present*, translated by APPLETON, Oxford, 1867).

The subject remained practically *terra incognita* till the appearance of DENIFLE's great work, *Die Entstehung der Universitäten des Mittelalters bis 1400* (Berlin, 1885), the first and only volume of a colossal undertaking which was never continued. I have expressed my sense of the value of this great work in the Preface.

18

Of the critics of Denifle the most important is GEORG KAUFMANN. His *Geschichte der Deutschen Universitäten* (Stuttgart, 1888–96) forms an interesting, well-written, and not unimportant contribution to the history of medieval universities in general. The controversy between him and DENIFLE (which was unfortunately violent) was conducted by KAUFMANN in *Göttingische Gelehrte Anzeigen* (1886, p. 97 *sq.*), *Zeitschrift d. Savigny-Stiftung* (VII. Germ. Abth. Heft i, p. 124 *sq.*), *Historisches Jahrbuch* (x, 1888, 349–60), *Deutsche Zeitschrift für Geschichtswissenschaft* (1889, I. i, 118 *sq.*); and by DENIFLE in *Hist. Jahrbuch* (x. 72–98, 361–75), *Archiv für Litteratur- und Kirchengeschichte des Mittelalters* (ii. 337 *sq.*).

LAURIE, *Lectures on the Rise and Early Constitution of Universities* (London, 1886), is a brilliantly written little book, but is unfortunately full of inaccuracies and misconceptions, old and new. MULLINGER's article on *Universities* in the *Encyclopaedia Britannica* (ninth edition) deserves mention as the first tolerably correct (though very brief) account of the subject which has appeared in English.

[The most suggestive contribution to the subject since 1895 is to be found in Giuseppe MANACORDA's *Storia della scuola in Italia*, vol. i; *Il medio evo*, in two parts, published in the series 'Pedagogisti ed Educatori' (Remo Sandron, editore, Milan, n.d. The preface is dated October 1913). This book, however, should be used with care, for MANACORDA's main contentions have been strongly criticized; see especially V. ROSSI's review in the *Giornale storico della letteratura italiana*, lxvi (1915), 182–99; reprinted in his *Scritti di critica letteraria*, iii. 71 *sqq.* Stephen D'IRSAY, *Histoire des universités françaises et étrangères des origines à nos jours*, volume i. (Paris, 1933), is good within its limits, and especially useful for the development of studies.

Among other recent works may be noted Ch.-V. LANGLOIS's essay in the first series of his *Questions d'histoire et d'enseignement* (Paris, 1902); C. H. HASKINS, *The Rise of Universities* (New York, 1923), a good popular sketch. Paul SIMON's rectorial address, *Die Idee der mittelalterlichen Universität und ihre Geschichte* (Stuttgart, 1932), is thoughtful and interesting.

The subject is treated at more or less length in the general histories of education: K. A. SCHMID, *Geschichte der Erziehung vom Anfang an bis auf unsere Zeit* (Berlin, 1884–1902); Th. ZIEGLER, *Geschichte der Pädagogik mit besonderer Rücksicht auf das höhere Unterrichtswesen* (3rd ed., Munich, 1909); cf. articles in WATSON's *The Encyclopaedia and Dictionary of Education* (4 volumes, London, 1920).]

Importance
of subject.

Sacerdotium, Imperium, Studium are brought together by a medieval writer[1] as the three mysterious powers or 'virtues', by whose harmonious cooperation the life and health of Christendom are sustained. This 'Studium' did not to him, any more than the 'Sacerdotium' or the 'Imperium' with which it is associated, represent a mere abstraction. As all priestly power had its visible head and source in the city of the Seven Hills, as all secular authority was ultimately held of the Holy Roman Empire, so could all the streams of knowledge by which the Universal Church was watered and fertilized, be ultimately traced as to their fountain-head to the great universities, especially to the University of Paris. The history of an institution which held such a place in the imagination of a medieval scholar is no mere subject of antiquarian curiosity; its origin, its development, its decay, or rather the transition to its modern form, are worthy of the same serious investigation which has been abundantly bestowed upon the Papacy and the Empire.

Its extent.

Like the Papacy and the Empire, the university is an institution which owes not merely its primitive form and traditions, but, in a sense, its very existence to a combination of accidental circumstances; and its origin can only be understood by reference to those circumstances.[2] But the subsequent development of each of these institutions was determined by, and reveals to us, the whole bent and spiritual character of the age to whose life it became organic. The university, no less than the Roman Church and the feudal hierarchy headed by the Roman Emperor, represents an attempt to realize in concrete form an ideal of life in one of its aspects. Ideals pass into great historic forces by embodying themselves in institutions. The power of embodying its ideals in institutions was the peculiar genius of the medieval mind, as its most conspicuous defect lay in the corresponding tendency to materialize them. The institutions which the Middle Age has bequeathed to us are of greater and more imperishable value even than its cathedrals. And the university is distinctly a medieval institution—as much so as constitutional kingship, or parliaments, or trial by jury. The universities and the immediate products of their activity may be said to constitute the great achievement of the Middle Ages in the intellectual sphere. Their organization and their traditions, their studies and their exercises affected the progress and intellectual development of Europe more powerfully, or (perhaps it should be said) more exclusively, than any schools in all likelihood will ever do again. A complete history of the universities of the Middle Ages would be in fact a history of medieval thought—of the fortunes, during four centuries, of literary culture, of the whole of the scholastic philosophy and scholastic theology, of the revived study of the civil law, of the formation and development of the canon law, of the faint, murky, cloud-wrapped dawn of modern mathematics, modern science, and modern medicine. Hardly more than a glance can be given at many of these subjects in the present work. Its paramount object will be to study the growth of the university as an institution, to trace the origin of the various universities, and to sketch the most important changes which passed over their form and their spirit during the period before us. Our attention will be for the most part confined to the parent or typical universities; no more than a slight sketch will be attempted of their derivatives or descendants. Even so, our subject is in some respects an inconveniently extended one. But if this diffusion of interest involves some sacrifice of that thoroughness in research, of that concentration of view, and that vividness of local colouring which might have been possible in a monograph on a single university, something will be gained if it becomes clear, as we compare Bologna with Paris, and Paris with Oxford or Prague, that the universities of all countries and all ages are in reality adaptations under various conditions of one and the same institution; that if we would completely understand the meaning of offices, titles, ceremonies, organizations preserved in the most modern, most practical, most unpicturesque of the institutions which now bear the name of 'university', we must go back to the earliest days of the earliest universities that ever existed, and trace the history of their chief successors through the seven centuries that intervene between the rise of Bologna or Paris, and the foundation of the new University of Strasbourg or of the new universities in England.

The word *universitas* is one to which a false explanation is often assigned for polemical purposes by controversial writers, while the true explanation of it at once supplies us with a clue to the nature and historical origin of the institution itself. The notion that a university means a *universitas facultatum*—a school in which all the faculties or branches of knowledge are represented—has, indeed, long since disappeared from the pages of professed historians; but it is still persistently foisted upon the public by writers with whom history is subordinate to what may be called intellectual edification. However imposing and stimulating may be the conception of an institution for the teaching or for the cultivation of universal knowledge, however imperative the necessity of such an institution in modern times, it is one which can gain little support from the facts of history. A glance into any collection of medieval documents reveals the fact that the word 'university' means merely a number, a plurality, an aggregate of persons. *Universitas vestra*, in a letter addressed to a body of persons, means merely 'the whole of you'; in a more technical sense it denotes a legal corporation[3] or juristic person; in Roman law (though in strictness a wider term) it is for most purposes practically the equivalent of *collegium*. At the end of the twelfth and beginning of the thirteenth centuries, we find the word applied to corporations either of masters or of students; but it long continues to be applied to other corporations as well, particularly to the then newly formed guilds and to the municipalities of towns; while as applied to scholastic guilds it is at first used interchangeably with such words as 'community' or 'college'. In the earliest period it is never used absolutely. The phrase is always 'University of Scholars', 'University of Masters and Scholars', 'University of

Meaning of *universitas*.

Study', or the like. It is a mere accident that the term has gradually come to be restricted to a particular kind of guild or corporation, just as the terms 'convent', 'corps', 'congregation', 'college', have been similarly restricted to certain specific kinds of association. It is particularly important to notice that the term was generally in the Middle Ages used distinctly of the scholastic body whether of teachers or scholars, not of the place in which such a body was established, or even of its collective schools. The word used to denote the academic institution in the abstract—the schools or the town which held them—was *studium* rather than *universitas*. To be a resident in a university would be *in studio degere* or *in scolis militare*. The term which most nearly corresponds to the vague and indefinite English notion of a university as distinguished from a mere school, seminary, or private educational *Studium* establishment, is not *universitas*, but *studium generale*; and *studium generale* *generale.* means, not a place where all subjects are studied, but a place where students from all parts are received. As a matter of fact, very few medieval *studia* possessed all the faculties. Even Paris in the days of her highest renown possessed no faculty of civil law; while throughout the thirteenth century graduation in theology was in practice the almost exclusive privilege of Paris and the English universities.[4]

Changes of   The term *studium generale* does not become common till the beginning meaning.   of the thirteenth century.[5] At that time the term was a perfectly vague one, as vague and indefinable as the English term Public School or the German *Hochschule*. In the main, however, the term seems to have implied three characteristics: (1) That the school attracted or at least invited students from all parts, not merely those of a particular country or district; (2) that it was a place of higher education; that is to say, that one at least of the higher faculties—theology, law, medicine—was taught there;[6] (3) that such subjects were taught by a considerable number—at least by a plurality—of masters. Of these ideas the first was the primary and fundamental one: a *studium generale* meant a school of general resort, but in its origin the expression was a wholly popular and extra-legal one. The question whether a particular school was or was not a *studium generale* was one settled by custom or usage, not by authority. There were, however, at the beginning of the thirteenth century three *studia* to which the term was pre-eminently applied and which enjoyed a unique and transcendent prestige: they were Paris for theology and arts, Bologna for law, and Salerno for medicine. A master who had taught and been admitted to the magisterial guild in one of those places was certain of obtaining immediate recognition and permission to teach in all other inferior studia, while these *studia* themselves would not receive masters from other schools without fresh examination. Thus to the original conception of a *studium generale* there was gradually added a vague notion of a certain ecumenical validity for the mastership which it conferred. But at the same time there was nothing to prevent any school which thought itself entitled to the designation from assuming it. In the thirteenth century many schools besides Bologna and Paris claimed the rank of *studium generale*: it was in fact—at least in Italy, where the term was most in use—assumed by any school which wanted to intimate that it gave an education equal to that of Bologna or Paris.[7] And the extension of this usage was facilitated by the fact that most of these early schools were founded by masters who had actually taught at one of these places.

In the latter half of the thirteenth century this unrestricted liberty of founding *studia generalia* gradually ceased; and the cessation brought with it an important change in the meaning of the term. It so happened that at about the same time the two great 'world-powers' of Europe conceived the idea of creating a school which was to be placed by an exercise of authority on a level with the great European centres of education. In 1224 the Emperor Frederick II founded a *studium generale* at Naples; in 1229 Gregory IX did the same at Toulouse; while in 1244 or 1245 Innocent IV established a *studium generale* in the Pontifical Court itself. These foundations would appear to have suggested the idea that the erection of new *studia generalia* was one of the papal and imperial prerogatives, like the power of creating notaries public. Moreover, in order to give the graduates of Toulouse (in so far as parchment and wax could secure it) the same prestige and recognition which were enjoyed by the graduates of Paris and Bologna, a Bull was issued (in 1233) which declared that any one admitted to the mastership in that university should be freely allowed to teach in all other *studia* without any further examination. In the course of the century other cities anxious to place their schools on a level with these privileged universities applied for and obtained from Pope or Emperor Bulls constituting them *studia generalia*. The earlier of these Bulls simply confer the position of *studium generale* without further definition or confer the privileges of some specified university such as Paris or Bologna. The most prominent practical purpose of such Bulls seems at first to have been to give beneficed ecclesiastics the right of studying in them while continuing to receive the fruits of their benefices[8]—a privilege limited by canonical law or custom to *studia* reputed 'general'.[9] But gradually the special privilege of the *ius ubique docendi* came to be regarded as the principal object of papal or imperial creation. It was usually, but not quite invariably, conferred in express terms by the original foundation-bulls; and was apparently understood to be involved in the mere act of erection even in the rare cases where it is not expressly conceded. In 1291–2 even the old archetypal universities themselves—Bologna and Paris—were formally invested with the same privilege by Bulls of Nicholas IV. From this time the notion gradually gained ground that the *ius ubique docendi* was of the essence of a *studium generale*, and that no school which did not possess this privilege could obtain it without a Bull from Emperor or Pope.[10] At the same time there were some of the older *studia*[11]—such as Oxford and Padua—which, without having been founded by Pope or Emperor and without having procured a subsequent recognition of their *ius ubique docendi*, had obtained a position as *studia*

The ius ubique docendi.

generalia too secure to be successfully attacked. Hence, with their habitual respect for established facts, the fourteenth-century jurists, to whom is chiefly due the formulation of the medieval ideas about universities, declared that such schools were *studia generalia* 'by custom' (*ex consuetudine*).[12]

The view of the fourteenth-century Italian jurists no doubt, on the whole, represents the dominant medieval theory on the subject. At the same time it is only natural to find that these ideas were less rapidly and less firmly established in countries which recognized the supremacy of the Holy Roman Empire at most in some shadowy and honorary way, and where the national Churches possessed most independence. Thus we find the Spanish kings erecting *studia generalia* without consulting Pope or Emperor. They do not, indeed, claim to confer a *ius ubique docendi*, which would be an absurd pretension on the part of a merely local sovereign. The jurists conceded to such universities all that they could possibly claim when they held them to be *studia generalia respectu regni*. If (as is insisted by Kaufmann)[13] there are instances of attempts on the part of a city republic to erect a *studium generale* without papal or imperial permission, if in one or two cases we even have diplomas granted by such bodies purporting to confer the *licentia ubique docendi*,[14] these are merely the exceptions which prove the rule. A claim on the part of officials or corporations chartered by a mere local authority to confer rights of teaching in universities which lay beyond their jurisdiction is too extravagant to have been seriously made, much less to have obtained general recognition.

The fluctuations of meaning which the term *studium generale* underwent in the course of the Middle Age make it no easy task in all cases to adjudicate upon the claims of particular schools to that title. In the thirteenth century we are obliged to include in the category of 'universities' all bodies which we find expressly styled *studia generalia* in medieval writers, though there were no doubt many schools (especially in parts of Europe where the term was less current) which had in point of fact quite as good claims to 'generality', in the sense in which it was then understood, as some of those to which the term is actually applied; and some of them may have been actually so called, though evidence of the fact does not happen to have come down to us.[15] But from the beginning of the fourteenth century I accept the juristic definition, and exclude from the category of universities all bodies which were not founded by Pope or Emperor. *Studia generalia respectu regni* are, however, included, but these in nearly every case sooner or later strengthened their position by a papal Bull.

A wrong impression would, however, be given of the whole matter if it were supposed that, even when the *ius ubique docendi* was most indisputably assured by papal or imperial authority, it really received the respect which juristic theories claimed for it. The great primeval universities perhaps never recognized the doctorates conferred by the younger bodies.[16] At Paris, even Oxford degrees failed to command incorporation without fresh examination and licence, and Oxford repaid the compliment by refusing admission to Parisian doctors, the papal Bull notwithstanding.[17] Even in less illustrious universities the statutes provide for some preliminary test before the reception of a graduate from another university which can hardly be distinguished from the 'examination' which the papal Bulls forbade,[18] since it is always implied that the university reserved the right of refusing permission to lecture and exercise other magisterial rights to any foreign graduate of whose competence it was not satisfied.[19] It should be added that in proportion as the real privileges of the mastership were restricted (as was eventually more or less the case in the majority of universities) to a limited body of salaried doctors, the ecumenical rights conferred by graduation in a *studium generale* came to possess a purely honorary value. The mastership was reduced to a universally recognized honour, but nothing more.[20]

It remains to point out the relation of the term 'studium generale' to the term 'universitas'. There was originally no necessary connexion between the institution denoted by the term *universitas* and that denoted by the term *studium generale*. Societies of masters or clubs of students were formed before the term *studium generale* came into habitual use; and in a few instances such societies are known to have existed in schools which never became *studia generalia*.[21] The university was originally a scholastic guild whether of masters or students. Such guilds sprang into existence, like other guilds, without any express authorization of king, pope, prince, or prelate. They were spontaneous products of that instinct of association which swept like a great wave over the towns of Europe in the course of the eleventh and twelfth centuries.[22] But in two places especially—Bologna and Paris—the scholastic guilds obtained a development and importance which they possessed nowhere else. And, as we shall see, nearly all the secondary *studia generalia* which arose spontaneously without papal or imperial charter, were established by secessions of masters or students from Paris or Bologna. The seceders carried with them the customs and institutions of their *alma mater*. Even in the few cases where the germs of a university or college of doctors may have originated independently of the influence of Paris and Bologna, their subsequent development was due to more or less direct and conscious imitation of the scholastic guilds of these two great schools. Thus it came about that a *universitas*, whether of masters or of students, became in practice the inseparable accompaniment of the *studium generale*—and a *universitas* of a particular and definite type formed more or less on the model of one of these great archetypal universities.[23] Thus in the later Middle Ages the term *studium generale* came practically to denote not merely a school with the *ius ubique docendi* (though this remained its legal and technical differentia), but a scholastic organization of a particular type and endowed with more or less uniform privileges. By the fifteenth century the original distinction between the two terms was pretty generally lost; and *universitas* gradually became a mere synonym for *studium generale*.[24] In the following pages the term

Universitas and studium generale; originally distinct, afterwards synonymous.

25

university will be used in this comprehensive sense except where it is necessary expressly to distinguish the *studium* from the *universitas* proper.

Paris and Bologna are the two archetypal—it might almost be said the
only *original* universities: Paris supplied the model for the universities of
masters, Bologna for the universities of students. Every later university from
that day to this is in its developed form a more or less close imitation of one
or the other of these two types, though in some few cases[25] the basis of the
organization may be independent. In the case of the earlier universities
the imitation was, with whatever adaptation to local circumstances, conscious and deliberate; while the most purely utilitarian of new universities
retains constitutional features or usages which are only explained by the
customs and institutions either of the Bologna students or of the Parisian
masters at the end of the twelfth or the beginning of the thirteenth centuries.
It is clear therefore that a somewhat minute study of these two typical bodies
is essential to a proper understanding of the university as an institution.

The two great parent universities arose at about the same time—during
the last thirty years of the twelfth century. They arose out of different sides
of that wonderful deepening and broadening of the stream of human culture
which may be called the Renaissance of the twelfth century. In Italy this
Renaissance found its expression most conspicuously in a revival of the study
of the Roman law, which started from Bologna; in France it took the form of
a great outburst of dialectical and theological speculation which found its
ultimate, though not its earliest, home in Paris. The Bologna university of students, though perhaps later than the first rudimentary germ of the Parisian
society of masters, completed its organization earlier. And though each
type of constitution was affected in its development by the influence of the
other, Bologna in all probability exerted more influence over Paris than
Paris over Bologna. Bologna therefore shall be dealt with first. With regard
to the derivative universities, it might seem natural to divide them into two
great classes, and to deal first with the universities of students, and then with
the universities of masters. When, however, we come to examine the various
constitutions in detail, it will be found that it is not always possible, without
a very arbitrary treatment, to assign a given university definitively either
to the Bolognese or the Parisian group. Many universities were influenced
both by Paris and by Bologna. For it must be remembered that, though at
Bologna the student-guild eventually established complete supremacy over
the magisterial body, the masters always had a college of their own, to
which alone belonged the right of admitting new masters or (in the modern
phrase) 'granting degrees'. There might therefore be, and in fact there were,
great variations in the distribution of academic power between the magisterial college and the student-guild. Moreover, this distribution might vary
at different times; so that some *studia* approximate at one period of their
history to the Bolognese, at another to the Parisian type. Hence, though a
classification into student-universities and master-universities would bring

Paris and Bologna the two archetypes.

Order of treatment.

into prominence the curious fact that the French universities are mostly children of Bologna rather than of Paris, and that the Scottish universities are in certain points more closely affiliated to Bologna than to Paris or Oxford, I have deemed it best on the whole (after dealing with the great model-universities) to group together the universities of each country in Europe, which naturally have certain features in common, though the differences between these national varieties are often far smaller than the fundamental distinction between the student and the magisterial type. Our own universities shall be reserved to the last, because, though belonging wholly to the magisterial type, and originally modelled on Paris, they exhibit from the first such marked constitutional peculiarities as almost to constitute a separate natural order of universities, distinct alike from the Bologna and the Parisian groups.

There is, however, one great *studium generale*, older in a sense than either Paris or Bologna, which stands absolutely by itself. Its original constitution, of which, indeed, not much is known, appears to have had little resemblance to that of any other; and it never enjoyed that reproductive power which is so remarkable a characteristic of Bologna and Paris. The Medical School of Salerno did not (so far as it is known) influence the constitution even of the medical universities or the medical faculties. Such treatment as can be given to it must precede our account of Bologna. But, before entering upon the universities in detail, it will be convenient to give some general sketch of the great intellectual movement out of which in a sense all the universities, though pre-eminently that of Paris, arose, and, as an introduction to it, of the state of European education, especially in France, before the rise of the universities proper. *(margin: Salerno.)*

Before closing this preliminary survey of our subject, it may be well to point out that the three titles, master, doctor, professor, were in the Middle Ages absolutely synonymous. At Paris and its derivative universities we find *magister* the prevailing title in the faculties of theology, medicine, and arts; the title *professor* is, however, pretty frequently, that of *doctor* more rarely, employed.[26] The teachers of law at Bologna, however, specially affected the title *doctor*; they were also called *professores* and *domini*, but not as a rule *magistri*. The same usage was transferred to Paris. In the Acts of the faculty of canon law, we find the term *doctor* habitually used. Thus, when letters are addressed 'Rectori, Magistris, *Doctoribus* et Scolaribus Universitatis Parisiensis', the order makes it plain that the theological teachers are included in the *magistri*, while the teachers of canon law are specially designated by the *doctores*. The same distinction was observed at Oxford; but in the fifteenth century—at least in the English universities—the practice gradually arose of appropriating the title *doctor* to all the superior faculties and reserving that of *magister* for the inferior faculties of arts and grammar. In Italy the term *doctor* soon spread from the faculty of law to all the other faculties. The same was eventually the case in Germany, where the master of arts is *(margin: The synonyms master, doctor, professor.)*

27

still styled doctor of philosophy. The purely accidental character of the distinction is strikingly illustrated by the fact that in the English universities the doctor of music, who in spite of his gorgeous plumage is not a member of Convocation and only ranks above the modest bachelor of arts, enjoys that imposing prefix of *doctor*, while his superior, the teacher of arts, is confined to the (in popular estimation) humbler style of *master*. German diplomas often confer the style 'Doctor of Philosophy and Master of Arts'.[27]

Notes

1 'Hiis si quidem tribus, scilicet sacerdotio imperio et studio, tanquam tribus uirtutibus, uidelicet uitali naturali et animali, sancta ecclesia katholica spiritualiter uiuificatur augmentatur et regitur. Hiis etiam tribus, tanquam fundamento pariete et tecto, eadem ecclesia quasi materialiter perficitur.' Jordan of Osnaburg, *De prerogatiua Romani Imperii*, ed. Waitz (1869), p. 70. [For the authorship of this tract see below, p. 23, where the passage is again cited.]

2 [The possibility that the medieval university owed much to conscious imitation from the Arabian system of education has been urged by the Spanish scholar, J. Ribera y Tarragó. See his collected *Disertaciones y opúsculos*, i. 243 (Madrid, (1928). He lays stress upon the rapidity of the development from the twelfth century, the mingling of papal direction with free institutions, suggesting a mingling of two types of civilization, and the grant of titles or degrees (cf. the *ichaza* or licence, *ibid.*, pp. 334–40). His argument is not convincing.]

3 Long after the rise of the scholastic universities, *universitas* is used (absolutely) of the town corporations or guilds. Thus Boniface VIII writes 'Universitatibus et populo dicti Regni' (Franciae). Even so vague a body as 'all faithful Christian people' is often addressed as 'Universitas vestra'.

4 Though nominally shared by Naples, Toulouse, and the university of the Roman Court. Bulls for the erection of *studia generalia* usually specified the faculties in which the *Facultas ubique docendi* was granted; or it was 'in quavis licita facultate'.

5 'Universale', and more rarely 'commune', are common synonyms for 'generale'. The allusion in Guibert de Nogent (†1124), *De vita sua*, l. i, c. 4 (ed. G. Bourgin, 1907, p. 13), 'Cum nocte dormiret in cubiculo, cuius et ego memini, in quo totius nostri oppidi generale studium regebatur, . . .', is clearly a non-technical use of the word. The earliest instance of the technical expression that I have noticed is in the Chronicle of Emo in relation to Oxford, *c.* 1190 (*Monumenta Germaniae Historica, Scriptores*, xxiii. 467; below, vol. ii, ch. xii, § 1), where the word is 'commune'. *Studium solempne* is sometimes used as a synonym for *generale*, but occasionally it seems to be distinguished from it, meaning an important or frequented school which was not technically 'general'. See Denifle and Chatelain, *Chartul. Univ. Paris.*, 1889, &c., ii, No. 1015, 'in nullo conventu, ubi non est studium generale aut aliud studium solempne'. See the definition in the Siete Partidas of Alfonso X of Castile, below, vol. ii, ch. vii, § 2. The Canonist 'Hostiensis' (Henricus de Segusia), writing at about the same time (†1271), discusses the limits of the privilege of dispensation from residence for the purpose of study, and lays it down: 'Hoc autem arg. potest hinc elici, quod istud intelligatur de generali, non de particulari. Et dicitur generale, quando triuium et quadriuium, Theologia et sacri canones ibidem leguntur. Sed certe et hoc putamus ad arbitrium bonijudicis redigendum,' &c. Hostiensis, *in Decretalium Libros*, ii, Venice, 1581, f. 13. The requirement that theology should be taught is curious, since Bologna

could only satisfy the test by its Friar doctors, who did not graduate at Bologna. He goes on to ask: 'Nunquid enim si propter guerram non audent ad presens ad scholas Bononie accedere, licebit eis citra montes etiam in castris si competentem magistrum habeant studere?' A gloss declares that the laws may be read anywhere: 'talis tamen locus non habebit priuilegium studii generalis, nisi ei concedatur a principe, vel consuetudine immemoriali, ut not. Bat.' &c. It was no doubt largely the necessity of defining a *studium generale* for the purpose of dispensation from residence on account of study which led to a definite and precise meaning being given to the term.

6 [Cf. the words of Pope Innocent VI, in his *privilegium* establishing a theological faculty at Bologna (1360): 'auctoritate apostolica statuimus et ordinamus quod in dicta civitate deinceps existat *studium generale in eadem theologica facultate*'; Ehrle, *I più antichi statuti della facoltà teologica dell'università di Bologna* (1932), p. 3.] There are at least two instances of a *studium generale* in arts only: (1) Saragossa, which Denifle somewhat arbitrarily excludes from the category of Universities—see below, vol. ii, p. 101; (2) Erfurt, which we learn from a document of 1362 was 'populari sermone' spoken of as a *studium generale*. Since the recognition is in this case equivocal, I have considered Erfurt as founded by the Bull of 1379. See below, vol. ii, p. 248.

7 There were many such schools in Italy during the thirteenth century, but most of them early died out. Where they maintained their ground, the later and more technical ideas about *studia generalia* were naturally applied to them, since the change in the meaning was gradual and unconscious. Out of Italy there were no doubt many schools which *de facto* were as much *studia generalia* as Arezzo or Vercelli, but the name does not happen to have been applied to them: hence when the technical interpretation of *studium generale* gained ground, they lost their claims to the privileges which it conferred. Such schools were Lyons and Reims, for whose inclusion Kaufmann is urgent.

8 The first Bull for a *studium* not actually created to forward some special purpose of Pope or Emperor was that for Piacenza in 1248, which conferred the privileges of Paris and other *studia generalia*. The Bull for Rome (*studium urbis*) in 1303 confers the right to receive fruits and other privileges, but no express *ius ubique*; those for Pamiers (1295) and Perugia (1308) simply create a *studium generale*. On the other hand, Montpellier (1289) and Avignon (1303) received the *ius ubique docendi*, which gradually became the usual form.

9 Honorius III in 1219 (Decretal. Greg. IX. lib. v, tit. 5, c. 5; cf. lib. iii, tit. 5, c. 32) provided that teachers *of theology* as long as they were teaching, or students for five years, might receive their fruits, and prelates and chapters were required to send 'docibiles' (i.e. canons) to study theology. There was no express limitation to *studia generalia*; but Honorius III clearly had recogized *scolae* in mind; and in 1207 Innocent III had ruled (Decretal. Greg. IX, lib. iii, tit. 4, c. 12) that the privilege of receiving the fruits of their prebends did not apply to those who 'se transferunt ad villas vel castella, in quibus nullum est vel minus competens studium literarum'. This was only intended to prevent fraud, but as time went on it could be interpreted to mean *studia* which were not general. (See the comment of Hostiensis, above, p. 6 note.)

Later, particular universities often obtained special Bulls confirming the dispensation from residence, and the right to receive all fruits except the 'daily distribution'.

10 The Bull for Paris is given in *Chartul. Univ. Paris*. ii, No. 578 (in Bulaeus, iii. 449, wrongly ascribed to Nicholas III); the Bologna Bull by Sarti, *De claris Archigymnasii Bononiensis Professoribus*, t. i, p. ii, Bologna, 1772, p. 59, renewed

by Clement V in 1310, *Reg. Clem. V*, Rome, 1885, &c., No. 5275. In the latter case the privilege extended only to the two legal faculties. Bologna never obtained this privilege for her faculty of medicine or arts, yet this made no difference in practice to the estimation of the degrees—an illustration of the anomalies with which the matter abounds.

11 Denifle holds (i. 777) that no *studium generale* arose without a Bull after the middle of the thirteenth century. There are one or two cases where this is doubtful: they are discussed in vol. ii.

12 In some cases these prescriptive *studia generalia* assumed the right of conferring the *licentia docendi hic et ubique*. This appears to have been done by Reggio as early as 1276 (see the diploma in Tacoli, *Memorie storiche d. Reggio*, iii. 215), a circumstance which would suggest that the formula was used at Bologna before the grant of the papal Bull. In other cases, however, no such change appears to have taken place, e.g. at Oxford, if we may trust the evidence of the extant *formulae*. Padua eventually (in 1346) obtained a Bull. (See below, vol. ii, p. 15.)

13 Kaufmann (*Die Gesch. d. deutschen Universitäten*, i. 371–409) labours to show that the papal or imperial brief was not necessary to the legitimacy of a *studium generale* according to medieval notions—that the essential thing was recognition by the sovereign of the place. This theory is put forward in opposition to Denifle's view, which I have, in the main, adopted. Upon Kaufmann's arguments I remark: (1) That the discussions by Baldus and Bartolus in the extracts which he gives (i. 383, 384) turn not upon the question what constitutes a *studium generale*, but upon the question whether the teaching of the civil law was still restricted, as the constitution *omnem* (Digesta, ed. Mommsen, Berlin, 1872, i. xvi) provided, to *civitates regiae*, and what constituted a *civitas regia*. No doubt this constitution, and the claims which Bologna based upon it, powerfully contributed to the growth of the custom of applying for papal and imperial Bulls of erection and to the eventual belief in their necessity. But to say that the laws might be taught 'ex permissione eius tacita vel expressa qui est princeps' is not the same thing as to say that any 'princeps' could create a *studium generale* (in the full sense, not merely 'respectu regni'). There were scores of Italian cities (as Denifle has shown over and over again) in which law was taught by a number of state-authorized teachers which never pretended to be *studia generalia*. (2) That all passages and instances taken from the thirteenth-century writers or documents are not *ad rem*. It is admitted that at this time no Bull or Brief was thought to be necessary. But then so far *studium generale* meant merely 'a place of higher education of European or more than local repute'. And equally little is there any general notion (though such a view is undoubtedly expressed by the *Siete Partidas*) that a *studium generale* required a charter from King or sovereign-city. Undoubtedly it might have been held that it required the sovereign's 'permissio tacita', though this might have been denied by a Hildebrandine Churchman. There was no more general agreement as to the limits of the authority of Church and State than there is at the present moment between Father Denifle and Prof. Kaufmann. The fact is that this whole discussion as to the educational right of 'the State' in the Middle Ages involves something of an anachronism. I am bound to say that Kaufmann's treatment of the subject is far more vitiated by an infusion of ideas suggested by the *Kulturkampf*, than Denifle's is distorted by any desire to find support for those of the Syllabus [1895].

(3) It is useless to quote documents in which a king or town purports to erect a *studium generale* without express allusion to Emperor or Pope, unless it is shown (*a*) that no Bull was actually applied for, and (*b*) that a school actually came into existence without such Bull which was looked upon as a *studium generale*. Royal charters for the erection of a university are usually expressed

in this form even where a Bull was applied for or already granted. It would be as reasonable to quote a written agreement between two persons to enter into marriage as evidence that they thought marriage would be legal without the intervention of priest or registrar. Even Denifle does not contend that it was considered lawful, or at all events possible, for the Pope to erect a university without consulting the local sovereign.

(4) The case of the Spanish universities is no exception to Denifle's view, since it is admitted that they were *studia generalia respectu regni.*

(5) Even if it could be shown that in isolated instances a city did purport to erect a *studium generale* without a Bull (after 1300), this would only show that they used the word in its older and less technical sense. In this older sense it is impossible to decide dogmatically what was a *studium generale* and what was not. It is therefore better to confine the word (in dealing with the period 1300–1500) to its technical sense of a *studium* which possessed the *ius ubique docendi* at least *respectu regni*—even if this sense of the word was not universally accepted. As to the impossibility of a mere city (even if really sovereign) granting such a right, I have said enough. The case of the Parmese diploma merely proves the arrogance or ignorance of the scribe who copied it from some diploma or form-book of a real university, even if it was not intended to apply for a Bull.

(6) The only evidence that may possibly require some modification of Denifle's view is the language used by the *imperial* Bull (the Papacy at this time always assumes the necessity of a Bull) in the foundation of Siena (1357), where the Emperor treats the *studium generale* of that place as already existing. But if its position as *studium generale* was established before 1250, Denifle would admit it to be *studium generale ex consuetudine.* Although Denifle does not admit this to have been the case, the correction involves no change of principle. See below, ch. vi, § 9.

(7) It must be conceded to Kaufmann that when Denifle, while fully admitting the imperial prerogative of founding universities, insinuates (i. 384) that 'Allein gerade dieses letztere Recht war theilweise durch das Gutdünken des Papstes bedingt', the Vatican Archivist does for once get the better of the historian. For Denifle's view of the whole question, see especially *Die Entstehung,* &c., pp. 763–91, and for his controversy with Kaufmann, the articles mentioned above, p. 1.

[We leave this characteristic note; but see the Additional Note at the end of the chapter.]

14 As to Reggio see above, p. 10, note 3; cf. below, vol. ii, p. 6.

15 Such as Lyons, Reims, Erfurt, &c. It is highly probable—and this must be conceded to Kaufmann—that in the thirteenth century these schools were sometimes or always called *studia generalia.* A Paris Statute of 1279 (Bulaeus, iii. 447; Denifle and Chatelain, *Chartul.* i, No. 485) requires candidates for the licence in arts to have determined either at Paris or in some other *studium generale* where there were not less than twelve regents: this points to the existence of many small *studia generalia.* But if we begin to include in our enumeration schools which are not expressly described as *studia generalia* or created such by Bull, it would be impossible to know where to draw the line.

16 When Paris complained of the rights given to the graduates of Toulouse, Gregory IX himself explained that the privileges of the new university were not intended to interfere with those of Paris. *Chartul. Univ. Paris.* i, No. 101. In granting the *ius ubique docendi* to Salamanca, Alexander IV expressly excepted Paris and Bologna. See below, vol. ii, p. 78.

17 'Qui Parisius uel alibi ubi Oxonienses a resumpcione maliciose excluduntur, necipsi Oxonie admittantur' (*Statuta Antiqua,* ed. S. Gibson, pp. 53, 54; see the comment in the introduction, p. cxviii and note), and Paris complains to the Pope that her

ius ubique docendi is not respected everywhere 'ut in Anglia et apud Montem Pessulanum'. *Chartul. Univ. Paris.* ii, No. 728. Attempts were made in 1296 and 1317 to procure the *ius ubique docendi* by papal Bull. Documents in Lincoln Register (Bishop Sutton's *Memoranda*, f. 141 *b*); Wood, *Hist. and Antiq. of Oxford*, ed. Gutch, i. 155; *Chartul. Univ. Paris.* ii, No. 756. As the attempt was not made at a later date, we may perhaps assume that Oxford was satisfied with its position as a *studium generale ex consuetudine*; yet Oxford never actually conferred the *licentia ubique docendi*, nor (of course) did she confer degrees 'Apostolica auctoritate'. At Bologna we find the personal intervention of Charles II of Naples necessary to obtain recognition for Jacobus de Belvisio, who had graduated at Naples in 1298 or 1299; and even then he appears to have gone through the ceremony of promotion *de novo*. Savigny, c. xlix.

18 See e.g. Kink, *Gesch. der Univ. Wien*, ii. 167. At Angers it is expressly provided that no graduates from another university shall lecture before 'per scholasticum et doctores examinentur diligenter', but 'si repetant alia examinatione non indigent'. Rangeard, *Hist. de l'Un. d'Angers*, ii. 221.

19 In 1321 Orleans enacted 'quod nullus doctor extrinsecus veniens, ad actum regendi ordinarie . . . in nostra Universitate admittatur, vel ad alios actus doctorales, nisi per collationem doctorum, ut moris est, fuerit approbatus, et hic insignia receperit doctoratus'—Fournier, *Stat. et privilèges des univ. françaises* (Paris, 1890) i, No. 78. It is true that there is a 'salvo honore . . . sancte sedis apostolice'. In 1463 (*ibid.*, No. 320) we find the Pope interfering to prevent a 'doctor bullatus', i.e. made by the Pope, from assuming the rights of a regent at Orleans. Cf. *Chartul. Univ. Paris.* ii, No. 1174.

20 Kaufmann (i. 366 *sq.*) has the merit of first pointing out the very limited respect which was actually paid to these papal Bulls.

21 Thus at Cremona it is provided by the town-statutes of 1387 'quod duo rectores possint eligi per scholares legum vel unus, secundum quod placuerit dictis scholaribus' (*Statuta Civ. Crem.*, Cremona, 1678, p. 135 [for the schools at Cremona see the bibliography in Manacorda, *op. cit.* ii. 295–6]); and the privileges accorded by the town are as ample as those enjoyed by masters and scholars in *studia generalia*. So at Perugia and at Pisa (see below, ch. vi, §§ 11, 12) before they became *studia generalia*. It should be added that a *studium privilegiatum* —even with papal privileges—was not necessarily a *studium generale*, unless the Bull expressly created it such. Thus in 1247 the Pope gave 'doctoribus et scholaribus universis Narbonne in studio commorantibus', the privilege of absence from benefices, as though they were scholars in a *studium generale*. *Reg. Innocent IV*, ed. Berger, Paris, 1884, &c., No. 2717. Fournier prints a Bull of 1329 exempting the *studium* of Arts at Gaillac from the control of the Bishop of Albi and 'rectoris et magistrorum studii Albiensis' (*loc. cit.*, No. 1573). As to Valencia, see below, vol. ii, p. 107.

22 Among general historians, no one has so fully appreciated this essential fact as the learned, if unsympathetic, Church-historian Mosheim: 'They who had satisfied all the demands of this academical law, and gone through the formidable trial with applause, were solemnly invested with the dignity of professors, and were saluted masters with a certain round of ceremonies, that were used in the societies of illiterate tradesmen, when their company was augmented by a new candidate. This vulgar custom had been introduced, in the preceding century, by the professors of law in the academy of Bologna; and in this century it was transmitted to that of Paris, where it was first practised by the divinity colleges, and afterwards by the professors of physic and the liberal arts.' *Ecclesiastical History*, trans. by Maclaine, 1826, iii. 137. This last distinction is, however, unfounded.

23 It is clear that graduation in its stricter sense could only exist where there was a *universitas*. A *licentia docendi* of purely local validity might of course have continued to be given by *studia* which were not general, but gradually the *licentia docendi* seems usually to have disappeared with the growing employment of university graduates to teach in the smaller *studia*. This seems to me a truer mode of statement than to say (with Denifle, i. 21) that *studia particularia* could only enjoy the 'Promotionsrecht' by special papal privilege or special custom.

24 The way for the identification was prepared by the intermediate term *universitas studii*, which was used at first distinctly of the society, as at Perugia in 1316, afterwards more loosely.

25 Chiefly some of the older French universities, such as Angers and Orleans. See below, vol. ii, ch. viii. Denifle will not admit this except in the case of Oxford, where the contention is doubtful.

26 That is, after the rise of the university. At an earlier period it had been common; *Hist. lit. de la France*, ix. 81. [It again became more frequent in the fifteenth century.]

27 In the above chapter, I am under exceptional obligations to Denifle, and have with some reserves adopted his position; but I have put the matter in my own way, and do not hold myself responsible for his views except so far as I have actually reproduced them. Denifle hardly recognizes sufficiently the prominence of the dispensation from residence in the earlier conception of a *studium generale*. See the Bull for Rome, cited below, vol. ii, p. 28 n., and above, p. 6, n. 2.

Additional note to Chapter I

[Rashdall in the main accepted Denifle's conclusions on the origin of universities. Later investigation has done little to shake these conclusions. It tends to emphasize the importance of the *licentia docendi* and to strengthen the connexion between the early universities and ecclesiastical authority. It suggests that the sharp distinction between the *studium* and the *studium generale* can easily be exaggerated and that it obscures the growing control of the Pope and the bishops over the whole field of educational activity in the twelfth and thirteenth centuries. Manacorda (*Storia della scuola in Italia*, I. i, c. vii) discusses the various views of previous writers and argues that, even in Bologna, where Denifle traced the origin of the university to the communal schools, the evidence for continuous intervention by the ecclesiastical authority, and particularly by the Pope, is considerable. His conclusion, anticipated on p. 165, that the medieval universities were in origin 'trasformazioni delle scuole vescovili', cannot be literally accepted as a universal truth. It is true of Paris, but it cannot be established, on existing evidence, in the cases of Oxford and Montpellier, nor is it clear that, in the early twelfth century, the masters who taught at Bologna had any connexion with an episcopal school (cf. Haskins, on the *dictamen* of Albert of Samaria, *c.* 1111–18, in *Studies in Mediaeval Culture*, Oxford, 1929, p. 175). On the other hand, Manacorda's main contention, that the continuity of the schools, in Bologna and elsewhere, was mainly due to the oversight of the diocesan authorities who gave the licence to teach, and whose powers at this time were steadily enforced, may be accepted, although, according to one view, Montpellier provides an exception (see below, vol. ii, p. 122). It should be remembered, in this regard, that the importance of the episcopal schools, especially north of the Alps, in the twelfth century has been better realized than it was when Rashdall wrote. Until late in the century Paris was by no means the outstanding centre of higher learning in France, nor was Oxford in England. Why the schools of Paris or Oxford grew into a university, while those of Chartres and Laon, of Exeter and Lincoln did not, is a separate problem, but the groups within which the university organization developed were in the twelfth century given permanence by the *licentia docendi*, and the licence was granted by the *magiscola*, chancellor or archdeacon, as the case might be.

In the formative period the schools were fostered by the ecclesiastical authority and, like the universities into which some of them developed, depended upon this authority for the right to exercise their activity. There were exceptional cases, and these should be regarded as exceptional. In Italy the city schools began too late to be responsible for early developments; outside Italy such schools hardly existed. In the later decades of the twelfth century ecclesiastical control of education was complete.

A long series of papal decrees provided for the creation of schools under episcopal control. It begins with a letter of Eugenius II (*c.* 826), embodied by Gratian in his *Decretum* (pars I, dist. xxxvii, c. 2). The control of education by the secular power in Carolingian times was first shared by, and then gave way to ecclesiastical control. By the end of the twelfth century the ecclesiastical sanction behind the licence to teach was undisputed. (The evidence for the undoubted existence of lay schools, and for the probable existence of lay masters, in the twelfth century is discussed by Manacorda in his fifth chapter; see below, p. 92, n. 1.) Pope Alexander III, in the third Lateran Council in 1179 (see *Decretals*, lib. v, tit. v, c. 1) and in various letters, emphasized the importance of the cathedral schools and laid down rules for the grant of the licence. (See Gaines Post, 'Alexander III, the *licentia docendi* and the rise of the Universities' in *Haskins Anniversary Essays*, Boston, 1929, pp. 254–77.) As Post points out, too much stress has been laid on the point that the licence was to be gratuitous; whether this injunction was observed or not is not really of great importance in the history of university development. The important matter is the continuous guidance and encouragement given by the Papacy. When, on 28 June 1219, Honorius III in a letter to Grazia, the archdeacon of Bologna, decreed 'ut nullus ulterius in civitate predicta ad docendi regimen assumatur, nisi a te obtenta licentia, examinatione praehabita diligenti', he was not initiating a new policy. Manacorda (p. 208) is probably right in urging that the novelty here is the insistence upon a careful examination, not in the application to Bologna of a general practice which had not hitherto prevailed in the schools of that city. (See his quotations from the published and unpublished *summae* of S. Raymond of Pennaforte and the other evidence cited; Post, p. 266, accepts the earlier view that Honorius III was using precedents to bring the Law School of Bologna 'within the papal system'; and see Rossi's criticism of Manacorda, noted in the bibliographical note above, p. 2.)

The papal position in the thirteenth century was defined by Clement IV, in his letter 'contra venerabilem fratrem' of 31 May 1268, addressed to James I, king of Aragon (Potthast, No. 20366; edited by Martène, *Thesaurus anecdotorum*, ii. 603; see Manacorda, *op. cit.*, p. 217 *passim*). The bishop of Maguellone had excommunicated a civilian who had, in accordance with earlier usage (cf. Post, p. 267), received the licence to teach from the king, after he had taken counsel with *iuris prudentes* in the faculty at Montpellier. The Pope rebuked the king for his rancour against the bishop and upheld the claim of the latter to grant the licence in the faculty of law as in the other faculties, in which the episcopal licence had been given *a largissimis retro temporibus*. He did not deny that it had been customary at Montpellier for the king to grant the licence to civilians: 'de licentiandis quibus doctoribus in scientiarum facultatibus aliud canonica iura diffiniunt, aliud principum sanctiones', for local custom had differed and the secular authority at one time had dealt even with matrimonial questions, when the 'censura ecclesiae non vigebat'. On the other hand, the policy of the Church has been laid down by Eugenius II and the general rule applies to new specific conditions, although the species did not exist at the time when the rule was made, just as, if new kinds of corn are grown, the old law of tithe applies to them. 'Cancellarius caput studentium, post episcopum, in quacunque legat vel doceat facultate, ab episcopo ordinatur.'

The issue in debate between Denifle and Kaufmann (above, p. 11, note) may best be considered from the historical standpoint taken by Pope Clement IV. In the thirteenth and fourteenth centuries the *studia* were regarded as ecclesiastical foundations. In S. Thomas's words the *collegium scholasticum* was a *collegium ecclesiasticum*. But this is to be interpreted in the light of the medieval conception that the Christian *ecclesia* was synonymous with Christian society. While the *studium* belonged to the *sacerdotium* rather than to the *imperium*, it was, like both, a part of the Christian society, which acquired a dignity of its own and deserved the fostering attention of *sacerdotium* and *imperium* alike. Thus, kings founded universities in co-operation with and after gaining the approval of the Popes (cf. Lérida, below, ii. 92). Where the spirit of co-operation existed, no burning question need arise if the chancellor was appointed by the king or bishop or masters. After expounding the curious historical view that Charles the Great had transferred the 'studium philosophiae et liberalium artium' from Rome to Paris, in part recompense to the king of the western Franks for the loss of his Empire (*regnum*), a German patriot (probably Alexander of Roes, in the year 1281) concludes: 'Hiis siquidem tribus, scilicet sacerdotio imperio et studio, tamquam tribus virtutibus, videlicet vitali naturali et animali, sancta ecclesia catholica spiritualiter vivificatur augmentatur et regitur' (*De translatione imperii*, ed. H. Grundmann, Leipzig, 1930, p. 27; cf. Cecil Woolf, *Bartolus of Sassoferrato*, Cambridge, 1913, p. 239). This wider conception made any dispute about the particular rights of lay or ecclesiastical authority a matter of local or temporary interest only, so long as the Pope and lay rulers co-operated in the foundation and development of universities. (F. von Bezold, following Gebhardt, has some pertinent remarks to this effect in his review of Kaufmann's work, *Aus Mittelalter und Renaissance*, Munich, 1918, p. 226.) An early instance of co-operation is the confirmation by Alexander III of the immunity granted by the Emperor Frederick I in 1158 to the students of Bologna (below, p. 145, n.). Just as the two powers co-operated in the repression of heresy, so they co-operated in the encouragement of learning. Papal privileges for the German universities, frequently founded by lay rulers, are found throughout the Middle Ages. That the grant of the licence was regarded as an ecclesiastical act is clear from the protest against the practice entered by Marsiglio of Padua: 'conferendi licentias in disciplinis iam dicto episcopo et alteri cuicumque presbytero ac ipsorum soli collegio debeat et licite potest revocari potestas. Est enim hoc humani legislatoris aut eius auctoritate principantis officium', and again, 'nolentes enim aut dubitantes viri literati suorum magisteriorum titulos perdere, appetitu commodi et gloriae consequentis, hosque sibi episcoporum Romanorum aut aliorum auctoritate advenisse, non aliunde, credentes, votis horum assequuntur' (*Defensor Pacis*, ii. xxi, ed. Previté-Orton, Cambridge, 1928, pp. 340, 341).]

That, as time went on, secular princes exercised authority over universities in virtue of their position as founders, or in the public interest, is undoubted; but it is important to distinguish action which can be construed as a deliberate interference with ecclesiastical or quasi-ecclesiastical privilege from co-operation which can be traced throughout the Middle Ages in all kinds of social activity, and which raised no controversial issues. It would not be difficult, if no regard were paid to this distinction, to show that the university of Oxford was under the control as well as the patronage of the king of England, and the more so, because the Chancellor was invested with a measure of temporal jurisdiction. Blackstone, indeed, traced the grant by the Crown of privileges to universities back to the Authenticum '*Habita*' or imperial constitution of 1158 (see Strickland Gibson, 'The Great Charter of Charles I', *Bodleian Quarterly Record*, vii. 1933).]

31

KNOWLEDGE ITS OWN END

John Henry Newman

Source: John Henry Newman, *The Idea of a University Defined and Illustrated*, London: Longmans, Green and Co., 1910, pp. 99–123.

A university may be considered with reference either to its Students or to its Studies; and the principle, that all Knowledge is a whole and the separate Sciences parts of one, which I have hitherto been using in behalf of its studies, is equally important when we direct our attention to its students. Now then I turn to the students, and shall consider the education which, by virtue of this principle, a University will give them; and thus I shall be introduced, Gentlemen, to the second question, which I proposed to discuss, viz. whether and in what sense its teaching, viewed relatively to the taught, carries the attribute of Utility along with it.

1.

I have said that all branches of knowledge are connected together, because the subject-matter of knowledge is intimately united in itself, as being the acts and the work of the Creator. Hence it is that the Sciences, into which our knowledge may be said to be cast, have multiplied bearings one on another, and an internal sympathy, and admit, or rather demand, comparison and adjustment. They complete, correct, balance each other. This consideration, if well-founded, must be taken into account, not only as regards the attainment of truth, which is their common end, but as regards the influence which they exercise upon those whose education consists in the study of them. I have said already, that to give undue prominence to one is to be unjust to another; to neglect or supersede these is to divert those from their proper object. It is to unsettle the boundary lines between science and science, to disturb their action, to destroy the harmony which binds them together. Such a proceeding will have a corresponding effect when introduced into a place of education. There is no science but tells a different tale, when viewed as a portion of a whole, from what it is likely to suggest when taken by itself, without the safeguard, as I may call it, of others.

Let me make use of an illustration. In the combination of colours, very different effects are produced by a difference in their selection and juxta-position; red, green, and white, change their shades, according to the contrast to which they are submitted. And, in like manner, the drift and meaning of a branch of knowledge varies with the company in which it is introduced to the student. If his reading is confined simply to one subject, however such division of labour may favour the advancement of a particular pursuit, a point into which I do not here enter, certainly it has a tendency to contract his mind. If it is incorporated with others, it depends on those others as to the kind of influence which it exerts upon him. Thus the Classics, which in England are the means of refining the taste, have in France subserved the spread of revolutionary and deistical doctrines. In Metaphysics, again, Butler's Analogy of Religion, which has had so much to do with the conver-sion to the Catholic faith of members of the University of Oxford, appeared to Pitt and others, who had received a different training, to operate only in the direction of infidelity. And so again, Watson, Bishop of Llandaff, as I think he tells us in the narrative of his life, felt the science of Mathematics to indispose the mind to religious belief, while others see in its investiga-tions the best parallel, and thereby defence, of the Christian Mysteries. In like manner, I suppose, Arcesilas would not have handled logic as Aristotle, nor Aristotle have criticized poets as Plato; yet reasoning and poetry are subject to scientific rules.

It is a great point then to enlarge the range of studies which a University professes, even for the sake of the students; and, though they cannot pursue every subject which is open to them, they will be the gainers by living among those and under those who represent the whole circle. This I conceive to be the advantage of a seat of universal learning, considered as a place of educa-tion. An assemblage of learned men, zealous for their own sciences, and rivals of each other, are brought, by familiar intercourse and for the sake of intellectual peace, to adjust together the claims and relations of their respec-tive subjects of investigation. They learn to respect, to consult, to aid each other. Thus is created a pure and clear atmosphere of thought, which the student also breathes, though in his own case he only pursues a few sciences out of the multitude. He profits by an intellectual tradition, which is inde-pendent of particular teachers, which guides him in his choice of subjects, and duly interprets for him those which he chooses. He apprehends the great outlines of knowledge, the principles on which it rests, the scale of its parts, its lights and its shades, its great points and its little, as he otherwise cannot apprehend them. Hence it is that his education is called "Liberal." A habit of mind is formed which lasts through life, of which the attributes are, freedom, equitableness, calmness, moderation, and wisdom; or what in a former Discourse I have ventured to call a philosophical habit. This then I would assign as the special fruit of the education furnished at a University, as contrasted with other places of teaching or modes of teaching. This is the main purpose of a University in its treatment of its students.

And now the question is asked me, What is the *use* of it? and my answer will constitute the main subject of the Discourses which are to follow.

2.

Cautious and practical thinkers, I say, will ask of me, what, after all, is the gain of this Philosophy, of which I make such account, and from which I promise so much. Even supposing it to enable us to exercise the degree of trust exactly due to every science respectively, and to estimate precisely the value of every truth which is anywhere to be found, how are we better for this master view of things, which I have been extolling? Does it not reverse the principle of the division of labour? will practical objects be obtained better or worse by its cultivation? to what then does it lead? where does it end? what does it do? how does it profit? what does it promise? Particular sciences are respectively the basis of definite arts, which carry on to results tangible and beneficial the truths which are the subjects of the knowledge attained; what is the Art of this science of sciences? what is the fruit of such a Philosophy? what are we proposing to effect, what inducements do we hold out to the Catholic community, when we set about the enterprise of founding a University?

I am asked what is the end of University Education, and of the Liberal or Philosophical Knowledge which I conceive it to impart: I answer, that what I have already said has been sufficient to show that it has a very tangible, real, and sufficient end, though the end cannot be divided from that knowledge itself. Knowledge is capable of being its own end. Such is the constitution of the human mind, that any kind of knowledge, if it be really such, is its own reward. And if this is true of all knowledge, it is true also of that special Philosophy, which I have made to consist in a comprehensive view of truth in all its branches, of the relations of science to science, of their mutual bearings, and their respective values. What the worth of such an acquirement is, compared with other objects which we seek,—wealth or power or honour or the conveniences and comforts of life, I do not profess here to discuss; but I would maintain, and mean to show, that it is an object, in its own nature so really and undeniably good, as to be the compensation of a great deal of thought in the compassing, and a great deal of trouble in the attaining.

Now, when I say that Knowledge is, not merely a means to something beyond it, or the preliminary of certain arts into which it naturally resolves, but an end sufficient to rest in and to pursue for its own sake, surely I am uttering no paradox, for I am stating what is both intelligible in itself, and has ever been the common judgment of philosophers and the ordinary feeling of mankind. I am saying what at least the public opinion of this day ought to be slow to deny, considering how much we have heard of late years, in opposition to Religion, of entertaining, curious, and various knowledge. I am but saying what whole volumes have been written to illustrate, viz., by a "selection from the records of Philosophy, Literature, and Art, in all ages and countries, of a body of examples, to show how the most unpropitious circumstances have been unable to conquer an ardent desire for the acquisition of knowledge."[1] That further advantages accrue to us and redound to others by its possession, over and above what it is in itself, I am very far indeed from denying; but, independent of these, we are satisfying a direct need of our nature in its very acquisition; and, whereas our nature, unlike that of the inferior creation, does not at once reach its perfection, but depends, in order to it, on a number of external aids and appliances, Knowledge, as one of the principal of these, is valuable for what its very presence in us does for us after the manner of a habit, even though it be turned to no further account, nor subserve any direct end.

3.

Hence it is that Cicero, in enumerating the various heads of mental excellence, lays down the pursuit of Knowledge for its own sake, as the first of them. "This pertains most of all to human nature," he says, "for we are all of us drawn to the pursuit of Knowledge; in which to excel we consider excellent, whereas to mistake, to err, to be ignorant, to be deceived, is both an evil and a disgrace."[2] And he considers Knowledge the very first object to which we are attracted, after the supply of our physical wants. After the calls and duties of our animal existence, as they may be termed, as regards ourselves, our family, and our neighbours, follows, he tells us, "the search after truth. Accordingly, as soon as we escape from the pressure of necessary cares, forthwith we desire to see, to hear, and to learn; and consider the knowledge of what is hidden or is wonderful a condition of our happiness."

This passage, though it is but one of many similar passages in a multitude of authors, I take for the very reason that it is so familiarly known to us; and I wish you to observe, Gentlemen, how distinctly it separates the pursuit of Knowledge from those ulterior objects to which certainly it can be made to conduce, and which are, I suppose, solely contemplated by the persons who would ask of me the use of a University or Liberal Education. So far from dreaming of the cultivation of Knowledge directly and mainly in order to our physical comfort and enjoyment, for the sake of life and person, of health, of the conjugal and family union, of the social tie and civil security, the great Orator implies, that it is only after our physical and political needs are supplied, and when we are "free from necessary duties and cares," that we are in a condition for "desiring to see, to hear, and to learn." Nor does he contemplate in the least degree the reflex or subsequent action of Knowledge, when acquired, upon those material goods which we set out by securing before we seek it; on the contrary, he expressly denies its bearing upon social life altogether, strange as such a procedure is to those who live after the rise of the Baconian philosophy, and he cautions us against such a cultivation of it as will interfere with our duties to our fellow-creatures. "All these methods," he says, "are engaged in the investigation of truth; by the pursuit of which to be carried off from public occupations is a transgression of duty. For the praise of virtue lies altogether in action; yet intermissions often occur, and then we recur to such pursuits; not to say that the incessant activity of the mind is vigorous enough to carry us on in the pursuit of knowledge, even without any exertion of our own." The idea of benefiting society by means of "the pursuit of science and knowledge" did not enter at all into the motives which he would assign for their cultivation.

This was the ground of the opposition which the elder Cato made to the introduction of Greek Philosophy among his countrymen, when Carneades and his companions, on occasion of their embassy, were charming the Roman youth with their eloquent expositions of it. The fit representative of a practical people, Cato estimated every thing by what it produced; whereas the Pursuit of Knowledge promised nothing beyond Knowledge itself. He despised that refinement or enlargement of mind of which he had no experience.

4.

Things, which can bear to be cut off from every thing else and yet persist in living, must have life in themselves; pursuits, which issue in nothing, and still maintain their ground for ages, which are regarded as admirable, though they have not as yet proved themselves to be useful, must have their sufficient end in themselves, whatever it turn out to be. And we are brought to the same conclusion by considering the force of the epithet, by which the knowledge under consideration is popularly designated. It is common to speak of "*liberal* knowledge," of the "*liberal* arts and studies," and of a "*liberal* education," as the especial characteristic or property of a University and of a gentleman; what is really meant by the word? Now, first, in its grammatical sense it is opposed to *servile;* and by "servile work" is understood, as our catechisms inform us, bodily labour, mechanical employment, and the like, in which the mind has little or no part. Parallel to such servile works are those arts, if they deserve the name, of which the poet speaks,[3] which owe their origin and their method to hazard, not to skill; as, for instance, the practice and operations of an empiric. As far as this contrast may be considered as a guide into the meaning of the word, liberal education and liberal pursuits are exercises of mind, of reason, of reflection.

But we want something more for its explanation, for there are bodily exercises which are liberal, and mental exercises which are not so. For instance, in ancient times the practitioners in medicine were commonly slaves; yet it was an art as intellectual in its nature, in spite of the pretence, fraud, and quackery with which it might then, as now, be debased, as it was heavenly in its aim. And so in like manner, we contrast a liberal education with a commercial education or a professional; yet no one can deny that commerce and the professions afford scope for the highest and most diversified powers of mind. There is then a great variety of intellectual exercises, which are not technically called "liberal;" on the other hand, I say, there are exercises of the body which do receive that appellation. Such, for instance, was the palæstra, in ancient times; such the Olympic games, in which strength and dexterity of body as well as of mind gained the prize. In Xenophon we read of the young Persian nobility being taught to ride on horse-back and to speak the truth; both being among the accomplishments of a gentleman. War, too, however rough a profession, has ever been accounted liberal, unless in cases when it becomes heroic, which would introduce us to another subject.

Now comparing these instances together, we shall have no difficulty in determining the principle of this apparent variation in the application of the term which I am examining. Manly games, or games of skill, or military prowess, though bodily, are, it seems, accounted liberal; on the other hand, what is merely professional, though highly intellectual, nay, though liberal in comparison of trade and manual labour, is not simply called liberal, and mercantile occupations are not liberal at all. Why this distinction? because that alone is liberal knowledge, which stands on its own pretensions, which is independent of sequel, expects no complement, refuses to be *informed* (as it is called) by any end, or absorbed into any art, in order duly to present itself to our contemplation. The most ordinary pursuits have this specific character, if they are self-sufficient and complete; the highest lose it, when they minister to something beyond them. It is absurd to balance, in point of worth and importance, a treatise on reducing fractures with a game of cricket or a fox-chase; yet of the two the bodily exercise has that quality which we call "liberal," and the intellectual has it not. And so of the learned professions altogether, considered merely as professions; although one of them be the most popularly beneficial, and another the most politically important, and the third the most intimately divine of all human pursuits, yet the very greatness of their end, the health of the body, or of the commonwealth, or of the soul, diminishes, not increases, their claim to the appellation "liberal," and that still more, if they are cut down to the strict exigencies of that end. If, for instance, Theology, instead of being cultivated as a contemplation, be limited to the purposes of the pulpit or be represented by the catechism, it loses,—not its usefulness, not its divine character, not its meritoriousness (rather it gains a claim upon these titles by such charitable condescension),—but it does lose the particular attribute which I am illustrating; just as a face worn by tears and fasting loses its beauty, or a labourer's hand loses its delicateness;—for Theology thus exercised is not simple knowledge, but rather is an art or a business making use of Theology. And thus it appears that even what is supernatural need not be liberal, nor need a hero be a gentleman, for the plain reason that one idea is not another idea. And in like manner the Baconian Philosophy, by using its physical sciences in the service of man, does thereby transfer them from the order of Liberal Pursuits to, I do not say the inferior, but the distinct class of the Useful. And, to take a different instance, hence again, as is evident, whenever personal gain is the motive, still more distinctive an effect has it upon the character of a given pursuit; thus racing, which was a liberal exercise in Greece, forfeits its rank in times like these, so far as it is made the occasion of gambling.

All that I have been now saying is summed up in a few characteristic words of the great Philosopher. "Of possessions," he says, "those rather are useful, which bear fruit; those *liberal, which tend to enjoyment*. By fruitful, I mean, which yield revenue; by enjoyable, where *nothing accrues of consequence beyond the using*."[4]

5.

Do not suppose, that in thus appealing to the ancients, I am throwing back the world two thousand years, and fettering Philosophy with the reasonings of paganism. While the world lasts, will Aristotle's doctrine on these matters last, for he is the oracle of nature and of truth. While we are men, we cannot help, to a great extent, being Aristotelians, for the great Master does but analyze the thoughts, feelings, views, and opinions of human kind. He has told us the meaning of our own words and ideas, before we were born. In many subject-matters, to think correctly, is to think like Aristotle; and we are his disciples whether we will or no, though we may not know it. Now, as to the particular instance before us, the word "liberal" as applied to Knowledge and Education, expresses a specific idea, which ever has been, and ever will be, while the nature of man is the same, just as the idea of the Beautiful is specific, or of the Sublime, or of the Ridiculous, or of the Sordid. It is in the world now, it was in the world then; and, as in the case of the dogmas of faith, it is illustrated by a continuous historical tradition, and never was out of the world, from the time it came into it. There have indeed been differences of opinion from time to time, as to what pursuits and what arts came under that idea, but such differences are but an additional evidence of its reality. That idea must have a substance in it, which has maintained its ground amid these conflicts and changes, which has ever served as a standard to measure things withal, which has passed from mind to mind unchanged, when there was so much to colour, so much to influence any notion or thought whatever, which was not founded in our very nature. Were it a mere generalization, it would have varied with the subjects from which it was generalized; but though its subjects vary with the age, it varies not itself. The palæstra may seem a liberal exercise to Lycurgus, and illiberal to Seneca; coach-driving and prize-fighting may be recognized in Elis, and be condemned in England; music may be despicable in the eyes of certain moderns, and be in the highest place with Aristotle and Plato,—(and the case is the same in the particular application of the idea of Beauty, or of Goodness, or of Moral Virtue, there is a difference of tastes, a difference of judgments)—still these variations imply, instead of discrediting, the archetypal idea, which is but a previous hypothesis or condition, by means of which issue is joined between contending opinions, and without which there would be nothing to dispute about.

I consider, then, that I am chargeable with no paradox, when I speak of a Knowledge which is its own end, when I call it liberal knowledge, or a gentleman's knowledge, when I educate for it, and make it the scope of a University. And still less am I incurring such a charge, when I make this acquisition consist, not in Knowledge in a vague and ordinary sense, but in that Knowledge which I have especially called Philosophy or, in an extended sense of the word, Science; for whatever claims Knowledge has to be considered as a good, these it has in a higher degree when it is viewed not vaguely, not popularly, but precisely and transcendently as Philosophy. Knowledge, I say, is then especially liberal, or sufficient for itself, apart from every external and ulterior object, when and so far as it is philosophical, and this I proceed to show.

6.

Now bear with me, Gentlemen, if what I am about to say, has at first sight a fanciful appearance. Philosophy, then, or Science, is related to Knowledge in this way:—Knowledge is called by the name of Science or Philosophy, when it is acted upon, informed, or if I may use a strong figure, impregnated by Reason. Reason is the principle of that intrinsic fecundity of Knowledge, which, to those who possess it, is its especial value, and which dispenses with the necessity of their looking abroad for any end to rest upon external to itself. Knowledge, indeed, when thus exalted into a scientific form, is also power; not only is it excellent in itself, but whatever such excellence may be, it is something more, it has a result beyond itself. Doubtless; but that is a further consideration, with which I am not concerned. I only say that, prior to its being a power, it is a good; that it is, not only an instrument, but an end. I know well it may resolve itself into an art, and terminate in a mechanical process, and in tangible fruit; but it also may fall back upon that Reason which informs it, and resolve itself into Philosophy. In one case it is called Useful Knowledge, in the other Liberal. The same person may cultivate it in both ways at once; but this again is a matter foreign to my subject; here I do but say that there are two ways of using Knowledge, and in matter of fact those who use it in one way are not likely to use it in the other, or at least in a very limited measure. You see, then, here are two methods of Education; the end of the one is to be philosophical, of the other to be mechanical; the one rises towards general ideas, the other is exhausted upon what is particular and external. Let me not be thought to deny the necessity, or to decry the benefit, of such attention to what is particular and practical, as belongs to the useful or mechanical arts; life could not go on without them; we owe our daily welfare to them; their exercise is the duty of the many, and we owe to the many a debt of gratitude for fulfilling that duty. I only say that Knowledge, in proportion as it tends more and more to be particular, ceases to be Knowledge. It is a question whether Knowledge can in any proper sense be predicated of the brute creation; without pretending to metaphysical exactness of phraseology, which would be unsuitable to an occasion like this, I say, it seems to me improper to call that passive sensation, or perception of things, which brutes seem to possess, by the name of Knowledge. When I speak of Knowledge, I mean something intellectual, something which grasps what it perceives through the senses; something which takes a view of things; which sees more than the senses convey; which reasons upon what it sees, and while it sees; which invests it with an idea. It expresses itself, not in a mere enunciation, but by an enthymeme: it is of the nature of science from the first, and in this consists its dignity. The principle of real dignity in Knowledge, its worth, its desirableness, considered irrespectively of its results, is this germ within it of a scientific or a philosophical process. This is how it comes to be an end in itself; this is why it admits of being called Liberal. Not to know the relative disposition of things is the state of slaves or children; to have mapped out the Universe is the boast, or at least the ambition, of Philosophy.

Moreover, such knowledge is not a mere extrinsic or accidental advantage, which is ours to-day and another's to-morrow, which may be got up from a book, and easily forgotten again, which we can command or communicate at our pleasure, which we can borrow for the occasion, carry about in our hand, and take into the market; it is an acquired illumination, it is a habit, a personal possession, and an inward endowment. And this is the reason, why it is more correct, as well as more usual, to speak of a University as a place of education, than of instruction, though, when knowledge is concerned, instruction would at first sight have seemed the more appropriate word. We are instructed, for instance, in manual exercises, in the fine and useful arts, in trades, and in ways of business; for these are methods, which have little or no effect upon the mind itself, are contained in rules committed to memory, to tradition, or to use, and bear upon an end external to themselves. But education is a higher word; it implies an action upon our mental nature, and the formation of a character; it is something individual and permanent, and is commonly spoken of in connexion with religion and virtue. When, then, we speak of the communication of

Knowledge as being Education, we thereby really imply that that Knowledge is a state or condition of mind; and since cultivation of mind is surely worth seeking for its own sake, we are thus brought once more to the conclusion, which the word "Liberal" and the word "Philosophy" have already suggested, that there is a Knowledge, which is desirable, though nothing come of it, as being of itself a treasure, and a sufficient remuneration of years of labour.

7.

This, then, is the answer which I am prepared to give to the question with which I opened this Discourse. Before going on to speak of the object of the Church in taking up Philosophy, and the uses to which she puts it, I am prepared to maintain that Philosophy is its own end, and, as I conceive, I have now begun the proof of it. I am prepared to maintain that there is a knowledge worth possessing for what it is, and not merely for what it does; and what minutes remain to me to-day I shall devote to the removal of some portion of the indistinctness and confusion with which the subject may in some minds be surrounded.

It may be objected then, that, when we profess to seek Knowledge for some end or other beyond itself, whatever it be, we speak intelligibly; but that, whatever men may have said, however obstinately the idea may have kept its ground from age to age, still it is simply unmeaning to say that we seek Knowledge for its own sake, and for nothing else; for that it ever leads to something beyond itself, which therefore is its end, and the cause why it is desirable;—moreover, that this end is twofold, either of this world or of the next; that all knowledge is cultivated either for secular objects or for eternal; that if it is directed to secular objects, it is called Useful Knowledge, if to eternal, Religious or Christian Knowledge;—in consequence, that if, as I have allowed, this Liberal Knowledge does not benefit the body or estate, it ought to benefit the soul; but if the fact be really so, that it is neither a physical or a secular good on the one hand, nor a moral good on the other, it cannot be a good at all, and is not worth the trouble which is necessary for its acquisition.

And then I may be reminded that the professors of this Liberal or Philosophical Knowledge have themselves, in every age, recognized this exposition of the matter, and have submitted to the issue in which it terminates; for they have ever been attempting to make men virtuous; or, if not, at least have assumed that refinement of mind was virtue, and that they themselves were the virtuous portion of mankind. This they have professed on the one hand; and on the other, they have utterly failed in their professions, so as ever to make themselves a proverb among men, and a laughing-stock both to the grave and the dissipated portion of mankind, in consequence of them. Thus they have furnished against themselves both the ground and the means of their own exposure, without any trouble at all to any one else. In a word, from the time that Athens was the University of the world, what has Philosophy taught men, but to promise without practising, and to aspire without attaining? What has the deep and lofty thought of its disciples ended in but eloquent words? Nay, what has its teaching ever meditated, when it was boldest in its remedies for human ill, beyond charming us to sleep by its lessons, that we might feel nothing at all? like some melodious air, or rather like those strong and transporting perfumes, which at first spread their sweetness over every thing they touch, but in a little while do but offend in proportion as they once pleased us. Did Philosophy support Cicero under the disfavour of the fickle populace, or nerve Seneca to oppose an imperial tyrant? It abandoned Brutus, as he sorrowfully confessed, in his greatest need, and it forced Cato, as his panegyrist strangely boasts, into the false position of defying heaven. How few can be counted among its professors, who, like Polemo, were thereby converted from a profligate course, or like Anaxagoras, thought the world well lost in exchange for its possession? The philosopher in Rasselas taught a superhuman doctrine, and then succumbed without an effort to a trial of human affection.

"He discoursed," we are told, "with great energy on the government of the passions. His look was venerable, his action graceful, his pronunciation clear, and his diction elegant. He showed, with great strength of sentiment and variety of illustration, that human nature is degraded and debased, when the lower faculties predominate over the higher. He communicated the various precepts given, from time to time, for the conquest of passion, and displayed the happiness of those who had obtained the important victory, after which man is no longer the slave of fear, nor the fool of hope . . . He enumerated many examples of heroes immoveable by pain or pleasure, who looked with indifference on those modes or accidents to which the vulgar give the names of good and evil."

Rasselas in a few days found the philosopher in a room half darkened, with his eyes misty, and his face pale. "Sir," said he, "you have come at a time when all human friendship is useless; what I suffer cannot be remedied, what I have lost cannot be supplied. My daughter, my only daughter, from whose tenderness I expected all the comforts of my age, died last night of a fever." "Sir," said the prince, "mortality is an event by which a wise man can never be surprised; we know that death is always near, and it should therefore always be expected." "Young man," answered the philosopher, "you speak like one who has never felt the pangs of separation." "Have you, then, forgot the precept," said Rasselas, "which you so powerfully enforced? . . . consider that external things are naturally variable, but truth and reason are always the same." "What comfort," said the mourner, "can truth and reason afford me? Of what effect are they now, but to tell me that my daughter will not be restored?"

8.

Better, far better, to make no professions, you will say, than to cheat others with what we are not, and to scandalize them with what we are. The sensualist, or the man of the world, at any rate is not the victim of fine words, but pursues a reality and gains it. The Philosophy of Utility, you will say, Gentlemen, has at least done its work; and I grant it,—it aimed low, but it has fulfilled its aim. If that man of great intellect who has been its Prophet in the conduct of life played false to his own professions, he was not bound by his philosophy to be true to his friend or faithful in his trust. Moral virtue was not the line in which he undertook to instruct men; and though, as the poet calls him, he were the "meanest" of mankind, he was so in what may be called his private capacity and without any prejudice to the theory of induction. He had a right to be so, if he chose, for any thing that the Idols of the den or the theatre had to say to the contrary. His mission was the increase of physical enjoyment and social comfort;[5] and most wonderfully, most awfully has he fulfilled his conception and his design. Almost day by day have we fresh and fresh shoots, and buds, and blossoms, which are to ripen into fruit, on that magical tree of Knowledge which he planted, and to which none of us perhaps, except the very poor, but owes, if not his present life, at least his daily food, his health, and general well-being. He was the divinely provided minister of temporal benefits to all of us so great, that, whatever I am forced to think of him as a man, I have not the heart, from mere gratitude, to speak of him severely. And, in spite of the tendencies of his philosophy, which are, as we see at this day, to depreciate, or to trample on Theology, he has himself, in his writings, gone out of his way, as if with a prophetic misgiving of those tendencies, to insist on it as the instrument of that beneficent Father,[6] who, when He came on earth in visible form, took on Him first and most prominently the office of assuaging the bodily wounds of human nature. And truly, like the old mediciner in the tale, "he sat diligently at his work, and hummed, with cheerful countenance, a pious song;" and then in turn "went out singing into the meadows so gaily, that those who had seen him from afar might well have thought it was a youth gathering flowers for his beloved, instead of an old physician gathering healing herbs in the morning dew."[7]

Alas, that men, in the action of life or in their heart of hearts, are not what they seem to be in their moments of excitement, or in their trances or intoxications of genius,—so good, so noble, so serene! Alas, that Bacon too in his own way should after all be but the fellow of those heathen philosophers who in their disadvantages had some excuse for their inconsistency, and who surprise us rather in what they did say than in what they did not do! Alas, that he too, like Socrates or Seneca, must be stripped of his holy-day coat, which looks so fair, and should be but a mockery amid his most majestic gravity of phrase; and, for all his vast abilities, should, in the littleness of his own moral being, but typify the intellectual narrowness of his school! However, granting all this, heroism after all was not his philosophy:—I cannot deny he has abundantly achieved what he proposed. His is simply a Method whereby bodily discomforts and temporal wants are to be most effectually removed from the greatest number; and already, before it has shown any signs of exhaustion, the gifts of nature, in their most artificial shapes and luxurious profusion and diversity, from all quarters of the earth, are, it is undeniable, by its means brought even to our doors, and we rejoice in them.

9.

Useful Knowledge then, I grant, has done its work; and Liberal Knowledge as certainly has not done its work,—that is, supposing, as the objectors assume, its direct end, like Religious Knowledge, is to make men better; but this I will not for an instant allow, and, unless I allow it, those objectors have said nothing to the purpose. I admit, rather I maintain, what they have been urging, for I consider Knowledge to have its end in itself. For all its friends, or its enemies, may say, I insist upon it, that it is as real a mistake to burden it with virtue or religion as with the mechanical arts. Its direct business is not to steel the soul against temptation or to console it in affliction, any more than to set the loom in motion, or to direct the steam carriage; be it ever so much the means or the condition of both material and moral advancement, still, taken by and in itself, it as little mends our hearts as it improves our temporal circumstances. And if its eulogists claim for it such a power, they commit the very same kind of encroachment on a province not their own as the political economist who should maintain that his science educated him for casuistry or diplomacy. Knowledge is one thing, virtue is another; good sense is not conscience, refinement is not humility, nor is largeness and justness of view faith. Philosophy, however enlightened, however profound, gives no command over the passions, no influential motives, no vivifying principles. Liberal Education makes not the Christian, not the Catholic, but the gentleman. It is well to be a gentlemen, it is well to have a cultivated intellect, a delicate taste, a candid, equitable, dispassionate mind, a noble and courteous bearing in the conduct of life;—these are the connatural qualities of a large knowledge; they are the objects of a University; I am advocating, I shall illustrate and insist upon them; but still, I repeat, they are no guarantee for sanctity or even for conscientiousness, they may attach to the man of the world, to the profligate, to the heartless,— pleasant, alas, and attractive as he shows when decked out in them. Taken by themselves, they do but seem to be what they are not; they look like virtue at a distance, but they are detected by close observers, and on the long run; and hence it is that they are popularly accused of pretence and hypocrisy, not, I repeat, from their own fault, but because their professors and their admirers persist in taking them for what they are not, and are officious in arrogating for them a praise to which they have no claim. Quarry the granite rock with razors, or moor the vessel with a thread of silk; then may you hope with such keen and delicate instruments as human knowledge and human reason to contend against those giants, the passion and the pride of man.

Surely we are not driven to theories of this kind, in order to vindicate the value and dignity of Liberal Knowledge. Surely the real grounds on which its pretensions rest are not so very subtle or abstruse, so very strange or improbable. Surely it is very intelligible to say, and that is what I say here, that Liberal Education, viewed in itself, is simply the cultivation of the intellect, as such, and its object is nothing more or less than intellectual excellence. Every thing has its own perfection, be it higher or lower in the scale of things; and the perfection of one is not the perfection of another. Things animate, inanimate, visible, invisible, all are good in their kind, and have a *best* of themselves, which is an object of pursuit. Why do you take such pains with your garden or your park? You see to your walks and turf and shrubberies; to your trees and drives; not as if you meant to make an orchard of the one, or corn or pasture land of the other, but because there is a special beauty in all that is goodly in wood, water, plain, and slope, brought all together by art into one shape, and grouped into one whole. Your cities are beautiful, your palaces, your public buildings, your territorial mansions, your churches; and their beauty leads to nothing beyond itself. There is a physical beauty and a moral: there is a beauty of person, there is a beauty of our moral being, which is natural virtue; and in like manner there is a beauty, there is a perfection, of the intellect. There is an ideal perfection in these various subject-matters, towards which individual instances are seen to rise, and which are the standards for all instances whatever. The Greek divinities and demigods, as the statuary has moulded them, with their symmetry of figure, and their high forehead and their regular features, are the perfection of physical beauty. The heroes, of whom history tells, Alexander, or Cæsar, or Scipio, or Saladin, are the representatives of that magnanimity or self-mastery which is the greatness of human nature. Christianity too has its heroes, and in the supernatural order, and we call them Saints. The artist puts before him beauty of feature and form; the poet, beauty of mind; the preacher, the beauty of grace: then intellect too, I repeat, has its beauty, and it has those who aim at it. To open the mind, to correct it, to refine it, to enable it to know, and to digest, master, rule, and use its knowledge, to give it power over its own faculties, application, flexibility, method, critical exactness, sagacity, resource, address, eloquent expression, is an object as intelligible (for here we are inquiring, not what the object of a Liberal Education is worth, nor what use the Church makes of it, but what it is in itself), I say, an object as intelligible as the cultivation of virtue, while, at the same time, it is absolutely distinct from it.

10.

This indeed is but a temporal object, and a transitory possession; but so are other things in themselves which we make much of and pursue. The moralist will tell us that man, in all his functions, is but a flower which blossoms and fades, except so far as a higher principle breathes upon him, and makes him and what he is immortal. Body and mind are carried on into an eternal state of being by the gifts of Divine Munificence; but at first they do but fail in a failing world; and if the powers of intellect decay, the powers of the body have decayed before them, and, as an Hospital or an Almshouse, though its end be ephemeral, may be sanctified to the service of religion, so surely may a University, even were it nothing more than I have as yet described it. We attain to heaven by using this world well, though it is to pass away; we perfect our nature, not by undoing it, but by adding to it what is more than nature, and directing it towards aims higher than its own.

Notes

1 Pursuit of Knowledge under Difficulties. Introd.
2 Cicer. Offic. init.
3 $T\acute{\epsilon}\chi\nu\eta\ \tau\acute{\upsilon}\chi\eta\nu\ \acute{\epsilon}\sigma\tau\epsilon\rho\xi\epsilon\ \kappa\alpha\grave{\iota}\ \tau\acute{\upsilon}\chi\eta\ \tau\acute{\epsilon}\nu\eta\nu$
                  Vid. Arist. Nic. Ethic. vi.
4 Aristot. Rhet. i. 5.
5 It will be seen that on the whole I agree with Lord Macaulay in his Essay on Bacon's Philosophy. I do not know whether he would agree with me.
6 De Augment. iv. 2, vid. Macaulay's Essay; vid. also "In principio operis ad Deum Patrem, Deum Verbum, Deum Spiritum, preces fundimus humillimas et ardentissimas, ut humani generis ærumnarum memores, et peregrinationis istius vitæ, in quâ dies paucos et malos terimus, *novis suis eleemosynis, per manus nostras*, familiam humanam dotare dignentur. Atque illud insuper supplices rogamus, ne *humana divinis officiant*; neve *ex reseratione viarum sensûs*, et accensione majore luminis naturalis, *aliquid incredulitatis* et noctis, animis nostris erga divina mysteria oboriatur," etc. *Præf*. Instaur. Magn.
7 Fouque's Unknown Patient.

LOSS AND GAIN

John Henry Newman in 2005

Sheldon Rothblatt

Source: Ann Lavan (ed.) *The University and Society: From Newman to the Market*, Conference Proceedings, UCD College of Human Sciences, University College Dublin, 2006, pp. 15–29.

There is a custom that pious founders must be recalled with, well, piety. I am not certain that Newman would have desired such enforced reverence. Not that he was especially humble, although in theological terms very likely so. He was a complex man and aware of human limitations. It is also doubtful that he actually was the founder of University College Dublin, as we notionally describe those who create institutions, nor—and of this I am certain—would he have recognised in the structure, administration and ethos of University College as part of a national system of mass higher education the type of university that he admired.

But let me hope that these opening remarks do not suggest that Newman's overall significance depends on his relevance to our times. Much history has been written in this mode, justifying the life and thought of a thinker by what he was able to anticipate. We need not establish that what Newman thought, said and did have validity primarily because he was, as the expression goes, ahead of his time. That sort of whiggishness was disparaged some seventy years ago by the Cambridge University historian Herbert Butterfield, who said that the past exists independently of the present. In a subsequent work published during World War II, Butterfield appeared to change his mind, but the whiggishness that resulted in a second book on the subject was of another character, an effort to capture the spirit or essence of a past achievement rather than laud its topical semblance. Or we might say that in retrieving the historical spirit of a seminal work, especially one that is fundamentally different from the convenient modes of present thought, we better understand our own assumptions.

Therefore I come in a mood neither to praise John Henry Cardinal Newman nor to bury him, but rather to situate him in time and place and to enquire (I'm not sure) as to just what such historicity may mean. Newman is an important figure, but not a conventionally important figure. I will suggest that although his outright impact on the history of universities in the English-speaking world is limited, he conveys through his writings more than through his example a unique moving authority, a capacity to stir the mind. He compels us, even against our wills, to see the academy as he saw it and to consider, as he asked, and we repeat today, 'what are we here for?'

He was by no means the only Victorian to ask that question; but he answered it more fully, with greater scope and passion, than his contemporaries. He lived at a time when the historic role of the ancient universities was being severely questioned and when newer institutions were responding to newer demands. The existing universities of England and Scotland had undergone and continued to undergo internal and external change. New universities were being founded all over the British Isles. Ireland itself was becoming a testing ground for experiments in higher education. Newman was in exile from his beloved Oxford and tried emotionally to prevent its disappearance, as he knew it, by reconstructing its essential features. He struggled mightily to retain a particular legacy by recording it before the curtain of history came crashing down forever. Oxford went on, in Alfred Lord Tennyson's railway image, to spin down the ringing grooves of change. Newman rode on railways, but I doubt he admired the technological mentality behind rail travel, nor was he pleased with a world popularly described in terms of iron, speed and smoke, but represented mysteriously by the famous painting of the Great Western Railway by Turner.

Readers of John Henry Newman's corpus will recognise that the title I have assigned to my lecture is taken from his novel published in 1848 and subtitled *The Story of a Convert. Loss and Gain* is an autobiographical work that is sometimes called the first of the university novels, a copious genre much contributed to by British and American writers from Newman's day to the present. While hardly uniquely British or American, the university novel nevertheless appears to be dominated by writers from anglophone countries. I am sure that more continental contributions will be found, as Marta Ronne in Uppsala has located more twentieth-century novels about university women in Sweden than previously supposed.[1] But probably the importance of the university novel to university history in English-speaking nations is attributable to the importance of a particular conception of undergraduate education deriving from English and Scottish sources. In the English, American and Scottish traditions, the undergraduate experience is a *rite de passage* for which the university is uniquely responsible, standing *in loco parentis* to the student. The style of this has varied by time and country and quite possibly, except for the remnants here and there, the university no longer holds itself particularly responsible for bringing adolescents to maturity. But a pastoral function was very much part of the Oxford that Newman knew, even if, in his opinion when a don at Oriel, it was undertaken inadequately.

If Newman is said to have written the first of the university novels, one needs to understand that he was not the first to actually depict undergraduates in novel form. That style went back at least to the 1820s, and undergraduates, in a picaresque mode, can be found in late Enlightenment novels. But the differences are profound. Newman was the first to make the university itself a primary character in the novel. He wrote a *Bildungsroman*. Before that, fictional undergraduates simply passed through on their way to somewhere else. After Newman the university becomes responsible for directing and shaping character and future. The novel ends with the protagonist rejecting Oxford, but clearly Newman regards that as a necessary loss. The question is whether the subsequent gain would compensate for that loss. The answer depends upon how one interprets Newman's subsequent life and work.

The irony of Newman's perpetual reincarnation is that none of the structural or even conceptual features of the university as he knew and loved them has survived him—not even this university which may on an occasion such as the 150th anniversary of UCD revere him as a spiritual ancestor. So Newman's continuing reputation is a conundrum. The whigs would say that if he was very much a man of his historical period, his reputation ought to have faded long ago. So do we gather today in partly reverential tone, a little bit of *Weltschmerz*, dreaming of a utopian world[2] which is so much a tendency in the history of universities—or have I overstated the difficulty? Do we actually owe Newman something? Does he still speak to us?

I will not answer that just yet. I ask for your indulgence in order to explore the theme just announced, that Newman is a conundrum because his name is recurrent, yet his ideas about a university largely fail to influence contemporary society. It is even possible to assert that his influence was never profound, however much he has been referenced by the modern world. I should also say that Newman's reputation has been fairly well confined to the English-speaking world. Once searching for foreign-language translations of his masterpiece, *The Idea of a University: Defined and Illustrated*, I could come up with none, only some tributes by French authors who, I must add, seem to have found much that was attractive in his argument— most notably, that the university is a *milieu*. This is a very fine rendering I believe of the Cardinal's use of the English word 'place' in the opening section of the Idea and in other of his writings.[3] The other great body of idealistic thinking about a university is German, so understandably that inheritance does not depend upon Newman. German conceptions such as *Bildung*, with its Scandinavian cognates such as the Danish and Norwegian danelse or the Swedish *bildning*, or *Kultur* or *Wissenschaft*, or the twin tag of *Lehrfreiheit* and *Lernfreiheit* owe nothing to Newman. And these notions play a larger role in American university history than does Newman, probably because they are more readily linked to the research university model and to the importance of the free-standing, secular or even faith-related American liberal arts college.

'Research' or 'Humboldtianism', both of which have variant readings unnecessary for now to the telling of this story, was starting to become an issue in the public domain when Newman was writing the lectures and essays that constitute a corpus larger than the *Idea of a University*. The 'discourses', as he called them, comprising the *Idea* are in published form a compendium that includes some chapters that were never actually given before an audience. Mark Pattison, the Rector of Lincoln College Oxford and a personality who appears or is thought to appear in famous Victorian novels (there are other candidates), was already a leader in what was called 'the endowment of research' movement. Whereas generations of dons before Newman had proclaimed the liberal arts, liberal learning or classical learning to be the core and fundamental nature of a university—ideas and sentiments much expressed during Newman's sojourn at Oxford, and which he certainly accepted—many of the strongest voices of the second half of the nineteenth century were arguing otherwise. His reform-minded contemporaries in Parliament were debating a raft of conceptions of a university quite distinct from the pastoral and moral perspectives that he held. They were focused on other issues: the university as a national (rather than a class) asset; the university in alliance with the state and no longer with an established church; the university as a German research university; the university as primarily a source of professional training.[4]

The opening of the *Idea of a University* appears to leave no doubt as to where Newman believed research belonged. In his Preface Newman quickly disposed of it. The function of a university being the teaching of universal knowledge, Newman wrote that if it were otherwise, if its object were the 'advancement of knowledge' or 'scientific and philosophical discovery, I do not see why a University should have students; if religious training, I do not see how it can be the seat of literature and science'.[5] But Newman's Irish episcopal sponsors, those who summoned him to John Bull's other island, wanted training, some element of professional preparation for a new élite, and so in the actual founding of the Catholic University Newman found a role for the professions.

The opening lines are often quoted. Most writers, and I include myself, take them quite literally, a possible mistake. I would be remiss if I did not mention the distinguished editor of Newman who sees the matter very differently. First, he observes that Newman is emphasising teaching, and the teaching of undergraduates, as a primary university responsibility because the Irish bishops who summoned him to Ireland wanted a seminary to protect Catholic youth from the nefarious influences of modernism. So there is a rhetorical purpose behind the ringing disclaimer. Second, the heart of Newman's university is the dissemination of universal knowledge, learning in all of its known contours. He could hardly be opposed to learning, nor was he, as the *Idea* amply demonstrates. And third, if we look beyond the *Idea*, Newman actually intended his Irish university to contain research institutes in science, medicine, technology and archaeology, whether or not students were present. This was not exactly the Oxford that he had known, where research as the Germans understood it was not yet a mandatory requirement for holding a professorial chair.[6]

I accept this clarification and rectification. Yet I would still like to maintain that the emotional core of Newman's university is not Humboldtian. It is not discovery, and certainly not the wrenching discoveries that led Strauss to write Leben Jesu and deny the divinity of the Christian messiah. Newman was more liberal-minded than his Irish sponsors, but he was not—and the *Idea* indicates this—about to open the floodgates to every kind of possible apostasy, which is exactly what an ethic of original inquiry invites. It allows the university to stand in a nervous relationship to its surrounding society, cooperative at times (depending upon subject) but also contrary. In other respects, soon to be mentioned, he was adamantly opposed to innovations that are now typical of the world's universities.

The notion that an institution as complicated in its multiple heritages as a university can nevertheless be discussed in terms of an 'idea' has proven immensely appealing. Almost every year it seems a book or article appears with the title 'Idea of a University'. Writing on this peculiarity some years back, I traced the practice back to philosophical idealism and particularly to German romanticism, or back slightly from there to Kant and Moses Mendelssohn, among others. In England it went to Samuel Taylor Coleridge, who was influenced by German thought.[7] Edmund Burke too can be considered a source. Newman may not have liked the German pedigree. He was not comfortable with things foreign, did not like foreigners such as the Irish (nor they he). The experience of Ireland was excruciatingly difficult, 'penance' he once said. 'No one knows but myself,' he wrote from Limerick in 1854, 'the desolateness of leaving Birmingham [the Oratory there where he worked], and being thrown among strangers. . . .'[8] And of course he had an unhappy experience with the Holy Congregation. His Roman Catholicism was suspect. He was sensed to be the convert whose heart lay in Anglican Oxford, the soul of English Protestantism, and, as it was becoming in his lifetime, a home for English political and religious liberalism, trends that turned him away from the colleges he so dearly loved. Liberal, Protestant and aesthetic Oxford, Newman thought, was impossible to resist. He could not resist it himself, but he tried. In the famous and poignant phrase appearing in his autobiography, once he left (or was more or less driven out), he never saw Oxford again, except for the dreaming spires from a speeding railway on its way to his new home in Birmingham.

Newer scholarship continues to detract from his personal reputation, taking the edge off his idealism. (That is to say, many of us have problems with cranky idealists.) But even a generation ago one could find historians who noted how difficult Newman could be in committee. Doubtless committee work often brings out the more irritating side of academics; but surely it is not improper to suggest that some colleagues are more bothersome than others? And now Colin Barr, who has consulted a body of new materials on the founding of the Catholic University of Ireland, has concluded that the Archbishop of Armagh, Paul Cullen, was the true founder and inspiration. Newman's arrival, contested by many but reluctantly approved by Cullen, who later, after a nervous breakdown attributable to Newman, regretted inviting him, caused endless trouble. Newman was not even present all that much in Ireland, being an absentee rector of the university he had been summoned to create. And he called upon other English converts to assist him, a decision that led to even greater Irish distrust.[9] Of course he was capable of making friendships, but he apparently did not like being crossed.

I mentioned a few paragraphs ago that even within the English-speaking world Newman's influence was limited. America appeared not to need him, although the nation welcomed the poet Matthew Arnold on his lecture tours. Arnold and Newman's thinking, or at least dispositions, are commonly linked, both coming up high on the list of Victorian 'sages' who spoke about 'culture'. Arnold and Newman shared much, as I wrote some forty years ago in *The Revolution of the Dons*, but Arnold proposed 'culture' as a metonym for religion. Newman made the study of religion, or rather theology, the centrepiece of a university curriculum much more in the spirit of the original universities of Europe. Both Newman and Arnold had a conception of a 'gentleman' as the product of liberal learning, and this *beau ideal* in both cases captured what might be termed a feminine view of character traceable to the eighteenth century and to novelists such as Jane Austen, or earlier to Fielding's *Amelia*. But once again Newman departed from his fellow high Victorian, for he explicitly noted that the gentlemanly ideal is secular and therefore inadequate as a full expression of a rounded personality. Both Julian the Apostate and Saint Basil received a liberal education, he announced, but how differently they used it.

The culture concept, however, was destined to have a rocky history, being so closely identified with words like 'gentlemanly', long associated with privileged élites in England, or New England Brahmins on the other side. Responding to Thomas Huxley's questions on behalf of the Royal Commission on Scientific Instruction and the Advancement of Science (the Devonshire Commission of 1872) whether 'it may be part of the business of a University, as distinguished from other teaching bodies, to set up a standard or model of culture', Mark Pattison answered that it was 'rather an abstract question'. Such a function might be 'usefully performed' by a university, but care had to be taken to see that the very concept of 'culture' was not a euphemism for social exclusion.

By the beginning of the twentieth century, in another work now considered a classic, the clergyman Hastings Rashdall's history of the medieval university,[10] the core of the university was 'rediscovered'. Liberal education was not its core. It was merely propaedeutic. A university was a 'place *par excellence* for professional and properly trained students, not for amateurs or dilettantes or even for the most serious of leisure'. And in words that hit directly at Newman's famous opening where discovery is dismissed as a primary activity, a university exists 'for the advancement of science; and not merely for its conservation or diffusion . . . and [is a place] where education and research advance side by side'.[11]

The Scots did not require Newman, having their own successful sets of historical ideas on the nature and meaning of a university. The Scots have been an extraordinary influence in higher education throughout the Anglophone world. The Victorian civic or regional university colleges of England, Wales and Ulster were directly modelled on Scottish types. The Scottish professorial system appeared to reformers of the Victorian era to be closer in spirit to the German view of a university than either Oxford or Cambridge where tutors predominated, especially at Oxford. The University of London in its first incarnation in the 1820s was denounced by hostile critics as a 'Scottish' university, meaning that detractors said that it had lower entry and educational standards than the reforming Oxford and Cambridge and was insufficiently aristocratic. It was also 'godless', a charge equally laid against Thomas Jefferson's newly founded University of Virginia. The suggestion that the universities of Scotland were of lesser educational rigour was possibly true of undergraduate education, for Scotland's universities in some respects drew mainly from undergraduates of secondary school age.

Scotland's influence on the United States was enormous. Throughout the eighteenth century the Scots were all over the colonies, serving as college masters and leaders, and Scottish moral philosophy had an extraordinary reign in the burgeoning colleges and universities of the new nation. The Scots can be said to have created the American universities long before German influence started to be felt, but in fairness to the English it can be said that the college residential idea, with tutors and high staffing ratios, was their contribution. In another direction, across the North Sea to Sweden, Scots gave their name to one of Sweden's universities, Chalmers, which began life as a technical institute but is today a recently semi-privatised university. The famous Scotto-Swedish families dating from the eighteenth century retain their special identity to this day.

Surely, we may ask, Newman's writings influenced American Roman Catholic higher education? Here I rely on the excellent Archbishop Gerety Lecture for 1997 given at Seton Hall University, a Roman Catholic institution in New Jersey, by Philip Gleason of Notre Dame University, America's premier Roman Catholic research university. The answer is a mixed one.

Nineteenth-century American Protestants generally ignored him. Their religion, after all, was what the historian Henry May has called 'progress'. As a Catholic, Newman was not seen to fit that generalised, liberal Protestant mould. Newman's reception by American Roman Catholic educators depends upon historical circumstances. In some periods he was regarded as too conservative, but in others as too liberal and identified with the Modernist opponents of the doctrine of papal infallibility. Nineteenth-century Jesuits were opposed to him, but twentieth-century Jesuits, sensing his support for classical modes of learning, were much more in favour. Insofar as Irish Catholics in America disliked the English, the Englishman Newman was as unacceptable as he was in Victorian Ireland itself. Up until the First World War there was some interest in Newman, often enough in his other writings narrating the corrosive effects of scepticism on received faith, but for many builders of institutions he was simply insufficiently practical. The conclusion may not have been fair, but that is how Newman came across.

The opening up of American colleges and universities to Roman Catholic undergraduates in the early decades of the twentieth century led to the formation of faith-related student organisations, and Newman became a household name to describe the pastoral activities associated with campus clubs for Roman Catholic students, as the historical teacher Hillel was associated with Jewish foundations. This was a correct tribute to Newman. He had managed to turn Oriel College Oxford upside down in the 1820s when he quarrelled with the provost over the conduct of tutorial classes. Oriel was turning liberal, moving just a bit away from a student-centred to a knowledge-centred conception of undergraduate education, and Newman was far more concerned with the moral health of his charges. He lost that quarrel then, but Americans remembered it, or remembered Newman's concern, and provided the necessary campus real estate to continue the work. However, understandably enough, many American Catholics were distressed by the circumstances leading to the advent of Newman Halls because they were founded on secular and Protestant campuses, exposing Catholic students to the types of influences that the original Catholic University in Ireland was supposed to combat.

According to Gleason, the golden age of interest in Newman occurred after World War I, extending up to about 1960. He was embraced by American educational reformers and intellectuals, became a staple of courses on Victorian literature and was invoked in the many discussions about liberal education that have never ceased to animate the American academic community, eager, since the Revolution, to explore the relationship between higher education and the making of a unique American character. Newman fit well in these discussions, and indeed, in any discussion bearing on anti-materialist themes, although it must be said that German ideas were also a source of such yearnings. Various Roman Catholic literary revivals also led to Newman. And it can even be noted that beginning with the twentieth century even the English began to take greater notice of their *bête noir*. *The Times* of London declared in 1915 that Newman was actually worth reading.

And so it can be said that Newman was rehabilitated in the twentieth century, or discovered, or found to be relevant in new educational but also religious contexts and more important to a Catholic intelligentsia, as well as serious authors generally. But as this was happening, the most significant statement about Newman was published almost quietly and in an utterly new context. How many understood its manifold emotional layers of meaning? The statement was not intended as a critique, but as an historical explanation of the passing of a recently-reconstructed Newman, the writer giving him oblique credit for having been influential in higher education. The author of a set of lectures given at Harvard in 1963 outlining the arrival of a new type of university was himself a Quaker and as passionate about education as Newman. His prose simple but effective, yet hardly as rich and full as Newman's, Clark Kerr, president of the campus federation known as the University of California, drew a picture of an institution which he termed, borrowing the word from another district, as a 'multiversity'.[12] The intended prototype was not California or Berkeley, however, but probably Harvard, America's oldest and presumably therefore most traditional institution. But this was hardly the case in 1963. Harvard had taken a major lead in higher education after 1945, throwing off its historical allegiance to the New England Brahmanate, disavowing its anti-semitic bigotry and embracing meritocracy.[13]

The multiversity was long in the making, and its sources in American life extended back certainly into the late nineteenth century. It was an institution devoted to the public good in its fullest dimensions, to serving every constituency irrespective of whether the service was validated by a specific history. Its standards were varied, as was its contribution to anything that could be called 'history'. The multiversity was divided into segments that were virtually separate fiefdoms loosely correlated with one another. Harvard's massive endowment, today placed at 23 billion dollars, was distributed and controlled by its separate satellites. The multiversity, said Kerr, was a fact of life, and it was an historical necessity. In retrospect, this appears to have been said without affection for the new type of institution, almost it can be imagined, defensively. Above all—and here was the denouement—the multiversity was not based upon a clear and identifiable historical 'idea'. It was rather a collection of ideas competing with one another. It was messy and chaotic. Liberal education was only one form of education offered within the multiversity, and it was problematic whether it was even the dominant one, or whether it could even be defined within the parameters of a contemporary university. Having no central core, the multiversity exhibited a peculiar kind of resilience; chopping off one part of the Hydra did not necessarily affect the others.

Let us now acknowledge a profound and tender irony. Kerr died at the age of 92 on 1 December 2003, very much alert until virtually the end. In his last years, he who had written of the multiversity and had offended those who thought that he was advocating rather than describing, was not thinking so much about multiversities as about his own special creation, the University of California at Santa Cruz. High in the mountains in a redwood forest overlooking the Pacific Ocean, Santa Cruz, created in 1960, was for Kerr 'Swarthmore in the Redwoods', a phrase that evoked the Quaker college in Pennsylvania where he had spent his own undergraduate years. For a public research university system to contain within it a collegiate structure devoted essentially to undergraduate instruction showed a touch perhaps of Newman, or of Newman's Oxford (or Cambridge, with its more centralised structure, not surprising in that Cambridge expatriates played an early part in establishing the Santa Cruz college system).

Kerr had written that the multiversity had no poets to sing its praises. He later wrote that the multiversity, meaning the central presidential leadership of such a system, had no heritage.[14] Without heritage, a university could not command loyalty. A university was a Campus Visible, not an administrative office. Newman knew that. He understood the deep importance of space, tactile, embracing, filled with symbols and associations that made supposedly inert institutions alive, players in the story of an undergraduate's coming of age. He knew the importance of *milieu*. Returning to Oxford after the absence of several years, Newman's alter ego Charles in *Loss and Gain* notices 'the silver Isis, the grey willows, the far-stretching plains, the dark groves, the distant range of Shotover. . . . wood, water, stone, all so calm, so bright, they might have been his, but his they were not; whatever he was to gain by becoming a Catholic, this he had lost'.[15]

Kerr had not after all given Newman a *coup de grâce*. Shall we interpolate that he had spent a lifetime wondering how to undo some of the mischief caused by his discussion of the multiversity, which he also termed the Federal Grant University? If the essence of the multiversity was that it had no essence, why then could it not also contain a world according to Newman? In the multiversity there are many mansions. About a year before he died Kerr summoned me to his home and asked me to write the history of the 'failure' of Santa Cruz. I could not do that, I explained, for I did not regard the campus as exactly a 'failure'. As he himself had noted, certain changes are the result of history, possibly logical but certainly unavoidable. However beautiful some aspects of the past may be, they slip away, held in the memory perhaps, but gone. There may indeed be many mansions in the multiversity, but the collegiate one came up against formidable fiscal, political and demographic odds.

In *Loss and Gain*, Newman's surrogate lost Oxford. He lost the dreaming spires that Newman so loved, the romantic images that he conjured up in his prose and poetry. He lost a place in the English Establishment, guaranteed for him as a graduate of an Anglican institution. He lost the intense conversation of common room and tutorial. And he nearly lost all of the educational history that followed. If Newman had really been profoundly and consistently influential, we would not have much of the machinery of administration, the structure and content of courses, the huge array of rules and regulations, the debates over access, over SAT scores in the US and A-levels and Highers in England and Scotland. We wouldn't be talking bureaucratically about 'seat time', 'enrolment targets', interactive teaching technologies, modular systems of instruction. Newman's vocabulary and conceptualisation would not have led us to discuss quality control mechanisms, student transfer, the relationship of further education to higher education, contract research, funding, loan policies, pension schemes for academics. Had he prevailed, we might even have had to modify our present conceptions of academic freedom and institutional autonomy, since he was a firmer believer in the boundaries imposed by faith than are we, although more flexible than most of his Roman Catholic contemporaries. If it is said in praise of thinkers that they were born out of their time and awaited the future for vindication, that cannot easily be said of Newman. He was absolutely a man of his time, or a man of his youth, when he walked along the roofs of the Oxford colleges in the gaslight of evening and dreamt of being a fellow of one of them, or noticed a red snapdragon rooting itself in the cold stone of the quadrangles.

So Newman lost his idealised university world, and we have most certainly lost his. The modern university world could not function as he would have wished. He knew that, or his opposition to the new London University would not have been so bitter. He did not care for market-driven instruction, which yielded, in an image he used, the cacophony and hawking of wares typical of an oriental bazaar.

Yes, assuredly, we lost what Kerr said we lost, the belief in the university as a unique educational institution, born with the corporate identity that was its heritage from the beginning when the Pandects of Justinian were recovered and provided the corporate genetic code that was henceforth to define a university, to transform its designation from a general Latin term for a collection of persons to an institution based on an 'idea'. Newman believed in that idea, but I must say that he could never really define it, precisely because no set of discourses, no discursive set of conversations, can fix ideas. The very form itself disallows it. But if we have multiversities, even liberal arts colleges in America that are mini-multiversities, the result of present-day graduate training, we have not lost one thing that Newman gave to us: a mode of understanding, an alternative approach to thinking about education, a method for beginning to make sense out of the anarchy of the modern university. Without an idea as starting place, we are reduced to petty rivalries, grumbling and unmitigated self-interest as we hawk our special wares.

I have written of what Newman himself lost. What did he gain as a convert to Roman Catholicism, or rather, what feature of his mind led him to renounce the faith he had hitherto followed and make conversion a necessity? It was no less than what he had argued all along, that obedience of some kind is necessary to clarity of mind. Matthew Arnold once said that great thinking takes place within an establishment where some sort of boundaries exist. In general, the cognitive processes rely on immense mental discipline. Subjects are called disciplines. We think in categories, concepts, frameworks, paradigms. We have come to feature 'method' as essential to understanding. Science and scholarship are highly controlled cerebral activities, 'unnatural' in the sense that our basic instincts (or inclinations) incline us to the random and to streams of consciousness. *The Idea of a University* works best as a series of discourses on the nature of the categories of knowledge. Neither Newman nor Arnold was a totalitarian thinker as we have come to understand the horrible effects of crushing orthodoxies. But both cautioned against what Arnold called 'the free swing of this and that'. Education depended upon discipline, culture depended upon discipline, and life depended upon a sense of limits.

Newman, I said, was a man of his time, or a man of his youth. His *Idea of a University* is derived from the experiences around him. Reading into his contemporaries, one understands how much he shared with them. But if he was not unique in the message that he conveyed, he did what other fine thinkers have done. He put together in readable and luxurious form, quotable insertions, an argument informed by passion and a particular slant on the human condition. His work is filled with the sentiments and beliefs of a world that had passed. He did this so successfully that in defiance of everything that he so dearly wanted, we still keep him on our shelves. And we almost always start with him. Hence Jaroslav Pelikan of Yale, a theologian himself, gave a learned set of lectures over ten years ago on *The Idea of the University*, a *Reexamination*, traversing the ground laid out by Newman.[16]

But even more than that, Newman has the power to summon up for us the world that we have lost. As a friend once said of Alexis de Tocqueville, the brilliant young Frenchman one day set out for the New World like a latter-day Aeneas, to found Rome while weeping for Dido. Before departing from this world, Clark Kerr, arguably America's greatest university president of the second half of the twentieth century, prime definer of the New World of the multiversity, wept for the heritage he had lost and could not regain. Certainly Newman could not be blamed for that. Although he himself lost much in leaving Oxford behind, he never abandoned the view that universities had a heritage. That, in fact, is the real 'idea' at the core of his *Idea of a University*.

Notes

1 Marta Ronne, *Två världar – ett universitet. Svenska skönlitterära skildringar 1903–1943. En genusstudie.* Uppsala, 2000. *(The Gendered Worlds of the University. Swedish University Fiction 1903–1943).*

2 Elaborated in the Hans Rausing Lecture for 2002 given at Uppsala University by Sheldon Rothblatt, *The University as Utopia*. Uppsala, 2003.

3 Jacques Dreze and Jean Debelle, *Conceptions de l'université*. Paris: Éditions Universitaires, 1968.

4 See, *inter alia*, the review article by Lawrence Goldman, 'Oxford and the Idea of a University in Nineteenth Century Britain', in *Oxford Review of Education*, vol. 30 (December 2004), 586–587.

5 John Henry Newman, *The Idea of a University, Defined and Illustrated*, ed. I. T. Ker. Oxford: Clarendon Press, 1976 edition, ix.

6 Ian Ker, 'Newman's *Idea of a University: a Guide for the Contemporary University?*', in *The Idea of a University*, ed. David Smith and Anne Karin Landslow. London and Philadelphia: Jessica Kingsley, 1999, 13–15.

7 Sheldon Rothblatt, *The Modern University and Its Discontents*, the *Fate of Newman's Legacies in Britain and America*. Cambridge: Cambridge University Press, 1997, chapter 1.

8 Louis McRedmond, *Thrown among Strangers: John Henry Newman in Ireland*. Dublin: Veritas, 1990, title page. (I am indebted to Cyril White for the reference.)

9 Colin Barr, *Paul Cullen, John Henry Newman and the Catholic University of Ireland, 1845–1865*. Notre Dame, IN: Notre Dame University Press, 2003.

10 Hastings Rashdall, *The Universities of Europe in the Middle Ages*. Oxford University Press, 1936 edition.

11 P. E. Mathison, *The Life of Hastings Rashdall, D.D.* Oxford, 1928, 74–75. (Quoted from Rashdall's *The Universities of the Middle Ages*, II. Oxford: Oxford University Press, 1969, 724ff.)

12 Clark Kerr, *The Uses of the University*. Fifth edition. Cambridge, MA: Harvard University Press, 2001.

13 The leading book on this theme is Morton and Phyllis Keller, *Making Harvard Modern, The Rise of America's University*. New York: Oxford University Press, 2001.

14 Clark Kerr, *Higher Education Cannot Escape History*. Albany, NY: State University of New York Press, 1994, 48.

15 John Henry Newman, *Loss and Gain: The Story of a Convert*. London: Longmans Green, 1906, 243.

16 Jaroslav Pelikan, *The Idea of the University, a Re-examination*. New Haven and London: Yale University Press, 1992. (Gordon Graham, (*Universities, the Recovery of an Idea*. Thoverton, Essex: Imprint Academic, 2002, 38) is surely correct to mention the ongoing utility of Newman's distinction between education and instruction.)

33

Excerpt from
THE ESSENCE OF
T. H. HUXLEY

T. H. Huxley

Source: Cyril Bibby (ed.) *The Essence of T. H. Huxley*, London: Macmillan and New York: St. Martin's Press, 1967, pp. 220–30.

The ideal university

Elected by the suffrages of your four Nations Rector of the ancient University [Aberdeen] of which you are scholars, I take the earliest opportunity which has presented itself since my restoration to health, of delivering the Address which, by long custom, is expected of the holder of my office. . . .

I have already done my best, and, as long as I hold my office, I shall continue my endeavours . . . to do what in me lies, to bring this University nearer to the ideal — alas, that I should be obliged to say ideal — of all Universities; which, as I conceive, should be places in which thought is free from all fetters; and in which all sources of knowledge, and all aids to learning, should be accessible to all comers, without distinction of creed or country, riches or poverty.

Do not suppose, however, that I am sanguine enough to expect much to come of any poor efforts of mine. If your annals take any notice of my incumbency, I shall probably go down to posterity as the Rector who was always beaten. But if they add, as I think they will, that my defeats became victories in the hands of my successors, I shall be well content. . . .

When I think of the host of pleasant, moneyed, well-bred young gentlemen, who do a little learning and much boating by Cam and Isis, the vision is a pleasant one; and, as a patriot, I rejoice that the youth of the upper and richer classes of the nation receive a wholesome and a manly training, however small may be the modicum of knowledge they gather, in the intervals of this, their serious business. I admit, to the full, the social and political value of that training. But . . . I am tempted to inquire what has become of the

64

indigent scholars, the sons of the masses of the people whose daily labour just suffices to meet their daily wants, for whose benefit these rich foundations were largely, if not mainly, instituted. . . .

As compared with other actual Universities, then, Aberdeen may, perhaps, be well satisfied with itself. But do not think me an impracticable dreamer, if I ask you not to rest and be thankful in this state of satisfaction; if I ask you to consider awhile, how this actual good stands related to that ideal better, towards which both men and institutions must progress, if they would not retrograde.

In an ideal University, as I conceive it, a man should be able to obtain instruction in all forms of knowledge, and discipline in the use of all the methods by which knowledge is obtained. In such a University, the force of living example should fire the student with a noble ambition to emulate the learning of learned men, and to follow in the footsteps of the explorers of new fields of knowledge. And the very air he breathes should be charged with that enthusiasm for truth, that fanaticism of veracity, which is a greater possession than much learning; a nobler gift than the power of increasing knowledge; by so much greater and nobler than these, as the moral nature of man is greater than the intellectual; for veracity is the heart of morality.

But the man who is all morality and intellect, although he may be good and even great, is, after all, only half a man. There is beauty in the moral world and in the intellectual world; but there is also a beauty which is neither moral nor intellectual — the beauty of the world of Art. There are men who are devoid of the power of seeing it, as there are men who are born deaf and blind, and the loss of those, as these, is simply infinite. There are others in whom it is an overpowering passion; happy men, born with the productive, or at lowest, the appreciative, genius of the Artist. But, in the mass of mankind, the Aesthetic faculty, like the reasoning power and the moral sense, needs to be roused, directed, and cultivated; and I know not why the development of that side of his nature, through which man has access to a perennial spring of ennobling pleasure, should be omitted from any comprehensive scheme of University education.

All Universities recognise Literature in the sense of the old Rhetoric, which is art incarnate in words. Some, to their credit, recognise Art in its narrower sense, to a certain extent, and confer degrees for proficiency in some of its branches. If there are Doctors of Music, why should there be no Masters of Painting, of Sculpture, of Architecture? I should like to see Professors of the Fine Arts in every University; and instruction in some branch of their work made a part of the Arts curriculum. . . .

The founders of Universities held the theory that the Scriptures and Aristotle taken together, the latter being limited by the former, contained all knowledge worth having, and that the business of philosophy was to interpret and co-ordinate these two. I imagine that in the twelfth century this was a very fair conclusion from known facts. Nowhere in the world, in those days, was there such an encyclopaedia of knowledge of all three classes, as is to be found in those writings. The scholastic philosophy is a wonderful monument of the patience and ingenuity with which the human mind toiled to build up a logically consistent theory of the Universe, out of such materials. And that philosophy is by no means dead and buried, as many vainly suppose. On the contrary, numbers of men of no mean learning and accomplishment, and sometimes of rare power and subtlety of thought, hold by it as the best theory of things which has yet been stated. And, what is still more remarkable, men who speak the language of modern philosophy, nevertheless think the thoughts of the schoolmen. 'The voice is the voice of Jacob, but the hands are the hands of Esau.' Every day I hear 'Cause', 'Law', 'Force', 'Vitality', spoken of as entities, by people who can enjoy Swift's joke about the meat-roasting quality of the smoke-jack, and comfort themselves with the reflection that they are not even as those benighted school men. . . .

But it is only fair to the Scottish Universities to point out that they have long understood the value of Science as a branch of general education. . . .

I do not know what the requirements of your examiners may be, but I sincerely trust they are not satisfied with a mere book knowledge of these matters. For my own part I would not raise a finger, if I could thereby introduce mere book work in science into every Arts curriculum in the country. Let those who want to study books devote themselves to Literature . . . be assured that no teaching of science is worth anything, as a mental discipline, which is not based upon direct perception of the facts. . . .

I am very strongly inclined to agree with some learned schoolmasters who say that, in their experience, the teaching of science is all waste time. As they teach it, I have no doubt it is. . . .

Within my recollection, the only way in which a student could obtain anything like a training in Physical Science, was by attending the lectures of the Professors of Physical and Natural Science attached to the Medical Schools. But, in the course of the last thirty years, both foster-mother and child have grown so big, that they threaten not only to crush one another, but to press the very life out of the unhappy student who enters the nursery; to the great detriment of all three. . . .

If I had the power to remodel Medical Education, the first two years of the medical curriculum should be devoted to nothing but such thorough study of Anatomy and Physiology, with Physiological Chemistry and Physics; the student should then pass a real, practical examination in these subjects; and, having gone through that ordeal satisfactorily, he should be troubled no more with them. His whole mind should then be given with equal intentness to Therapeutics, in its broadest sense, to Practical Medicine and to Surgery, with instruction in Hygiene and in Medical Jurisprudence; and of these subjects only — surely there are enough of them — should he be required to show a knowledge in his final examination. . . .

We are told that the medical man ought to be a person of good education and general information, if his profession is to hold its own among
other professions; that he ought to know Botany, or else, if he goes
abroad, he will not be able to tell poisonous fruits from edible ones; that
he ought to know drugs, as a druggist knows them, or he will not be
able to tell sham bark and senna from the real articles; that he ought
to know Zoology, because — well, I really have never been able to
learn exactly why he is to be expected to know zoology ... And there is
a scientific superstition that Physiology is largely aided by Comparative
Anatomy....

I hold as strongly as any one can do, that the medical practitioner ought
to be a person of education and good general culture; but ... I would urge,
that a thorough study of Human Physiology is, in itself, an education broader
and more comprehensive than much that passes under that name. There is
no side of the intellect which it does not call into play, no region of human
knowledge into which either its roots, or its branches, do not extend; like
the Atlantic between the Old and the New Worlds, its waves wash the
shores of the two worlds of matter and of mind; its tributary streams flow
from both; through its waters, as yet unfurrowed by the keel of any
Columbus, lies the road, if such there be, from the one to the other; far
away from that North-west Passage of mere speculation, in which so many
brave souls have been hopelessly frozen up....

In thus proposing the exclusion of the study of such branches of knowledge as Zoology and Botany, from those compulsory upon the medical
student, I am not, for a moment, suggesting their exclusion from the University. I think that sound and practical instruction in the elementary facts and
broad principles of Biology should form part of the Arts curriculum:
and ... I have no sort of doubt that, in view of the relation of Physical
Science to the practical life of the present day, it has the same right as
Theology, Law, and Medicine, to a Faculty of its own in which men shall be
trained to be professional men of science....

The establishment of a Faculty of Science in every University, implies
that of a corresponding number of Professorial chairs, the incumbents of
which need not be so burdened with teaching as to deprive them of ample
leisure for original work. I do not think that it is any impediment to an
original investigator to have to devote a moderate portion of his time to
lecturing, or superintending practical instruction. On the contrary, I think it
may be, and often is, a benefit to be obliged to take a comprehensive survey
of your subject; or to bring your results to a point, and give them, as it were,
a tangible objective existence. The besetting sins of the investigator are two:
the one is the desire to put aside a subject, the general bearings of which
he has mastered himself, and pass on to something which has the attraction
of novelty; and the other, the desire for too much perfection, which leads
him to

> Add and alter many times,
> Till all be ripe and rotten;

to spend the energies which should be reserved for action in whitening the decks and polishing the guns.

The obligation to produce results for the instruction of others, seems to me to be a more effectual check on these tendencies than even the love of usefulness or the ambition for fame. . . .

Examination — thorough, searching examination — is an indispensable accompaniment of teaching . . . but my admiration for the existing system of examination and its products, does not wax warmer as I see more of it. Examination, like fire, is a good servant, but a bad master; and there seems to me to be some danger of its becoming our master. I by no means stand alone in this opinion. Experienced friends of mine do not hesitate to say that students whose career they watch, appear to them to become deteriorated by the constant effort to pass this or that examination . . . They work to pass, not to know; and outraged Science takes her revenge. They do pass, and they don't know. . . .

Again, there is a fallacy about Examiners. It is commonly supposed that any one who knows a subject is competent to teach it; and no one seems to doubt that any one who knows a subject is competent to examine in it. I believe both these opinions to be serious mistakes . . . Examination is an Art, and a difficult one, which has to be learned like all other arts.

Beginners always set too difficult questions — partly because they are afraid of being suspected of ignorance if they set easy ones, and partly from not understanding their business . . . A practised Examiner will seek for information respecting the mental vigour and training of candidates from the way in which they deal with questions easy enough to let reason, memory, and method have free play.

No doubt, a great deal is to be done by the careful selection of Examiners, and by the copious introduction of practical work, to remove the evils inseparable from examination; but, under the best of circumstances, I believe that examination will remain but an imperfect test of knowledge, and a still more imperfect test of capacity, while it tells next to nothing about a man's power as an investigator. (*Universities: Actual and Ideal*, 1874)

The actual work of the University founded in this city [Baltimore] by the well-considered munificence of Johns Hopkins commences tomorrow, and among the many marks of confidence and goodwill which have been bestowed upon me in the United States, there is none which I value more highly than that conferred by the authorities of the University when they invited me to deliver an address on such an occasion. . . .

University education should not be something distinct from elementary education, but should be the natural outgrowth and development of the latter. Now I have a very clear conviction as to what elementary education ought to be; what it really may be, when properly organised; and what I think it will be, before many years have passed over our heads, in England and in America. Such education should enable an average boy of fifteen or sixteen to read and write his own language with ease and accuracy, and with a sense of literary excellence derived from the study of our classic writers: to have a general acquaintance with the history of his own country and with the great laws of social existence; to have acquired the rudiments of the physical and psychological sciences, and a fair knowledge of elementary arithmetic and geometry. He should have obtained an acquaintance with logic rather by example than by precept; while the acquirement of the elements of music and drawing should have been pleasure rather than work. . . .

But it is of vital importance to the welfare of the community that those who are relieved from the need of making a livelihood, and still more, those who are stirred by the divine impulses of intellectual thirst or artistic genius, should be enabled to devote themselves to the higher service of their kind, as centres of intelligence, interpreters of Nature, or creators of new forms of beauty. And it is the function of a university to furnish such men with the means of becoming that which it is their privilege and duty to be. To this end the university need cover no ground foreign to that occupied by the elementary school. Indeed it cannot; for the elementary instruction which I have referred to embraces all the kinds of real knowledge and mental activity possible to man. The university can add no new departments of knowledge, can offer no new fields of mental activity; but what it can do is to intensify and specialise the instruction in each department. Thus literature and philology, represented in the elementary school by English alone, in the university will extend over the ancient and modern languages. History, which, like charity, best begins at home, but, like charity, should not end there, will ramify into anthropology, archaeology, political history, and geography, with the history of the growth of the human mind and of its products in the shape of philosophy, science, and art. And the university will present to the student libraries, museums of antiquities, collections of coins, and the like, which will efficiently subserve these studies. Instruction in the elements of social economy, a most essential, but hitherto sadly-neglected part of elementary education, will develop in the university into political economy, sociology, and law. Physical science will have its great divisions of physical geography, with geology and astronomy; physics; chemistry and biology; represented not merely by professors and their lectures, but by laboratories, in which the students, under guidance of demonstrators, will work out facts for themselves and come into that direct contact with reality which constitutes the fundamental distinction of scientific education. Mathematics will soar into its highest regions; while the high peaks of philosophy may be scaled by those whose aptitude for abstract thought has been awakened by elementary logic. Finally, schools of pictorial and plastic art, of architecture, and of music, will offer a thorough discipline in the principles and practice of art to those in whom lies nascent the rare faculty of aesthetic representation, or the still rarer powers of creative genius.

The primary school and the university are the alpha and omega of education. Whether institutions intermediate between these (so-called secondary schools) should exist, appears to me to be a question of practical convenience. If such schools are established, the important thing is that they should be true intermediaries between the primary school and the university, keeping on the wide track of general culture, and not sacrificing one branch of knowledge for another. . . .

One half of the Johns Hopkins bequest is devoted to the establishment of a hospital, and it was the desire of the testator that the university and the hospital should co-operate in the promotion of medical education. . . .

What is the object of medical education? It is to enable the practitioner, on the one hand, to prevent disease by his knowledge of hygiene; on the other hand, to divine its nature, and to alleviate or cure it, by his knowledge of pathology, therapeutics, and practical medicine. That is his business in life, and if he has not a thorough and practical knowledge of the conditions of health, of the causes which tend to the establishment of disease, of the meaning of symptoms, and of the uses of medicines and operative appliances, he is incompetent, even if he were the best anatomist, or physiologist, or chemist, that ever took a gold medal or won a prize certificate. . . .

It may be taken for granted that I should be the last person in the world to object to the teaching of zoology, or comparative anatomy, in themselves; but I have the strongest feelings that, considering the number and the gravity of those studies through which a medical man must pass, if he is to be competent to discharge the serious duties which devolve upon him, subjects which lie so remote as these do from his practical pursuits should be rigorously excluded. The young man, who has enough to do in order to acquire such familiarity with the structure of the human body as will enable him to perform the operations of surgery, ought not, in my judgment, to be occupied with investigations into the anatomy of crabs and starfishes. . . .

All knowledge is good. It is impossible to say that any fragment of knowledge, however insignificant or remote from one's ordinary pursuits, may not some day be turned to account. But in medical education, above all things, it is to be recollected that, in order to know a little well, one must be content to be ignorant of a great deal.

Let it not be supposed that I am proposing to narrow medical education, or, as the cry is, to lower the standard of the profession. Depend upon it here is only one way of really ennobling any calling, and that is to make those who pursue it real masters of their craft, men who can truly do that which they profess to be able to do, and which they are credited with being able to do by the public. And there is no position so ignoble as that of the so-called 'liberally-educated practitioner', who may be able to read Galen in the original; who knows all the plants, from the cedar of Lebanon to the hyssop upon the wall; but who finds himself, with the issues of life and death in his hands, ignorant, blundering, and bewildered, because of his ignorance of the essential and fundamental truths upon which practice must be based. Moreover, I venture to say, that any man who has seriously studied all the essential branches of medical knowledge; who has the needful acquaintance with the elements of physical science; who has been brought by medical jurisprudence into contact with law; whose study of insanity has taken him into the fields of psychology; has *ipso facto* received a liberal education. . . .

Up to this point I have considered only the teaching aspect of your great foundation, that function of the university in virtue of which it plays the part of a reservoir of ascertained truth, so far as our symbols can ever interpret nature. All can learn; all can drink of this lake. It is given to few to add to the store of knowledge, to strike new springs of thought, or to shape new forms of beauty. But so sure as it is that men live not by bread, but by ideas, so sure is it that the future of the world lies in the hands of those who are able to carry the interpretation of nature a step further than their predecessors; so certain is it that the highest function of a university is to seek out those men, cherish them, and give their ability to serve their kind full play.

I rejoice to observe that the encouragement of research occupies so prominent a place in your official documents, and in the wise and liberal inaugural address of your president . . . Many seem to think that this question is mainly one of money; that you can go into the market and buy research, and that supply will follow demand, as in the ordinary course of commerce. This view does not commend itself to my mind. I know of no more difficult practical problem than the discovery of a method of encouraging and supporting the original investigator without opening the door to nepotism and jobbery. My own conviction is admirably summed up in the passage of your president's address, 'that the best investigators are usually those who have also the responsibilities of instruction, gaining thus the incitement of colleagues, the encouragement of pupils and the observation of the public'. . . .

It appears to me that what I have ventured to lay down as the principles which should govern the relations of a university to education in general, are entirely in accordance with the measures you have adopted. You have set no restrictions upon access to the instruction you propose to give; you have provided that such instruction, either as given by the university or by associated institutions, should cover the field of human intellectual activity. You have recognised the importance of encouraging research. . . .

You have enunciated the principle that, 'the glory of the university should rest upon the character of the teachers and scholars, and not upon their numbers or buildings constructed for their use'. . . .

I constantly hear Americans speak of the charm which our old mother country has for them, of the delight with which they wander through the streets of ancient towns, or climb the battlements of mediaeval strongholds, the names of which are indissolubly associated with the great epochs of that noble literature which is our common inheritance; or with the bloodstained steps of that secular progress, by which the descendants of the savage Britons and of the wild pirates of the North Sea have become converted into warriors of order and champions of peaceful freedom, exhausting what still remains of the old Berserk spirit in subduing nature, and turning the wilderness into a garden. But anticipation has no less charm than retrospect, and to an Englishman landing upon your shores for the first time, travelling for hundreds of miles through strings of great and well-ordered cities, seeing your enormous actual, and almost infinite potential, wealth in all commodities, and in the energy and ability which turn wealth to account, there is something sublime in the vista of the future. Do not suppose that I am pandering to what is commonly understood by national pride. I cannot say that I am in the slightest degree impressed by your bigness, or your material resources, as such. Size is not grandeur, and territory does not make a nation. The great issue, about which hangs a true sublimity, and the terror of overhanging fate, is what are you going to do with all these things? What is to be the end to which these are to be the means? You are making a novel experiment in politics on the greatest scale which the world has yet seen. Forty millions at your first centenary, it is reasonably to be expected that, at the second, these states will be occupied by two hundred millions of English-speaking people, spread over an area as large as that of Europe, and with climates and interests as diverse as those of Spain and Scandinavia, England and Russia. You and your descendants have to ascertain whether this great mass will hold together under the forms of a republic, and the despotic reality of universal suffrage; whether state rights will hold out against centralisation, without separation; whether centralisation will get the better, without actual or disguised monarchy; whether shifting corruption is better than a permanent bureaucracy; and as population thickens in your great cities, and the pressure of want is felt, the gaunt spectre of pauperism will stalk among you, and communism and socialism will claim to be heard. Truly America has a great future before her; great in toil, in care, and in responsibility; great in true glory if she be guided in wisdom and righteousness; great in shame if she fail. I cannot understand why other nations should envy you, or be blind to the fact that it is for the highest interest of mankind that you should succeed; but the one condition of success, your sole safeguard, is the moral worth and intellectual clearness of the individual citizen. Education cannot give these, but it may cherish them and bring them to the front in whatever station of society they are to be found; and the universities ought to be, and may be, the fortresses of the higher life of the nation.

May the university which commences its practical activity to-morrow abundantly fulfil its high purpose; may its renown as a seat of true learning, a centre of free inquiry, a focus of intellectual light, increase year by year, until men wander hither from all parts of the earth, as of old they sought Bologna, or Paris, or Oxford.

And it is pleasant to me to fancy that, among the English students who are drawn to you at that time, there may linger a dim tradition that a countryman of theirs was permitted to address you as he has done today, and to feel as if your hopes were his hopes and your success his joy.

34

T. H. HUXLEY'S IDEA OF
A UNIVERSITY

Cyril Bibby

Source: *Universities Quarterly* X (1955–6): 377–90.

The lifetime of T. H. Huxley, from 1825 to 1895, spans the great period of university reform in Britain. While he was yet an infant, London's University College was opened in Gower Street and King's College founded in opposition to that godless institution; before he had started school the *Edinburgh Review* launched its second series of attacks on the ancient universities of England; as the young medical student of twenty published his first paper Newman seceded from the Established Church and threw Oxford into turmoil; as the brilliant biologist of twenty-five was selected for Fellowship of the Royal Society the older universities were about to be investigated by their first Royal Commissions. In 1854, when Huxley was settling down as lecturer at the School of Mines in Jermyn Street, the Catholic University was receiving its first students in Dublin; by 1870, when he began to build the great science school at South Kensington, the University of London had consolidated its position as an immense imperial examining body and the older universities had begun to make substantial provision for the newer studies. When Huxley retired in 1885, religious tests had been largely abolished and women's colleges accepted at both Cambridge and Oxford, the sexes were admitted on equal terms to degrees at London, half a dozen provincial towns had their own University Colleges, and the work of university extension was started. Before he died, both Redbrick and Oxbridge had taken recognizably modern form, and in the last years of his life the movement to provide London with an effective teaching university took firm shape. Living through these decisive decades, and ever immersed in science and education, Huxley could scarcely fail to think about the problems of university education.

The context of his thinking was different from that of most nineteenth-century reformers. He had not trod the upper-class path from public school

74

to ancient university, nor had he wealthy and well-placed relatives to ease his way. Leaving school at the age of ten and thereafter (apart from three years as a Free Scholar at Charing Cross Hospital) educating himself, he had no preconception of the university as a sort of *haut lycée* or finishing school for the sons of the well-to-do. Apprenticed at fifteen to an East End physician, and always vividly aware of the educational handicap of poverty, he took it for granted that universities should be open to the children of the poor. Member of the Scottish Universities Commission and Rector of Aberdeen, intimately connected over forty years with the University of London, Governor of Owens College in Manchester, Huxley's thought was never straight-jacketed by any assumption that universities must be built of residential colleges. Friend of Jowitt and Mark Pattison and Goldwin Smith at Oxford, of Gilman at Johns Hopkins and Fiske at Harvard, of Brown-Sequard at Paris and Haeckel at Jena, he had every opportunity to consider the values of different traditions of university organization. And, increasingly as the years went by exerting great influence on Britain's cultural development, his idea of a university was of more than private significance.

Almost inevitably one examines Huxley's idea against the background of Newman's, and it is an interesting coincidence that Thomas Henry's father once taught the young John Henry at Dr. Nicholas's school at Ealing.[1] On the fundamental issue of the Church's ultimate regency over education there could be no compromise between the coiner of the word 'agnostic' and the man he described as 'the slipperiest sophist I have ever met with'. And, although Newman welcomed poor scholars at Dublin, his essentially aristocratic attitude was in marked contrast to that of Huxley. 'I ought to be thankful at the style of youths I have got', wrote Newman, '—the French Vicomte, the Irish Baronet, and our own Lord R. Kerr': it was in very different language that Huxley declared, 'I am a plebeian, and I stand by my order' and congratulated Aberdeen on not becoming 'a school of manners for the rich; of sports for the athletic; or a hot-bed of high-fed, hypercritical refinement'. For the one, poor students should be admitted as a charitable concession to an inferior class; for the other, the wealthy had simply filched the universities from their proper beneficiaries. There were many in those days who demanded that the cost of a university education be brought within the purses of the middle classes, but few like Huxley urged their opening to 'the sons of the masses of the people whose daily labour just suffices to meet their daily wants.'

Yet, Huxley had much in common with Newman. Children both of England in her hey-day, proud of their Englishness and even somewhat insular in it, they each had a passionate regard for truth and intellectual integrity and each was contemptuous of all merely human authority. They were similar, too, in the universality of their respect for learning, and the same puritan morality dominated the lives of Catholic convert and arch-agnostic. 'J.H.N. was simply a sceptic who backed out of it', wrote Leslie Stephen, and the *Spectator* once headed an article 'POPE HUXLEY'. Perhaps, after all, it is not so surprising that the two men's ideas of a university bore so many resemblances.

In his 1874 Rectorial Address at Aberdeen, Huxley spoke of his ideal of all universities:

> which, as I conceive, should be places in which thought is free from all fetters; and in which all sources of knowledge, and all aids to learning, should be accessible to all comers, without distinction of creed or country, riches or poverty. . . .
>
> In an ideal university, as I conceive it, a man should be able to obtain instruction in all forms of knowledge, and discipline in the use of all methods by which knowledge is obtained. In such a university, the force of living example should fire the students with a noble ambition to emulate the learning of learned men, and to follow in the footsteps of the explorers of new fields of knowledge. And the very air he breathes should be charged with that enthusiasm for truth, that fanaticism of veracity, which is a greater possession than much learning; a nobler gift than the power of increasing knowledge; by so much greater and nobler than these, as the moral nature of man is greater than the intellectual; for veracity is the heart of morality.

Not only the general line of thought, but in places the very words, remind us of Newman's description of a university as 'An assemblage of learned men, zealous for their own sciences' creating 'a pure and clear atmosphere of thought, which the student also breathes, though in his own case he only pursues a few sciences out of the multitude' and of his insistence that 'What I would urge upon everyone . . . is a great and firm belief in the sovereignty of Truth. Error may flourish for a time but Truth will prevail in the end'. One would suspect Huxley of plagiarism were it not that he does not seem to have possessed a copy of the Dublin discourses[2] and did not include a line from them among his thirty folios of notes from Newman's writings.

Both men took the traditional view of the university as a place of teaching universal knowledge, the coping stone of the general educational system, and Huxley expressed this opinion clearly at the official opening of Baltimore's new university in 1876:

> University education should not be something distinct from elementary education, but should be the natural outgrowth and development of the latter . . . the university need cover no ground foreign to that occupied by the elementary school. Indeed it cannot; for the elementary instruction which I have referred to embraces all the kinds of real knowledge and mental activity possible to man.

> The university can add no new departments of knowledge, can offer no new fields of mental activity; but what it can do is to intensify and specialise the instruction in each department. . . . The primary school and the university are the alpha and omega of education.

Just as Newman, himself a classical scholar, planned to establish a Faculty of Science at Dublin, so Huxley, although tireless in urging the universities to grant science its proper place, never failed to recognize the claims of literary studies. 'An exclusively scientific training', he declared at the opening of Sir Josiah Mason's College in Birmingham, 'will bring about a mental twist as surely as an exclusively literary training. The value of the cargo does not compensate for a ship's being out of trim; and I should be very sorry to think that the Scientific College would turn out none but lopsided men'.

This Mason College speech of 1880 has been the cause of a good deal of misunderstanding. When Huxley approved of the exclusion of 'mere literary instruction and education' he meant by that phrase 'the ordinary classical course of our schools and universites' which would lead merely to 'the introduction of the ordinary smattering of Latin and Greek', and his attack on the assumption that a liberal education was synonymous with instruction on classical antiquity was in no sense a criticism of literary studies. Connell's remark that in his 1882 Rede Lecture Matthew Arnold 'had no difficulty in showing that Huxley had not fully comprehended his concept of culture' does not take sufficient account of Huxley's specific exculpation of 'our chief apostle of culture' and his clear statement that he was criticizing only certain sentences capable of a narrow interpretation. The particular point at issue was Arnold's definition of culture as knowing 'the best that has been thought and said in the world', and in fact he wrote to Huxley admitting that his wording had been unsatisfactory:

> I remember changing the word *said* to the word *uttered*, because I was dissatisfied with the formula for seeming not to include art, and a picture or a statue may be called an *utterance* though it cannot be called a *saying*: however I went back to *said* for the base reason that the formula runs so much easier off the tongue with the shorter word.

There was, of course, some real disparity; and Arnold could never have said, as Huxley did to the House of Commons Select Committee of 1868, 'Oxford and Cambridge put . . . science outside and underneath, which I conceive to be wrong; I am of opinion that physical science ought to be the primary instrument and subject matter of education, and literary culture secondary'. Yet, when an effort was made in 1886 to ensure that the new Chair of English Literature at Oxford should not be diverted to philology, the scientist gave stronger support than the poet.

Standing firm on the traditional ground that 'universities should be learning and teaching bodies devoted to art (literary and other), history, philosophy, and science, where anyone who wanted to learn all that is known about these matters should find people who could teach him and put him in the way of learning for himself', Huxley drew the logical conclusion that no arbitrary limits should be placed on the range of university studies:

> All universities recognize literature in the sense of the old rhetoric, which is art incarnate in words. Some, to their credit, recognize Art in its narrower sense, to a certain extent, and confer degrees for proficiency in some of its branches. If there are doctors of music, why should there be no masters of painting, of sculpture, of architecture? I should like to see professors of the fine arts in every university.

Once again, it is interesting to note that Newman thought so similarly that he had a Chair of Fine Arts in his university at Dublin.

Sharing Newman's view that 'A thorough knowledge of one science and a superficial acquaintance with many, are not the same thing', Huxley declared at Johns Hopkins University:

> It is obviously impossible that any student should pass through the whole of the series of courses of instruction offered by a university. If a degree is to be conferred as a mark of proficiency in knowledge, it must be given on the ground that the candidate is proficient in a certain fraction of those studies. . . . The important points to bear in mind, I think, are that there should not be too many subjects in the curriculum, and that the aim should be the attainment of thorough and sound knowledge of each.

And, in Huxley's own science school at South Kensington, the course was so arranged that students could at different stages concentrate their attentions fairly closely on specified areas of the whole field of study. But Huxley also believed with Newman that 'Any one study, of whatever kind, exclusively pursued, deadens in the mind the interest, nay the perception of any other', and it is fitting that his memorial in the Ealing Public Library bears the motto 'Try to learn something about everything, and everything about something.'

It was a quarter of a century before Huxley spoke at Baltimore that Newman had sympathized with 'those earnest but ill-used persons, who are forced to load their minds with a score of subjects against an examination', and in the intervening years examinations had proliferated in England: Kingsley's 'Isle of Tomtoddies' resounded all day to the praises of the great idol Examination, and in the University of London and the Department of Science and Art Huxley served the idol well. But not uncritically. 'Examination – thorough, searching examination – is an indispensable accompaniment of teaching . . .', he told the assembled University of Aberdeen, 'but my admiration for the existing system of examination and its products, does not wax warmer as I see more of it. Examination, like fire, is a good servant, but a bad master; and there seems to me to be some danger of its becoming our master . . . students . . . work to pass, not to know; and outraged Science takes her revenge. They do pass, and they don't know.' Not surprisingly, his feeling was 'distinctly against any absolute and defined preliminary examination, the passing of which shall be an essential condition of admission to the university', but it was to be many years before the universities' somewhat narrow and rigid matriculation requirements were to be relaxed in the way that he would have wished.

Newman's prescription for avoiding the ill effects of specialization and examination was residence and tutorial superintendence. To the former, Huxley's writings scarcely refer; but he sent his own son to Balliol and, in a man who ever lay about him with vigour at everything of which he disapproved, perhaps the absence of reference to residence implies approval combined with recognition of its impracticability in the universities with which he was most concerned. About the merits of close tutorial supervision Huxley had no doubts, and in 1868 he told the Select Committee on Scientific Instruction that an important defect in the School of Mines was that 'the entire business of teaching is thrown upon the professors . . . that is to say, we have not the tutorial system as well as the professorial system, though both of these systems ought to be combined in any completely organized course of instruction'. And it was he who at South Kensington adapted the tutorial system to the requirements of scientific work in a manner now almost universal in the world's teaching laboratories.

The extent of agreement between Huxley and Newman is less surprising when one notes the faith of both in the potentialities of a liberal education. A liberally educated man, said Newman in Dublin, 'will not indeed at once be a lawyer, or a pleader, or an orator, or a statesman, or a physician, or a good landlord, or a man of business, or a soldier, or an engineer, or a chemist, or a geologist, or an antiquarian, but he will be placed in that state of intellect in which he can take up any one of the sciences or callings I have referred to, or any other for which he has a taste or special talent' (which leaves little warrant for Judges's remark that a liberal education is 'that which by Newman's definition is useless'). It was in very similar terms that Huxley in Baltimore asserted that with a liberal school education 'and with no more than is to be obtained by building strictly upon its lines, a man of ability may become a great writer or speaker, a statesman, a lawyer, a man of science, painter, sculptor, architect, or musician'. So far as professional education was concerned, Huxley held that 'the Faculties of Theology, Law, and Medicine, are technical schools, intended to equip men who have received general culture, with the special knowledge which is needed for the proper performance of the duties of clergymen, lawyers, and medical practitioners', and he would have students pass through the Faculty of Arts before entering on their professional studies. Indeed, according to his evidence to the Cowper Commission in 1892, it was 'a matter of indifference whether the technical schools for the professions . . . are called faculties or not' for 'The primary business of the universities is with pure knowledge and pure art – independent of all application to practice; with progress in culture, not with increase of wealth'.

But, while holding the traditional view of the essential function of a university, Huxley insisted that in one respect the modern university must be quite different from that of earlier days. 'The mediaeval university', he wrote to Lankester, 'looked backwards: it professed to be a storehouse of old knowledge, and except in the way of dialectical cobweb-spinning, its professors had nothing to do with novelties. Of the historical and physical (natural) sciences, of criticism and laboratory practice, it knew nothing. Oral teaching was of supreme importance on account of the cost and rarity of manuscripts. The modern university looks forward, and is a factory of new knowledge: its professors have to be at the top of the wave of progress. Research and criticism must be the breath of their nostrils; laboratory work the main business of the scientific student; books his main helpers.' Truscot is scarcely fair to Newman in suggesting that his view would 'exclude research from the university altogether', and it is even doubtful if Judges was justified in speaking of his 'distaste for research', but undoubtedly here is a major difference of emphasis between Newman and Huxley. The former held that 'To discover and to teach are distinct functions, they are also distinct gifts, and are not commonly found united in the same person'; the latter agreed with the view 'that the best investigators are usually those who have the responsibilities of instruction, gaining thus the incitement of colleagues, the encouragement of pupils, and the observation of the public'. And, although Newman spoke of the university as 'the high protecting power of all knowledge and science, of fact and principle, of inquiry and discovery, of experiment and speculation', research and criticism were never the breath of his nostrils as they were of Huxley's.

Although Huxley held that the university 'is neither an institution for testing the work of schoolmasters, nor a machinery for ascertaining the fitness of young men to be curates, lawyers or doctors', he had no Simon Pure fear that the universities would be contaminated by undertaking new tasks; and, when towards the end of his life the great educational topic was the reorganization of the University of London, he set down on nine foolscap sheets his idea of how a modern metropolitan university might be constituted. Especially interesting is the proposal to organize the university in 'Colleges' (with a note that, to distinguish these 'Colleges' from the existing institutions such as University College and King's College, we 'want some other name') of the following types:

Institutions giving instruction for purposes of:

   i. General Education (Arts).
  ii. Professional education in
      (*a*) Law
      (*b*) Medicine
      (*c*) The Industrial Professions
      (*d*) The Scholastic Professions
      (*e*) Painting, Sculpture and Architecture
      (*f*) Music.
 iii. Research in any of the Schools.

The three different types of 'College' (which were to share a common university chest) are clearly depicted as teaching institutions, either single or of a federal nature, and are not to be confused with the groupings of the university teachers in 'Schools' (*v. infra*). There is an obvious resemblance to a fairly common type of American university structure, with its Liberal Arts College and Professional Colleges and Graduate College, developed mainly in the present century, and this element in Huxley's plan is an interesting expresion of his awareness of the educational needs of an emerging industrial society. The Senate, which would have 'Supreme power in all affairs . . . with appeal to the Privy Council', was to include considerable professorial representation; but Huxley, ever anxious to avoid the establishment of an academic episcopate, notes the 'importance of having no seats on Senate attached *ex officio* to chairs in existing or future Collegiate Institutions'. Graduates were to have some share in university government, but that share was to be limited, as indicated by the note 'Convocation to have a right to be heard on any question by the Senate – and if necessary to appeal to Privy Council – but no veto'. Huxley's scheme contained no provision for a University Court, but he would stiffen the professorial body by some extra-academic representation on the Senate itself. Out of the Professoriate the Senate was to constitute 'Boards of Studies', which would, subject to the Senate's over-riding authority, consider questions of curriculum and examination. These 'Boards of Studies' would have exercised the functions of the present Boards of Studies and some of those of the present Boards of Faculties, while others of the functions of the latter would have been exercised by his 'Colleges'.

The students of the 'College of General Education', which was to be responsible also for Extension work, were to be examined by the university as such; while the 'Professional Colleges' were to have a semi-autonomous position, each arranging its own scheme of instruction and examination (under the joint supervision of representatives of the 'College' and of the appropriate 'Schools' of the University) and presenting its students to the university on an *ad eundem* basis for the award of its professional 'degrees'.

The 'Research College' in Huxley's sense would include not only institutions concerned solely with research, but also the non-professional research departments of other university institutions; and the degree of Doctor of Philosophy (which was in fact not to be instituted in England for nearly another thirty years) was 'to be conferred on the production of a good piece of original work – the sufficiency of which agreed to by the professors of the appropriate School of the University'.

As an example of how the Professional Colleges might be constituted, Huxley notes 'London Schools & Colleges of medicine organised into one body = *College of Medicine of the University*', and some further insight of the sort of structure he envisaged is given by a much earlier scheme for the professional preparation of science eachers. Some notes of 1869 include the following jottings:

London Training College organization—Dean, etc. . . .
Provincial Training Colleges
Examining Body for the whole formed by selection from the professors of all the Colleges—

_____

Nominated for 5 to 7 years

_____

Examining body not to be called a University—

_____

National Institute

_____

Degrees granted by Minister on recommendation of Examiners.

At that time there was no network of provincial universities to provide nodes of regional organization, but by 1892 Huxley was prepared for the university instead of the Minister to grant 'degrees' on the recommendation of the 'Institute' or 'Professional College' – a somewhat remarkable anticipation of our modern Institutes of Education.

On the thorny question of the professional education of the clergy, he writes, 'There are obvious objections to the admission of a College of Theology among the Institutions for professional education recognized by the University if Theology is to be taken as the special theology of any particular Church or Sect – On the other hand, I conceive it is very much to be regretted that the study of Philosophy, History and Philology – which stand in the same relation to Theology as the Institutes of Medicine[3] to Medicine – should be ignored in any University . . . assuredly there is room enough and to spare in these subjects not only for learning but for research –'. But, he concludes a little regretfully, 'I am afraid however that it is quite hopeless to expect that the various theological institutions in London would combine into a 'College' as the Medical Law and other Professional Institutions may be reasonably expected to do.' In the event, the Inns of Court were to remain outside the university, while some theological institutions were to enter in. Today, with the successful example of the University of London Institute of Education before us, it might perhaps be well to consider the possibility of developing Huxley's 1892 scheme in connection with other fields of professional preparation. There might, for example, be an 'Institute of Music' (with the Royal College, the Royal Academy and Trinity College as its principal constituents), an 'Institute of Theology' (including not only the four colleges and schools recognized in the existing Faculty of Theology, but also the clergy training colleges in the university's area), an 'Institute of Art', and so on – each awarding certificates and diplomas under the university's aegis as the Institute of Education does. But such speculations cannot be pursued further here.

Cutting across the organization of the teaching institutions into 'Colleges', the teachers themselves were, according to Huxley's plan, to be grouped and meet in 'Schools' as follows:

   i. Philosophy (incl. Psychology, Logic, Metaphysics, Ethics, Jurisprudence)
   ii. Mathematical and Physical Sciences
   iii. History (Archaeology – General and Special History, Political Economy)
   iv. Philology (General and Special)
   v. Literature
   vi. Painting, Sculpture and Architecture
   vii. Music. –

Huxley's 'Schools' correspond approximately, but only approximately, to what are now called 'Faculties'. He had no 'Schools' of Medicine, Law, Engineering, Pedagogy, or Theology: the teachers in such professional subjects were to belong to his 'Schools' of Philosophy, Science, History, etc., according to their special studies. And it may be that, for example, the regular meeting of philosophers (irrespective of whether they are concerned with professional training in theology or pedagogy or general education in arts or science) or of scientists (irrespective of whether they engage in professional trainin in medicine or engineering or general education in science) would be a very good thing. Unfortunately, such a dual organization of teaching institutions on the one hand and of teachers on the other cannot be regarded as a practicable possibility for the London University of today.

What then, may we say of Huxley's idea of a university? He built no monumental literary structure as Newman did in his Dublin discourses. In his deep concern for the proper recognition of the natural sciences he merely shared the views of many in his day. In his dislike of the aristocratic atmosphere of Oxford and Cambridge he had many contemporary allies and not a few predecessors. In his contempt for the petty pedantry of the grammarians he was in communion with all the leading spirits of the day. In his objection to religious tests he simply shared the views of all agnostics and nonconformists, and of the forward-looking anglicans also. In his insistence on a democratic form of university organization he was but the representative of an age becoming conscious of the meaning of democracy. Indeed, scarcely a view that he expressed on the nature of universities was an original one. It would, however, be very misleading to leave the matter at that: there may be novelty not merely in elements but in the mode of their composition, and it is in its composition that Huxley's idea of a university had significance for his time and has it still today.

If Huxley urged that natural science be given a proper place in the university, he did so in no partisan way but in full recognition of the value of other studies. He showed an awareness of the historical tradition of universities and an appreciation of their essential spirit, but he was also deeply conscious of the changes demanded by a complex modern society. Recognizing the dangers of a narrow scientific education, he perceived equally the perils of a narrow education in other specialities; but, seeing also the futility of fragmentary and superficial knowledge, he insisted on the virtues of specialization. In his objections to rigid matriculation requirements, he anticipated modern provisions for the admission of capable students whose earlier education has not followed the orthodox path; in his insistence that those who know a subject well are not necessarily qualified to teach it in a university or to conduct examinations in it, he made a point that still needs making. He urged the development of the professorial system, but he valued the tutorial system and showed how to adapt it to the needs of practical studies. He agreed that its teachers should have a large share in the conduct of a university, but he saw also the desirability of some degree of general lay participation in control. He recognized the ancient supremacy of the Faculty of Arts as the coping stone of the education of the citizen, but he also wanted a more thorough development of university professional education. On every major issue Huxley seems to have sided with those who were forward-looking, but on each issue he avoided partisan extremes.

Huxley's idea of a university contained no novel element, but his sensitivity to the immediate needs and future trends of an emerging industrial society enabled him to foresee many developments and to suggest patterns of organization which might yet prevent the squeezing out of the essential life of a university by the enormous weight of modern social requirements.

Notes

1 According to Father Henry Tristran (personal communication, 2. iii. 1953).
2 The book is not listed in Sotheby's catalogue of H.'s library, nor does Mrs. Leonard Huxley remember seeing it among the books her husband inherited.
3 'Institutes of Medicine' is an old term for the foundation studies basic to the practice of medicine.

References

The major source of unpublished material is the collection of Huxley's papers at the Imperial College of Science and Technology, to whose Governing Body gratitude is expressed for facilities granted. Particular references may be traced by the following volume and folio numbers:

Matthew Arnold to H. (17. x. 80)–10. 163

Leslie Stephen to H. (8. iv. 89)–27. 57

H. to E. R. Lankester (11. iv. 92)–30. 148

Draft of H.'s evidence to Cowper Commission (26. x. 92)–42. 93 *et seq.*

H.'s notes on possible constitution for University of London (c. 8. xi. 92)–42. 110 *et seq.*

H.'s notes of conversation *re* teacher training (30. xi. 69)–42. 194

H.'s notes from Newman's writings–47. 196 *et seq.*

The main published sources are Huxley's lectures *Universities: Actual and Ideal* (1874), *Address on University Education* (1876) and *Science and Culture* (1880), all reprinted in Volume III of his *Collected Essays* (Macmillan, London, 1893). Particular references may be traced on the following pages of this volume: 141, 153, 191, 202, 203, 204, 206, 215, 228, 237, 238, 239, 241, 242, 243, 255.

Other sources are:

Huxley, '[Newman is] the slipperiest sophist . . .' *Life and Letters of T. H. Huxley*, by Leonard Huxley (Macmillan, London, 1900), II, 226.

—— 'universities should be learning and teaching bodies . . .' *id.*, 308.

—— 'I am a plebeian . . .' *Anglo-American Memories*, Ser. II, by E. W. Smalley (Duckworth, London, 1912), p. 19.

—— 'Oxford and Cambridge put . . .' *Report from the Select Committee on Scientific Instruction*, etc., Published by Order of the House of Commons, 15 July 1868, Answer 8026.

—— 'the entire business of teaching . . .' *id.*, Answer 7957.

—— 'is neither an institution . . .', *The Times*, 7. vii. 92.

Newman, 'the French Vicomte . . .', *Newman's University: Idea and Reality*, by F. McGrath (Longmans, London, 1951), p. 347.

Connell, '[Arnold] had no difficulty . . .', *The Educational Thought and Influence of Matthew Arnold*, by W. F. Connell (Routledge, London, 1950), p. 199.

Judges, 'that which by Newman's definition . . .', and 'distaste for research', *Pioneers of English Education*, ed. A. V. Judges (Faber, London, 1952), p. 33.

Truscot, '[Newman] would exclude . . .', *Redbrick University*, by Bruce Truscot (Penguin edn., 1951), p. 142.

Article, 'Pope Huxley', *Spectator*, XLIII, 135; 29. i. 70.

Chair of English Literature at Oxford, *Pall Mall Gazette*, 22. x. 86.

No bibliographic references are given for the better-known passages from Newman.

35

THE IDEA OF A MODERN UNIVERSITY

Abraham Flexner

Source: A. Flexner, *Universities: American, English and German*, London: Oxford University Press, 1930, pp. 3–36.

I

Seventy-five years ago, an eminent Oxonian, Cardinal Newman, published a book entitled *The Idea of a University*. I have adopted in a modified form the title of that volume. I am undertaking in this chapter to discuss the idea of a *modern* university. In inserting the word "modern" I am endeavouring to indicate in the most explicit fashion that a university, like all other human institutions — like the church, like governments, like philanthropic organizations — is not outside, but inside the general social fabric of a given era. It is not something apart, something historic, something that yields as little as possible to forces and influences that are more or less new. It is, on the contrary — so I shall assume — an expression of the age, as well as an influence operating upon both present and future. I propose to elaborate this point of view and, as I proceed, to ask myself to what extent and in what ways universities in America, in England, and in Germany have made themselves part of the modern world, where they have failed to do so, where they have made hurtful concessions, and where they are wholesome and creative influences in shaping society towards rational ends.

Quite obviously I am assuming that to some extent, however slight, we are masters of our fate. The modern world is developing under the pressure of forces that reason cannot readily control. Pitted against these forces, our abilities may for the moment seem feeble and ineffectual. But the existence of universities implies there is something, perhaps much, in the past for which it is worth while to fight, to which it is worth while to cling; and that there is something — no one knows how much — which we may ourselves do to mould to our liking the civilization of the future. Man, as Professor Woodbridge has admirably said, "is not content to take nature as he finds her. He insists on making her over."[1] But the modern world — no matter how new we think it to be — is rooted in a past, which is the soil out of which we grow, a past during which poets and scientists and thinkers and peoples have accumulated treasures of truth, beauty, and knowledge, experience, social, political, and other, which only a wastrel would ignore. On the other hand, science, democracy, and other forces steadily increasing in intensity are creating a different world of which universities must take account.

II

Universities differ in different countries; if, as Lord Haldane says, "it is in universities that . . . the soul of a people mirrors itself,"[2] then it would be absurd to expect them to conform to a single pattern. Moreover, as a matter of history, they have changed profoundly — and commonly in the direction of the social evolution of which they are part. The Paris of 1900 has little in common with the Paris of 1700; the Oxford of the twentieth century, externally so largely the same, is nevertheless a very different thing from the Oxford of the eighteenth century; Althoff's Berlin is not Wilhelm von Humboldt's, though they are separated by hardly a hundred years; very different indeed is the Harvard, of which Mr. Eliot became president in 1869, from the Harvard which he left on his retirement in 1909. Historians have traced certain aspects of this evolution in detail; and nothing in their stories is more striking than the adjustments — sometimes slow and unconscious, sometimes deliberate and violent — made in the course of centuries by institutions usually regarded as conservative, frequently even as the stronghold of reaction. I say then that universities have in most countries changed; but have they latterly changed profoundly enough, or have they been so intelligently modified as to be the effective and formative agencies which are needed in a society that is driven it knows not whither by forces of unprecedented strength and violence? An American sociologist has invented the term "social lag." Institutions as such tend for quite obvious reasons to lag behind the life which they express and further. To what extent are the universities of America, England, and Germany hampered by "social lag"?

III

There is danger at precisely the opposite end of the line. I have spoken of the intelligent modification of universities — of their modification in the light of needs, facts, and ideals. But a university should not be a weather vane, responsive to every variation of popular whim. Universities must at times give society, not what society wants, but what it needs. Inertia and resistance have their uses, provided they be based on reasonable analysis, on a sense of values, not on mere habit. In response to the criticism that universities lag, instances in plenty can — and will — be given by way of showing

that universities are up to date or even ahead of the times. But the two characteristics are not mutually exclusive. Universities are complex and organic
institutions: their arms may be sound, while both legs may be broken. They
may lag fundamentally, even while superficially catering to whim or fashion;
they may lag fundamentally at the very moment when at this or that point they
are as expert as newspapers and politicians in catching the current breeze. A
proper amount of critical resistance, based on a sense of values, would — as
we shall see — save them from absurd, almost disastrous blunders.

IV

Of all this, more hereafter. In the present chapter, I shall not discuss universities, but merely the idea of a university, and I am going to procure a free
field for speculation by assuming the impossible and, indeed, the undesirable; suppose we could smash our existing universities to bits, suppose we
could remake them to conform to our heart's desire, what sort of institution
should we set up? We should not form them all alike — English, French,
American, German. But, whatever allowances we might make for national
tradition or temperament, we should see to it somehow that in appropriate
ways scholars and scientists would be conscious of four major concerns:
the conservation of knowledge and ideas; the interpretation of knowledge
and ideas; the search for truth; the training of students who will practise and
"carry on." I say, to repeat, "the major concerns" of scholar and scientist.
Of course, education has other and important concerns. But I wish to make
it plain at the outset that the university is only one of many educational
enterprises. It has, in the general educational scheme, certain specific functions. Other agencies discharge or should discharge other functions. We shall
see whether universities now discern and discharge their special functions or
whether they meddle with functions which do not constitute their proper
business.

The conservation of knowledge and ideas is and has always been recognized as the business of universities, sometimes, perhaps, as almost their
only business, occasionally, even today, as too largely their business. In any
event, universities have always taken this to be one of their functions; and
however universities may change, no reconstruction will or should deprive
them of it. But one should add this: conservation and interpretation are
one thing in institutions that are concerned with merely or chiefly that; they
are a different thing in a university where fresh streams of thought are constantly playing upon the preserved treasures of mankind.

Original thinkers and investigators do not therefore represent the only
type of university professor. They will always be the distinguished figures;
theirs will usually be the most profound and far-reaching influence. But
even universities, modern universities, need and use men of different stamp
— teachers whose own contributions to learning are of less importance than

their influence in stimulating students or their resourcefulness in bringing together the researches of others. Michael Foster was not the less a great university professor, though he was not himself a great original thinker: in subtle ways that defy expression, he created the great Cambridge school of physiology. So, too, Paulsen was not the less a great university professor, though he was not himself a great original thinker, but rather a broad and profound scholar of sound judgment and beautiful spirit who helped hundreds, struggling with the perplexities of life and thought, to find themselves. But, be it noted, both did this not for boys, but for mature students, under conditions that threw upon them responsibility for efforts and results. And this is a university criterion of first-rate importance. The university professor has an entirely objective responsibility — a responsibility to learning, to his subject, and not a psychological or parental responsibility for his students. No fear that he will in consequence be dehumanized. What could be more charming, more intimate, more personal, more coöperative than the relations between the great continental masters and their disciples during the best part of the nineteenth century?

It is, however, creative activity, productive and critical inquiry — all in a sense without practical responsibility — that must bulk ever larger and larger in the modern university. Conservation continues to be not only important, but essential alike to education and to research; but, as other educational agencies improve and as our difficulties thicken, it is destined, I think, to become incidental to the extension of knowledge, to training at a high level, and to a critical attempt to set a value upon the doings of men.

Of the overwhelming and increasing importance of the study and solution of problems or the advancement of knowledge — they are interchangeable phrases — one can readily convince one's self, no matter where one looks. Let us consider for a moment the social and political situation within which we live, and I take this realm first, because it is the realm in which universities are doing least, the realm which is most difficult and dangerous to approach, the realm which is for these reasons perhaps the most important to master. Democracy has dragged in its wake social, economic, educational, and political problems infinitely more perplexing than the relatively simple problems which its credulous crusaders undertook to solve. Society cannot retreat; whatever may happen sporadically or temporarily in Italy or Spain, we shall in the end probably fare better, if the adaptations and inventions requisite to making a success of democracy are facilitated. But adaptations in what ways? Statesmen must invent — not statesmen, fumbling in the dark or living on phrases, but statesmen equipped by disinterested students of society with the knowledge needed for courageous and intelligent action. Now the postulates, ideas, terminology, phraseology, which started the modern world on new paths, have become more or less obsolete, partly through their own success, partly through changes due to science and the industrial revolution. To be sure, men have always acted blindly, ignorantly;

but for the time being at least, the chasm between action, on the one hand, and knowledge, on the other, is widening rather than contracting. Practice cannot be slowed down or halted; intelligence must, however, be accelerated.

This contention could be equally well illustrated by Germany, France, England, or the United States. What has happened in the United States? There was between 1776 and 1790 a revolution based upon a simple philosophy. Time, even a brief century, brought changes; but the philosophy had meanwhile crystallized. A thin rural population living on the seaboard had increased beyond a hundred millions spread over an empire; steam and electricity had transferred importance from agriculture to industry; huge cities had grown up; enormous discrepancies of wealth had been created. But the documentary basis of government and society remains essentially the same. We find ourselves therefore now enmeshed in a phraseology that is discordant with the facts. The phraseology tends to hold things fixed; but readjustments have somehow to be effected. Publicists and jurists have therefore been forced to make inherited formulae mean something that they do not mean and could not have meant. The easy and effective reconceiving and rewording of theory and ideas are thus gravely hampered. Somewhere, away from the hurly-burly of practical responsibility and action, the social and political problems involved in these discords must be exposed. The "great society" must and wants to understand itself — partly as a matter of sheer curiosity, partly because human beings are in a muddle and cannot get out unless they know more than they now know. Towards fundamental knowing the newspaper cannot help much; men of action — politicians and business men — help but slightly. They themselves know too little; they are not disinterestedly concerned with finding out; they have usually their own axes to grind. Almost the only available agency is the university. The university must shelter and develop thinkers, experimenters, inventors, teachers, and students, who, without responsibility for action, will explore the phenomena of social life and endeavour to understand them.

I do not mean to say that this is altogether a novelty. Great scholars have in all countries in fragments of time snatched from routine duties made important contributions to political and economic thought: "in fragments of time snatched from routine duties" — from administrative burdens, from secondary instruction, from distracting tasks undertaken to piece out a livelihood. But though individuals differ in their requirements, no university in any country has made really adequate provision or offered really adequate opportunity and encouragement. I have not in mind the training of practical men, who, faced with responsibility for action, will do the best they can. That is not the task of the university. Between the student of political and social problems and the journalist, industrialist, merchant, viceroy, member of Parliament or Congress, there is a gap which the university cannot fill, which society must fill in some other way. Perhaps no outright educational institution should be expected to fill it; educated men can be allowed to do some things for themselves — though, at the moment, we appear to be under a different impression.

One may go further: a study of mediaeval charters, of the financing of the Napoleonic Wars, of the rise of Prussia, of the origins of local government in the American Colonies, of the ideas of Plato, Aristotle, or Hobbes — these topics — just slightly musty — would be generally regarded as appropriately academic, for they may be investigated in a library. But is it equally good form — academically speaking — to study Mr. Keynes rather than Ricardo, the war debts with which successive commissions have wrestled rather than the repudiated state debts which most Americans quite wrongly prefer to regard as possessing merely historic interests, the present-day consequences of the industrial revolution rather than its early evolution? A field expedition to unearth an Assyrian palace is admittedly a proper undertaking for university professors; but should coal strikes, Indian unrest, rubber, oil, and American lynchings be for the present mainly left to journalists, travellers, and politicians? Do they become proper subjects of academic interest only when they approach the post-mortem stage? Quite the contrary: with all the difficulties arising from contemporaneousness, the task of the scientist, dealing with present social phenomena, is probably easier than that of the Hellenist or mediaevalist, intent upon reconstructing the past. "Think of the happiness of the scholar if he could see a Greek republic or a Roman colony actually living under his own eyes — granted that he recover from the havoc of some of his best established delusions!"[3]

I have said that data of one kind or another are not so difficult to obtain. But generalization is another matter. The social scientist may resent the premature generalizations of his predecessors. He will himself not get very far unless he himself tentatively generalizes; unless, in a word, he has ideas as well as data. Essays and investigations may be piled mountain high; they will never by themselves constitute a science or a philosophy of economics, psychology, or society. The two processes — the making of hypotheses and the gathering of data — must go on together, reacting upon each other. For in the social sciences as elsewhere generalization is at once a test of and a stimulus to minute and realistic research. The generalizations will not endure; why should they? They have not endured in mathematics, physics, and chemistry. But, then, neither have the data. Science, social or other, is a structure: "a series of judgments, revised without ceasing, goes to make up the incontestable progress of science. We must believe in this progress, but we must never accord more than a limited amount of confidence to the forms in which it is successively vested."[4]

The task, then, of finding a basis and providing a methodology for the social sciences, is today more pressing than it has ever been because of the accelerated rate of social change and the relatively more rapid progress in the physical and biological sciences: "The events of 1914–1918, to quote a single example, showed that the statesmen, the social scientists, the moral and religious teachers of Europe, to whom belonged, as their main duty, the preservation of peace, failed utterly; the directors and inventors of the physical sciences had assigned to them as their main duty the killing of as many of the national enemies as possible, and they succeeded magnificently. Twenty years hence the same situation may recur; and unless the two disciplines concerned can meanwhile come to an understanding, half the population and all the accumulated wealth of Europe may be destroyed with even more complete efficiency."[5]

As long as evolution proceeded slowly over centuries, men could feel their way and make adjustments imperceptibly on an empirical basis. But the restraints which for centuries slowed down or limited adjustments have been largely removed. Societies have to act — intelligently, if possible — if not, then unintelligently, blindly, selfishly, impulsively. The weight and prestige of the university must be thrown on the side of intelligence. If the university does not accept this challenge, what other institution can or will? In this present-day world, compounded of tradition, good and bad, racial mixtures, nationalistic and internationalistic strivings, business interests, physical forces of incredible power for good or ill, emancipated workers and peasants, restless Orientals, noisy cities, conflicting philosophies — in this world rocking beneath and around us, where is theory to be worked out, where are social and economic problems to be analysed, where are theory and facts to be brought face to face, where is the truth, welcome or unwelcome, to be told, where are men to be trained to ascertain and to tell it, where, in whatever measure it is possible, is conscious, deliberate, and irresponsible thought to be given to the task of reshaping this world of ours to our own liking, unless, first and foremost, in the university? The wit of man has thus far contrived no other comparable agency.

The urgency of the need is not, as I have said, without its dangers. The history of the more manageable sciences contains a warning which the social scientist will do well to heed. Chemistry made no progress as long as men were concerned immediately to convert base metal into gold; it advanced when, for the time being, it ignored use and practice. Today chemical theory and chemical practice are continuously fertilizing each other. So, again, medicine stood almost still until the pre-clinical sciences were differentiated and set free — free to develop without regard to use and practice. The same situation has more recently developed on the clinical side; disease is most likely to be understood — and ultimately combatted — if it is approached as a phenomenon, and patients and problems must be selected on the basis of the clinician's interest, in so far as he is engaged in investigation. The social sciences have not yet developed far enough to win assured scientific status. A sympathetic onlooker is fearful lest the frail theoretic or scientific structure is being subjected to a practical strain that it is not competent to bear. To be sure, the social scientist must find his material in the thick of events; but qua scientist, he must select and approach and frame his problems, from the viewpoint of science, without incurring responsibility for policies. In the social as in the physical sciences, the university is, in so far as scientific effort to understand phenomena is concerned, indifferent to the effect and use of truth. Perhaps, in due course, use and theory may in the social sciences also prove mutually helpful; perhaps social experimentation, involving application, may prove the only laboratory. But even so, it is one thing to incur responsibility for policies, and quite another to set up an experiment primarily in the interest of ascertaining truth or testing theory. The modern university must neither fear the world nor make itself responsible for its conduct.

I have been urging that universities maintain contacts with the actual world and at the same time continue to be irresponsible. Are the two attitudes incompatible? Can they really take an objective position in reference to social, political, and economic phenomena? Can they study phenomena without wanting to tell legislatures, communities, municipal authorities, and chambers of commerce what they ought to do at any particular moment about some particular thing? I think they must and can. It is a question of ideals and organization.[6] For experimental purposes they may, without sacrifice of intellectual integrity, make suggestions and watch results; but this is different from running a city government or a political party, involving, as such responsibilities do, compromises of principle that are fatal to fearless thinking. The analogy of the medical clinic, already mentioned, is not complete, but it is suggestive. The professor of medicine needs patients, just as the social scientist needs his environment. The professor of medicine ought to be thoroughly humane, realizing fully that he is dealing with, and in that sense responsible for, human life. But the professor of medicine is primarily a student of problems and a trainer of men. He has not the slightest obligation to look after as many sick people as he can; on the contrary, the moment he regards his task as that of caring for more and more of the sick, he will cease to discharge his duty to the university — his duty to study problems, to keep abreast of literature, to make his own contributions to science, to train men who can "carry on." The greatest and most productive of American surgical thinkers lived his entire scientific life in this fashion: he was considerate and humane in the care of his patients; he trained a group of remarkably competent surgeons; but his central thought and activity never swerved from the study of problems; one problem after another yielded its mystery to him; but having solved a problem, he ceased to occupy himself actively with it; other persons could do that, while he pushed on to something new, important, unknown. "We are still, as you know, groping more or less in the dark," he once wrote, "and always shall be, I trust; for otherwise there would be no game in medicine. There are, however, light spots back of us, where before there was darkness."[7] In those words the university professor spoke — the professor of surgery, of medicine, of law, of economics, of all subjects whatsoever.

Industry has found ways of utilizing the sheerest scientific research — it does not require that of the university; medicine is groping about for a similar connecting link — the medical faculty would be ruined if it served in both capacities. The social sciences must be detached from the conduct of business, the conduct of politics, the reform of this, that, and the other, if they are to develop as sciences, even though they continuously need contact with the phenomena of business, the phenomena of politics, the phenomena of social experimentation.

V

The situation is not essentially different in respect to the so-called "exact sciences," though universities have in the more vigorous western countries become more hospitable to their cultivation for their own sake. These sciences — mathematics, physics, chemistry, and biology — have made greater progress in the last century than in many preceding centuries. Even so, they are still in their infancy. In what is usually called their "pure" form — I mean their cultivation without reference to application — they have now so securely established themselves, theoretically at least, that I need not emphasize their importance. It is, however, not so generally realized that science, pure or applied, creates more problems than it solves. First, on the theoretic or philosophic side: we have become increasingly and painfully aware of our abysmal ignorance. No scientist, fifty years ago, could have realized that he was as ignorant as all first-rate scientists now know themselves to be. It was but recently that we believed that Newton had arrived at rock-bottom! It is a disquieting change from that complacent state of mind to the attitude of Charles Peirce, who described the laws of nature as habits or customs; or to the attitude of Gilbert Lewis who asks: "Can we not see that exact laws, like all the other ultimates and absolutes, are as fabulous as the crock of gold at the rainbow's end?"[8] The theoretic consequences of scientific discovery may thus be very disconcerting; for the scientist, bent perhaps merely upon the gratification of his own curiosity, periodically and episodically destroys the foundations upon which both science and society have just become used to reclining comfortably. We listen nowadays not to one Copernicus — a voice crying in the wilderness — but to many, and their voices are magnified and transmitted through the entire social and intellectual structure. Physics and chemistry, viewed as merely intellectual passions, will not stay "put"; they have an elusive way of slipping through the fingers of the investigator.

I have spoken of the theoretic consequences of scientific progress and of the need of a place in which calm, philosophic reflection can be brought to bear upon them. Consider now the practical consequences of scientific advance, the problems thus created, and the need of opportunities for their consideration and solution. Medicine offers an obvious example. Whether out of humanitarian or sheer scientific interest, men study the phenomena of disease. What happens? A problem is solved — the problem of this or that infection or contagion. Quite unexpected consequences ensue. One problem is solved; other problems are created. Life is lengthened. Thereupon we are confronted by a new crop of diseases, almost negligible as long as the infancy death rate was high and the expectation of life limited to the thirties; thus has medical science increased, not diminished, its own burden. But this is not all: men live longer and more safely; they live more healthily and contentedly in huge cities than in small villages or in the open country. At once, serious social problems, involving education, government, law, custom, morality, arise from the congestion of population following improved sanitation. Nor is this all. There are more people — many more. They must be fed and clothed. Raw materials are needed; the excess of manufactured products must be marketed. Competition becomes more and more intense — for raw materials, for colonies, for markets. War is no longer a solution — it merely creates additional problems. Thus science, in the very act of solving problems, creates more of them. Such are the consequences of progress in a portion of the physical and biological sciences in a small corner of the western world. Inevitably, the sciences will be more thoroughly and more widely cultivated. What new problems will be thereby created, we are powerless to conceive. But so much at least is clear: while pure science is revolutionizing human thought, applied science is destined to revolutionize human life. We are at the beginning, not at the end, of an epoch. Problems therefore abound and press upon us — problems due to ignorance, problems created by knowledge. They must be studied before intelligent action can be taken. Hand-to-mouth contrivance does not suffice. Who is going to study them? Who and where? There will be, of course, from time to time a lonely Mendel or a lonely Darwin, who may do epochmaking things. But more and more the worker needs co-workers and facilities such as the individual is not likely to possess; he needs, also, soil in which to grow. However deeply the flash of genius may penetrate, the bulk of the world's work in research and teaching will be done in universities — if universities are what they ought to be.

VI

Our world is not, however, merely a matter of democracy and science. Indeed, if some sort of cultural equilibrium is to be attained, the humanistic disciplines, in which philosophy is included, necessarily become of greater rather than less importance; and by humanistic disciplines I refer not only to the humanities as such, but to the human values inherent in a deep knowledge of science itself. With the quick march of science, philosophy and humanism have gone under a cloud; when they assert themselves, they are prone to do so apologetically, on the ground that they too are, or can be, scientific. To be sure, they are and can; I shall in a moment have a word to say on that point. But quite aside from their pursuit in a scientific spirit, the world has not lost, and, unless it is to lose its savour, will never lose the pure, appreciative, humanistic spirit — the love of beauty, the concern for ends established by ideals that dare to command rather than to obey. Now science, while widening our vision, increasing our satisfactions, and solving our problems, brings with it dangers peculiarly its own. We can become so infatuated with progress in knowledge and control — both of which I have unstintedly emphasized — that we lose our perspective, lose our historic sense, lose a philosophic outlook, lose sight of relative cultural values. Something like this has happened to many, perhaps to most, of the enthusiastic, clear-headed, forward-looking, perhaps too exclusively forward-looking, and highly specialized young votaries of science. They are, culturally, too often thin and metallic; their training appears technological rather than broadly and deeply scientific. I have urged that science, quâ science, is indifferent to use and effect. Taste and reason do not intervene to stop the scientist prosecuting his search for truth; they do sit in judgment on the uses to which society puts the forces which the scientist has set free. I say, our younger scientists not infrequently appear to have been dehumanized; so also do some humanists. In the modern university, therefore, the more vigorously science is prosecuted, the more acute the need that society be held accountable for the purposes to which larger knowledge and experience are turned. Philosophers and critics, therefore, gain in importance as science makes life more complex — more rational in some ways, more irrational in others.

But there are other senses in which humanism must be promoted by modern universities. For humanism is not merely a thing of values — it has, like science, consequences. At first sight, what can be more innocent than the resurrection of a dead language? But every time a dead language is exhumed, a new nationality may be created. The humanists, not merely the Turks or the politicians or the newspapers, are at least partly responsible for the Balkanization of Eastern Europe and for the recrudescence of Celtic feeling. Like the scientist, the humanist creates as well as solves problems; he helps to free the Serbs and the Greeks from Turkish rule; he helps both to create and to solve the Home Rule problem in Great Britain — irresponsibly in either instance; he assists powerfully in stimulating self-consciousness in India, in Egypt, in China, and among the American Negroes; he finds himself one of the causes of an exacerbation of nationalism and racialism which no one has yet learned to mollify or cure. He has, I repeat, no practical responsibility for the trouble he makes; it is his business and duty to preserve his independence and irresponsibility. But he must go on thinking; in that realm his responsibility is of the gravest. And, perhaps, in the fullness of time, the very licence of his thought may, without intention or forethought on his part, suggest inventions or profoundly influence solutions, as it has done heretofore.

I cannot presume, even if I had space, to enumerate all the reasons for desiring a vigorous renascence of humanistic studies. But I must touch on one more point. During the last century, palaeontologist and historian have shown us how little we know of the story and import of man's career on this planet. A tremendous gap remains to be filled by archaeologists, philologists, and palaeographers — by Greek and Latin scholars working in libraries and in the field, by Orientalists, digging at Megiddo, in the Nile Valley, at Dura, and elsewhere. The story of the Athenian Empire will have to be rewritten in the light of recent readings of the pieced-together fragments of a few Greek tablets; who knows what will happen when the Agora discloses its secrets? And were the Hittite, Sumerian, and Malay languages and remains properly cultivated, we might arrive at very different conceptions than are now accepted as to the origin, development, and spread of culture. I need not labour the point by dwelling on the importance of a humanistic development covering mediaeval and modern times. Suffice it to say that further study of mediaeval and modern art, literature, music, and history will inevitably revise notions formed on the basis of the defective data which have hitherto controlled our thinking.

Intensive study of phenomena under the most favourable possible conditions — the phenomena of the physical world, of the social world, of the aesthetic world, and the ceaseless struggle to see things in relation — these I conceive to be the most important functions of the modern university. We shall get further with the physical world than with the social world or the aesthetic world; but the difference is only one of degree — all are important, all are worth while — worth while in themselves, worth while because they have bearings, implications, uses. But the university will not exhaust its function when it piles up its heaps of knowledge. Within the same institution that is busy in ascertaining facts, intelligence will be at work piecing facts together, inferring, speculating. There will be a Rutherford, breaking up the atom, and a Whitehead or Eddington, trying to make out what it all means; a Virchow demonstrating cellular pathology, and a Banting bringing from the four corners of the earth the various bits that, fitted together, produce insulin. When the late Jacques Loeb was asked whether he was a chemist or physiologist, he is reported to have replied, "I am a student of problems." It is fashionable to rail at specialization; but the truth is that specialization has brought us to the point we have reached, and more highly specialized intelligence will alone carry us further. But, of course, specialization alone does not suffice; there must somehow be drawn into the university also minds that can both specialize and generalize. The philosophic intelligence must be at work, trying new patterns, trying, however vainly, to see things in the large, as new material is accumulated. And this process should go on in the university more effectively than anywhere else, just because the university is the active centre of investigation and reflection and because it brings together within its framework every type of fundamental intelligence.

VII

A modern university would then address itself whole-heartedly and unreservedly to the advancement of knowledge, the study of problems, from whatever source they come, and the training of men — all at the highest level of possible effort. The constitution of the stars, the constitution of the atom, the constitutions of Oklahoma, Danzig, or Kenya, what is happening in the stars, in the atom, in Oklahoma, what social and political consequences flow from the fact that the politician is becoming more and more obsolescent while the business man and the idealist are playing a larger part in determining the development of society — all these are important objects to know about. It is not the business of the university to *do* anything about any of them. The university cannot regulate the weather in Mars, it cannot run business, it cannot directly influence what happens at Westminster or Washington. But neither can it hold itself aloof.

There are dangers to be encountered in modernizing universities, in the sense in which I have used the term. Quite obviously, such a modern university has more things to think about than a mediaeval institution given to expounding Aristotle, the Fathers, and the classic philosophers. But precisely because modern universities have many interests, they must be extremely critical of every claimant. Now, men — especially mediocre men — do not always distinguish the serious from the trivial, the significant from the insignificant. A university, seeking to be modern, seeking to evolve theory, seeking to solve problems, may thus readily find itself complicating its task and dissipating energy and funds by doing a host of inconsequential things.

There is a second danger. The moment a real idea has been let loose, the moment technique has been developed, mediocrity is jubilant; the manufacture of make-believe science flourishes. Learning has never been free from pedantry or from superficiality. But the modern world, what with its abundant facilities for publication and its ridiculous fondness for "learned" degrees, groans under a tropical growth of make-believe. Now, as against this tendency, against the tendency towards specialization of a mechanical or technological kind, we need to remember that universities depend on ideas, on great men. One Virchow, one Pasteur, one Willard Gibbs can change the entire intellectual order in his respective sphere. But great men are individuals; and individuals and organizations are in everlasting conflict. The university is an institution. It cannot, on the one hand, be amorphous or chaotic. Neither, on the other, can it flourish unless it is elastic enough to supply the different conditions that different productive individuals find congenial. It may well turn out that these conditions are just as favourable to somnolence as to productivity. It does not much matter that some persons go to sleep, provided only enough others are wide awake and fertile at the maximum of their powers. The important thing is not that a few persons doze or loaf or are ineffectual; the important thing is that a Hertz, a Maxwell, a Mommsen, and a Gildersleeve find within the university the conditions that suit them as individuals — conditions favourable to their own development and to the development of a varied group of co-workers.

VIII

I do not wish now to anticipate what I shall have to say of American, English, and German universities. But it must be obvious already that my criticism will cover two points, viz., what universities do not now touch, what they have no business to touch. The program which I have sketched is surely not lacking in extent or difficulty; its successful execution would call for more talent and more money than any university now possesses. Moreover, the kind of work that such universities should do requires proper conditions — books, laboratories, of course, but also quiet, dignity, freedom from petty cares, intercourse at a high social and intellectual level, a full and varied life, nicely adjusted to individual idiosyncrasies. We shall have occasion in subsequent chapters to consider with how much intelligence universities nowadays draw the line in these matters. Let me concede, for the purpose of argument (and for that only), that all the things that universities do are in themselves worth doing — a very large concesssion. Does it follow that universities *should* do them? Does it follow that universities *can* do them? I answer both questions in the negative. If universities are charged with the high functions that I have enumerated, they will do well to discharge them effectively — do well to assemble the men, to gather the money, to provide the facilities that are requisite to their performance. I think it can be shown that universities do not yet discharge these functions well; that they assume obligations that are irrelevant and unworthy. If the functions, against which I should draw the line, are really worth discharging, society must find other ways of discharging them. Of course there is nothing sacrosanct about the three or four traditional faculties or the traditional subjects. As the world has changed, new faculties have been needed; new subjects have from time to time been created. But even in the most modern university a clear case must be made out, if for no better reason than the fact that expansion means increase of professors and students — the former difficult to obtain, the latter likely through sheer size to destroy the organic character of the institution. And the case, as I see it, must rest on the inherent and intellectual value of the proposed faculty or the proposed subject. Practical importance is not a sufficient title to academic recognition: if that is the best that can be said, it is an excellent reason for exclusion. A university is therefore not a dumping ground. Universities that are held to their appropriate tasks will be unfit to do other tasks. A far-reaching educational reconstruction may thus become necessary. In no two countries is it going to be brought about in identical fashion. Indeed, it need not be uniformly accomplished in any one country. But, however this may be, the reorganization of universities, in order that they may do supremely well what they almost alone can do, may accomplish much by forcing the reorganization of the rest of the educational system.

IX

On the basis which I have discussed, the pursuit of science and scholarship belongs to the university. What else belongs there? Assuredly neither secondary, technical, vocational, nor popular education. Of course, these are important; of course, society must create appropriate agencies to deal with them; but they must not be permitted to distract the university.

With merely technical, merely vocational, or merely popular education we shall encounter no difficulty in dealing; but the term "secondary education" is so vague and so variously used that I must explain the sense in which I shall use it throughout these pages. To my mind, the difference between secondary and university education is the difference between immaturity and maturity. Secondary education involves responsibility of an intimate kind for the student, for the subject-matter that he studies, even for the way in which he works, lives, and conducts himself — for his manners, his morals, and his mind. The university has no such complicated concern. At the university the student must take chances — with himself, with his studies, with the way in which he works. The freedom of the university does not mean either that the professor is indifferent or that at the very outset the student should attack a piece of research independently: on the contrary, he has, while free, to work through a difficult apprenticeship before he attains independence. In the same way, the entire texture of secondary education need not be uniform. Freedom and responsibility may be increased, as adolescence advances; in one way or another, the peculiar character of the secondary school may taper off, as the university approaches. But in any event, there will be a break, a jolt, a crisis, precisely as there is a break when a grown boy or girl leaves home. It is not the business of education to avoid every break, every jolt, every crisis. On the contrary, the boy having become a man, a jolt tests his mettle; unless he survives and gains in moral and intellectual strength, the university is no place for him, for the university should not be even partly a secondary school.[9]

Of the professional faculties, a clear case can, I think, be made out for law and medicine;[10] not for denominational religion, which involves a bias, hardly perhaps for education, certainly not at all for business, journalism, domestic "science," or library "science," to which I shall return in detail later.[11] It is true that most physicians and most lawyers are mere craftsmen; it is even true that their training largely occupies itself with teaching them how to do things. I should go further: I should add that an unproductive faculty of law or medicine is no whit the better for being attached to a university; it has no business there; it would do as well by society and by its students if it were an independent vocational school.

How are we to distinguish professions that belong to universities from vocations that do not belong to them? The criteria are not difficult to discern. Professions are, as a matter of history — and very rightly — "learned professions"; there are no unlearned professions. Unlearned professions — a contradiction in terms — would be vocations, callings, or occupations. Professions are learned, because they have their roots deep in cultural and idealistic soil. Moreover, professions derive their essential character from intelligence. Of course, the surgeon uses his hands; the physician uses a stethoscope; the lawyer uses a clerk and an accountant. But these are the accidents of activity. The essence of the two professions resides in the application of free, resourceful, unhampered intelligence to the comprehension of problems — the problems of disease, the problems of social life, bequeathed to us by history and complicated by evolution. Unless legal and medical faculties live in the atmosphere of ideals and research, they are simply not university faculties at all.

Professions may be further distinguished by their attitude towards results. The scientist or the scholar who takes shape in the physician or the jurist has objects to accomplish. The achievement of these objects incidentally brings in a livelihood; but the livelihood is, theoretically at least (and for many centuries practically too), of secondary or incidental, even though to the individual, of essential, importance. Professions have primarily objective, intellectual, and altruistic purposes. A profession is therefore an order, a caste, not always in fact free from selfish aims, but in its ideals at least devoted to the promotion of larger and nobler ends than the satisfaction of individual ambitions. It has a code of honour — sometimes, like the Hippocratic oath, historically impressive.

It will become clear, as we go on, that, compared with present theory and practice, the conception of the university which I have outlined is severe. Have I lost sight of the importance of "training" — training college teachers or educational administrators or candidates for governmental posts? I think not. I have merely assumed that persons who have had a genuine university education will emerge with disciplined minds, well stored with knowledge, possessing a critical, not a pedantic edge, and that such persons may thereafter for the most part be safely left to their own devices. I suspect, if I must tell the whole truth, that persons who sacrifice broad and deep university experience in order to learn administrative tricks will in the long run find themselves intellectually and vocationally disadvantaged. From the standpoint of practical need, society requires of its leaders not so much specifically trained competency at the moment as the mastery of experience, an interest in problems, dexterity in finding one's way, disciplined capacity to put forth effort. Lower or special schools or experience itself will furnish technique, if that is what students desire.

X

The emphasis which I have placed upon thinking and research may create the impression that I am really discussing institutes of research rather than universities. Such is not the case. Institutes of research, as we know them, differ in certain respects from universities as I am trying to conceive them. In the first place, the research institute stands or falls by its success in research, whereas, in projecting the modern university, I have been careful to associate training with research. The history of research institutes throws light upon this point. The modern research institute was first set up in Paris for Pasteur, because within the French university of Pasteur's time one could not procure the conditions requisite to scientific research. The movement broadened in Germany under the influence of Friedrich Althoff, the forceful and fertile administrator who from 1882 to 1907 was the guiding spirit of the Prussian *Cultus Ministerium*. A jurist and a bureaucrat, Althoff was especially interested in medicine; and to some extent at least, his general program was governed by his ideals of medical education and research. He strove with tireless energy and splendid success to equip all the faculties of the Prussian universities, so that they might, under modern conditions, realize and develop the conception of training and research which had been embodied in the University of Berlin at its origin. Althoff perceived, however, that even under ideal university conditions a small number of rare geniuses might squander in teaching or administration rare abilities that ought to be concentrated upon research. He was thus led to plan a series of institutes in which the most fertile minds might be devoted to research in fields in which fundamental progress had already been made — fields, in which the basic sciences had already attained definiteness and solidity, in which problems, theoretic as well as substantive, could be clearly formulated, in which personnel of high quality had already been trained. The feasibility of the research institute was thus pretty narrowly circumscribed. It does not follow that, because the research institute is feasible and timely in physics, chemistry, or medicine, it is either feasible or timely in less well developed fields of interest, however urgent the need.

The points just mentioned suggest at once the strength and the weakness of the research institute. The research institute is a sort of flying column, that can be directed hither or yon, wherever results seem attainable, wherever personnel of exceptional character is available. But so specific is the research institute that its particular activities depend on an individual or a small group. Whatever the institute be called, its energies centre about a person. The important things are not subjects, but persons; when the person goes, the subject goes. If a university chair is vacated, it must usually be filled — with a productive scholar and teacher if possible, with a scholar, at any rate, if a productive scholar is not obtainable. Not so, the research institute. In 1911, an institute of experimental therapeutics was set up at Dahlem for Wassermann; when Wassermann died in 1920, there was no successor, or the situation had changed. His institute was turned over to Professor Neuberg as an institute of bio-chemistry. What happened was not that one institute was abolished and another created; what really happened was that Wassermann died, and that Neuberg was enabled to carry on his own work. The research institute does not have to include all subjects within a definite field; it can demobilize as readily as mobilize. The university may have to employ makeshifts temporarily; the research institute, never.

From the standpoint of progress under favourable conditions, these are great advantages. But there are disadvantages. Forecasting in *The New Atlantis* a foundation aiming to obtain "the knowledge of causes," Bacon conceived an institution equipped with the paraphernalia of what we term research, including fellows and "novices and apprentices that the succession do not fail." The university has at hand a student body from which "novices and apprentices" may be drawn by professors who have had opportunity to ascertain their merits. The research institute, lacking a student body of its own, must seek out young men, possessed of ability and training. If financially strong, it can take the risk; but its "novices and apprentices" are rarely known at first hand, as they may easily be within the university.

Again, in the complexity of modern science, there is no telling from what source the magic fact or the magic conception will come. The very breadth of the university increases greatly its potential fertility. The research institute may therefore be hampered by limitations consequent upon intense concentration. Too highly specialized institutes, especially if somewhat practically minded, are likely to be fruitless. Althoff foresaw this danger. "If," says his recent biographer,[12] "the research institute is detached from the university and made directly accountable to the ministry, this idea must not be too narrowly interpreted. All these institutions serve the purposes of the university, namely, teaching and investigation. Indeed, the Prussian educational authorities are so strongly convinced of the soundness of the universities that all the most recent organizations are in some way or other more or less intimately connected with the universities." Thus a research institute, set up within or in connection with a modern university, might escape some of the limitations to which the isolated institute is exposed.

There is a further point on which I must touch. The research institute enjoys, I have said, the advantages of concentration and mobility. Yet Althoff was right in opposing a narrow conception. Too definite a conception or formulation may eliminate the element of surprise — important to both teaching and research. Both research institute and university laboratory are engaged in solving problems; both are engaged in training men. Is the head of a research division only seeking knowledge? By no means. He has about him a group of assistants — younger men whom he sifts and trains, precisely as does the university professor. His students are simply more advanced, more highly selected. Thus the research institute might be described as a specialized and advanced university laboratory, enjoying certain marked advantages and not free from possible disadvantages. Successful research institutes are no substitute for universities. Indeed, they cannot succeed, unless universities furnish them a highly trained personnel — a debt, I hasten to add, which they repay as they give further training to men and women, many of whom become university teachers. Far more hopeful, in my opinion, than the rapid multiplication of research institutes at this moment would be the freeing of existing universities from inhibitions and encumbrances, and their development into instruments competent to perform well their proper functions.

XI

So much in general. I began by saying that in this chapter I should discuss the idea of a university that would answer the intellectual needs of this modern age. It is the idea, not the organization that I have been speaking of. To organization excessive importance is likely to be attributed. Nevertheless, organization or lack of organization is not entirely immaterial. We shall see in subsequent chapters how in one country excessive organization and in another poor organization obstruct the realization of the idea of a university. In all countries university reform is now the subject of earnest discussion. In all countries, history, traditions, vested interests hamper reconstruction. Obstacles are not always bad: a rich and beautiful past may interfere with reconstruction, while at the same time offering considerable compensation. When therefore the moment for action arises, one needs to view existing realities against the background of a clearly defined general principle. We shall find both conditions and possibilities highly varied — absurdities that may easily be eliminated, sharp corners that need to be cautiously turned, preconceptions that need to be vigorously combatted, historic values that must not be sacrificed, practical commitments that can only be gradually shifted to other agencies. In the end, when reconstruction has been achieved, we shall find ourselves not with a standardized, but with a very varied result — in no two countries alike, and total uniformity in not even one. Our chances of meeting the needs of modern life will be better, if we are content to accept anomalies and irregularities, though there are also anomalies and irregularities which are intolerable. The line is not easy to draw; different countries, different individuals may draw it in different places; but the precise point at which it is drawn is of relatively little importance, as long as the main function of the modernized university stands out with sufficient prominence.

Notes

1 Frederick J. E. Woodbridge, *Contrasts in Education* (New York, 1929), p. 17.
2 Viscount Haldane, *Universities and National Life* (London, 1912), p. 29.

3 Salvador de Madariaga, *Aims and Methods of a Chair of Spanish Studies* (Clarendon Press, Oxford, 1928), p. 12.

4 Duclaux, *Pasteur — The History of a Mind* (translated by Smith and Hedges, Philadelphia and London, 1920), p. 111.

5 Graham Wallas, *Physical and Social Science* (Huxley Memorial Lecture 1930, London), p. 1. The quotation is slightly paraphrased.

6 The present British Government has set up an Economic Advisory Council, an academic group which discusses, from the academic or theoretic point of view, economic and political questions; the Council does not decide policies: that is left to the Government.

7 Extract from a letter written by Dr. William S. Halsted, Professor of Surgery, Johns Hopkins Medical School, 1889–1922.

8 G. N. Lewis, *The Anatomy of Science* (Yale University Press, 1926), p. 154.

9 It is clear, for example, that, as I employ the term, the American high school is not co-extensive with secondary education: on the contrary, in the United States, "secondary education" would swallow not only the high school, but much, perhaps most of the college. See p. 53.

10 I do not in this volume discuss schools of law or schools of technology, for the simple reason that I have never studied them. The omission implies no opinion of any kind.

11 See pp. 158–9, 172.

12 Arnold Sachse, *Friedrich Althoff und Sein Werk* (Berlin, 1928), p. 294.

36

ADAPTATION TO A
DEMOCRATIC AGE

Albert Mansbridge

Source: A. Mansbridge, *The Older Universities of England: Oxford and Cambridge*, London: Longmans, Green and Co., 1923, pp. 172–95.

University administrators and teachers have always been afraid lest they should conform too rapidly, or too weakly, to the religious, social, or political movements in the world about them. When men feel that they have proved a thing and found it good, they are reluctant to give it up. It is also too true that the possessors of vested interests in knowledge, as in material things, tend to fight furiously against those who would introduce a new order. Anyone who has considered the history of Universities must have come to the conclusion that in these matters they are no exceptions to the general rule. But always the reflection must be made that in both Oxford and Cambridge instances of almost every kind of human action can be discovered; they are so vast and comprehensive in the area of their thought and influence. Thus, there could at any time have been found men who resisted every change, however good, side by side with others who were eager to embark on new adventures and enterprises, careless of their own interests, or indeed of the lesser interests of the society, simply because they were full of a passion for the extension of the bounds of knowledge. During the time intervening between the last of the nineteenth-century Commissions and the twentieth-century Commission there are abundant instances of the working of two forces, one of which would retain Oxford and Cambridge as they are, and the other which would make them responsive to the legitimate aspirations of the community.

Now let it be said at once that Oxford and Cambridge have no right to do anything in connection with the world outside them unless by so doing they strengthen themselves, not in their material resources but in the purity and power of their mind and spirit. This is ultimately the test by which the admission of women students to full membership, and the extension of the teaching activity of the University to towns remote from their immediate areas, must be judged. Equally, also, the abolition of Greek as an inviolable requirement of admission to degree courses must submit to the same test. These are the matters we propose to consider, and, as in duty bound, we shall devote by far the greater amount of attention to problems bound up with the extension of University teaching to working men and women.

But, first, the abolition of Greek as a condition of matriculation, which came into effect at Cambridge by a Vote passed on January 17, 1919, and at Oxford by a Statute passed on March 2, 1920, after much heartburning and discussion, opens the Universities to students of a type that found the language an obstacle. Of course, a boy who had not learned Greek, if he obtained admission to the University on other grounds, in a very few months could learn sufficient either to pass Responsions at Oxford or the Little-Go at Cambridge, but it was not a dignified procedure, and it did not strengthen Classics at either University. At the same time, the finest education which England has yet devised for certain minds is that ending in the School of 'Greats' at Oxford, which is preponderantly classical. If the stream of under-graduates with suitable abilities feeding this School became narrower, then an irreparable evil would be perpetrated; but this need not be so if those who believe in classical education will be up and doing, and will prove its virtues to the English people. It should be established thoroughly in schools which are within the reach of every child, not because of University require-ments but because it is necessary to the very advancement of education in the nation. That schools are dropping elementary Greek, that in some Public Schools it is at any rate made an optional subject, is an actual fact; but a diminution in the numbers of those studying Greek need not concern us, provided always that those who ought to study it do so. The English working man is interested in Ancient Greece and Rome; left to himself he is attracted by it as by few other things. If the Society for Hellenic Studies or the Clas-sical Association will see that opportunities for hearing and learning about Greek and Roman history and philosophy are widespread, they will secure ultimately that classical studies are placed within the reach of every child.

The appearance of Oxford has greatly changed since 1920, when women were admitted to full membership and privileges. 'They study every subject,' writes the Sub-Rector of Exeter, a hostile critic, 'they obtain every degree. Damsels adorned with attractive academic cap and less engaging academic gown cycle furiously and dangerously through every street.' There are five societies of women at Oxford, all flourishing, yet all poor. They have on their books 700[1] undergraduates. Their admission was accepted after years of long struggle, without obvious opposition, but there are many yet who shake their heads sadly and look with longing to Cambridge, where women are not yet admitted to full membership. 'Hence it is,' writes one of them, 'that Oxford's beautiful sister Cambridge can complacently allude to herself as "the man's University." And "the man's University" gains thereby in

popularity with and in the esteem of many a normal English schoolboy.'
The battle for the admission of women at Cambridge burst into full fury in
December 1920, when Cambridge rejected a Grace providing for the admission of women largely by the influence of the outvoters and of those, so it is
claimed, who are not most competent to give an opinion. The analysis of the
voting showed that, of the resident members of the University who voted,
226 approved the Grace and 137 opposed it, whereas the full vote, including
non-residents, was 904 against the Grace and 712 for it. All sorts of reasons
for the result were, of course, alleged; some said that the London hospitals
were searched for those who did not approve the admission of women to the
medical profession; others suggested that even theological motives were
brought into play; but, whatever is said and done, the residents pronounced
in favour. That is the vital fact which the Royal Commission of 1919 must
have had before it when it stated, in terms that admit of no misconception,
that 'ample facilities should be offered both at Oxford and Cambridge for
the education of women and their full participation in the life and work
of the University.' The Commission itself, however, did not decide upon the
alternative courses whereby this might be brought about—whether by Act
of Parliament or by the action of a reformed constitution which would
allow the resident vote to have full play.

We have had little or no opportunity to record the growth of the education of women at Cambridge by the development of Girton and Newnham,
and at Oxford by the work of Lady Margaret Hall, Somerville, St. Hugh's,
St. Hilda's, and the Society of Home-Students. The whole movement for
women's education was, after all, the direct and natural result of efforts
for general educational reform. When women teachers, led by Miss Anne
Clough and Miss Emily Davies, secured the admission of their pupils to the
Oxford and Cambridge Local Examinations, the desire for participation in
all the benefits of University and College life followed inevitably. Cambridge,
characteristically perhaps, was first. With the help of men like Kingsley, Lightfoot, Maurice, and Sidgwick, Girton was founded first at Hitchin in 1869 and
Newnham in Cambridge in 1875. At Oxford, the first steps in the education
of women were made by a group of University teachers, who formed the
Association for the Advancement of the Education Women and undertook
to coach a few women residents, several of whom were married (the result
of the change of rule for Fellows). With the active encouragement of
Mark Pattison, Walter Pater, Dr. Stubbs, Dr. Creighton, Arnold Toynbee,
Dr. Jowett, Henry Nettle-ship, and others, the work progressed rapidly and
unobtrusively until one by one University examinations were opened to
women and their societies were founded. No names of Founders stand out
conspicuously; it was essentially a group movement. But Oxford women
look back with special gratitude to the first two Principals, Miss Shaw-Lefevre of Somerville and Miss Elizabeth Wordsworth of Lady Margaret
Hall, herself the Founder of St. Hugh's College,[2] while the members of

St. Hilda's Hall owe their College more directly to Miss Dorothea Beale's keen concern for the education of girls and her sense of all the intangible gifts which Oxford has in store for teachers.

The women's Colleges have in every case shown themselves to be animated by the same spirit and to possess the same academic power as the men's Colleges. Indeed, in the old competitive days at Cambridge, Mrs. Montagu Butler was placed 'above the Senior Classic' and, later, Miss Phillipa Garrett Fawcett 'above Senior Wrangler.' The achievements of their students, having regard to the limited numbers and the narrow opportunities open to women, are as remarkable as those of any of the men's Colleges, even in their best years. It is inevitable, since women are admitted already to the studies, examinations, and even to titular[3] degrees, that Cambridge should admit women to full membership, however long or short the time they take in the process. The wish has been strongly expressed that England would create, when this is done, a University solely for men and a University solely for women, because a full variety of educational experiment is needed above all things, and every possible standard by which to test the development of the most difficult thing a nation has to do—the education and training of the best, mentally and spiritually, of its sons and daughters—should be secured.

Happily, in the question of extra-mural work there has never been any disputation concerning the equal rights of men and women. In University Extension Lectures, in University Tutorial Classes, and in Vacation Schools, they have sat side by side on terms of absolute and unquestioned equality. Of course, no University privileges of any marked character are accorded the students in any of these types of education; but, even so, the students in the University Extension Centres, as well as in the University Tutorial Classes, feel themselves a part of the Universities in a real sense. This feeling of theirs was encouraged by the then Vice-Chancellor of the University of Oxford, Sir Herbert Warren, President of Magdalen, when he sent a welcoming message to the first Tutorial Class students at Rochdale and Longton, regarding them as actually of the University of Oxford itself, although resident in towns far remote.

This brings us right face to face with the problems of the education of working men and women, which can never properly be carried out apart from the rest of the community. The whole idea of University education is democratic, in the sense that anyone who has the capacity and the goodwill —no matter what his previous experience has been, or what his father was before him—shall have full and free opportunity to develop his mental faculties. It is clear that the policy of providing University education for working men and women must not be taken as omitting others in the community; but at the end of the nineteenth century there was so much leeway to be made up in the provision of facilities adapted to wage-earners, and there were so many of them, that a special effort—even in an exaggerated way—was necessary and was desired by the most far-sighted men in Oxford and Cambridge. The encouragement to working men to develop their attitude towards the Universities came unmistakably from the most capable and highly-placed of University administrators and teachers. Yet they could do nothing unless working men themselves supplied the dynamic of the ideas. This they did; the Universities then concurred, and the most significant of Oxford and Cambridge movements in recent years was set on foot. In a remarkable manner the establishment of University Tutorial Classes has redounded to the credit of Universities, and has helped to renew their life and to strengthen their studies. These are large claims to make, but they can be substantiated, and indeed three separate Royal Commissions have identified such work as inalienable from the true purposes of Universities. 'We are even more impressed by the true spirit of learning, the earnest desire for knowledge, and the tenacity of purpose which have been shown by the students,' said the Commissioners sitting in London. 'These men and women desire knowledge, not diplomas or degrees; and we think that no University ... would justify its existence that did not do its utmost to help and encourage work of this kind.'

The recent Royal Commission on Oxford and Cambridge, after expressing its approval of the work of extra-mural University education (so fully and recently discussed in the Report of the Adult Education Committee, and approved by the Royal Commissions on University Education in London and in Wales), made elaborate provisions for the development of the work and suggested a specific grant from public funds for the purpose of strengthening the Universities to carry it out effectively. The University of Cambridge, before the Report of the Commission was published, adopted, largely as a result of the Report of the Ministry of Reconstruction[4] on Adult Education, a new form of organisation for its extra-mural teaching work, and those responsible for similar work in the University of Oxford have given unmistakable signs that they are in agreement. Nothing is wanting now but the necessary money.

It must not be supposed, from what has been said, that everyone in the University agrees; some are fearful. There never was a time in any University when everyone agreed about anything. Societies which express themselves in an intellectual manner seldom do agree; there are so many sides to the truth. The present Vice-Chancellor of the University of Oxford, Dr. L. R. Farnell, Rector of Exeter College, is manifestly afraid. 'This is an admirable movement,' he said, in addressing Convocation on October 11, 1922, 'offering a most useful career to our young men who have not the aptitude for our higher intra-mural, more concentrated work, and who can go forth as our missionaries. But the same men never do or can fulfil both functions at once; and if our higher teachers are constrained to attempt it, they will lose that leisure and spirit of research which the Commissioners strongly desire them to possess. We must therefore be watchful in guarding our true prerogative.'

But though even supporters of the work who are not of the University would not desire that overworked teachers should add railway journeys and extra teaching to their University duties, there is no doubt that most teachers at some time or other, especially early in their experience, would inevitably find it a means of inspiration and of acquiring knowledge not to be obtained in any other way, if they went out to study with the keen students of our industrial towns. There is practically no divergence from the unanimous testimony of those who have actually done this; they have been encouraged when they needed it, and have been inspired by a strength and keenness which, strange as it may seem, they had never experienced in academic society. There is at least one eminent professor in the University of Oxford who was saved for his subject, to the lasting gain of the community, because, at a time when the fires of his enthusiasm were low, he met a class of working men who fanned them into flame again. Professors of mature years and ripe attainment have passed through the same experience; the memory of W. M. Geldart, Vinerian Professor of English Law at Oxford, is of one who lost no opportunity of discussing law with working men after he had met a group of them in a Vacation School at Balliol College; and, although Sir William Anson never actually taught them, yet he was always ready to discuss subjects of topical importance with working men and women. This is the spirit which, constantly expressed as it is by leading men in the University, will make Oxford and Cambridge live in the mind of democracy. For Cambridge is no whit behind Oxford in this; to its honour it can claim, through Professor James Stuart, the foundation of one form of extramural teaching by the establishment of external lectures in 1873.[5]

It is significant that in the report of the 1850 Commission there is no recognition of any interest that working men had, or might have, in the Universities. They were doubtless not forgotten in the general consideration of 'poor scholars,' but, in fact, though probably unintentionally, their handicap, or that of their sons, was made greater by the abolition of the close scholarships attached to local and unimportant grammar schools.

The strength of both Universities was drawn from the middle and upper classes, as represented by boys from the Public Schools or the more powerful of the town grammar schools. This made it difficult for them to discover the new class which was open to them, consisting of wage-earners and other adults, who had missed the opportunities of an undergraduate career but who possessed both capacity and hunger for scholarship in its higher reaches. The roots of the Universities, in order to draw sustenance and strength from such a source, would of necessity have to be struck over a wide area, even though it is improbable that any large number of adult students would seek to enter a College or to become members of the non-collegiate body. Most students of this kind would attend local classes and Vacation Schools, and would remain, and be content with remaining, extra-mural; but nevertheless the direct result of their work would be a greater interest and belief in the Universities as such, leading to discriminating support and growing confidence. The real value of such a striking of the roots is inherent in the necessities of academic studies which demand the assistance of every conceivable piece of knowledge, and the inspiration arising out of the life of every right-living man.

It is strange that Universities should have been so blind, or so inert, as not long ago to have benefited by the mind and experience of the manual labourer; so often has intellectual and spiritual power been not only associated with but inspired by physical toil. At times it almost seems that every great prophetic advance derives its impetus directly from the power of physical labour. Most certainly any community or institution which shuts itself off from the physical operations necessary to its health and development and relegates them to an under-class, whether of slaves or servants, cannot possibly live at its highest, and must inevitably become degenerate.

There are many applications of this dictum which may be considered, but only one concerns us now. If the Universities are to become even a shadow of what they might be in the twentieth century, they must permeate the very minds and hearts of working men and women. The ground has been left free and open for this democratic development by the almost complete overthrow of the barriers of creed and sex. As for class distinctions, they exist but weakly, if at all, in the Colleges themselves. There are, in all societies, snobs and selfish or self-important members, but even the obvious adult workmen found themselves one in the fellowship and unity of the twentieth-century Colleges.[6] The days have long since passed when 'Noblemen' and 'Fellow Commoners' strutted through the quadrangle and honoured the University by condescending to take a Degree after two years of radiant yet unenlightened residence.

The extra-mural work of a University has been justified in the main, quite incompletely, on the ground that it is a means whereby people who cannot come to the University may participate in its advantages. This is excellent enough, but the chief purpose of an academic society as it grows more powerful in its inherent nature is to develop and reveal knowledge and truth. The recognition of this has induced men of high academic position, whose minds and sympathies are excellent though narrow, and who are unable to distinguish every true source of power, to utter warnings concerning the undue dissipation of the energy of the University on external activities.[7] If extra-mural work is to be justified as an integral and essential activity of a University, it must be because it is a source both of strength and of knowledge which cannot be achieved in any other way. This does not mean that the intra-mural work is not supremely more important: it is indeed the end of all University aspiration and effort. But it does mean that the full flower and fruit are unattainable without extramural work. Even if it be that only one per cent. of the whole intellectual product can result from the conduct of University Extension Lectures and Tutorial Classes, yet the importance of this unit cannot be exaggerated.

An examination of the whole situation from the point of view of the workman-scholar will help the impartial or even prejudiced reader to decide as to the importance of, or even necessity for, this new twentieth-century order. 'They pursue learning,' said Professor Gilbert Murray, 'in the spirit of the great scholars of the Renaissance, or almost in that of the three Kings of the East.'

The opening years of the twentieth century witnessed a new phenomenon. Mature and experienced working men and women adopted a definite attitude towards the Universities which had as its aim the development of their own education. They showed by this attitude a full appreciation of the mission and purpose of a University. They saw both Oxford and Cambridge as the consecrated homes of sound learning and of steady work for the advancement of knowledge. With a shrewd insight which was in itself prophetic, they saw that the purest mental and spiritual influences which come from rightly conducted labour must be assimilated by a University if it is ever to fulfil the high purposes of its foundation. They felt themselves to be drifting hither and thither without real knowledge and the power which it gives, and devoid of a constructive plan for achieving it. They could not hope, they knew, to take their rightful place in the life of the community unless they possessed the power in their own ranks, and unless the knowledge they achieved was illumined by devotion to truth and was in real unity with all the best in human life. They instinctively felt that, in spite of past departures from sound procedure and the undue adhesion to the ideals of the English country-house, the Universities were indeed in their essence the expression of a spirit which could control and direct knowledge and the possessors of it, to legitimate and splendid ends, to the welfare and development of the life of the whole community.

The University Extension Movement, which had been founded at Cambridge in 1873 by James Stuart, had been untiring in its attempt to help working men and women. In some places and at some periods it achieved marked success, but on the whole its influence was limited by the fact that it was supported to too great an extent by men and women, chiefly the latter, of the middle classes only. Yet nothing could have exceeded in enthusiasm and power the efforts of the early lecturers, whether from Oxford or from Cambridge. They felt that they were missionaries; indeed, it is impossible to put too high an assessment upon the value of their labours in English education. They were instrumental in developing a spirit in England which led directly to the development of the new University movement and popularised the idea of a University apart altogether from its connection with resident undergraduates and scholars.

It is easy to visualise the University Extension lecture at its best in an industrial city—an eager audience of many hundreds of working men and women crowded together in the hall of the Co-operative Society, eagerly intent upon every word, taking notes, feeling that they also were scholars. The lecturer, Fellow of his College, ardent, well-informed, often eloquent, is vibrant with eagerness to absorb and harmonise with the inspiration flowing to him from the mass of inquiring minds before him. The lecture over, the majority of the audience pass out, but the fire of questions then commences; it is the period allotted to the class, and in it, at all times, there is eager discussion and there is insistent manifestation of that fearless, inquisitive character so much to be encouraged in the English industrial worker. When the class is over, the time arrives for a word or two of spoken appreciation or criticism of the essays which have been written previously by the keenest of the students and now are given back. These essays bear their part as one item of the work on the basis of which a final award may be made by the University, after written examination at the conclusion of the course. It may be that some of the audience, with the aid of scholarships or otherwise, will attend at Oxford or Cambridge in the summer, and there will feel themselves to be of the company of all students of the glorious past. 'The impressions of those grand old College buildings linger in my mind,' writes a house decorator of the North, 'and impel me to acknowledge that, after all, Cambridge is Cambridge, the home of scholars and saints.' Such are the advance guard of a new order.

It was during a Summer Meeting of this kind that the new movement was confirmed. A few trade unionists and co-operators gathered together in the conviction that education amongst working men and women must be carried out by co-operation between the Universities and their own organisations. It must ever be to the credit of Oxford and Cambridge that they understood and sympathised with the first thought and expression of this small and, to unseeing eyes, insignificant group. Thus it was that representatives of Universities, trade unions and co-operative societies met at Oxford on August 21, 1903, to confirm and establish an 'Association to Promote the Higher Education of Working Men,' which afterwards became famous as 'The Workers' Educational Association.' The working man, fresh from his industrial city, was by no means a mere worshipper at the shrine of Oxford or Cambridge; he saw in them the promise of a fuller life which it was his duty to achieve for his comrades of the mine or factory. One man, a general labourer and an ardent Socialist, could not restrain his tears as, standing upon New College tower, he gazed upon the incomparable beauty of Oxford. 'I want my comrades to see this,' he said; he really meant that, in season and out of season, he would strive with all his power to make the dingy, gloomy, crowded town in which he lived as near to the ideal of beauty as ever it was in his power to do. 'That visit to Cambridge made me a rebel,' said a prominent trade unionist in a Midland town, 'a rebel against all mean and ugly conditions in our municipal life.' There was never any bitterness in their minds. To look forward with generous enthusiasm to the finer life to be is characteristic of the thoughtful English workman.

Year by year, under the influence of the new movement, the number of working men and women attending the Summer Courses increased until a sudden development took place in 1906. This was due in part to an eager group of weavers and labourers in the town of Rochdale. Under the influence of the Workers' Educational Association, they began again to use the University Extension Lectures; they enjoyed them; they asked awkward questions of the lecturers; they found in them the suggestion of better education. They appreciated the short courses on Dante and on the stars, but short courses were not enough for them. They wanted to know all that there was to be known about the subject of their choice, and they were prepared, with all that spirit of independence and persistence which English northerners possess, to make any sacrifice, if only their object could be achieved. 'Give us a teacher who will come to us for two years and we will attend every lecture: we will write essays, we will read all the books he tells us to read. We will do everything, having regard to our economic position and conditions, that is possible for us to do in the pursuit of learning in the true spirit.'

Oxford once again proved that it had not merely the listening ear but the sympathetic mind. The New College of William of Wykeham, out of a favourable financial opportunity, had decided to make a grant of £300 for the education of working men and women. It was a prophetic grant, and perhaps one of the most important made by any College in modern times. It enabled Dr. Strong, Dean of Christ Church, to say to the eager, pressing group of Rochdale workmen who invaded the Deanery that they should have their class. The meeting of these weavers and the high dignitary of Church and College was a meeting of new and old, but they understood one another in a flash because they were alike consecrated to a cause higher than themselves. In a very short time a group of Longton potters and miners, infected by the example of Rochdale, met in a similar way and formed another group; thus what is known throughout the world as the University Tutorial Class Movement came into existence. Both groups decided to study Economic History, and the services of a tutor[8] of rare ability and devotion were secured. The interest of the statutory educational bodies was awakened. The Board of Education, then under the sympathetic and far-seeing control of Sir Robert Morant, the greatest English educational administrator of modern times, began the work of adapting its regulations to meet the new needs. The Local Education Authority at Rochdale made a contribution, and the Longton Authority took the full financial responsibility.

The records of both these classes are notable in the history of English education. One persisted for four years and the other for seven years. There were very few withdrawals from slackness, and a high standard of work was achieved from the outset. In a short time every English University and

University College commenced to work with one or more of the numerous groups which were arising in all parts. In 1914, at the outbreak of the Great War, there were 140 classes; during the War they dropped to 95; immediately the War was over they started to increase once more, until in 1921–22 there were 342 classes.

A visitor who is present at a tutorial class will find that often the students gather together as early as possible before the time fixed for opening, and talk and discuss, not merely with one another, but with the tutor, if they have the good fortune to find him. The class begins on a note of happiness and closes two hours later without a trace of boredom. There has been one hour's exposition, not uninterrupted by questions, and in the hands of certain teachers developing almost into a Socratic dialogue, then there has followed an hour of eager discussion. But the close of the class is not the end of the evening's work. It is often midnight before the last members of the group break up; they remain in the class-room as long as possible; they frequently continue their discussion in the street or adjourn to some favoured room or place where they can drink coffee, or smoke, and still argue. It is a poor class which confines its activities to the two hours of the schedule.

The study of Philosophy was continued regularly, at one time, by practically the whole of a Birmingham class on a certain sidewalk until an energetic policeman informed the tutor that if he persisted in making an obstruction every Thursday night after ten o'clock he would have to invite him to visit the police station. On another occasion the tutor was accompanied by his class to the railway station; the train came in; part of the class, as many as dared, got into the train, and the last of the class for that evening was a group of students running by the side of the train with the tutor projecting from the window. The last sentence was broken off in the middle and had to be mended next week.

In the summer vacation students go to Oxford and Cambridge, as well as to other Universities, for periods of intensive study. This gives an opportunity to professors, who desire to meet them, to do so, and the students are often so far advanced as to need the help of specialists. Men or women may thus attend classes in their own locality in the winter and also year by year study for a brief period at Oxford or Cambridge. Such a one, keen and passionate, burst free for a week from distasteful and coercive employment in a factory he should never have been allowed to enter, but in which he worked patiently and well, with a high standard of honour. He was extreme, even revolutionary in his politics, but the spirit of Oxford called to his spirit. The home of scholarship had an abiding place in the heart of the man who could only visit it for a brief week.

He writes the following recollections of his visit:

Although it is now some few years ago since I was a student of the W.E.A. at Oxford, the memory of it is still pleasantly vivid, and joyously dear to my memory. I can honestly say that, except for not having my family with me, it was the finest, happiest and most intellectual treat I had ever enjoyed. For, at least part of my life has been a bitter struggle against poverty and accidents; at one time, as a child glad and thankful to gather garbage from ash buckets from the streets to get a meal;—but, to get back to Oxford. There I met kindred souls aflame with enthusiasm and an unquenchable desire for knowledge. Not for the purpose of material gain, not for their own advancement over their fellows, but because they realised that here was the fountain of knowledge for the thirsty soul and they could drink, and drink, and yet they were still dry. Because it was good for the mind. It was good for the body. It was good for the very soul. It would help us to be real true men and women, beautiful in trying to attain to a well-balanced mind; freed from the petty things of life and getting to grips with the great, high and noble thoughts of life and nature generally. We were rising from the tiny beings of mundane things to what Carlyle says: 'Ye are the Gods if ye did but realise it.' Oh, the joy of listening to those great lecturers! Then the greater joy still of the discussions, when our minds and thoughts were struggling with the professors to get to rock bottom with the facts and truth! Sometimes one side won, then the other. All through these mental tussles the only aim was to get the best out of each and to arrive at the truth for all. We were railway-workers, cotton-mill workers, miners, labourers in ordinary life, but, as Whittier said, and never more truly said:

> 'True pioneers and labourers
>   Up the encumbered way,
>   With hands that dig for knowledge,
>   And eyes that watch for day.'

On the other side were the College people, whose only experience had been the great seat of learning. We battled day after day—me for a week, what an awfully short time—on Trade Union Law, Ethics, Literature, Philosophy, etc. After the lectures and discussions in the room, we would chum up with groups of kindred-spirited pals and seize a passing lecturer, take him a willing prisoner under some shady tree, and so pursue further the subject that was most fascinating and enchanting to the particular group. In the evenings there were the socials, where each according to his talents gave of his best for the pleasure of all. There, too, was a cementing of the bonds of friendship and fraternity, which will live for many years to come. Oxford itself is still the Oxford of yore. It changes so slowly that what changes there are, are almost imperceptible even after a visit with a lapse of years between. It is a real seat of learning, so much so that one can almost feel and taste the desire and atmosphere of knowledge as soon as one enters its environs. When all is said and done, one can only say that Learning is Oxford, and Oxford is Learning, and finally, Oxford *is* really and truly Oxford—there is and can be no other Oxford. I am glad that I had that one opportunity to attend these lectures, and I shall carry the memories of loving friends, comrades and professors, lectures and socials, rambles and discussions with me to the end, for I can honestly say that, through and by these, I am and have been a better, brighter and happier man. They have, and are still, helping me mentally to keep my feet firmly planted on the road of desire for knowledge for truth's sake. That, and that alone, can make us manly in the true sense of the word. What more epitaph can anyone desire than that it shall be said of him,' He was in very truth a man.'

The best comment on so enthusiastic an utterance is: 'Wisdom lifted up the head of him that is of low degree and maketh him to sit among great men.'[9]

If Oxford seems to have meant too much to him, then the background of a starved life must be brought into the picture. Such students also were the Midland factory girls who set to work to raise money by means of a dramatic representation for Lady Margaret Hall, the College of their tutor. They too were of Oxford.

There has been no more inspiring spectacle in English educational effort than the sight of men and women attending lectures, classes and Summer Schools, and while suspicious and afraid at first of all that a University connotes, finding with rapidity that they are of use as students and have a real place in University life. 'I certainly regarded the Universities with great suspicion,' writes a mine surface worker, 'and this was only eliminated by personal experience and contact with people in them, until I am now convinced that anything reactionary about them belongs mainly to tradition and can be borne down by the sheer weight of a demand for a democratic educational system, as soon as such a demand is made with sufficient strength.'

The days are too young to justify a valuation of all the effort in terms which would convince the most deaf or blind of those members of the University who still remain sceptical. There is little doubt, at any rate, that any danger that the Universities might be damaged as a result of political and social power passing into the hands of working men and women is definitely overpast. This ought in itself to convince those who claim to be the guardians of a University's interest—but which of them can fail to be inspired by the knowledge that thousands of men and women are participating, according to their degree and strength, in the studies which they themselves pursue?

In the near future those who are mainly concerned with the extra-mural work of Oxford and Cambridge will have to decide how far and in what way they will encourage adults to undertake lengthened courses of intra-mural study. It would seem that, for most men and women who have entered fully into an occupation or way of living, the local class and the Summer School provide the best means of developing their powers, and equipping them fully for the service of the community. For the rest, if any student ought quite clearly to work in the University because of exceptional ability, and can do so without breaking up or even endangering his home life, then he should have opportunity. He ought, however, not to be received as, or classed with, the eighteen-year-old undergraduate. Unless he joins the non-collegiate body, his conspicuous ability (and no ordinary ability in this connection need be considered) should justify a place in college with the post-graduate students at least. Yet such adult working men as have entered Colleges as ordinary undergraduates have found them altogether to their liking. Their ages have been as a rule anything up to forty years. The oldest student of them all, who is over fifty, is uncontrolled in his enthusiasm for the life of the non-collegiate undergraduate. It is indeed the realisation of a dream to one who, though a scholar by nature, became a bleacher in a textile works, until, through a University Tutorial Class, he reached the Oxford of his desire. There is no reason why the best of such students should not enter the Universities as teachers, but before this happens they must have proved themselves indubitably; as, for instance, did Thomas Okey,[10] a workman, before he was invited by Cambridge to occupy the Chair of Italian.

The development of Ruskin College, founded at Oxford in 1899 by two citizens of the United States, Walter Vrooman and Charles Beard, and of the Roman Catholic Labour College at Oxford, founded in 1921, cannot be discussed at any length. Yet it is important to notice that not a few students of Ruskin College take with distinction the University Diploma in Economics and Political Science, and that the College maintains a friendly attitude to the University while preserving jealously its complete independence.

There is likely to be a development of Labour Colleges in the near future, for in spite of all that has been done in connection with Universities there is ever present in men and women a desire for self-expression and self-government. Probably the greatest good will result from such colleges if they can federate with one another and have some organised connection with the Universities. They will be able to take advantage of University Tutorial Classes and of lectures, and will through this medium exercise such influence as they ought on the centres of English learning.

The older Universities in a democratic age have special significance for the men and women who are engaged in the ordinary tasks of the community, whether tasks of labour or of government. The problems which confront society at the present time are both complicated and elusive. Their solution demands the finest powers of humanity, strengthened and fortified by sound learning. Such powers cannot be acquired by the people during their limited school training. The problems can only be appreciated and understood by mature minds illumined by advanced education.

At all times the mission of a University is to be an intellectual centre, but this mission is specially important in the present age. There are growing up all kinds of institutions and activities which can only be kept strong and clear in their work if they remain in vital contact with Universities as the intellectual repositories of all their experience and knowledge. As a result of this contact by a process of action and reaction, the Universities and the institutions of the people, whatever they may be, will both become stronger as they realise more fully their true place in the community, which, when all is said and done, is not a congeries of divided and unrelated groups, but is one body.

The world has passed recently through overwhelming and shattering times. The future is full of immense possibilities, both as a result of scientific discovery and of new social ideas, and these possibilities can only be translated into increased power and health for humanity if the citizens of the various countries, and particularly of the British Commonwealth of Nations and the United States, are unremitting in their pursuit of knowledge inspired by spiritual forces. Thus, although everyone, even in a democratic age, cannot and ought not to reside at a University, yet in some way or other they should be brought into contact with its extra-mural work or the institutions which are helped or directed by it. Mr. A. L. Smith, the Master of Balliol, writing as Chairman of the Adult Education Committee, in its final report said: 'The necessary conclusion is that adult education must not be regarded as a luxury for a few exceptional persons here and there, nor as a thing which concerns a short span of early manhood, but that adult education is a permanent national necessity, an inseparable aspect of citizenship, and therefore should be both universal and lifelong.'

Now let us summarise in a different way the whole of the argument for extra-mural studies, pursued by working men and women. The ideal University is supported in its spiritual and intellectual aspects, as surely as in its material, by the good-will and active co-operation, nay more, by the fusion of the whole community. It may be argued that this view of things is mystical and not practical. Most surely it is both. These two forces are dependent the one upon the other for their very health, if not for their existence.

Roughly, then, the problem is one of making the maximum contact between the members of the University proper and the great world outside. Fortunately, the very fact that the Universities are not, and never have been, monastic, has kept them in the world and of it, but their seizure, or at least their usage, by clearly defined classes of people has denied them the advantages of co-operation with the largest section of the community—the ordinary labouring people, in intimate contact not only with the hardest but with the truest part of English life.

It is from labour that all true intellectual and spiritual force ascends. The proof of this assertion does not lie in the production of the records of scholars who have laboured themselves, or whose fathers have done so (this would be convincing enough), but in the mere recognition of the fact that manual toil is, or should be, the lot of all but a few men and women. It is a condition, indeed, of right living. On the other hand, there is so much manual work in modern civilisation that is not of a creative character, and machinery is making possible so enormous an output, that few men will perform that which is health-giving in its nature. The rectification of this will lie, can only lie, in the right use of leisure. Men whose powers are being either misused or used below their true level during the hours of work must have sufficient leisure allowed them to develop their own faculties, and they must seize the opportunity, or the civilisation of which we boast and with which we struggle will end in disaster.

Notes

1 The numbers of Women Undergraduates actually in residence at this time (Hilary Term, 1923) are as follows: Lady Margaret Hall, 103; Somerville College, 140; St. Hugh's College, 145; St. Hilda's Hall, 95; Society of Oxford Home-Students, 215.

2 Miss Wordsworth is still living, to watch with keen interest and sympathy the progress of her two Colleges.

3 The Grace of the Senate, admitting women to the Title of Degrees, and the right to wear the corresponding academic costume, was passed on March 3, 1923. The advocates of the admission of women to full privileges stated that they were unable to regard this as a settlement or even a contribution to a serious settlement of the matter. At the time of writing it seems probable that Parliament will pronounce a decision, thus overruling the University. From many points of view this would be unfortunate, if inevitable.

4 *Ministry of Reconstruction; Adult Education Committee; Final Report*, 1919. H.M.S.O. [Cmd. 321.] 1s. 9d. net.

5 The University of Cambridge is calling together the representatives of Universities in the British Empire and in the United States of America to celebrate the Jubilee of this work from July 6 to July 10 in this year (1923).

6 The West Riding County Council have granted exhibitions annually to adult workmen, tenable either at Ruskin College or at a College of Oxford University. The Council made its last award of a scholarship tenable at Ruskin College in 1919. Up to and including that year nine exhibitions had been awarded. Since then two exhibitions have been awarded to two ex-University Tutorial Class students, one tenable at Wadham College and the other at Christ Church. These two exhibitioners have met with much success. Both obtained the Diploma in Political Science and Economics; the one obtained Honours in the School of Modern History, and the other is at present preparing a thesis for the degree of B.Litt. No exhibition was awarded in 1922 owing to restrictions upon financial expenditure. It may be hoped that the scholarship will be renewed at no distant date.

7 *See* p. 179.

8 R. H. Tawney, B.A., formerly Scholar and Fellow of Balliol.

9 Ecclesiasticus.

10 Thomas Okey, born 1852, was appointed Professor of Italian in 1919. He was a working basket-maker for many years, and attended evening classes and lectures at Bethnal Green, the London Working Men's College, Birkbeck College, and Toynbee Hall.

37

AN EXPERIMENT IN DEMOCRATIC EDUCATION

R. H. Tawney

Source: *The Political Quarterly* (May 1914): 62–84.

I. The idea

The affairs of man in all their departments are carried on by two kinds of activity. The first is that which sustains, elaborates, and improves the existing order, in so far as improvement is possible without substituting new objects and assumptions for those which already obtain. The second is that whose innovations are matters of kind not of degree, which proceeds not by modifying methods but by introducing a new order of ideas, and which far off from the wavering front of affairs, where the small moves are made and inches won or lost, in remote and unsuspected places marshals a silent array of new presuppositions, the future criteria of failure and success. In the world of education it is easy to discover the working of the first of these two kinds of endeavour. It consists of the opinion held as to educational method by those whose immediate task is some kind of educational function, by teachers, by most experts and professional exponents of educational principles, by Universities, Education Authorities, and the Board of Education. Open-minded and alert in its own sphere, critical, even destructive, in its discussion of means, this opinion is usually highly conservative as to ends, waits reverently on the established order and the triumphant fact, and is occupied principally with laying down machinery, with elaborating organization, with the important task of perfecting the technique of education. As though they had purchased a kind of immunity against idealism by the mild virus with which they have been inoculated in their youth, many educationalists are apt to regard its intrusion into the practical affairs of their profession as a thing improper, and to dislike in particular the coarse questioning of presuppositions which disturbs the sacred whisperings of their art by the suggestion that it has not exhausted the possibilities of human nature. Doctors may disagree by the rules of science. But the patient who disagrees with them all is a vulgar fellow, especially if he protests that the cure of his disease is more light, more air, and more food; for these are things that can be imparted with advantage to very ordinary persons, and what, then, would become of the *arcana*, of the mysteries, of the 'educated classes' themselves? On the natural incapacity of the majority of mankind to profit by higher education, on the disastrous consequences which would follow from its too wide diffusion, on the serious danger of disturbing the social atmosphere with which in England it is often associated, the children of this world, who have a bad reputation for materialism, have hitherto had much to learn from the children of light.

It is at once the triumph and the penalty of all spiritual forces that, in proportion to their power, they add fuel to a temper which is critical of themselves. Education has this at least in common with religion, that its effect on those whom it has influenced is to make them regard it as too intimate a matter to be relegated entirely to experts, and that they seek to express in it, however imperfectly, a general philosophy of life. There is always at work therefore, as a second force, whose effect is less immediate and more profound, the conception which men take of themselves and of their place in society. It is the expansion of this conception which is the creative force in working-class education to-day. Its effect upon education is indeed only one, and not the most obvious, aspect of its influence. To no generation is it given to read the secrets of its own heart, and this is not the place, if there is a place, for the futile and presumptuous task of diagnosis. But one may suggest that when the wheels have ceased rumbling and the dust has settled down, when the first generation of historians has exhausted the memoirs and the second has refuted the memoirs by the documents, and the time has come for the remorseless eye of imagination to be turned on the first two turbulent decades of the twentieth century, it is perhaps less in the world of political and economic effort than in the revival among large masses of men of an Idea that their dominant *motif* will be found. That idea is very old, very commonplace, much thumbed and soiled since the world began—one of those notions at which learned men smile wearily, 'because', they say, pointing to their shelves, 'we knew it before'. For want of a better name it may be called the sentiment of the sanctity of human personality. Yet, trite as it is, it is a kind of lamp by which a host of squalid oppressions are being examined. The *clichés* of economists and politicians, the rise in prices, the tightening of the screw upon the wage-earners, the preposterous inflation in the wealth of the income-tax paying classes, derive half their significance from the new spiritual standards by which those material monstrosities are being tried. The minds of an ever-growing number of men and women are passing through one of these mysterious bursts of activity which make some years as decisive as generations, and of which measurable changes in the world of fact are the consequence rather than the cause. May that wonderful spring not be premature! It is as though a man labouring with a pick in a dark tunnel had caught a gleam of light and had redoubled his efforts to break down the last screen. The attack on the mere misery of poverty is falling into its place as one part of a determination that there shall be a radical reconstruction of human relationships. Not merely poverty, but economic privilege and economic serfdom is seen to be the enemy; not merely a wider diffusion of riches, but equality and freedom the goal. The material for something like a new Declaration of the Rights of Man is being silently prepared. To thousands of wage-earners there has come in the last few years the corroding discovery that they are treated not as persons but as things, as tools which are the more troublesome because they happen to be animated, as cogs in a devouring mechanism which grinds material wealth out of immortal spirits. The discovery outrages their humanity. With what reluctance it is made, with what silent despair in some, what bitterness of heart and angry determination in others, let him who has not seen imagine. The discovery is likely to be disturbing. 'The blessings of Judah and Issachar will never meet, that the same people or nation shall be a lion's whelp and an ass between burdens.'

It is most obviously disturbing because of the mine which it digs beneath economic arrangements; for it is in relation to economic affairs that the objective order of society is most violently in contradiction to men's subjective conception of right. But it may be expected to have an equal, though less immediately conspicuous, effect upon education. It is surely a very barren kind of pedantry which would treat education as though it were a closed compartment within which principles are developed and experiments tried undisturbed by the changing social currents of the world around. The truth is that educational problems cannot be considered in isolation from the aspirations of the great bodies of men and women for whose sake alone it is that educational problems are worth considering at all. The way in which the educational policy of a period reflects its conceptions of human society and of the proper object of human endeavour is well illustrated by the part which has in the past been played, and is still played to-day, by two ideas, the idea of status and the idea of the career open to talent. The former would adjust the character and duration of education in rough accordance with the social class of those for whom education is being provided. The latter would qualify the resultant rigidity of social stratification by creating special machinery to enable intellect to climb from one stratum to another. The first gave us the early elementary schools, in which the 'labouring poor' were to acquire learning 'suitable to their status'. The second was a potent force behind the reform of the older Universities in the middle of the nineteenth century, and has influenced in varying degrees more recent scholarship systems. Historically opposed on many a ringing field, they are both often used to-day to suggest the same conclusion: that the single and all-sufficient test of the education which a group is to receive is the probable professional avocation of the majority of its members, provided that movement between different groups is sufficiently free to prevent the potential barrister or doctor being set to the bench. Society can be divided, it is thought, into those who work with their brains and those who work with their hands, and this division offers a decisive guide to educational policy. It is worth while to provide University education for the former. It is not worth while to provide it for the latter. 'A University', said a distinguished professor in the presence of the writer, 'is simply the professional school of the brain-working classes.'

Now it would, of course, be folly to deny that there are large fields of education in which this statement has considerable truth. The majority of men—one may hope an increasing majority—must live by working. Their work must be of different kinds, and to do different kinds of work they need specialized kinds of professional preparation. Doctors, lawyers, engineers, plumbers, and masons must, in fact, have trade schools of different kinds. The point at which this theory of the functions of the Universities is challenged by the educational movement of labour is its doctrine that education which cannot, except by an unnatural distortion of terms, be called technical or professional, should be organized with a similar regard to the existing economic divisions of society, in particular its placid and impudent assumption, so popular with many educated people, that a 'humane education' is suitable for persons entering a certain restricted group of professions, to which attempts are now being made to add the direction of business, but that it is a matter with which the manual working classes have nothing to do. Such a misinterpretation of the meaning of educational specialization is felt to be intellectually an imposture. If persons whose work is different require, as they do, different kinds of professional instruction, that is no reason why one should be excluded from the common heritage of civilization of which the other is made free by a University education, and from which, *ceteris paribus*, both, irrespective of their occupations, are equally capable, as human beings, of deriving spiritual sustenance. Those who have seen the inside both of lawyers' chambers and of coal mines will not suppose that of the inhabitants of these places of gloom the former are more constantly inspired by the humanities than are the latter, or that conveyancing (*pace* the kindly shades of Maitland) is in itself a more liberal art than hewing. And the differentiation of humane education according to class is felt to be worse than a mere intellectual error on the part of those by whom such education has hitherto been managed. It is felt to be one of those blunders which reveal coarseness of spirit even more than confusion of mind. It is felt to be morally insulting. On the lips of many of its advocates it *is* morally insulting. Stripped of its decent draperies of convention, what it means is that there is a class of masters whose right it is to enter at manhood on the knowledge which is the inheritance of the race, and a class of servants whose hands should be taught to labour but whose eyes should be on the furrow which is watered with their sweat, whose virtue is contentment, and whose ignorance is the safety of the gay powers by whom their iron world is ruled. 'What', said an educated man to the writer, 'you teach history and economics to miners and engineers? Take care. You will make them discontented and disloyal to us.' That division of mankind into those who are ends and those who are means, whether made by slaveholders or by capitalists, is the ultimate and unforgivable wrong, with which there can be truce neither in education not in any other department of social life. To such wickedness only one answer is possible, *Ecrasez l'infame*.

But, it will be urged, secondary education is being improved. Rungs to connect it with the elementary schools at one end and with the Universities at the other are being constructed. In time every clever child will have a chance of winning a scholarship and passing from the elementary school to the University. What more do you desire? Now, it need hardly be said, the creation of such increased facilities is a matter for congratulation, especially if it is accompanied by a provision for the scholarship winner sufficiently generous to overcome the heavy burden entailed upon his family by the loss of his earnings. How meagre these facilities are at the present time in proportion to the need for them, how illusory is the idea that more than a tiny fraction of the children qualified to make the best use of higher education receive it, what infinite misapplication of human capacity results from the fact that of the children leaving elementary schools less than 5 per cent. pass each year to secondary schools, no one who has seen anything of working-class conditions of life needs to be told. It may truly be said that wisdom cries in the street and no man regards it, unless indeed it is so tired after ten hours in a mill that it cries at home. It is certainly not the case, however, that the only avenue to humane education of the highest kind ought to be that which consists in a career of continuous school attendance from five to eighteen. In this matter we are still far too much at the mercy of the dogma of selection through competitive examinations which dominated the last half of the nineteenth century. Such selection has its use, and its use is to determine who are most suitable for a limited number of posts. But no one dreams of determining who shall enter elementary schools by a process of selection. On the contrary, we provide elementary education for all on the ground that it is indispensable to good citizenship. In the same way, side by side with the selective system created by means of scholarships, there ought to be a system of higher education which aims at, even though it cannot attain, universal provision, which is accessible to all who care to use it, and which is maintained not in order to enable intellect to climb from one position to another, but to enable all to develop the faculties which, because they are the attributes of man, are not the attributes of any particular class or profession of men. To suppose that the goal of educational effort is merely to convert into doctors, barristers, and professors a certain number of persons who would otherwise have been manual workers is scarcely less unintelligent than to take the Smilesian advice, 'Remember, my boy, that

your aim should be to be master of that business,' as an all-satisfying formula of economic progress, or to regard the existence of freedmen as making
tolerable the institution of slavery. Selection is wanted to save us from
incompetence in high places: if only one could add to the scholarship system
by which capacity travels up, a system of negative scholarships which would
help incapacity to travel down! Universal provision is wanted because society
is one, because we cannot put our minds in commission, because no class
is good enough to do its thinking for another. The ideas are not mutually
exclusive: they are mutually complementary. It is not enough, for example,
that some children should be removed from elementary schools, where classes
are overcrowded and teachers overworked, to secondary schools where conditions are better. We want *all* the children to be given individual attention
in the elementary schools. It is not enough that a few working-class boys
and girls should be admitted to Universities, and that many more will be
admitted in the future. We want as much University education as we can get
for the workers who *remain* workers all their lives. The idea of social solidarity which is the contribution of the working classes to the social conscience
of our age has its educational as well as its economic applications. What it
implies is not merely *la carrière ouverte aux talents*, indispensable though
that is, but *égalité de fait*, not simply equality of opportunity but universality of provision. Perhaps our educationalists have not hitherto allowed
sufficiently for the surprising fact that there is no inconsiderable number
of men and women whose incentive to education is not material success
but spiritual energy, and who seek it, not in order that they may become
something else, but because they are what they are. The oversight is not
unnatural. The attitude is not one which is common in the ordinary semi-
naries of youth.

II. The organization

The impulse which such ideas imperfectly express has come not from
the authorities but from the rank and file, and because it has come from the
rank and file it has been not simply an addition but an innovation. While
the experts have been engaged in the necessary task of preparing machinery, the new spirit has been finding its way into higher education from those
who have hitherto been accustomed to see their educational destinies settled
over their heads. Almost for the first time in English educational history
the sedate rows of statistics which appear in Government Reports have
suddenly begun to walk, to assert intellectual appetites, to demand that they
shall be satisfied, to organize themselves in order to insist that they shall be
satisfied—in short, to behave like men and women. The result, partially
revealed in different ways by Ruskin College, by the Central Labour College, by the growth of innumerable classes and reading circles whose existence
is almost unknown except to their members, perhaps, finds its completest

expression in the Workers' Educational Association. Not, of course, that the Association is labouring at an untilled field. Behind it lies a century of working-class educational effort, whose history, as yet almost unrecorded, may be read in the forthcoming book of Mr. A. E. Dobbs. The high landmarks which stand out and are known to all, the educational work of the Co-operative movement, the rush to found Working Men's Colleges in the 1850's, the earlier years of University Extension in the north of England, rise from foundations laid by the faith of countless pioneers, humble men and women whose names are remembered lovingly in their own little towns and villages, who would have called themselves anything but educationalists, whose students were disciples rather than pupils, and whose influence an itinerant teacher can here and there trace to-day in the unexpected warmth of the welcome accorded him. Such was an old Yorkshire Chartist, who, when the world turned dark in 1848, laid his pike among the rafters, but still believed that the cause would triumph, and in the meantime kept the spark alight by gathering a group of friends for study; such a co-operator to whom co-operation still meant not dividends but the new moral world of its founder; such a trade unionist who caught the distant gleam of a brotherhood of craftsmanship beyond the grey and scarcely ended days of persecution. Like all working-class movements the Workers' Educational Association moves in a path worn smooth by the vanguard of the anonymous.

Founded in 1903 by a group of trade unionists and co-operators, the Workers' Educational Association is a federation which at the present time includes a very large number[1] of working-class and educational organizations. Owing mainly to the inspiration of its founder and general secretary, Mr. Albert Mansbridge, its organization has grown in the last few years with remarkable and rather disconcerting rapidity. Its affiliated societies, which in 1906 numbered 283, were, at the date of its last Report, 2,164; its local branches have risen from 13 at the earlier date to 158 at the later. The branches are grouped into districts, of which there are now eight, and these districts, together with societies and individual members affiliated to the Central Association, appoint representatives to a Council by which the affairs of the whole Association are transacted. But each branch, and each district, is autonomous, and it is within the branches and districts that the real life of the Association moves. Like trade unions, co-operative societies, and mediaeval gilds, the Workers' Educational Association is not limited by any articles of association to one specific purpose. Its aim is to articulate the educational aspirations of Labour, to represent them to the proper authorities, to stimulate into activity, when it exists, the organization through which they can be satisfied, to create it when it does not. Necessarily, therefore, the work of the Association is in a constant state of transformation, and there are already signs of a widening in its horizon which is likely to cause it in the future to give increased attention to questions connected with the education of children and young persons. During the first ten years of its existence, however, its main task has been to create, with the assistance of the proper authorities, the nucleus of that system of humane education for adult workers, both men and women, which has attained some celebrity under the name of the University Tutorial Class movement. The establishment of University Tutorial Classes is not by any means the only outcome of its labours. An energetic branch of the Association forms the centre of those educational activities of a district which, because they are not supported out of public money, do not fall within the province of the Local Education Authority, and offers a medium through which they are kept in communication with each other. The University spirit exists outside University cities, and such activities, at any rate in the north of England, are more numerous and more vigorous than might at first be supposed. A successful branch of the Workers' Educational Association secures the affiliation of all bodies carrying on any educational work, as well as of the local trade unions, trades councils, and co-operative societies which are its main support. With the assistance thus obtained it can take steps to meet the educational needs of different sections of the population in ways which vary according to the conditions of different localities, but which normally consist of the organization of lectures, classes, and reading circles. The strength of the movement is that by casting a wide net it is able to draw together all the educational forces of a district, to give the demand for higher education the support of a representative and democratic organization, and to build from within instead of borrowing from without. To build from within, to help men to develop their own genius, their own education, their own culture, that is the secret. The first task, indeed, of any such society as the Workers' Educational Association is to lay to rest that smiling illusion which whispers that 'culture' is something that one class—'the educated'—possess, that another—'the uneducated'—are without, and that the former, when sufficiently warmed by sympathy or alarm, can transfer to the latter in pills made up for weak digestions. How venerably is this superstition, mentioned by Bacon in his tedious, though not exhaustive, list of the *Idola Universitatis*,[2] rooted in the historical organization of English education! With what affection is it regarded by that not inconsiderable number of persons who possess sufficient money to be able to dispense with any other test of intellectual attainments! With what triumphant logic has the beautiful English arrangement by which wealth protects learning and learning in turn admits wealth as a kind of honorary member of its placid groves, enabled the upper classes to meet their inferiors! 'You see, my good friends, it is no use fighting against science. We govern you because we are wiser, because we have more knowledge, because we are *better educated* than you are'! The time appears to be coming when these inferiors do not listen so patiently as of old. 'Very well,' they say, 'granted for the sake of argument that you govern us because you are educated, and we are not educated because you have hitherto governed us, and made laws upon (among other matters) the subject of education, then we will have our own education. We will show what we can make of it, and what it will do for us.' Of that answer the branches of the Workers' Educational Association are the first, not yet wholly self-confident, voices. Men meet and discuss. There is hesitation, curiosity, interest, eagerness for knowledge. We ought to have learned about that; can't we learn about it? we *will* learn about it, and we will find a man to help us if a man is to be found. Fortunate teacher, who is sought and not avoided! Thus the medium is created; the spirit finds a body; the solitary student discovers that he is one of a crowd.[3] Education is not put on like varnish. It springs like a plant from the soil, and the fragrance of the earth is upon it.

Such work is at once educational and propagandist. It meets some of the needs of those who are beginning to demand higher education, and it creates a body of students who desire more advanced, systematic, and continuous study. The provision made for such students, or for some among them, consists of the University Tutorial Classes. A University Tutorial Class is really the nucleus of a University established in a place where no University exists. Its organization is simple. It consists of a group of not more than thirty students who agree to meet regularly once a week for twenty-four weeks during each of three successive winters for the purpose of study under a tutor appointed by a University, to follow the course of reading outlined by the tutor and to write fortnightly essays. For the purpose of managing these classes ten Universities and University Colleges have appointed joint committees consisting of equal numbers of University representatives and of representatives of working-class organizations, and three others have established committees, which, though similar in purpose, differ somewhat in composition from the ordinary joint committee. These Committees receive applications for the establishment of classes and appoint the tutors, who are paid partly by the Universities concerned, partly out of the grants which are paid to the classes by the Board of Education. The classes meet every week for two hours at a time, of which the first normally consists of a lecture and the second of questions and discussion by the students. Books are obtained from the Universities and from local libraries. The subjects of study are chosen by the classes themselves after consultation with the tutor. In the earlier years of the movement they consisted almost entirely of economic history and economics. But these subjects were interpreted in a very catholic sense, and included the consideration of a good many matters which would not, perhaps, figure largely in a University course on economics. At the present time the scope of the classes is tending to widen, and though economic history and economics still probably predominate, there are classes in literature, political science, general history, biology, psychology, and philosophy. And the classes *are* classes, not lectures. Thanks to the fact that they are small, tutor and students can meet as friends, discover each other's idiosyncrasies, and break down that unintentional system of mutual deception which seems inseparable from any education which relies principally on the formal lecture. It is often before the classes begin and after they end, in discussions round a student's fire, or in a walk to and from his home, that the root of the matter is reached both by student and tutor. The students themselves are drawn from almost every occupation, but the majority of them are manual workers.[4]

Judged by the increase in their numbers, the University Tutorial Classes have met with a success unanticipated by the pioneers of the movement. In 1908 the University of Oxford provided a teacher for two classes, composed of some sixty students. At the present time[5] thirteen Universities and University colleges in England and Wales conduct 142 classes, including about 3,500 to 4,000 students. The expectation that only in certain selected areas would a body of workers be found sufficiently enthusiastic and alert to give their evenings to study after a hard day's labour in the factory or in the mine has been quite falsified by the event. Though harassed by unemployment, by the habitual and scandalous abuse of overtime which obtains in certain industries, and by the paralysing insecurity which is the grim background of every working-class movement, the Tutorial Classes, which began in Lancashire and North Staffordshire, have now spread to almost every part of the country. In London, the desert where so many brightly-running streams are lost, there are now thirty. In Wales there are four. The ready optimism of Scotland was at first sceptical as to the existence of any considerable number of persons who had not opportunities for obtaining all the higher education which they could desire, but several classes have now been established in connexion with the University of Edinburgh, and there are three in Ireland. Parts of rural England are taking up the movement, and though no Tutorial Classes have as yet been established in villages, the way has been prepared for them by numerous classes of a less exacting kind. There are, therefore, no signs that the movement[6] has miscalculated its possibilities or mistaken the interest of a few enthusiasts for a widespread demand. On the contrary, requests for the establishment of Tutorial Classes have to be refused because the money to finance them is not forthcoming. In six years the students in the Tutorial Classes have increased from 60 to nearly 4,000. In another ten years they could be increased from 4,000 to 12,000 if the men and the money needed to conduct the classes were available. If there was ever any truth in the saying that English people do not care for higher education—how should they when it was almost unattainable?—it has been disposed of by the simple process of offering them higher education for which they care. There are not a few social difficulties which might wisely be met in a similar manner.

If the University Tutorial Classes have shown that there is a wide demand for higher education of a humane type among the workers, it has shown also that there is a large number of workers who need only the opportunity to reach a very high level in their studies. It is as to the quality of the work done in the classes that the academic critic will naturally feel the greatest curiosity, and by which the movement will necessarily be judged by educationalists. The classes are fortunate in having from the first been closely watched by high academic authorities and by the inspectors of the Board of Education. The disposition, which was occasionally shown in their earlier years, to regard them as an amiable but quixotic attempt to provide cheap culture 'for the masses', by popularizing subjects which lose their meaning when they lose their austerity, has, therefore, been brought from the beginning to the test of facts, and is no longer held by persons whose experience or attainments entitle them to consideration. The verdict given[7] in their Report to the Board of Education by Professor L. T. Hobhouse and Mr. Headlam, after an exhaustive examination of a large number of classes, that their work was 'in some respects better, and in others not so good, as that of an Oxford or Cambridge undergraduate', that the classes 'tend to accustom the student to the ideal of work familiar at a University', and that 'as regards the standard reached, there are students whose essays compare favourably with the best academic work', is substantially that of most observers who have had experience of teaching in a University and who have seen the work of the Tutorial Classes at first hand. It is, of course, true that in most classes there are one or two students whose mental machinery fell out of gear in the critical interval between fourteen and twenty, and who find it difficult to set it in motion when the interests of manhood bring an intellectual awakening, just as there are one or two dunces in any sample of thirty undergraduates taken at random in a University. It is also true that the work of the students suffers severely from the unfavourable economic conditions under which many of them carry it on. To attempt to strike a balance between drawbacks such as these and the advantage of the students' maturity—their average age is probably about thirty—and from the fact that what induces them to submit to a somewhat arduous course of study is not custom or professional advancement, but the desire for knowledge, is neither profitable nor necessary. Though they are susceptible, in more favourable circumstances, of much improvement, the Tutorial Classes have at least proved that work of a University character can be done by men who labour with their hands all day. Of course, 'work of a University character' is a vague enough phrase. But if University study means, above all, facing difficulties, testing accepted theories, shedding conventions, and going to sources, then the work of most of the classes, though of course they differ, is certainly University education in the highest sense of those words.

Such a development means more than the addition of a few thousands to the ranks of University students. It means that we are approaching a period, such as existed sixty years ago, when it will be necessary to revise the meaning of the word University. The new interpretation of the meaning of a University education will be wider in two respects than that which has obtained hitherto. The conception of a University as the 'professional school of the brain-working classes' will not disappear, but it will be broadened to admit as genuine University students those who are not studying for the purpose of any profession except that of a reasonable and humane conduct of life. If the whole object of a University were to prepare those who enter it for specialized avocations, then it would indeed be the case that University education could never be enjoyed by men and women who depend on manual labour for their living, though it still might and should be far more accessible to their children than it is at present. But is it? What is actually happening to-day is that the study under University teachers of the subjects taught in Universities by the methods pursued in Universities is being demanded and obtained by a growing number of men and women quite apart from the professional interests which it is one of the legitimate aims of a University to encourage. And since it will hardly be contended that a man obtains a University education when he studies history and philosophy in order to enter the Civil Service, and does not obtain it when he studies the same subject merely because he enjoys doing so, we must revise our conception of a University education so as to include in it all those, whatever, their occupations, who are pursuing a regular course of University studies under the guidance of a University teacher. And we must find room in our idea of a University for students of mature years, who carry on their education in the midst of the routine of their working life. That education is never ended is one of those gracious commonplaces which mankind seems to have agreed to learn in its youth in order that it may disregard them when it reaches the age at which they become applicable. Certainly the conventional conception of education in England is of a continuous course of whole time study from about the age of seven to that of twenty-one or twenty-two, and of University education as the final plunge in the bath of ideas before men 'turn from books to life'. This view of the place of University education, admirably adapted as it is to the needs of those from whom the demand for University education has hitherto principally come, need not be discarded. But it requires to be supplemented by a realization of the function which Universities can fulfil in providing for the needs of those whose economic career is moulded on a different framework from that of the professional classes. To make University education accessible to men and women who have already begun the work by which they obtain their livelihood is not to lower the standard of Universities, but to increase their opportunities by throwing open to them wide continents of experience of whose very existence they are sometimes unaware. Certainly nothing is more likely to invigorate the branches of learning which are concerned with the study of human society than to create opportunities for cross-fertilization through intercourse between the experience of the workshop and the experience—for it also is experience—of the University. University Tutorial Classes are not, in short, an alternative to a University education, a *pis aller* for those who cannot 'go to a University'. Nor are they merely a preparation for study in a University, though that is not, of course, incompatible with thinking it right for some students to go from them to residence in a University, just as in Germany men go regularly from one University to another. They are themselves a University education, carried on, it is true, under difficulties, but still carried on in such a way as to make their promotion one among the most important functions of a University. If this is not yet fully recognized it is because one of the besetting sins of those in high places in England—it is not that of the working classes—is the bad utilitarianism which thinks that the object of education is not education, but some external result, such as professional success or industrial leadership. It is not in this spirit that a nation can be led to believe in the value of the things of the mind. In the matters of the intellect, as in matters of religion, 'High Heaven rejects the lore of nicely calculated less or more.' And it is, perhaps, not fanciful to say that the disinterested desire of knowledge for its own sake, the belief in the free exercise of reason without regard to material results and because reason is divine, a faith not yet characteristic of English life, but which it is the highest spiritual end of Universities to develop, finds in the Tutorial Classes of the Workers' Educational Association as complete an expression as it does within the walls of some University cities. To these miners and weavers and engineers who pursue knowledge with the passion born of difficulties, knowledge can never be a means, but only an end; for what have they to gain from it save knowledge itself?

While the development of facilities for adult education has occupied a great part of the energies of the Workers' Educational Association during the past ten years, it has, as a federation of working-class organizations, the function of forming and expressing the opinion of labour upon matters which concern the education not only of adults but of children. That a body which can act as an organ of criticism in educational matters has an indispensable function to perform, few who have practical experience of the educational service of the country will deny. There are still a large number of Authorities which do little more than comply with the bare minimum required of them by the law. Side by side with much devoted public service there is nearly everywhere an influential group of councillors whose principal anxiety, expressed often quite frankly to the inquirer, is to see that whatever must be provided—teachers, medical inspection, school accommodation— is bought in the cheapest market, that nothing at all is spent on providing anything the absence of which will not entail a loss of grant, and that the development of public education is not allowed to conflict with their desire to secure a sufficient supply of cheap juvenile labour. It is best to be candid in facing disagreeable facts, and it must be admitted at once that hitherto labour organizations, in spite of some notable exceptions, have in most places entirely failed to grasp the responsibility which the development of a system of public education imposes on them. Partly through ignorance of the steps which are being taken by the most enlightened Authorities, partly through a natural absorption in industrial questions, partly because they themselves have not altogether escaped from the bad economic philosophy which in public they repudiate, they have been too ready to acquiesce in the control of education by their masters, and to allow conditions to be maintained in the schools which would produce a strike in any properly organized workshop. A society which will focus on the pressing needs of public education the best opinion of the world of labour has a career of infinite possibilities before it. Such a body, if it is to do its work effectively, must be representative. It must be in touch with educational administration in many different parts of England, and have facilities for obtaining information as to recent developments. And it must be free from official influence. Given these three conditions, it should be in a position to assist the creation of an intelligent opinion and policy on educational matters by stimulus, encouragement, and criticism. There is indeed one further condition of success: that sufficient funds should be forthcoming to enable it to discharge its work. The Workers' Educational Association has been hampered throughout its career by financial difficulties. It cannot hope—what educational organization can?—to be entirely self-supporting, and it is perhaps not too bold to suggest that it has proved its value as an educational instrument sufficiently to deserve a grant from the State such as is made to other pioneer organizations. One noticeable development in the work of the Association in recent years has been, in spite of its lack of funds, the increased attention which its members have found themselves compelled to pay to questions of elementary and secondary education. By conferences, by discussions at its annual meeting, by local inquiries as to educational conditions, the Association is helping to develop the educational conscience whose growth has perhaps scarcely kept pace with the recent astonishing development of educational machinery. It is evident that the natural reluctance of Education Authorities to spend money in improving public education is not likely to be overcome unless the classes whose children have most to gain by its improvement and most to lose by its deficiencies show that they are as intent upon raising the standard of educational as of economic conditions. The observer who reflects on such matters as the size of classes in elementary schools, the provision for medical treatment and school feeding, the age at which exemption from compulsory attendance is permitted, the provision of scholarships to secondary schools, the conditions upon which the teaching staffs are employed, and who then compares the practice of an average Authority with that of the best, and that of the best with that which might be, can hardly escape a sense of desolation at the waste of opportunity, of intelligence, of human potentiality. Historians tell us that decadent societies have been revivified through the irruption of new races. In England a new race of nearly 900,000 souls bursts upon us every year. They stand on the threshold with the world at their feet, like barbarians gazing upon the time-worn plains of an ancient civilization, and if, instead of rejuvenating the world they grind corn for the Philistines and doff bobbins for mill owners, the responsibility is ours into whose hands the prodigality of Nature pours life itself, and who let it slip aimlessly through the fingers that close so greedily on material riches.

To do more than labour at the foundations, to create the faith to use the weapons that knowledge has put into our hands and the courage which will dare to be extravagant in matters where the true extravagance is a mean and sightless parsimony, is not given to any organization, however comprehensive and enthusiastic. It is not indeed with organization that the final word on these high issues rests. The Workers' Educational Association can, at least, do the humble and necessary work of serving as a vehicle to express the best thought upon educational matters of the plain people on whose attitude the future of English education principally depends.

Notes

1 E.g. 790 trade unions, trade union branches and trades councils, 326 co-operative education committees, 254 adult schools and classes, 163 working men's clubs and institutes, 61 teachers' associations, 20 University bodies, 15 local education authorities, and a number of miscellaneous working-class organizations.

2 Apparently not included in his published works.

3 E.g. One W. E. A. branch arranged in 1912–13 over 1,000 lectures (mostly in course of from 3 to 6) for trade unions, adult schools, co-operative guilds, &c., in the district. Nearly all of some 150 branches are doing similar work on a smaller scale.

4 The following figures relate to the year 1912–13. They are not complete as some classes did not make full returns.

The classification is obviously very rough. If London be omitted, the number of clerks is reduced by one-third. In this, as in other respects, London is abnormal.

610 Clerks, telegraphists, &c.	30 Potters.
191 Textile workers.	66 Insurance agents, &c.
182 Miners and quarrymen.	57 Labourers.
278 Teachers.	72 Railway servants.
94 Metal workers.	24 Postmen and policemen.
160 Printers.	16 Commercial travellers.
195 Engineers, &c.	59 Boot and shoe trades and leather
113 Shop assistants.	workers.
134 Women working at home.	45 Food workers.
98 Carpenters and joiners.	53 Warehousemen.
81 Building trades.	34 Foremen and managers.
80 Tailors and dressmakers.	304 Miscellaneous.
144 Factory workers.	Total 3,176.

5 1913–1914.

6 The work of Tutorial Classes has attracted the attention of Australian Educational Administrators. The State of New South Wales, in its University Amending Bill, laid it upon the University to construct Tutorial Classes. Almost simultaneously, the Trades and Labour Council of Sydney, New South Wales, decided to establish the Workers' Educational Association, whilst the Australian Delegates to the Congress of the Universities of the Empire were so impressed by the statement on Tutorial Classes that they decided to invite the General Secretary to Australia for the purpose of developing the work there. The result of his visit, carried out from July to October, 1913, is that the Workers' Educational Association has

been started and that Tutorial Classes are at work in many places. The University of Sydney has appointed a Director of Tutorial Classes and the University of Tasmania a Lecturer in Economic History for that purpose. These Universities have been aided by their respective Governments. It is expected that further appointments will be made. Australia has heard little of non-vocational education until this visit.

In Canada, the Universities are turning their attention to the work, and, at Toronto, a Tutorial Class has been established.

Representations have been made from various quarters of South Africa.

7 Report to the Board of Education on Tutorial Classes. It is reprinted in *University Tutorial Classes*, by Albert Mansbridge, App. III (Longmans & Co., 2s. 6d.), which gives a full account of the movement.

38

THE NATURE AND AIMS OF A MODERN UNIVERSITY

Bruce Truscot

Source: B. Truscot, *Red Brick University*, London: Faber and Faber, 1943, pp. 45–56.

What is a university? That is a question which the Oxbridge freshman must often ask himself, on his introduction to a place so different in every respect from the school which he has left three months earlier. It will be some time before he can give the question a satisfactory answer, and he will probably not be helped by an extraordinary definition, surely inspired by some demon of irony, to be found in the *Students' Handbook* to Cambridge:

'The University of Cambridge is a corporation which, in addition to the usual powers of corporations, such as the ownership of property, possesses the rights of exercising disciplinary authority over its members, returning two representatives to Parliament and conferring degrees.'[1]

Even at the tender age of nineteen he may have an inkling that knowledge is more important than proctors or M.P.s. Later, when he has gone down, and is able to take a more objective view of his university and to appreciate its merits and defects in a way no undergraduate can, he might evolve a definition which, though undoubtedly imperfect, is perhaps as satisfactory as it is possible to find. The definition would be framed in words something like these:

A University is a corporation or society which devotes itself to a search after knowledge for the sake of its intrinsic value.

Each phrase of this definition needs consideration. Let us deal with each in ascending order of importance.

(1) *A corporation or society.* Not, it will be observed, an 'organization' or (as they often say in the United States) an 'institution' or 'school';[2] still less a 'place'. A University may be domiciled in one town or city, or even housed in a single group of buildings within a limited area, and it is often most convenient that this should be so. But it may equally well consist of several groups of teachers and students each housed in a separate town. Or, as

139

sometimes happens on the Continent, two or three of its Faculties may be domiciled in one place and the remainder in another. Or again, the main body may have distant colleges affiliated to it, which are in a real sense a part of it. Or the whole of its members may be dispersed among twenty or thirty colleges, each with a separate individuality. We all know the story of the foreigner who, after being taken round all the colleges at Oxford (or was it at Cambridge?), inquired of his guide, 'But where is the University?' And it was no foreigner, but an intelligent undergraduate very near the end of his university course, who once remarked to me in genuine bewilderment: 'What I have never understood is, who *owns* the University?'

To both these questions the history of the word supplies the best answer. The medieval Latin word *universitas* meant a corporation, society or community of any kind, a body of persons collectively organized and considered in their corporate aspect. It could be used in a broad sense, to embrace all Christian people; it could be used in a narrow sense, to denote a relatively small group of captives languishing in a foreign prison.

When used in the particular sense of *studium generale* (a phrase which embodies the nearest conception in existence in the Middle Ages to our modern conception of a university), it would invariably be delimited by an appropriate phrase of qualification, such as *magistrorum et discipulorum*. More and more frequently scholars began to group themselves together to form a kind of guild for the purposes of mutual defence and protection, and it soon became sufficient to refer to such a guild simply as a *universitas*. For this reason our word 'university' properly denotes 'a body of teachers and scholars'—nothing less and nothing more. Yet the common conception held of it is that of a building, or of a set of buildings, *attended by* teachers and scholars, and nobody realizes that, in saying 'This bus passes the University', he means that it passes the buildings used or inhabited by the University, or that, if the buildings were all burned to the ground, the University would still remain.

There is a further important point to be made here. Many people talk of universities as if their name indicated that every kind of subject under the sun ought to be studied in them and they were places where knowledge in its most 'universal' aspect should be sought, a college of the liberal arts and a technical and commercial school all rolled into one enormous whole, with a syllabus in *x* large volumes. This is as erroneous a supposition as that the *studium generale* concerned itself only with knowledge of the most 'general' kind and specialized in nothing. The 'general' or 'universal' concept underlying each of these terms has reference not to the subjects studied but to the people who study them. These associations could be joined by anyone capable of profiting by them—i.e., without distinction of class, or age, or rank, or previous occupation—as they may still, with even fewer restrictions than of old. It is quite incorrect to think that every kind of subject should be studied at a university, and it is surely astonishing that Newman should not only have been so vague about the history of the word, but should have been so easily content to adopt the popular sense in which it is used and say 'that a University should teach universal knowledge',[3] asking

'What ought the term University to mean, but a place where every science is taught which is liberal, and at the same time useful to mankind?'[4]

(2) *For the sake of its intrinsic value.* If some would assent to the first part of the definition, a few would frankly disagree with the second, while many more would misunderstand it. Dr. Lowell, one of the great Harvard Presidents, once drily defined a university as a place where nothing useful is taught. I would not go as far as that; to the extent that it was meant to be taken seriously, it was intended as a sharp corrective to the mentality, only too common in America, which (to quote an equation which I have actually seen in print) puts the cultural value of modern language study on a level with that of typewriting. I can see nothing inconsistent with the nature of a university in the inclusion in the curriculum of frankly vocational teaching, provided this be recognized as an addition to the university's essential work and not claimed as a part of it. A technical college, a secretarial or domestic science school, a cramming institution are all quite distinct from a university. Both deliberate technical training and a certain amount of cramming may legitimately be indulged in during the course of university instruction, but education in a much broader and humaner sense must be the chief and ever-present aim.

(3) *The search after knowledge.* Here we come at once to the most vital, and yet to the most contentious part of our definition. Let me say at once that I must diverge fundamentally from the position of Newman, to whom the university is 'a place [*sic*] of *teaching* universal knowledge', and its object, 'the diffusion and extension of knowledge rather than the advancement'. 'If its object were scientific and philosophical discovery,' he adds, 'I do not see why a University should have students':[5] that we shall discuss later on.

That the search after knowledge is the essential function of the university is to me a basic article of faith; and if this book does no more than convert a handful of university teachers to that belief it will have fully repaid the time spent on it. It is in so far as our universities have declined from, forgotten or denied that ideal that they have failed in their duty. The definition is true historically: it was to *advance* knowledge, indeed to *possess all knowledge for themselves*, and not in the least to diffuse it abroad and convey it to others, that the earliest universities were established. It also holds together logically—for if existing knowledge is only to be diffused, let local authorities found *studia generalia* as they found elementary and secondary schools: they will only need to appoint superior types of school teacher, and these are plentiful enough, as any scholastic agency will testify.

No: the primary aim of the university must be search for knowledge— research, as we call it to-day: not merely actual discovery, not merely even the attempt to discover, but the creation and cultivation of the spirit of discovery.

Imagine a group of men, in any age, retiring from the life of the world, forming a society for the pursuit of truth, laying down and voluntarily embracing such discipline as is necessary to that purpose and making provision that whatever they find shall be handed on to others after their deaths. They pool their material resources; build a house; collect books; and plan their corporate studies. This, in its simplest form, is the true idea of a university.

But to do all this is not sufficient for them. Not content with discovering and leaving dissemination to others, they want to disseminate too. And, not content with doing this by means of books, they want to do it through living channels. So they seek contact with others, especially with the young, who are like-minded with themselves, and train them, first and foremost, to be discoverers of fresh knowledge—i.e., researchers—and secondarily, to be diffusers of the knowledge which they give them as part of their self-imposed task. And, as the effectiveness of a teaching inspired by such high ideals becomes manifest, more and more come to them to be taught—including many who have not the ambition, nor perhaps the capacity, to embrace research as a vocation, but who value, and desire, what we term 'the hall-mark of a university career'.

Here, as a natural development from the essential idea of the university, we discover its teaching function. In the original truth-seekers and the young people with whom they make contact we have the *socii* (the 'Fellows', now pretentiously termed 'Professors' and 'Lecturers'—words which obscure their main duty) and the *discipuli* (the 'Scholars', as they were called when part of a foundation, corresponding to the 'students' or 'undergraduates' of to-day).

One more detail has still to be added. The young scholars must not only be instructed, trained, educated, before they are ready to engage in research, or, in their turn, to instruct others; they must be tested, licensed and given some status which will be a guarantee of their competence and fitness. Hence the lowest degree, that of Bachelor, and the successive degrees of Master and Doctor, the power to confer which can be bestowed on a society only by high authority—in this country by Royal Charter—and is recognized, almost the world over, as the seal of the university, differentiating it from any other educational institution, from elementary school to 'University College'.

But to the idea of a university only the 'Fellows', the researchers, are essential. There could perfectly well be a university which, like All Souls' College, Oxford, had no undergraduates at all; and, instead of teaching, replenished its ranks by the choice of scholars who had been taught else-where, devoting itself entirely and exclusively to the pursuit of knowledge. But there could never be a university which had no researchers at all and which engaged in nothing but teaching. A secondary school can never be a university, though in its highest forms, given scholarly teachers, there can be much of the university spirit. A university without research would be nothing but a super-secondary school.

Here, then, are the university's two aims: (1) *research*—patient and unremitting—including the cultivation of the spirit of research in even the youngest; (2) *teaching*—systematic and methodical, but also rich, stimulating and thought-provoking, so much so that again and again one finds the two aims merging and becoming temporarily indistinguishable the one from the other. Ruling and dominating each of these activities is the formation, both in *socii* and in *discipuli*, of character. For the discipline of conscientious teaching and application to learning cannot but make men better. And the discipline of research is as much more beneficent than this as research itself is a nobler activity than teaching and learning. Here one discovers that method, mental retentiveness, quickness of apprehension and skill in argument are of less moment than selflessness, humility, sincerity and balance of judgement. Here, without knowing it, one grows in honesty, generosity and love of truth—or fails as a scholar.

There still remains one concept to be elucidated and clarified—that of 'knowledge'. Admittedly the word is unsatisfactory: whenever it is used there insinuates itself the age-old antithesis between 'knowledge' and 'wisdom'. But the acquisition of knowledge does not mean the mere amassing of facts, either in the memory or in books and monographs, nor even the mere discovery of facts previously unknown or the rediscovery and restatement of facts forgotten. The prevalence of this factual conception of knowledge is, as we shall see later, largely responsible for the disrepute into which, in some circles, research has fallen, though, as far as my own experience goes, those who speak slightingly of it have not themselves always great originality or breadth of mind. As soon as one considers in some detail all that the pursuit of knowledge comprehends, its nobility and supreme worth at once become manifest. It includes, on the lowest plane, collation, comparison, revaluation and the shedding of new light on facts previously known, always provided that these activities are carried out in an eager and questing spirit. It includes the study, in the same spirit, of backgrounds to facts and events with the object of attaining a juster perception of them. It includes adventures, both critical and creative, into the unknown, whether with objectives envisaged beforehand or for purposes of pure exploration. It includes the interpretation of knowledge, whether factual or conceptual, hitherto available only to one class, community or language-group, for the benefit of others. It includes the perfecting of method, so that unknown lands may be provisionally charted by those who are unable to embark on voyages of discovery. It includes the re-examination, in the light of modern knowledge, of views and conceptions held by past ages; and not infrequently this activity, besides correcting the past, will reillumine the present and even light up the future.

All that has been said can claim only to be a partial definition of a university, but it will at least give some idea as to what kind of person the *socius* and the *discipulus* should be. The *socii*, who have embraced university work as a vocation, will continue their pursuit of knowledge for as long as their powers allow. Compulsory superannuation may free them from their teaching duties and from the contractual obligation to engage in research, but they can no more regard their vocation as having ceased than can an aged monk, or a retired priest or doctor. Throughout their lives, too, they will attempt to stimulate the spirit of discovery in others—and this not so much of set purpose as because they cannot do otherwise. Their passion for knowledge should be infectious: none who know them should fail to be aware of it. The *discipuli*, apart from those who have found the vocation within the university, will, after a few years have passed, go out into the world, either to teach others, some of whom will, in due course, follow in their footsteps, or to pursue some other profession, which may take them far from the university atmosphere or may keep them near it. The extent of the influence of their years of study will therefore vary. But of all of them we can say this: when they go out from the university they should feel fuller, and yet emptier, than when they entered it; they should have an increased power, yet at the same time a keener sense of their own weakness; above all, they should be afire with a passion to discover and explore.

II

This is the 'idea of a university' held by many teachers who regard university work, not as a means of gaining a comfortable stipend for only a few hours' work every week, but as a vocation to which their ideals and talents pledge them. But, both in the ancient and the modern universities, it is an idea in grave danger of disappearance. Some of the *socii*, who in the enthusiasm' of youth were faithful to it, have allowed it to fade from their minds, and hence to evaporate from their teaching. As to the *discipuli*, the growing stress of life, the increasing difficulty of obtaining employment, the constant irruptions of worldly interests into the realms of the spirit, all tend to crush, in those who pass only three or four years in the university, the idea that their essential task there is to pursue learning for its intrinsic value. Only a few years ago the late Ramsay Muir, that well-known Manchester historian who to the great loss of academic life abandoned it for politics, said that he used to think his undergraduates 'had come to the university not as to a factory of ideas but as to a mere knowledge-shop; not to be forced to think about life, but merely to acquire the necessary fragments of dull and uninteresting knowledge which were required for examination purposes and therefore might open the way to some unim-aginative mode of livelihood.'[6] The reality in many cases is worse than that. Too often, not only at Oxbridge but also at Redbrick, the student is caught up in a whirlwind of lectures, games, examinations, dances, debates, friendships, vacations, worries—and who knows what else?—and, between preoccupation with the present and uncertainty as to the future, not only the most vital aspect, but any serious aspect, of a university career is forgotten.

Most freshmen come up to the university with two main ideas. One, a very clear idea, is that they have to amass a great deal of specialized knowledge in order to pass examinations, success in which will be important to them hereafter. This idea alone has been dinned into them both at school and at home, and, quite apart from that, it is a perfectly natural one, since lessons and examinations have been their principal concern at school, and the university appears to them as a kind of continuation school, and nothing more. The other idea, a much vaguer one, but very attractive to the adolescent and often the more potent of the two, is that the real purpose of the university is to broaden the undergraduate's experience, to enable him to pick up scraps of all kinds of knowledge and to give him something often vaguely described as 'general culture'. He hears little about this at school, except perhaps from some young master whose 'Varsity' days are not long past; whether he hears about it at home depends very much on the home itself; where he chiefly imbibes it is from former schoolfellows who have preceded him to the university. When he arrives there, he finds that Vice-Chancellors, Deans, tutors and all who deliver the well-known hortatory addresses to freshmen give this idea their most emphatic benediction; sometimes, in fact, they seem almost to be apologizing for the existence of lectures and examinations at all. The average undergraduate's reaction is to join every society, to attend every religious or political meeting, to read voraciously scraps from every kind of book and to discuss anything and everything with all and sundry. This phase, usually accompanied by neglect of academic work and by the most perfunctory attendance possible upon lectures, generally lasts until the examination lists at the end of the first year administer an already half-anticipated shock. The result of this shock, according to the strength of it, and to the temperament of the student, is either a reaction towards excessive specialization, or the feeling that academically all is now lost, leading to a slightly diluted and disillusioned pursuit of 'general culture' for the remainder of the undergraduate's career.

Much of the responsibility for all this lies at the door of those who fail to point out that a truly liberal education, and the acquisition, not only of knowledge, but of a thirst for knowledge, are best attained through a conscientious self-application to the subject or subjects in which one has elected to specialize in all their varying aspects, together with a rigidly self-controlled study, over the greater part of the university course, of a limited number of other subjects, chosen either from their connection with one's main interests or as providing a pure rest and relaxation from them. Thus an undergraduate reading for Honours in French would naturally select for subsidiary study Modern History, English Literature and another language; his societies might be the International Affairs Discussion Circle and the Dramatic Club; and his hobbies, photography and botany. A specialist in

Social Science might well read widely in the foreign language or languages he already knows, learn the elements of one other, join the Social Service Club and one or more of the political and religious societies and make a hobby of painting or music. If to these activities be added a care for physical fitness and attendance at debates or public meetings of current interest, the result should be an education both broad and deep, the maintenance of the sacred flame of desire for knowledge brightly burning, undimmed either by dilettantism, by ennui or by physical or mental fatigue. It should be impossible for anyone organizing his university career in this way to go down with the feeling that, on the one hand, he knows as much as he wants to of his special subjects, and, on the other, with a palate vitiated, through over-much tasting, for knowledge in general. 'Good-bye to all that' is the unhealthiest of cries which can come from a student after graduation. American universities significantly and inspiringly style their graduation day 'Commencement'.

<h1 style="text-align:center">III</h1>

The foregoing section applies with approximately equal force both to Oxbridge and to Redbrick, though Oxbridge, with its numerous social engagements and its long and alluring list of famous speakers, is more apt to breed the dilettante, and Redbrick, where the alternatives to lectures are less inviting, the dull and narrow specialist. But there are other reasons why the essential and inspiring central idea of the university is apt to be forgotten at Redbrick—or even never heard of. To each of these we must pay some attention.

(1) First, although, as we have said, the private lives of undergraduates differ very widely, in the average Redbrick home there is a severer economic pressure and the undergraduate is never away from his family for long enough to be free from it. Anyone at all intimate with students' homes will be familiar with the types of reminder that, often in quite a kindly way, are for ever being hammered into them:

'Well, Aggie knows *we* can't do anything more for her.'

'This is her only chance to get on in life and she'd better make the most of it.'

'We've all pinched and denied ourselves to send you to college, my boy, so you just see you do well in your exams.'

'Tom'll have to help us with the expenses when he's finished at the University so it's to be hoped he'll get a good job.'

What boy or girl of nineteen or twenty can be expected to think of acquiring knowledge for its intrinsic value when young life's song has to be sung to a dad-or-mum obbligato of that nature? And how incumbent it is on the professor, going home each Friday afternoon to his warm, comfortable and quiet study, where he can pursue knowledge undisturbed over a long week-end, to imbue his students with this counter-ideal and keep it continually before them!

(2) Freshmen, again, are apt to be misled by the superficial similarity between the modern university and the secondary school which leads to it. Walking or cycling to the university, just as they did to school, they are apt to think of lecture-rooms as class-rooms, of lectures as classes, of professors and lecturers as teachers and of the Vice-Chancellor as a kind of super-Headmaster. The differences seem trivial: the lectures are fewer than the classes were and on occasion can be cut without penalty. Professors seem to know more than the masters did and are unimpressed by that argument previously considered irrefutable: 'The book says so.' There are about three half-holidays a week as well as the whole of Saturday. And so on. But too often undergraduates go through the greater part of their course without suspecting that there is more in it than this. And the university itself—by means of compulsory lectures, register-marking, class examinations, etc. —unconsciously underlines the 'continuation school' idea. No-one tells the unsuspecting students that they are now members of a society with a common aim, toward which seniors as well as juniors are working; that upon them falls the onus of organizing their own work, both in term and in vacation; that every question they ask can no longer be answered with a 'Yes' or a 'No'; that they should learn how to use a library and aim at building up a small one of their own; that they should lose no opportunity of discussing their work, both with their contemporaries and with their seniors, so as to make it more real and living. These things it is surely the duty of the professor and lecturer to tell the student: how else can he be expected to learn them?

(3) Were the modern universities all residential, they could move out, as has been said, to the greatest good of the greatest number, into the suburbs of the great cities, or even into the country. But as, for generations to come, most of them are destined to be set in the heart of city life, the pull in the vocational direction which their environment gives must continue to be considered a drawback. Even indirectly, the constant roar and surge of city life puts the undergraduate continually in mind of his future. And direct reminders are more numerous and more potent still. Lectures are given on vocational topics in the Students' Union; the claims made by the Education Department upon undergraduates who depend for their maintenance on a Board of Education grant are always before them; the Department of Commerce, one of the modern adjuncts of the university course proper, organizes visits to works and factories; connections of all kinds are made with local leaders of industry. The world, students exclaim, is too much with them: little do they see that is theirs in the ideal of disinterested study—they have given their hearts (not to say their souls) away to the vocationists, who henceforward can lead them hither and thither at their will.

IV

So we come—rather despairingly, it would seem—to the crucial question: Is it possible, in a city university, to preserve and inculcate, in anything approaching its pure state, the fundamental idea which we have been considering? Provided the officers and teachers of the university themselves are true to the idea, I believe that it is. Some ways in which it can be done may be briefly suggested:

(1) The officers and teachers must not only hold the idea intellectually but must illustrate it by their own example. As we shall see later, the ideals of scholarship can be much better inculcated by practice than by precept and it is not only the brightest and most suggestive students who model their attitude to their work upon what they sense to be the attitude of their professor.

(2) We must lose no opportunity of stressing the double aim of the university—research and teaching—and of putting research first. It is possible to fight the 'continuation-school' idea from the outset and it should be so fought. No-one is more susceptible than an adolescent to a fresh moral ideal, provided it be attractively presented.

(3) We must make it clear how closely scholarship is related to character, leadership and virtue. That sounds priggish, but only because it is unfashionable to write of such things in a natural way. The point is: Do we ourselves firmly believe that there is such a relation? If we do, we have no need to compose addresses or lectures on the subject—the fact will become obvious in our whole attitude to the subjects we teach, in our individual tuition, in the correction of essays, in chance conversations. The adolescent at the university is less sensitive to atmosphere and impression only than the child in the home: he often respects one professor, is indifferent to another, and despises a third without having the least idea why. It is largely a matter of latent ideals—or the absence of them.

(4) Far from stifling vocational aspirations, we must encourage students to speak of them, relating both scholarship and vocation to the ideal of service, for which all true universities, in the past and in the present, have ever stood. 'The university', remarked a great American college president once, 'is the resting-place of those activities, those scholarly aspirations, those intellectual endeavours which make for spiritual insight, spiritual depth and spiritual beauty, but which cannot be transmuted into any coin less base than highest human service.'[7] In the ideal of service all three functions—research, teaching and vocational training—have their natural meeting-place.

(5) We must try to clarify in the undergraduate's mind the concept of 'general culture' and urge upon him the adoption of a definite policy of self-education. Dilettantism must be vigorously deprecated and its deleterious effects made plain. The linking together of interests and the importance of

intellectual relaxation must be insisted upon. This is a matter primarily for the psychologist; and it would be useful to arrange, in every October term, a short course of lectures for freshmen, to be attended perhaps by second-year students as well, to which the usual hortatory address already referred to could be the introduction. Two or three of these lectures, at least, should be given by a practical psychologist.

Notes

1 Ed. 1935–6, p. 1.
2 In many parts of the United States, especially in the Middle West and West, undergraduates habitually refer to their university or college as 'school'.
3 Newman, p. 20.
4 Op. cit., p. 161.
5 Op. cit., p. ix.
6 N.U.S., 1939, pp. 14–15.
7 Nicholas Murray Butler, *Scholarship and Service*, New York, 1921, p. 63.

39

CHANGING CONCEPTIONS OF THE UNIVERSITY'S TASK

Walter Moberley

Source: W. Moberley, *The Crisis in the University*, London: SCM Press, 1949, pp. 30–49.

How has the university arrived where it is? Within the last century there has been more than one revolution in the conception commonly held of its fundamental aim and methods. But perhaps 'conception' is hardly the right word, since our concern is rather with underlying assumptions, largely unconscious. What really counts is, less opinions consciously adopted and maintained than, what is silently and unreflectingly taken for granted. As T. E. Hulme pointed out, there are certain doctrines which have become so much a part of men's minds that they are never really conscious of them. 'They do not see them but other things *through* them.' Any change in such a body of basic acceptances tends to be slow and imperceptible; it easily escapes notice like the setting of the tide. Yet it is that, rather than the swimmer's own efforts or the waves he breasts, which determines his progress. So we have to recognize that, by the very fact that they are articulate and self-conscious, the representative thinkers from whom we must draw our illustrations are not quite representative.

1 Christian-Hellenic

For the greater part of the nineteenth century Oxford and Cambridge exemplified a highly distinctive type of university, based on Christian and Græco-Roman traditions. In various respects this type has become inadequate to the modern world. But it represents the most characteristic English contribution to 'the idea of the university,' and it is of the first importance to understand and appreciate it. Its classical statement occurs in Newman's *Idea of a University* and is inimitable. But, in substance, it is by no means peculiar to Newman, and there is nothing about it that is specifically Catholic. He is drawing on his recollections of Oxford and is painting its characteristic

150

excellences. What he depicts, is Jowett's ideal of Oxford quite as much as it is his own. A somewhat more pedestrian exposition of a view substantially the same had been given fifteen years earlier by Whewell in the sister university, and some of its most important features are to be found fifteen years later in J. S. Mill's Rectorial address to the students of St. Andrew's.

On this view the chief duty of the university is to produce good citizens. It should train an élite who are to be the future leaders in affairs and in the learned professions. Thus it differs from a seminary, a technical college, or a research institute. For neither training in the technique of particular callings, whether ecclesiastical or secular, nor the advancement of knowledge is its primary function, though it may contribute to each. The training it gives is an initiation of select young people into their cultural inheritance. In Matthew Arnold's words it seeks to familiarize them, with 'the best that has been thought and said in the world' and so to bind together the generations through their sharing in a common intellectual estate.[1]

Such education has the following characteristics. First, it is 'liberal' as opposed to 'servile.' That is, it aims at mental development for its own sake and not for any ulterior end. It seeks, not to make the student an effective tool to serve someone else's purpose or to give him power to make tools of others to serve his own purpose, but to train him to recognize, to respect and to delight in, what is intrinsically true, good and beautiful. It does so simply because this is a want of man's nature and in its satisfaction he fulfils himself. It encourages the student to master the Greek language, not because 'it not infrequently leads to positions of considerable emolument,' nor even because familiarity with Thucydides may make him a more capable statesman in after-life, but in order that he may appreciate and enjoy Homer or Plato for their own sake. By exposing young men to the acknowledged masterpieces of human thought and knowledge, it evokes a culture which is valuable for what it is rather than for what it does, and which is inseparable from mental health in all who are capable of it, since without it they would be less than fully human. Thus refinement rather than effectiveness is its direct aim; and yet, in a large view, it is just the people who have achieved refinement who are also the most effective and excel in practical judgment and knowledge of life. 'A cultivated intellect, because it is good in itself, brings with it a power and a grace to every work and occupation which it undertakes.'[2]

Secondly, this education is general as opposed to specialized. 'The man who has been trained to think on one subject only will never be a good judge even in that one';[3] while if he ventures to express opinions outside his own narrow field, he will be like a schoolboy or a ploughman presuming to judge a prime minister. The student needs to gain a synoptic view, like a man who possesses a map of the country or one who gets up on to high ground to see the panorama. Henceforward he will have some catholicity of outlook and sense of proportion; however intensively he studies any particular subject he will see it in its relation to the whole scheme. 'Not to know the relative disposition of things is the state of slaves or of children.'[4] But he does not necessarily acquire this sense through having a very wide curriculum. That in itself may be a snare. The dilettante is no better than the narrow specialist; a smattering in a dozen branches of study is not enlargement but shallowness. True enlargement is got rather from the fact that the student is a member of a community in which the whole range of knowledge is being studied and is in intimate association with those whose speciality differs from his own. Thus 'he apprehends the great outlines of knowledge, the principles on which it rests, the scale of its parts, its lights and its shades, its great points and its little, as he otherwise cannot apprehend them.'[5] In this way he avoids provincialism.

Thirdly, this education is systematic. There must be no stuffing with knowledge, no passive reception of scraps, no 'unmeaning profusion of subjects.' What is important is, not the amassing of facts but their grasp, not cramming but mental digestion. Hence a habit of method must be formed. The student must learn to start from fixed points, to make good his ground as he goes, to distinguish clearly what he knows from what he does not know, to relate what he learns to what he knows already. Further he is being made acquainted with a world of intellectual order and not of intellectual anarchy and with a hierarchy of intellectual values in which some are fundamental and others subsidiary. He is introduced to laws and principles which are objective and independent of fashion or individual caprice. 'Universities' says Whewell, 'so far as they are schools of *general* cultivation, represent the permanent, not the fluctuating elements of human knowledge . . . They have to transmit the civilization of past generations to future ones, not to share and show forth all the changing fashions of intellectual caprice and subtlety.'[6] Or, to adapt an aphorism of Burke's, one object of a university education is to make the student independent of his own private stock of reason which, in the nature of the case, is small and to make available to him 'the general bank and capital of nations and of ages.'

So much for the traditional aims of our older universities, but what of the methods by which they have sought to achieve them? These are based on the fundamental principle that the university, as a community of teachers and learners, is to be regarded as a family. Or, in words whose felicity has caused them to become a familiar possession, 'a university is . . . an Alma Mater, knowing her children one by one, not a foundry, or a mint, or a treadmill.'[7] In accordance with this principle, the bulk of the teaching has been tutorial or catechetical and has involved the direct impact of person on person. The student is required to answer questions, to write compositions or essays, or to engage in disputations. He is to be, not only a passive recipient of instruction, but an active co-operator in the process. His mental enlargement entails 'the mind's energetic and simultaneous action upon and towards and among those new ideas which are rushing in upon it.'[8]

In conformity with the family analogy, the relation between staff and students is regarded as being paternal on the one side and filial on the other. The student is under authority. He is subjected to rules and regulations, not many or burdensome but inescapable. He lives in a world of definite duties requiring of him some degree of self-restraint and self-regulation[9]; and this is part of his preparation for life. On the other side the teacher's is, to some extent, a pastoral office. He has a responsibility towards his pupils as human beings which extends far beyond his formal obligations as an instructor.

But the most potent educational influence of Oxford and Cambridge has been found outside lecture room or laboratory and even outside the private hour with the tutor. It arises, indirectly, from the character of the community life. No passage in Newman is better remembered or more frequently quoted than that in which he depicts and extols the influence of students on one another and asserts that, if he had to choose between one system in which students lived a corporate life but received no formal teaching and were submitted to no examination and another in which they were rigorously examined but lived no corporate life, he would unhesitatingly prefer the former. It is in this perhaps that Oxford and Cambridge have differed most decisively from Berlin or Tübingen. To live in college and so to be thrown together with others who come from different regions and different types of home, with different temperaments and interests and subjects of study, is a continuous exercise in mutual understanding and adjustment. Meeting one another in Hall, in Chapel, in Common or Combination Room, on the river or playing fields, and most of all in their own rooms, they acquire insensibly some appreciation of points of view other than their own, and some power of living and dealing with other people. The outside world has dimly sensed this. It has not enquired minutely what course the Oxford or Cambridge graduate has taken or even what class in an Honour School he has gained. It has been content to feel that, by the very fact of his residence in the university during his undergraduate years, he has undergone a peculiarly enriching type of experience.

Of course it is not simply by being communities that Oxford and Cambridge have exercised their educative influence. It is because they are communities which possess an extremely distinctive and inspiring, historic tradition. Their 'atmosphere' is the result of many centuries of corporate life. To wander among green lawns and stately buildings of crumbling grey stone or mellow red brick—such as the garden front of St. John's College, Oxford or the street front of St. John's College, Cambridge—to dine in Hall with its walls lined with the portraits of great men and its tables loaded with old silver, and to take part in the time-honoured ritual of university ceremonies—all these have made the undergraduate feel himself the citizen of no mean city and the inheritor of an illustrious tradition. They have conduced to expansion and elevation of mind and to that 'energy of the soul' in which Aristotle found the essence of true well-being.

In this tradition one of the most pervasive and characteristic ingredients has been religion. For far the greater part of their history, Oxford and Cambridge have deliberately set themselves to be 'places of religious and useful learning.' The two universities and their colleges were originally religious foundations and manifold traces of this origin still persist. Every college has its chapel, in which in term time there are daily and weekly services. The universities have their 'University Churches,' to which the dignitaries go weekly in state. But behind these expressly religious activities, the whole genius of the place and the view of man and of the world which it has, half-unconsciously, disseminated have been Christian. Even small things like the formula for the conferment of degrees or the saying of grace in Hall have borne witness to this. Much of it, no doubt, is conventional and very unlike the New Testament. Signs of any strong wind of the spirit have been rare. The Christianity which the ordinary undergraduate drank in was extremely diluted. Yet, such as it was, the atmosphere of the place was impregnated with it. Anyone going from Oxford or Cambridge to a modern and thoroughly secularized university must at once be conscious of the difference. Till quite lately the ancient universities have in this respect been in tune with the temper of our national life. Less than a hundred years ago it was possible for Newman to appeal confidently to the self-evident fact that belief in God was 'the secret assumption, too axiomatic to be distinctly professed, of all our writers.'[10] Only too obviously that situation has changed. But, until comparatively recent times, the work and recreation and common life of Oxford and Cambridge, however little directly religious, have been carried on within the setting of an ultimate Christian commitment.

At their best the older English universities have admittedly had success in turning out men fit to exercise responsibility, and this is no easy task. Some years ago one who carried large responsibilities in connection with appointments in the public service said, 'I can get any number of men with "First Classes," but what I want and find it hard to get, is "round" men.' To produce 'round' men, in his sense of the word, is exactly what the older universities, through their traditional mental discipline, based on classics and mathematics, set themselves to do. What they have cultivated and valued most highly is neither technical expertise nor prodigious learning but, as Newman puts it, the quality of judgment or the power to grapple with any subject and to seize the strong point in it. This, he says, is 'the education which gives a man a clear, conscious view of his own opinions and judgments, a truth in developing them, an eloquence in expressing them, and a force in urging them. It teaches him to see things as they are, to go right to the point, to disentangle a skein of thought, to detect what is sophistical, and to discard what is irrelevant. It prepares him to fill any post with credit, and to master any subject with facility. It shows him how to accommodate himself to others, how to throw himself into their state of mind, how to bring before them his own, how to come to an understanding with them, how to bear with them.'[11] In the same vein the authors of the recent Harvard Report on *General Education in a Free Society* define 'the abilities to be sought above all others in a general education,' as being 'to think effectively, to communicate thought, to make relevant judgments, to discriminate among values.'[12] In so doing, they echo Newman and imply that the qualities at which Oxford and Cambridge aimed in the middle of the nineteenth century are still of major importance in the middle of the twentieth. The fine flower of such training has been seen in men such as Balfour and Baldwin, Asquith and Milner, Curzon and Lang; and perhaps most of all in Gladstone, of whom it was truly said in a recent broadcast that he 'habitually lived from day to day in communion with the highest peaks of the human spirit' and, from that, derived much of his strength. Naturally the average product fell far behind such outstanding figures. But this is the type which Oxford and Cambridge endeavoured to foster and, with the better of their alumni, did in some measure achieve.

2 Liberal

Even in Oxford and Cambridge the traditional ideal has been largely displaced by a newer one. In the other universities of this country, as in Scotland, Germany and the United States, the triumph of the new ideal has been complete. It has been reached by giving a still stronger emphasis to some features in the Christian-Hellenic conception and by the total omission of others. Its own most salient traits are the following.

First, investigation matters more than instruction. The advancement rather than the communication—or, as some critics unkindly put it, the embalmment —of knowledge is the primary business of the university. The former is essential, the latter only incidental. It has been well said that Socrates, Plato and Aristotle were resorted to, not because they had made teaching their business, but because they were believed to have made philosophy their business. It is indeed a reproach to the British universities that, till comparatively recently, the great figures in our intellectual history have worked outside and not within them. This is true among philosophers of Hume, Bentham, Mill and Spencer; among historians of Gibbon, Hallam, Grote and Macaulay; and among scientists of Dalton, Davy, Faraday and Darwin. In Germany,on the other hand, Kant and Hegel, Niebuhr, Ranke and Mommsen, Jhering and Savigny, Liebig, Helmholtz and Virchow were all university professors; and so they incurred less danger of a certain amateurishness, wastefulness and freakishness, which is liable to come from isolation. Moreover the quality of the education itself is greatly heightened by its linkage with the great masters. From such a man, 'if he have also in any measure the special gifts of a teacher, all will come forth with a life and love, a power, fullness and freshness, which you will look for in vain from the man whose main business is to communicate, and not to possess something worth communicating.'[13]

Secondly, learning for learning's sake is the proper business of the university. This is a worthy, satisfying, and wholly self-justifying activity. As President Eliot of Harvard put it at the outset of his forty years' reign, the dominating idea should be 'the enthusiastic study of subjects for the love of them and without any ulterior motive.'[14] The savant's is a high calling. Like the poet,

> He lives detachéd days
> He serveth not for praise
> For gold
> He is not sold.

Alike in Germany and in Scotland this is recognized and he receives something of the esteem which the Indian villagers felt for Kipling's *Lama*. Here is implied an austere ideal of knowledge and a new type of scholar. In one of his books E. F. Benson, writing of Cambridge as it was sixty years ago, draws a vivid contrast between Walter Headlam and the ordinary college tutor. The ordinary classical tutor was widely read and an accomplished writer of elegant compositions; but his knowledge, though more extensive, was essentially of the same order as that of the better among his pupils. But 'Walter Headlam's knowledge of Greek began where theirs left off.' Now such mastery involves concentration and specialization. 'A man who is not capable of, so to speak, putting on blinkers, and of working himself up into the idea that the fate of his soul depends on whether, shall we say, his conjecture about this particular passage in a manuscript is correct—then that man had better keep away from scholarship.'[15]

Thirdly the function of the University as a community of science and learning is quite distinct from that of Church or State or of commerce and industry, and it should never be subservient to them. It has its own business which it understands better than any outsider can do. Its proper task is to promote neither money-making, nor good citizenship nor holiness, but simply sound learning. So, Dr. Doerne argues,[16] the duty of the university is not to make but to interpret history, not to produce leaders of Germany but to be the guardians of pure knowledge in a time of fanaticism. So far as training goes, it is the training of the graduate rather than of the undergraduate that is the university's primary concern. A master and his disciples were the nucleus out of which the earliest universities grew. So Socrates trained Plato and Plato trained Aristotle; the training of Alcibiades or Critias for public life was, by comparison, incidental and secondary. In terms of American organization, the 'college' is only a kind of junior department; the 'university' proper consists of its graduate schools. On this view Oxford and Cambridge in the nineteenth century contrasted unfavourably with the German universities, since a hundred years ago they trained graduates hardly at all, and fifty years ago only to a small extent. They might indeed be regarded as finishing schools rather than universities, and Paulsen's irony is thinly veiled when he writes of them, 'The general aim is to give a gentleman that broader and deeper culture with which custom demands that he should be equipped.'[17] Things are very different now. Even apart from the genuine researcher, the engineer or works manager who had come anywhere near Rutherford in Cambridge, the civil servant or business man who had come near Tout in Manchester, was often raised to a higher plane of intellectual life. As Paulsen wrote of the German situation at an earlier day, 'Though only a limited number of students succeed in doing original scientific work, yet the majority have at some time or other been seized with the impulse to seek after the truth. This longing remains in the souls of many, they become permanently interested in science and scientific life. Even in their callings they regard themselves as parts of the academic world; the teacher in the gymnasium, the clergyman, the physician, the judge, all seek to keep in touch with science, and not a few succeed not merely in following the stand-ard of science as sympathisers and sharers in its glories, but in serving under it, here and there, as active co-workers.'[18]

Fourthly, the academic thinker must have a completely open field and he should approach it with a mind free from antecedent bias or presupposition. For him all questions are open, all assumptions tentative, all conclusions provisional. There is no fixed framework of thought within which he must operate, no authoritative premises which must be the starting point of his reasoning and which it would be impious to question. He may and must follow the argument whithersoever it leads. 'For the academic teacher and his hearers there can be no prescribed and no proscribed thoughts.'[19] Each science is autonomous. In particular it must be free from all religious supervision. Neither the historian nor the physicist need look nervously over his shoulder to see what the theologian has to say of his hypothesis. The Darwinian theory, or any suggested modification of it, must be dis-cussed on the basis of the scientific evidence and judged by biological canons. The discussion must not be cramped or bedevilled by any pressure to accommodate it to the Book of Genesis. *Lehrfreiheit* is sacred and every kind of 'test' is inadmissible. In the words of President Eliot, 'The worthy fruit of academic culture is an open mind, trained to careful thinking, instr-ucted in the methods of philosophic investigation, acquainted in a general way with the accumulated thought of past generations, and penetrated with humility.'[20]

Fifthly, the university must cultivate detachment. It must keep itself clear of matters of current practical controversy in fields, such as the political or the religious, which excite passion. The heat and turbidity and partisanship which these engender are incompatible with the objectivity and serenity inherent in a scientific attitude. A university is a 'thought-organization' not a 'will-organization,' and its aim is understanding rather than action. It is a society for the pursuit of knowledge and not for the promotion of this cause or the prevention of that abuse. The only fanaticism permissible is 'the fanaticism of veracity.'

No doubt this emphasis is due to long experience of the distorting influence of the *odium theologicum* on the one hand and of 'reasons of state' on the other. The moral has been drawn in two, slightly different, ways. Some modern universities have played for safety by excluding altogether from their purview the fields in which controversies are most liable to arise. Others, without such drastic self-mutilation, have insisted that their treatment, e.g., of religious or political issues, must be in quite a different temper and perspective from that of those engaged in the hurly-burly. This difference is very clearly expressed by Matthew Arnold in his essay on 'The Function of Criticism at the Present Time.' There he deprecates the tendency of the young and ardent to see everything in inseparable connection with politics and practical life, and he asserts the value of criticism which is disinterested in the sense that the critic has no axe to grind, however altruistic. True criticism, he says, requires a free play of mind, and writing eighty years ago, he found it existing in France, in the *Revue des Deux Mondes.* But by contrast in England—'we have the *Edinburgh Review,* existing as an organ of the old Whigs, and for as much play of mind as may suit its being that; we have the *Quarterly Review,* existing as an organ of the Tories, and for as much play of mind as may suit its being that; we have the *British Quarterly* existing as an organ of the political Dissenters and for as much play of mind as may suit its being that, we have the *Times,* existing as the organ of the common satisfied, well-to-do Englishman, and for as much play of mind as may suit its being that.'[21] The disinterestedness and free play of mind which Arnold here requires of the critic are precisely the characteristics which, on the Liberal conception, should mark contributions from the universities to the discussion of major issues.

This view is expressed very clearly by Paulsen writing at the turn of the century and by Dr. Flexner thirty years later. 'The scholars' says Paulsen 'cannot and should not engage in politics.' This is because some of the qualities required in the thinker are the opposite of those which the practical politician should possess. The latter must be a man of resolute will and even a certain one-sidedness, who having chosen one path, follows it without *arrière pensée.* The thinker must look at a question from all sides and must constantly return to his starting point to make sure that no error has crept into the argument though, in action, this would produce some indecisiveness.[22] Dr. Flexner makes the same point. It is for the university to apply 'free, resourceful, unhampered intelligence to the comprehension of problems,' but it must preserve its 'irresponsibility.' By this of course he does not mean that the university is irresponsible absolutely; any theoretical advance in the field of the social sciences is likely to have practical repercussions. But immediate short-term applications are not its business: to concern itself with these would deflect it from its proper work. The professor 'has no practical responsibility for the trouble he makes . . . But he must go on thinking.'[23]

Sixthly, the university should be highly selective and even fastidious in regard both to the subjects it treats and the methods it employs. It should abhor mediocrity: its business is with an intellectual aristocracy. Energy can too easily and insidiously be dissipated in a multiplicity of interests. The university should therefore look critically at all new claimants for the provision of professional training. (Here Dr. Flexner's devastating criticism of the lengths to which some American universities have allowed the 'service-station' conception of their function to carry them is much in point.) The criterion to be employed is not the social importance of the proposed faculty or subject but its inherent and intellectual value. It is only the 'learned professions' or those that have intellectual content in their own right[24] with which the universities should concern themselves. So also they should eschew all that is half-baked or concerned with the shop-window. The public opinion to which the professor is rightly sensitive is that of his peers,

> Like Verdi when at his worst opera's end,
> He looks through all the roaring and the wreaths
> Where sits Rossini patient in his stall.

Seventhly, in the university there should be plenty of elbow-room. It should not be rigidly organized or regimented. Members of its staff should have the greatest possible freedom of choice in regard to what they are to teach, and how, and when. A great deal of wastage can and should be tolerated, so long as a congenial atmosphere is provided for a Mommsen or a Rutherford.

Finally, the liberty, initiative and adult status of the student are strongly emphasized. To the *Lehrfreiheit* of the teacher corresponds the *Lernfreiheit* of the student. The extreme example of this is the 'elective system' as it has flourished in the United States. This represents a violent reaction against the rigid curricula of earlier days. It is based on the principle that at all points the decision what to study and how hard to study should be made by, and not for, the student himself. His menu is to be 'à la carte'; or, as Professor Morison says of President Eliot, 'he wished every man's curriculum to be tailor-made.'[25] The curriculum is to be fitted to the student and not the student to the curriculum. It matters little what you study, provided you are interested. So it is for the university to offer the widest possible variety of choice. At one time in Harvard, 'the Bachelor's degree could be earned by passing eighteen courses, no two of which need be related.'[26] Similarly it is the student's own affair whether he works or idles. No official pressure should be put on him; that is appropriate only at the schoolboy stage. The university is not a kindergarten. Admittedly such liberty may, and in some cases will, be abused, but that is part of the price of freedom. Again, if the student is to be regarded as an adult, his morals are his own affair. They are outside the cognizance and jurisdiction of the university. It is a part of his education that he should himself bear this responsibility. At the student stage it is true, as never before or after, that 'the student belongs to himself, he is responsible to nobody and for nobody but himself.'[27] As Dr. Flexner has it, 'one wonders, not whether character and manners are unimportant, but whether, like cleanliness or clear speech, they may not now more or less be taken for granted.'[28] Accordingly the traditional, pastoral function and obligations of the staff are repudiated. The professor has an objective responsibility for his subject but not a parental responsibility for his students. Such an office as that of a 'moral tutor' is misconceived.[29]

The original source of this 'Liberal' conception was the French 'Enlightenment'; and, through such a man as Jefferson, this had some direct influence on the American universities. In Great Britain the change was somewhat delayed through antipathy to the Revolution. Here, as in America during most of the nineteenth century, the operative influence was the achievement and prestige of the German universities. This is seen in Sir William Hamilton's slashing *Edinburgh Review* attacks on Oxford in the early thirties and a generation later, in two almost simultaneous publications, Mark Pattison's *Suggestions for Academical Reorganization* and Matthew Arnold's *Schools and Universities on the Continent*. A generation later again it found a persuasive missionary in Lord Haldane. Even to-day this is probably 'the idea of the university' to which most academic people would subscribe. It is true that, under the surface, it is in process of being eaten away by newer forces, and it is no longer even the avowed creed of many of the younger men. Here, as in so many other fields, the twilight of liberalism seems to have set in. But a spirited note of recall to its ideals is sounded in such books as Flexner's *Universities, American, English, German*, and the various writings of the author who styles himself 'Bruce Truscot.'

3 Technological and democratic

Since the heyday of Liberalism new influences have been at work, and have acquired an enormous, and for many purposes a dominating, importance. These are the rise of applied science and technology and the growing democratization of the universities. For the moment it is the former with which we are concerned.

It is hard to exaggerate the significance for the universities of the growth and achievements of applied science. It is not merely that the balance of studies has been altered and that large sections of staff and students are now engaged in training as engineers or in the many large-scale applications of chemistry which in the old days hardly existed and certainly found no place in a university curriculum. Far more crucial is the fact that it is just in these fields that the universities are genuinely in touch with 'culture,' understood as the system of vital ideas of the age.[30] It is just here that they treat of what is of living interest to the world outside and to the mass of students themselves before they enter, and after they quit, the universities. It is this scientific culture that determines the categories in which people normally and naturally think. It determines also the issues which challenge their interest and attention, and to which they will really apply their minds because they readily see the point. For example the average schoolboy is familiar with, and keenly interested in, the mechanism of a motor bicycle, far more than in the story of human behaviour told in history or literature. It is such things as this which come alive to him and give him 'the pungent sense of effective reality.' It is by them that his mind is formed. In this way, within the universities as outside, the intellectual climate has been, insensibly but radically, altered.

Such studies are distinctive both in their aim and in their methods. Their aim is predominantly practical and utilitarian; it is conquest of nature for the satisfaction of human needs. The ends pursued are not mysterious, high-flown or elusive, but plain, practical, earthy and popular. It is these rather than theoretical curiosity which give the drive behind scientific discovery and invention. As Francis Bacon expressed it, its aim is 'fruit'; it abhors sterile argumentation. It endeavours, not to storm the sky but to minister to human convenience, or, in Macaulay's words, 'not to make men perfect but to make imperfect human beings comfortable.' It seeks to overcome admitted evils such as hunger and cold, disease and death. Its hero, or archetypal figure, is the man who makes two blades of grass grow where one grew before. Naturally this entails a sharp change in the valuation of handwork and bookwork. Traditionally handwork was looked down on as plebeian and 'banausic,' but now the technician is exalted and the mechanic becomes the truly representative man. Even the small change of the new culture consists of gadgets rather than of phrases.

But it is in its methods that the new culture is most distinctive, that is in the general lines on which problems are tackled. First it is empirical. It relies on observation and experiment rather than on general reasoning; it asks what actually is rather than what ought to be or what must be. The scientist is distrustful of authority and endeavours to put himself in the way of stubbing his toe on a fact. 'Hippocrates may say what he likes, but the coachman is dead.' He is chary of appealing to first principles or to intuition. He deals less in axioms than in provisional hypotheses, very tentatively held and readily modified or abandoned in face of new evidence. He lays immense stress on verification and reaches anything like firm conclusions only from thoroughly tested data. In the words of the Harvard Report, he is 'tough-minded, curious and ready for change.' Education on this pattern has a mental discipline of its own, different from that engendered by Latin prose or by Euclid but, in its way, quite as real. It enjoins submission to fact in despite of all preconceptions and predilections.

Secondly it is analytic. In order to bring things to the test of experiment, it endeavours to break up what is composite into its simple elements which can be isolated and controlled. A motorbicycle which can be taken to pieces and put together again or a machine-gun which can be stripped and re-assembled are the kinds of entity with which it can deal most successfully. It requires clarity and precision, and it steers clear of all that is cloudy, grandiose and emotionally coloured.

Thirdly it is deliberately selective. It discriminates between those fields and methods which promise practical results and those which do not. The things with which it has learned that it can deal are those that admit of being measured and weighed and counted and where the results of enquiry can be represented in graphs and statistical tables. It is by such discrimina-tion that it has progressed beyond the pretentious futilities of the alchemist and the astrologer. It turns its attention away from issues where enquiry is likely to be fruitless because the conditions of testing do not exist.

From such aims and methods there results a prevailing mental attitude which is at once activist and optimistic. The unparalleled increase in human power over environment, which the new knowledge has produced, has stimu-lated a strong drive for the removal of preventible evils, coupled with a recognition that a large part of those evils hitherto regarded as inevitable is in fact preventible. Many years ago Sir Alfred Zimmern drew attention to this change.[31] He observed that the women of Galilee and of Attica con-tinued as a matter of course, generation after generation, the old accustomed methods of 'grinding at the mill,' whereas no intelligent Lancashire mill-girl would tolerate them for many months without some attempt to find labour-saving devices. Resignation ceases to be a virtue and becomes a vice. One of Stevenson's fables, 'The Penitent,' well illustrates this change.

'A man met a lad weeping. "What do you weep for?" he asked.

"I am weeping for my sins," said the lad.

"You must have little to do," said the man.

The next day they met again. Once more the lad was weeping.

"Why do you weep now?" asked the man.

"I am weeping because I have nothing to eat," said the lad.

"I thought it would come to that," said the man.'

To a much larger extent than the subjects previously studied in univer-sities, the applied sciences require large-scale organization, for they often depend on bulky and expensive equipment and involve the co-operation of large numbers of workers. There is less scope for the free-lance, going his own way at his own time and purely on his own initiative. At present the back-wardness of the social sciences is in marked contrast with the triumphs of the natural sciences, and the demand is growing for the application to social problems of the methods which have succeeded so well in the other field.

Of course what here concerns us is to understand, not the aims and methods of scientists in themselves, but those elements in them which have entered deeply into contemporary culture and thus are affecting the minds of university teachers generally and still more of students. Three of these are particularly significant. The first is the concentration of interest. "To an amazing extent people's environment has come to consist of machines and man-made things.'[32] Beside the invention of the combustion engine, the discovery of insulin or penicillin, the splitting of the atom, with their obvious and stupendous consequences for human welfare, such pursuits as literary criticism, philosophical speculation or historical research are apt to seem secondary, remote and ineffectual. Secondly there is a new, and almost intoxicating, sense of power.

> Why then? The world's mine oyster
> Which I with sword will open.

To many the Russian experiment is a symbol and a pledge of the possibilities of social engineering. To a wholly unprecedented degree, men can and will determine their own destiny. Thirdly the colossal achievements of applied science have engendered a strongly optimistic temper. Professor Bernal goes so far as to enumerate among the major tasks to be undertaken the ultimate conquest of space, of disease, and death. 'Salvation by the acquisition and application of knowledge' seems on the way to becoming the religion of modern man.

The stream of influence derived from technological preoccupations coalesces with another. This springs from the change in the clientèle from which students, and in a rather lesser degree staff, are drawn. In the nineteenth century Oxford and Cambridge were predominantly upper-class institutions. The great majority of undergraduates were sons, not indeed of noblemen or plutocrats but, of the better-to-do professional men, country parsons, etc. They and their teachers shared a common social and cultural background. In their homes were space, books, a certain modicum of leisure and of intellectual interest. Their destiny was politics, the higher ranks of the Civil Service, the Bar, the Church, or the life of a country gentleman and landowner. The students of German universities were commonly drawn from a somewhat lower social stratum. But, there too, hardly any were of working-class origin, and in a broad sense, they expected to enter the ruling class of society.[33] To-day a large proportion of the students at modern universities in this country, and a substantial proportion at Oxford and Cambridge, come from working and lower middle-class homes, and have begun their education in the public elementary schools. To-morrow this change is likely to be carried a good deal further still; for one of the chief motive-forces in education to-day is a determination, based on a new sense of social justice, to achieve a far greater measure of equality of opportunity.

For large numbers of students to-day, to get to the university at all is a hardly-won achievement and by no means a matter of course. They are therefore more highly selected than their predecessors in the sense that they have been subjected to more exacting tests. On the average they certainly know more and they probably have more intellectual ability. Potentially therefore they are better material. On the other hand they are apt to suffer from handicaps which we have not yet found the way fully to overcome. They have not the background of culture which could once be assumed and often lack interest outside their prescribed subject. They have, as it were, been conducted over a prescribed route by forced marches, which leave them tired and with small inclination or energy for exploring by-roads, and so too often they have little initiative or resilience. At the same time their aim is utilitarian. To them the university is, first and foremost, the avenue to a desirable job, that is to one which promises some measure of economic security and social consideration. Success in examinations is therefore of dominating importance. The gay and carefree atmosphere and the absence of pressing material preoccupations which gave so much of its distinctive character to university life is disappearing. 'Redbrick' University has always been, and 'Oxbridge' is fast becoming, the university of the busy.

These changes in the provenance and character of their students naturally affect the universities' own aims and methods. They call in question older ideals, whether christian-hellenic or liberal. For instance the demands of equity challenge the cult of those particular excellences which have been associated either with Oxford or with Heidelberg, on the ground that they are essentially aristocratic and sacrifice the many to the few. Questions such as the following are asked. Should not universities cease to concentrate on the training of the ruling classes or of *Gelehrte,* i.e., either of a political or an intellectual aristocracy? Should they not think more of furnishing recruits for the middle-grades of business and industry? Does not the absence of regulation, the suffering the average student to be idle provided that the outstanding student gets the maximum stimulus, involve an unjustifiable sacrifice of the many to the few? However attractive the products, are they not hothouse plants? Does not the whole system presuppose in the student a background of culture such as is impossible without a high degree of economic privilege? Is not disdain for the bread-and-butter motive a luxury of the well-to-do? Formerly the universities were avowedly intended to buttress the existing social order; but was not their error, not as liberals would hold in attachment to any particular social order, but simply in attachment to the wrong one? In a democratic age ought they not to be engines of a beneficent social revolution? Should they not help to effect the transfer of power and of the chief right to consideration from the classes to the masses? Is not this indeed what the abler and more altruistic students, those who are leaders in bodies such as the National Union of Students, do in fact demand? In the war the universities directed all their resources to furthering the national cause; and in an age which is setting itself to achieve a juster social order, should they not repudiate the cult of aloofness and neutrality, and deliberately adopt a democratic orientation?

Within the universities as without, these two influences, the technological and the proletarian, are in course of producing a new culture; and this differs sharply from that in which universities originally were nourished and took their shape. It condemns liberalism as being aristocratic and fastidious rather than equalitarian, detached rather than 'mucking in,' and as exalting a sterile scholarship rather than being frankly occupational and utilitarian. It regards 'learning for learning's sake' as an idol to be demolished. In its light the Renaissance humanist is as little a model as the medieval schoolman, Dr. Gilbert Murray and Mr. 'Bruce Truscot' are out of date equally with Cardinal Newman and Dr. Whewell. As yet this new culture is articulate only in some of the younger teachers (e.g. the Association of Scientific Workers) and of the leading students (e.g. the National Union of Students). But, under the surface and only half-consciously, it is widely diffused. There is thus a widening gulf between the official and traditional professions of the universities and what, for large and growing sections of them, are the actually operative motives and beliefs. And here time seems to be on the side of the rebels, for it is they who are in tune with the movement of ideas in the contemporary world. To adapt a simile used by Gierke in a different connection, we may say, 'Within the liberal husk we see a scientific-utilitarian kernel. Always waxing, it draws away all vital nutriment from the shell and in the end that shell is likely to be broken.'

Notes

1 Whewell, *On The Principles of English University Education*, p. 34.
2 Newman, *op. cit.* p. 167.
3 *ibid*, p. 173.
4 *ibid*, p. 113.
5 *ibid*, p. 101.
6 *Op. cit.*, pp. 127–8.
7 Newman, *op. cit.*, p. 145.
8 *ibid.*, p. 135.
9 Whewell, *op. cit.*, p. 79.
10 *Op. cit.*, p. 68.
11 *Op. cit.*, p. 168.
12 *Op. cit.*, p 65.
13 Scott, *Introductory Lecture on the opening of Owen's College, Manchester*, p. 22.
14 Morison, *Three Centuries of Harvard*, p. 328.
15 Max Weber, quoted by Stirk in *German Universities through English Eyes*, p. 33.
16 'Problems of the German University' in *The University in a Changing World*, 1932.
17 *The German Universities and University Study*, E.T., p. 1.
18 *Op. cit.*, p. 169.
19 Paulsen, *op. cit.*, p. 228.
20 Morison, *op. cit.*, p. 330.

21 *Essays in Criticism*, p. 19.
22 *Op. cit.*, p. 55.
23 *Universities, American, English, German*, p. 22.
24 Hutchins, *The Higher Learning in America*, p. 56.
25 *Op. cit.*, p. 343.
26 *Op. cit.*, p. 346.
27 Paulsen, *op. cit.*, p. 266.
28 *ibid.*, p. 224.
29 These principles have been carried to a much less extreme point in Great Britain than in the United States and in Germany. Certain combinations of subjects have generally been prescribed, and the idler who passes no examinations is not allowed to prolong his stay indefinitely. Even in the United States the elective system has been modified.
30 See Ortega, *op. cit.*, p. 44.
31 *The Greek Commonwealth*, p. 218.
32 *General Education in a Free Society*, p. 15.
33 *cf.* Paulsen, *op. cit.*, pp. 126–7, 265.

40

Excerpt from
THE UNIVERSITIES
IN TRANSITION

H. C. Dent

Source: H. C. Dent, *The Universities in Transition*, London: Cohen and West, 1961, pp. 15–28.

PAST

Chapter one

1

*As the darker ages passed away, and men's thoughts turned to learning
once again, searching for a rule of right even in days of violent wrong-
doing, searching for reasons to satisfy the doubter even in days when
authority and dogma were supreme, the power of the teacher, never
altogether lost, revived. Students gathered with strange enthusiasm,
and if the records may be trusted, in surprising numbers, wherever
famous teachers made a school, travelling up from lonely districts,
voyaging from distant countries, amid the daily perils of mediaeval life.
The chief of these resorts sprang into European fame.* – SIR CHARLES
MALLET.[1]

The first two centres of learning in Europe to take the shape of universities
were both in Italy: at Salerno in the south and Bologna in the north. The
former, which was well established, and highly reputed, by the middle of the
eleventh century, was a school of medicine. The latter, which rose to fame in
the early decades of the twelfth century, was a school of civil law. Neither of
these subjects was to be found in the curricula of the cathedral and monastery schools, at that time almost the sole purveyors of education; hence the
necessity to seek instruction in them elsewhere. The third university to emerge,
at Paris about 1150–70, had a different origin; it grew out of the cathedral

schools in the city, and attracted students by its teaching of philosophy and theology.

The fact that Salerno and Bologna were devoted exclusively to single fields of knowledge, and Paris in the first instance to no more than two, may serve to clear away at once a widespread misunderstanding about the function of a university. It is not, and never has been, to teach all subjects. A university is not, as has so often been incorrectly assumed, a place of universal knowledge. The word 'university' had, in fact, originally nothing whatever to do with subjects of study; it had to do with persons organised as a corporate body. It came to be attached to bodies of scholars because the students at Bologna (little is known about the organisation at Salerno), lacking the protective matrix of a cathedral or monastery, and being most of them strangers in a strange land, in an age when foreigners were by no means always welcome, and in any case were accorded no political or civic rights, felt impelled to band themselves together into a guild, or corporation, for mutual protection against robbery and violence, and in order to secure for themselves some corporate rights and privileges. There was nothing unusual in such action; all the skilled trades similarly banded themselves together for the same reasons. The current Latin term, used in all documents of incorporation, for any such guild or corporation, was *universitas vestra*, meaning simply 'all of you'.

Other universities followed the example of Bologna, and for some reason the name *universitas* became attached particularly to guilds of scholars. But it was not until the latter part of the fourteenth century that it was reserved exclusively to them. Before that, the term usually employed to designate a university was *studium generale*. Again, the name had at first no reference to the subjects taught. It had reference to the absence of restriction upon the localities whence students came. A *studium* was, quite simply, a place of study, a place where organised teaching and learning went on. (I avoid use of the word 'school', because today this invariably implies permanent buildings, whereas many *studia* had none.) If a *studium* became sufficiently well known and highly regarded to attract scholars from considerable distances it was referred to as a *studium universale*, or *studium commune*, or, most often, a *studium generale*.

At least, that was what happened in the case of the earliest universities. But it was not long after the emergence of Bologna and Paris (and Oxford in England) before there were many claimants to the title *studium generale*, some of them with but modest pretensions to higher learning; and consequently questions of status and of academic standards began to be matters of serious concern.

Bologna, and later Paris and Oxford, had become *studia generalia* by 'general recognition' (*ex consuetudine*, as the phrase was), that is, because scholars all over Christendom knew them to be places of learning of the highest rank. But early in the thirteenth century it began to be felt that certain conditions should be satisfied before the title of *studium generale* could be assumed: for example, that attendance should not be restricted to natives of any particular town or country; that the *studium* must teach not only the seven liberal arts but also at least one of the higher studies of law, medicine, and theology; and that it must have a sufficient, and sufficiently well qualified, staff. And it was felt that there must be some means of guaranteeing that such conditions were, in fact, satisfied.

The obvious means was the official sanction of an acknowledged public authority. By the end of the thirteenth century it had become accepted that the title of *studium generale* could be conferred upon an institution only by the Pope, the Emperor of the Holy Roman Empire, a king, or the municipal authority of a city republic. Even between these awards there was a crucial distinction; only the Pope and the Emperor had the power to confer upon a *studium generale* the right to grant the *ius ubique docendi*, that is, the right to grant degrees which entitled their holders, without further examination, to teach in any *studium generale*. Thus originated, six centuries ago, two conventions which, though modified in particulars, have in essence persisted to this day in the United Kingdom and many other countries. In our own country no university institution can be created save by Royal Charter, and the right to confer degrees is reserved exclusively to such chartered university institutions.

To earn the high distinction of being a Master of Arts, possessing the 'right to teach anywhere', the mediaeval student had to pursue a long and rigorous course of study, divided into two parts which together compassed all the seven liberal arts. These arts were arranged in two groups, the *Trivium* and the *Quadrivium*. Starting normally at about the age of fourteen the student, who had previously acquired a working knowledge of Latin, the universal language of scholarship throughout Christendom, applied himself for three years (or longer) to the subjects of the *Trivium:* grammar (the Latin language and literature), logic, and rhetoric. At the end of this period, if he emerged successfully from the public 'disputations' (academic arguments on set topics) which were the mediaeval equivalent of external examinations, he became an 'incepting' (*i.e.,* commencing) Bachelor of Arts, and could go on to the four-year course of the *Quadrivium*. The subjects in this were called arithmetic, geometry, music, and astronomy – though it is perhaps hardly necessary to say that the subject matter under each of these heads was vastly different from that which goes under the same name today. At the end of this course the Bachelor had again to undergo the ordeal by disputation; if he survived he became an 'incepting' Master, eligible to receive the degree of Master of Arts and the 'right to teach anywhere'. If he wished then to specialise, he could embark upon a course, lasting eight years or longer, leading to a doctorate in canon law (*i.e.,* ecclesiastical law), civil law, medicine, or theology. But he was not allowed to undertake any of these specialised studies until he had successfully completed the general 'arts' course; that was obligatory upon all students.

The story of how systems of government developed at the universities of Bologna and Paris must be sought elsewhere. But one point of extreme importance must be mentioned here before restricting this narrative to the English universities. At Bologna it was the students – many of them grown men, and lawyers with established practices – who formed themselves into a *universitas* or, to be strictly accurate, into several *universitates*. Bologna, therefore, developed as a *universitas scholarium*, a corporation of students, which employed and paid its teachers – and incidentally reduced them to a sorry state of subjection. But at Paris it was the teachers who banded themselves together, and so Paris became a *universitas magistrorum* – a very different type of institution. Oxford, and all subsequent British universities, copied the Paris model. It is intriguing to try to imagine what our universities would be like today had Oxford copied Bologna; they would certainly be quite unlike what they are!

2

. . . there grew up at Oxford a great school or Studium, which acquired something of the fame of Paris and Bologna. – R. S. RAIT.[2]

It is customary, and proper, to begin the story of the British universities with the birth of a *studium generale* at Oxford during the latter half of the twelfth century. But it is, I think, essential to realise that this birth did not occur fortuitously. To continue the metaphor, not only had the child living parents, but a home had been prepared and was standing ready to receive it. Moreover, this child, which was later to grow into something unique, was not in its infancy much unlike other children that had previously been born into the same family. In other words, the emergence of a *studium generale* at Oxford, epoch-making though it was to prove, was at the time of its occurrence no more than a particular development in a tradition of scholarly learning which had persisted in Britain for many centuries.

That tradition had been sustained and expressed in three principal ways. First, in monasteries, where individual scholars or groups of scholars engaged in a rudimentary form of what we now call research, studying and transcribing the Scriptures, and writing commentaries and other learned works. The best known, and the most illustrious, example is the monastery at Jarrow during the time when it was adorned by the Venerable Bede, but monasteries at Canterbury, Glastonbury, and Lindisfarne – to name but three – had also produced work of scholarly distinction. Secondly, in the Grammar schools which were established as integral parts of all cathedral and collegiate churches. At their best these were very much more than 'schools' in the sense that we understand the word today; they taught pupils of all ages, and covered in their curricula the greater part of the field of learning known to the Middle Ages. 'In the middle of the eighth century', wrote A. F. Leach many years ago, 'University and Grammar School were one';[3] and no one who has read Alcuin's famous, and oft-quoted, description of the programme of studies of the cathedral school at York under his predecessor Aethelbert (or Albert) can doubt the truth of that assertion.

> There he (Albert) moistened thirsty hearts with divers streams of teaching and varied dews of study; busily giving to some the arts of the science of grammar (*grammaticae rationis artes*), pouring into others the streams of the tongues of orators; these he polished on the whet-stone of law, those he taught to sing in Aeonian chant, making others play on the flute of Castaly, and run with the lyre over the hills of Parnassus. But others, the said master made to know the harmony of heaven and the sun, the labours of the moon, the five belts of the sky, the seven planets, the laws of the fixed stars, their rising and setting, the movements of the air and the sun, the earth's quake, the nature of men, cattle, birds and beasts, the different kinds of number and various (geometrical) figures: and he gave sure return to the festival of Easter; above all, revealing the mysteries of holy writ, for he opened the abysses of the old and rude law.[4]

Thirdly, a growth which arose apparently much later in time, there were the 'schools' which sprang up spontaneously in already established centres of learning when the fame of individual scholars of eminence drew thither students from distant parts, 'travelling up from lonely districts, voyaging from distant countries, amid the daily perils of mediaeval life', as Sir Charles Mallet put it. These spontaneous gatherings of scholars were the immediate progenitors of the earliest universities, for the 'daily perils' – by no means confined to travel – were among the strongest reasons which impelled scholars to form themselves into self-protective and self-assertive guilds, after the fashion of the times. But the contributions made by the other two forms of organised learning and teaching to the idea of a university, as distinct from its organisation, should be neither overlooked nor underestimated, for they have remained among its essential elements. The monastic cell handed on the tradition and techniques of research, the Grammar school those of systematic teaching on a prescribed syllabus. Moreover, the Grammar school, relinquishing any claim to be itself a university, has continued to this day to carry out the indispensable task of giving youth that sound elementary training in the academic disciplines without which no one can confidently embark upon university studies.

Many examples of all these three forms of higher learning were to be found in England in the twelfth century – a period of great intellectual activity throughout Europe. Most numerous, probably, were the cathedral and collegiate schools, some of which, as my colleague Professor W. H. G. Armytage has recorded in his invaluable book *Civic Universities*[5] (to which I am most greatly indebted), had so broadened and deepened their curricula that they approached nearly to the mediaeval concept of a *studium generale*. Exeter, Lincoln, St. Paul's in London, Hereford, Salisbury, and York all possessed schools of this calibre. Why, then, it may be asked, did England's first University arise at Oxford rather than at one of these or other centres of learning?

Until further evidence than has as yet been unearthed becomes available – and so industrious have scholars been that the possibility seems remote – all discussion of this fascinating question must be more than a little speculative. The reason now generally accepted why the monastic and other schools which had existed at Oxford since the early decades of the twelfth century quite suddenly expanded, in or about 1167, into a *studium generale* is that this was a direct consequence of the quarrel between Henry II and his Archbishop, Thomas à Becket. As one of his moves in that quarrel, about 1167 (the exact year is uncertain) the King issued ordinances forbidding English clerics to travel to and from the Continent without his express permission, and ordering all those abroad who held benefices in England, and wished to retain them, to return home within three months. More or less coincidentally Louis VII of France, no friend of Henry II at any time, and currently supporting Becket, issued an edict expelling all alien scholars from France. As most of the English clerics in France at the time were students or teachers at the University of Paris, the result of these two royal commands was a considerable exodus – how large is disputed – of English scholars from France.

Now comes the interesting sequel. Once in England, a great many (though probably not all) of these scholars seem to have made direct for Oxford. Why there, rather than to any other of the well-known centres of learning? So long as the evidence remains not entirely conclusive the temptation to speculate is almost overwhelming – and I shall not entirely resist it. But, first, the evidence, as adduced by recognised authorities. Oxford was readily accessible from all parts of the country, and no great distance from London, the capital. It was a flourishing market town, with good communications by road and river, and situated in a rich agricultural district; it could therefore be expected to be usually well stocked with supplies of food: no unimportant consideration in days when the threat of famine was never far distant. It was well known as a centre of learning; doubtless many of the immigrants had previously studied there. Finally, and perhaps decisively, it was a 'royal city', and not merely that, but one much beloved by the reigning monarch, who frequently resorted to his castle there. Consequently, a community of scholars lodged at Oxford might reasonably expect to enjoy the personal protection of a monarch known to be not only favourably disposed to learning but keenly aware of the practical advantages of having intellectuals at his side, and on his side.

It is at this point that I begin to speculate. The English clergy in general supported Henry in his quarrel with Becket, and Henry was far too astute a statesman to ignore the danger of losing their goodwill. The Paris scholars, all of whom were clerics, had been uprooted at his behest, and some of them, at least, might well be expected to resent having to move, and to harbour a grudge against the King for causing them to do so. Left to their own initiative the immigrants would have had to make individual arrangements for finding new places in which to teach and learn; and this would undoubtedly have involved much breaking up of schools and separation of friends. What more feasible than that Henry, in some way or another, 'guided' the steps of the immigrants towards Oxford, indicating that here was a city where all would find appropriate accommodation in congenial circumstances – and where, incidentally, he could count henceforth upon a solid phalanx of grateful, and valuable, adherents?

There is another possible speculation. Oxford was not a cathedral city, and therefore not the seat of a bishop. Scholars at Paris knew from experience how irksome to academic freedom a bishop – who had absolute control over all forms of education – could be. Did the thought of being remote from this over-riding authority (the bishop's seat was at Lincoln) make Oxford seem yet more attractive?

3

...the habit of gregarious migration characteristic of medieval scholars. – HASTINGS RASHDALL.[6]

Though the scholars went to Oxford, that was no guarantee they would remain there. Universities were in their early days extremely insecure and unstable bodies. They were liable to be suspended or closed down if they fell foul of high authority, be it regal or ecclesiastical; they tended to disperse, at least temporarily (they usually returned), when threatened by local peril or controversy; and they were perpetually subject to defections by disgruntled teachers or students, or as the result of internal strife. Migration, whether by the whole or part of a university, was easily effected, because for long (in the case of Oxford for a century) universities and their members owned little in the way of buildings or equipment.

All the foregoing eventualities except permanent closure occurred at Oxford. Among the many migrations three must be mentioned, because the first and third of these were followed by momentous consequences, and the second failed only by a narrow margin, and after a considerable period of time, to be equally important. In all three cases both royal and ecclesiastical authority played important parts; in two the former decided the issue.

173

Independence of Church and State was far from being a characteristic of the early universities.

The first migration, in 1209, gave birth to the University of Cambridge. At Oxford a student killed a townswoman. He could not be found, so the town authorities arrested his fellow lodgers, and sought authority from the King to hang them. John, his country under interdict by Pope Innocent III, and himself either excommunicate or threatened with excommunication, was in no mood to make more enemies. He agreed. Two – possibly three – students were hanged. The University, filled with alarm, at once took flight, its members scattering far and wide. Some, it is said, returned to Paris; others went to nearby Reading, where there was a Cluniac abbey, to Canterbury, Maidstone, and – no one seems to know quite why – to Cambridge. There must, one imagines, have been schools there which attracted them, but if so history has left no record of them. All that is known is that there had long been in Cambridge an Augustinian priory, and that in the surrounding fens, at no great distance from the town, stood the great monasteries of Anglesey, Croyland, Ely, and Ramsey.

Except that some 'profane masters' are said to have remained, and to have 'irreverently lectured', there was no university in Oxford for five years. Then, King John having sought and received pardon from the Pope, the University returned in triumph. Its re-entry into the city was heralded by an Ordinance from the Pope's Legate which imposed drastic penalties upon the civic authorities for their part in the 1209 affray (and punishments upon the 'profane masters') and conferred upon the University rights and privileges which, with others acquired later, eventually made it the supreme authority in the borough.

The second great migration, in 1238, was the result of even more direct royal intervention. Again, a killing was the initial cause, but this time it was of a Papal Legate's brother, in an unseemly brawl between students and the Legate's servants which took place at the monastery at Oseney near Oxford, where the Legate was spending the night. The Legate, not unnaturally, protested to the King. Henry III responded by promptly suspending the University, which equally promptly packed up and left Oxford. Some of the scholars went to Salisbury and some to Northampton; and though most returned before very long, some remained. Had the wheel of fortune turned only slightly farther in favour of Northampton and Salisbury both of these cities might today be the homes of universities almost as ancient as Oxford and Cambridge.

There was at Salisbury a very famous school of theology. With the accession of the immigrants from Oxford this expanded into something approaching a *studium generale;* and this appears to have maintained itself for some forty years. After that it declined, though Salisbury remained for centuries a seat of learning, possessing two colleges, of which one may have had academic connections with Oxford.

The *studium* at Northampton had a somewhat shorter but more exciting life. Scholars from Cambridge joined the Oxford migrants, and, apparently with the encouragement and support of King Henry III, university studies proceeded steadily for nearly a quarter of a century. In 1261 there was a dramatic development. Following a serious disturbance at Cambridge, members of that university joined with Oxford migrants in petitioning the King to grant a licence for the foundation of a university at Northampton. Henry III at first listened favourably, but later changed his mind. Shortly after he was overwhelmed by the troubles which culminated in his defeat by Simon de Montfort at Lewes in 1265. This event was quickly followed by the abrupt termination of the life of the *studium generale* at Northampton. For Simon took serious heed of the complaint of the university and town of Oxford that their joint interests were being threatened by the continued existence of the Northampton *studium*, and, with the support of the ecclesiastical authorities of the day, ordered the teachers and scholars at Northampton, in the King's name, to return to Oxford. Some apparently refused, and were joined three years later by more scholars from Cambridge. But it was of no avail. Oxford, supported by both Church and State, was too powerful. Any chance of a University of Northampton was at an end.

The third, and the last, of the great migrations from Oxford was to Stamford in 1338. The cause of this was entirely different from those of the previous two, being the result of dissension within the University. In all the early universities there had grown up the practice for the scholars to group themselves together in 'Nations', according, usually, to the countries whence they came. At Oxford (and at Cambridge) there were two Nations, the Northerners (*Boreales*) and the Southerners (*Australes*), whose members came respectively from north or south of the river Trent. Frequent and furious fights took place between the Nations. It was one of these which, developing into a battle involving the town as well as the University, had prompted the Cambridge petition in 1261 for a University at Northampton. It was another which caused the Northerners at Oxford, worsted in a bloody strife, to secede to Stamford.

Universities in those days rarely hesitated to seek the aid of Church or State if they thought they would benefit thereby. In this case both sides appealed to the King. The Southerners, wiser in their generation, wrote on behalf of the University not only to the King, but also to the Queen and to the diocesan bishop of Lincoln. Edward III took their side decisively; he did not wish, he wrote, 'that schools or studies should be kept elsewhere within our realm except in the places where Universities are now in some sense held . . .'[7] And he forbade the holding of a university anywhere else. But the Northerners refused to budge, though the King repeated his orders, and sent the Sheriff of Lincoln to Stamford to proclaim them in person. Finally, some twelve months after their migration, the Northerners had to be evicted by force.

The incident had consequences of extreme importance not only for the universities but also for the country. As has been stated above, in his orders to the Stamford 'rebels' Edward III made it clear that he would allow in his kingdom no universities but those at Oxford and Cambridge. As soon as Stamford had been closed Oxford took steps to make this statement of royal policy effective. The University issued Ordinances making it compulsory from then on upon all its incepting Masters of Arts to swear a solemn oath that they would neither study nor lecture at Stamford, 'as in a university, seat of learning, or general college'.

> *Tu iurabis quod non leges nec audies Stamfordiae tanquam in universitate studio aut collegio generali.*[8]

And 'so', says Professor Armytage, 'the door was finally closed on any further foundations of a university character outside Oxford and Cambridge'. It remained closed for nearly 500 years. Incredible though it may seem, Oxford continued to exact this oath from all its Masters until 1827. And, though several serious attempts were made, notably in the seventeenth century, to found other universities, and a number of institutions, including the Gresham College in London, established in 1596, and some at least of the eighteenth century Dissenting Academies, conducted studies at university level, no institution received a charter conferring upon it university status until 1829.

Whether or not this long-enduring Oxbridge monopoly was to the country's benefit is disputed. Professor Armytage thinks it was:[9]

> Thus, by the concentration of academic energies, England avoided the dilution which characterised other countries, and as a result Oxford and Cambridge established a tradition for national as opposed to regional scholarship which has only recently been challenged.

Dean Hastings Rashdall, in his monumental work on the mediaeval universities, took a precisely opposite view:

> It is impossible to doubt that the cause of learning in England has been injured by the paucity of its universities, or that the stagnation of Oxford and Cambridge at certain periods of their history has been aggravated by the total absence of competition.[10]

Where the authorities differ so violently I would not dare to venture an opinion. What is, however, incontrovertible is that the centuries of monopoly enabled Oxford and Cambridge to acquire such eminence and esteem as to render it virtually impossible for the emerging university institutions of the nineteenth century to be regarded as even potentially their equals, in status or in scholarship. And, though the nineteenth century university colleges have now all achieved, on their merits, full university rank, this problem remains with us still, some people think in an even more acutely difficult form than in the nineteenth century.

Notes

1 Sir Charles Mallet, *A History of the University of Oxford*, Methuen, 1924, Vol. I, p. 2.
2 *Life in the Medieval University*, Cambridge University Press, 1912, p. 6.
3 In *The Schools of Mediaeval England*, Methuen, 1915, p. 59.
4 Quoted from Leach, op. cit., pp. 58–9.
5 Benn, 1955. See pp. 31–4.
6 *The Universities of Europe in the Middle Ages*, edited by F. M. Powicke and A. B. Emden, Oxford University Press, 1936, Vol. III, p. 30.
7 Quoted from A. F. Leach, *Educational Charters and Documents 598 to 1909*, Cambridge University Press, 1911, p. 287.
8 Quoted from Mallet, op. cit., Vol. I, p. 157 n.
9 Op. cit., p. 45.
10 Op. cit., Vol. III, p. 90.

41

THE IDEA OF THE IDEA OF A UNIVERSITY AND ITS ANTITHESIS

Sheldon Rothblatt

Source: S. Rothblatt, *The Modern University and its Discontents*, Cambridge: Cambridge University Press, 1997, pp. 1–49.

Introduction: ideas of a university

The subject of this chapter is the history of the 'idea of a university', or rather, it is the history of the idea that a university derives its identity from an idea. The subject is puzzling. Why does a university require an 'idea'? Quite simply, it does not. The historical answer, however, is more interesting. Whether or not a university needs an 'idea', it has been assigned one, more than one, in fact. For two centuries a particular kind of debate has gone on, revived in every generation, concerning the role and purpose of a university and the education it provides. The debate has been inconclusive. Yet what is significant about the history of the idea of a university is the search for one, the striving after an ideal that must satisfy two conditions: it must be pure, like a platonic ideal, and it must be lasting, superior to all apparent transformations.

By 'idea', then, is meant an inherent purpose, embedded, as it were, into the university and possibly its history – but this is not always clear from debate. An 'idea' is also a genetic code that dictates the subsequent development of a university; but like all such inheritances, the signals are not always recognised.

Metaphors such as these come readily to mind, for the history of the idea of the idea of a university lacks precision. There is no clear linear development such as intellectual historians prefer, no Darwinian evolution from one idea to another. A single idea of a university has never truly existed, although in some periods fewer alternatives were available. There have been emphases. In approximately 800 years of history, the university as an institution has served many different cultures and societies. Its transmogrifica-tions are nearly as numerous as the historical changes occurring in western society; but because there appears to be continuity between past and present – costumes, rituals and ways of self-government and the organisation of studies seem recognisable – it is convenient to deduce that universities have always shared an essential element.

It is both natural and unnatural to discuss institutions as if they embody an abiding, single purpose that provides a compass for decision-making. It is natural because complex institutions are otherwise unmanageable, adrift and open to all competing pressures. But it is unnatural for precisely the same reason. Highly differentiated organisations can be limited to key objectives only if they are inherently stable and unchanging. Universities are neither, which is why discussions today are more likely to focus on 'chang-ing roles' and 'future challenges', categories that bypass the question of an institutional essence.[1] Yet any discussion of 'changing roles' inevitably invites a backward look. That look always encounters two stubborn traditions of idealising universities, the first English and the second German. Critics of universities appeal to both traditions. Those who believe universities are resistant to innovation point to bottlenecks created by the 'idea of a univer-sity'. Those who are saddened, or angered, by twentieth-century trends towards diversification and differentiation, appeal for help to the same source. This being the case, the history of a way of thinking about institutions is worth examining.

Quite probably those who live and work in universities, churches, govern-ments or corporations carry with them some everyday conception of institutional purpose. Intermixed with an obvious career interest is a refer-ence to a higher objective, often moral or at least elevating, self-justifying in some cases, but also uplifting. Ordinary occupational service is raised to a superior level. It is possible to speak about the idea of public service, the idea of corporate loyalty and cooperative effort, the idea of self-sacrifice and honour (as in military service), but few of these ideas, except for those associated with the history of religions, have as clear an historiography and available reference manual as do universities. The 'idea of a university' is a signature immediately recognisable.

A distinction can be made between 'idea' as a thing in itself and particular kinds of 'ideas'. For the sake of argument we might say that the idea of a university is education, but what kind should it be? Liberal, vocational, technical, research-related? Is the object culture, citizenship, leadership or career? Are the recipients young men, young men and women, 'mature' students, postgraduates? Do they attend full or part time? The idea of a university can be negative. A university is not the place for this or that purpose because it is the place for something else.

In the absence of an idea of a university, there would exist no reason to dispute its nature. A university would simply be another institution, changing as circumstances allow, assuming new identities as easily as actors on the stage, with no particular aggregate commitment to any of a large number of easily assumed roles. We cannot deny that this occurs often in the history of universities. It seems to be the situation today. But such continuities as universities enjoy, such aspirations as they have to be a moral force in modern society, or at least a unique voice, are attributable to the odd and special history of the idea of the idea of a university. Even when that idea can no longer be discerned, it remains an intrusion, a method for organising thoughts about the essential purpose of higher education. It is consequently both inspiring and mischievous. An idea can elevate routine life to a higher realm, transposing mere occupations into callings; but its seductions can also channel energy into what appears to be hackneyed and sterile debate.

'Idea' is a useful but elusive word. Ambidextrous, it is of Greek origin and ranges in meaning from 'thought', 'opinion' or 'belief' to 'scheme' and 'project'. It descends into murkier depths yet to find itself only an 'inkling'. In short, 'idea' rivals 'thing', to which Dr Samuel Johnson, in his celebrated *Dictionary*, gave priority of place as the 'vaguest of all words'. Yet no matter how hazy or imprecise, or possibly because it is genuinely flaccid, no other word in the English language has had a comparable influence on discussions of what a university is, could or ought to be. And although other institutions have from time to time also been examined for their underlying 'idea' – the idea of a national Church, the idea of the State, the idea of an intelligentsia – no one of them has inspired a literature that continually builds upon itself, repeats itself almost desperately and is itself an inextricable and living part of the institution to which it refers. Futhermore, the 'idea of a university' is not merely a method for analysing the basic functions or missions of a university as if their fundamental utility is simply a matter of going down a list. The 'idea' of a university is invariably, one might say inevitably, a moral one, so that departures from it, or modifications of it, are a form of betrayal to be repented or an act of treason to be punished. Thus Julien Benda, in an argument parallel to that used to discuss universities, invoked the idea of an intellectual when he denounced activist ideology as *traison* in his famous book on the betrayal of intellectuals.

We need to begin the history of the idea of the idea of a university with a summary of the different if overlapping ways in which the university as an institution has been both defined and typified:

1   according to its forms of internal governance, in which case it is often referred to as a self-governing guild or corporation of junior and senior members, or masters and students;
2   according to its broadest existing social characteristics or identifications, in which case it can be called, *inter alia*, aristocratic;
3   according to its principles of entry, which bear upon its funding and staffing ratios, in which case it is elitist, meritocratic, or mass-access or open;

4   according to its geographic location or outlook, so that it is civic or municipal, provincial, metropolitan, urban, suburban or exurban, local, regional or national;

5   according to its legal or constitutional status or principal source of financial support, in which case it is state-supported, or publicly maintained, or private or quasi-private (as in the case of Cornell University in New York State), although, being one or the other, it sometimes simulates its opposite in part or full, as Berkeley is said to behave like a private university or the inner-city Roman Catholic universities of America act like public institutions;

6   according to its missions or functions, such as graduate research, undergraduate or collegiate instruction, professional education, vocational training, or, more vaguely, 'service';

7   more recently, according to the educational tier or sector to which it belongs, whether, for example, it is an autonomous campus or a federal component of a larger system, linked in a number of different ways to a central administrative authority.

These are largely convenient bureaucratic or sociological descriptions, categories and organisational matrices. None of them evokes the majesty or nobility of universities as does the simple reference 'idea'. For that reason it is now necessary to trace the process by which the idea of a university having an idea first emerged and became a significant feature of university history.

Origins of the 'idea' of a university

Nothing can be known unless it has a name. According to a *midrashic* commentary on the Book of Genesis, Adam was commanded to name the plants and beasts in Eden to bring into the world an order subject to human speech and comprehensible to human agency. This was a primal act. Naming things, as naming demons, is necessary for exorcising them. Consequently it appears almost natural for us to speak about institutions as if they have a primal identity, or incorporate some essential truth, purpose or essence. In this way, institutions are hypostatised. They are assigned the power of thinking because they have an 'idea'.[2] Furthermore, the casualness with which institutions are assigned an identity and made to think disguises the point that what truly requires explanation is not just the idea that may lie at the back of an institution but the very idea of an institution having an idea. And precisely because one of the characteristics of ideas is the ease with which they are manipulated once abstracted from their original historical contexts, it is astonishingly simple to forget that the process of assigning an idea to an institution usually implies a pre-history.

The pre-history of the idea of an idea of a university properly begins in the English-speaking world with the writings of the philosopher Edmund

Burke. His principal successor is commonly and quite properly regarded as Samuel Taylor Coleridge, poet, littérateur, thinker and opium-eater. Burke is commonly associated with his denunciation of the French Revolution and those aspects of Enlightenment thought which he associated with revolution, but prior to 1789 he was a significant reformer and also a supporter of the 'English liberties' of American subjects of the Crown. After 1789 he saw his special problem as defending ancient institutions like the Church and ancient estates like the aristocracy but without at the same time becoming merely an apologist for inherited and illegitimate privilege. To do this Burke spoke more about the spirit of institutions, the spirit of religion, for example, or the religious idea of which the Church of England itself was merely an embodiment. For Coleridge, educated under the influence of Cambridge rationalism in the 1790s, against which he rebelled, and living on into the nineteenth century when the first major challenge to aristocratic leadership was being politically organised, the intellectual problem was similar: not to defend an older world against all criticism nor to forestall change, but to find a middle way that allowed for both continuity and reform. In practical terms this entailed finding an institutional structure that would be sufficiently independent to resist the inherent instability and unpredictability of social and economic change. This in turn led to a clear educational challenge, the desirability of educating leaders who would be able to steer between outmoded practices and passing fads and fancies.

The idea of an institution having an idea therefore came into being as a means of stabilising establishments at a revolutionary moment in European history, defending them against arguments that all existing institutions served narrow vested interests. The enemies were the advocates of revolutionary institutional change – Unitarian radicals, Paineites and Philosophical Radicals, the last being the followers of the Utilitarian philosopher, Jeremy Bentham, whose articulated but clothed skeleton surmounted by a wax head is still imprisoned in a cabinet outside the office of the Provost of University College London.

As a functionalist critique, Utilitarianism was a powerful ally of radicals and detractors. For Utilitarians, the test of any institution's worth was whether it served the general interest or satisfied public opinion, conditions illustrated by the successful overthrow of imperial rule in North America. Neither Burke nor Coleridge could accept Utilitarianism as a philosophical justification for change. Neither believed with the Benthamites that the measure of the success of an institution was whether it provided happiness for the greatest number of people or met some criterion of the general interest. Yet both were utilitarians in another sense, in that they believed that institutions were and had to be functional, and therefore could be dysfunctional, and, if so, needed to be changed and reformed. For Burke, the basis upon which reform could be undertaken was not in reference to some abstract eighteenth-century theory, such as natural rights, or the happiness of the

generality of mankind, but rather in relation to something far more fundamental and, we might say, anthropological, which he called human wants or
needs – the need to be loved, the need to be sheltered, the need for security.
Reform was clearly not revolution, since it was not necessary to demolish
an institution in order to make it functional. For Romantics like Burke
and Coleridge – for now we must label them as such – Utilitarianism was
willy-nilly change. The 'general interest', 'public opinion', 'happiness' were
crude terms, and no more firmly established as intellectual categories than
'spirit' or 'needs'.

After the French Revolution, particularly the Terror and the adventures
of the famous Corsair, revolutionary alternatives did not seem so attractive,
even to those small numbers of the intelligentsia (to use an anachronism)
who had looked with favour upon the dawning of a new age in France. The
English national course was set in the direction of gradual change, ultimately
revolutionary but assimilable in the short run, allowing room for a great
variety of opinion on how change was to be conducted, at what pace and with
what consequences and with due but not slavish regard for what might be
designated 'traditional', itself a word that would require continual definition.

As a middle way, Coleridge's method, to examine institutions with regard
to their essence, was perfectly conceived for the historical circumstances of
the 1820s. So great were its attractions that John Stuart Mill, carefully
groomed by his lugubrious father James Mill as a Utilitarian and follower
of Bentham, was deeply attracted to it almost from the moment of its
publication in the seminal work *On the Constitution of Church and State*
(1829). Across the Atlantic, where the Jacksonian populist transformation
of American society was in full cry, an alarmed New Haven circle of scholars at Yale University also saw in Coleridge an opportunity to introduce
purposeful reforms into the college curriculum without compromising what
they regarded as the essential weight and mission of a university.[3]

It is not necessary to review in detail the intricacies and ultimate philosophical sources of Coleridge's thinking. A short presentation could scarcely
do justice to it in any case, and only a few emphases are required to bring us
to that point in the 1850s when John Henry, Cardinal Newman, adopted
Coleridge's method for analysing the function of institutions to universities
and wrote what remains the singlemost influential book on the meaning of
a university in the English language. It was Newman who transformed the
inherited legalistic description of a university as a corporate body possessing
endowments and privileges pertaining to learning into a thrilling emotion-
laden, higher order conception of education.

Coleridge was born into the clerical establishment, was sent, *inter alia*, to
one of the great boarding schools, Christ's Hospital, and went up to Jesus
College, Cambridge in 1791 as a sizar or poor scholar. He reacted strongly
to Cambridge rationalism with its heavy dose of mathematics, classical
philology and William Paley's Utilitarian theology. Most of his career was

spent as a poet and man of letters. His interests in philosophy developed early. He read the neo-platonist Plotinus while at school and visited Germany with borrowed money as early as 1798, publishing a translation of Schiller's *Wallenstein* in 1800.

He began his philosophical search for an 'idea' by a convoluted, rambling and one suspects opiated investigation and refutation of John Locke's epistemology, which, he was suggesting, was responsible for Utilitarianism. He began discussion with a rather perverse reading of Locke, arguing that he could not be taken seriously because his philosophy was derived from Descartes. Locke was hardly a Cartesian, although his epistemology certainly fell into the broad category of materialism. Locke and his disciples on the Continent had produced a theory of knowing which, eventually elaborated and refined into the doctrine of the association of ideas, had managed to find its way into all the major controversies of the Enlightenment.

At the core of any theory of change, when philosophers discuss change, lies an epistemology, an explanation of how we learn or know which subsequently serves as a basis for advocating social and institutional change. Epistemologies also have the advantage of furnishing educators with formidable pedagogical tools. This is the case whether we discuss phrenology or Piaget. But epistemologies can benefit more than one master at the same time. This was no less true for Locke. His ideas served either reformist or conservative ends. Thus the doctrine of the association of ideas became an article of faith to the Utilitarians because it justified radical change by rendering all knowledge, all establishments, all accepted and conventional ways of believing, merely relative to environment. Alter environment, and one alters belief. Tradition was only an excuse for inherited privilege. All religiously sanctioned systems of morality were but the power of the few over the timidity of the many. Even the appeal to self-sacrifice was a hypocritical justification for the status quo, for only those who protested against injustice were expected to desist. There was only one test of the value of an institution, or a social class, or a religious system, and that was a democratic but also a totalitarian principle: did the institution or moral system currently in vogue support the general public interest, creating the greatest good for the greatest number?

Although he had flirted with all manner of radical thought, joining other Romantics like the poet Robert Southey in a pantisocratic communitarian scheme for Pennsylvania, or becoming for a time a Unitarian minister, Coleridge ultimately gave up freethinking. He turned towards Platonism and the various traditions of idealist philosophy in a search for an alternative epistemology to Locke's. Where the associationists and Utilitarians made ideas subordinate to external stimuli received through the senses even when transformed in or by the mind, the Platonists or intuitionists made them independent of time and circumstances. Ideas about things were not relative. On the contrary, because they existed *a priori*, ideas possessed their own reality. It was no more evident that our mind was passive than that it was active. There were, Coleridge reasoned, according to the philosophical tradition he followed, pre-existing ideas of the world in the mind that could influence the interpretation of sensory data. The idealists could draw on the investigations of Bishop George Berkeley who had once demonstrated in his writings on vision that the senses were easily fooled. Does a paddle bend when inserted into water? It appears to do so. Nevertheless, in the context of revolutionary Europe a theory of knowing based on what we see, hear, taste, feel or smell was more immediately persuasive than its opponent doctrine. It does not matter, as a practical consideration, whether an object is ultimately real if it is contingently so, as Dr Johnson demonstrated by kicking a chair in a famous anecdote. If a chair can be kicked, it hardly matters whether it disappears when our backs are turned. It only matters when we want the Invisible to be actual.

Coleridge himself had great difficulty with the theory of pre-existing knowledge. In a notebook entry for 1808 he wrote 'of that abominable word, Idea/how have I been struggling to get rid of it, & to find some exact word for each exact meaning'. In yet another place he confessed to a 'mad metaphysician's Soliloquy', and in yet another, reviewing his wandering thoughts, he noticed that 'they may be thought to resemble the overflow of an earnest mind rather than an orderly premeditated composition',[4] to which even the most dedicated Coleridgean must immediately assent. Some years later Cardinal Newman, in his own effort to define the idea of an institution, interrupted the writing of his second lecture on 'Theology a Branch of Knowledge' by admitting that he too had plunged into a 'maze of metaphysics, from which I may be unable to heave myself'.[5]

Coleridge's particular version of the doctrine of innate ideas is close to and may have owed much to Kant. Ideas, Coleridge appeared to say, are certainly not dependent upon external stimuli as received through our senses, but neither are they strictly speaking innate. Rather ideas exist in the mind, to be recovered whenever awakened by stimuli or experiences received from the outer world. He distinguished between an idea and a conception (a distinction he attributed to Richard Hooker). The latter was a deduction from history and from circumstances. Because it was posterior, we tend to mistake the present 'form, construction, or model' of an institution for its original appearance. An idea was quite different. It was antecedent to history and circumstances and, unlike a conception, could not be 'abstracted from any particular state, form, or mode, in which the thing may happen to exist at this or at that time, not yet generalised from any number of succession of such forms or modes'.[6] Occasionally he used 'principle' as a synonym for 'idea'. A conception might follow from an idea without being coterminous with it, as the conception of a heliocentric universe was made possible by the idea or principle of gravity, which in the language of Plato was a 'law'. From the realm of social thought, Coleridge cited the example of an original social contract. No less than Bentham, he was scornful of the historical existence of a compact between governing and governed and called it an 'operatical farce . . . acted by the Illuminati and Constitution-manufacturers' of the late eighteenth century. As a theory Coleridge described the social contract as senseless and as a conception impossible. Yet as an 'idea' he pronounced it certain, and even more than certain, as indispensable, for without it no fundamental distinction between a servile polity and a commonwealth could have ever evolved. The idea of a social contract, therefore, was quite separate from the theory and conception of it. The first captured its essence, which was liberty, while the latter two tried to elaborate its essence into a working constitution, which was demonstrably false. Furthermore, while the existence of an original social contract was inaccessible to proof, the existence of an idea of liberty of which its exponents might not even be conscious could be found in discussions of any number of issues, such as the question of labourers' wages and poor rates.

Introducing yet another term, Coleridge maintained that an idea was a 'power' that constituted its own reality and was known when we have learned to recognise the 'ultimate aim' of a given institution.[7] But how does one discover that an institution has an 'ultimate aim'? Coleridge rejected pure functionalism as proof of the existence of an ultimate aim, calling functionalism a conception not an idea. He rejected historical reasoning, at least in one form, by refusing to admit that an institution's idea could be derived from its particular manifestation in the past. Of course he was correct in one respect. How, from amidst the welter of facts and details pertaining to the history of a given institution or situation could we ever spot the precise essential idea, the one thing needful, that clearly exposed its ultimate purpose?

Coleridge answered that we know the antecedent idea buried in an institution from the conduct of those associated with it, by the actions that they take or refuse to take, by the beliefs they hold or reject, by the institutional forms they adopt or oppose. He cited labour conflicts over wage and poor rates as evidence for the existence of the idea of liberty, a conclusion that historians might find dubious. He turned to history after all and argued that we can grasp the antecedent idea by the gradual realisation of related objectives over time, the past record containing a thread or consistency. Here we see why, in these borrowings from Hegel and Kant, John Stuart Mill in a famous discussion called this mode of understanding the Germano-Coleridgean school.[8]

Enter Confusion. We gather the purpose of an institution from its antecedent idea, we know its antecedent idea from its ultimate aim, we deduce its ultimate aim from a great many pieces of historical information, but the method requires us to maintain at all times a careful distinction between an idea, sometimes called a principle, and a conception. Ideas may be embedded in certain institutions – liberty in the social contract – but the latter is false, only the former true. For most readers this is casuistry, at best tautology, but in any case hardly the grounds upon which to argue today. We would not find the method useful for explaining how universities ought to function. Yet the young renegade philosophical radical, John Mill, found the method an enormous help in understanding how institutions could be accommodated to change, and in the Coleridgean habit of asking, 'What is the meaning of it?' he found a vast improvement over the Benthamite practice of saying, 'What is the use of it?' And is the Coleridgean mode of questioning really so alien today? It may not be far in spirit from the present social science method of looking beneath the obvious for a more general underlying principle or pattern, or from Freudian psychology with its stress on the unconscious, or from modern physics where ideal laboratory conditions are created in order to study natural phenomena, or from economic forecasting that also incorporates a teleological aspect and inevitably evaluates the present according to an ultimate aim.

But these rhetorical questions are not meant as a defence of Coleridge. They are intended to be an assist in explaining, if briefly, the rise of a habit of thinking about institutions as if they embodied an idea, whether we wish to call that idea a 'power' antecedent to history but understood through it, or a 'conception' deducible from the appearance of institutions and the actions of individuals in particular contexts. Both ideas and conceptions have informed the subsequent history of the method, even if Coleridge's distinction between them has not been customarily preserved. What has lasted is the persistent utility of his approach – the seductive influence of the inclination to see ideas existing at the heart of institutions.

His was the approach that received such remarkable application from Newman in the work that is the palladium of all such methods of reasoning and has inspired analyses about the role and purposes of universities for over a hundred years, mainly in English-speaking countries but occasionally elsewhere in a minor way as in France.[9] Since Newman the belief that universities possess a core idea or have an historical undertaking or a special responsibility and trust beyond the moment – we can state this essence in any number of ways – has remained a constant part of the process of institutional self-evaluation and internal debate.

Newman employed Coleridge's method for summarising the purposes of a university. He wrote his *Idea of a University* in the 1850s as a programme for a proposed new Roman Catholic university in Ireland; and the expanded book version, consisting of the original addresses, or as he called them 'discourses', and additional materials appeared in the 1870s. He also produced another work, much less well known than the *Idea*, which contains an analysis of a second kind of higher education institution denoted a 'college'.[10] In his view they were complementary not antagonistic institutions, and they were of course exactly the pairing existing at the ancient universities of Oxford and Cambridge. Newman was an undergraduate at Oxford, and was elected Fellow of Oriel, a college that in the 1820s led the way in revitalising a university that was not, by comparison to the old and new universities of Germany, intellectually distinguished; but intellectual distinction, as measured by the standard of original inquiry, was not the primary mission of an English university in Newman's formative years. Many of the great names of Victorian scholarship, Richard Porson in classical philology, for example, or Charles Darwin in biology, his cousin Francis Galton in genetics or Thomas Babington Macaulay were not regular members of the university despite other kinds of affiliations and relationships.

Newman loved Oxford. In his letters, as well as in the letters of other undergraduates of his generation, we find an intense personal identification with the physical beauty of the ancient quadrangles and courts and the beginning of that romantic mystique that takes us from the moonlit courts of Oxford and Cambridge in the first third of the nineteenth century to the cultivation of ivy in America in the first third of the twentieth century.[11]

In formulating his idea of a university, Newman incorporated what he considered to be the finest features of the Oxford of his day, and it is correct to say that Newman's idea is also, at least in inspiration, both the Oxford and the English idea of a university. That is the positive side of his thinking. There is also a negative side. If Newman loved what he wanted Oxford to stand for, he also passionately disliked a new and rival conception of a university that had arisen in the metropolis in the late 1820s, the University of London.[12] We must bear this situation in mind as we proceed to understand just what the Cardinal meant when he said that a university – and he meant all universities – contained, that is *should* contain, an idea.

The famous definition of the *Idea* as stated in Newman's Preface is that a university is a place for teaching universal knowledge – 'Such is a University in its *essence*'.[13] The function of a university is teaching, or, as it was called in the middle decades of the nineteenth century, the dissemination of knowledge.

Newman was not the first of Oxford's devotees to speculate on the basic purpose of a university. He had heard or read some of the arguments before, never so wonderfully elongated as in his own prose, but certain points were part of the Oxford apology. We need go no farther back than to Edward Tatham's remarks on the creation of the Oxford Honours examination at the turn of the century. The Rector of Lincoln maintained that 'An University is . . . the place of *Universal Teaching*, which is its first and most important duty'. However, there is a twist to the argument, for Tatham also asserted that,

> An University is the seat of *Universal Learning* increasing and to be increased, from the nature of men and things, with the lapse of time . . . *Its Discipline should, accordingly, be adapted to the Increase or Advancement of Learning improving and to be improved according to the times.*

Why? Because, 'otherwise it may occupy young-men in studies that are obsolete and in errors that are exploded'. Yet to admit that previous teaching and learning may have contained serious errors is dangerous doctrine in times of war and ideological disagreement, when the work of the *philosophes* was so evident in revolutionary Europe. And so Tatham takes another step in his argument on the proper relationship between knowledge and teaching that brings him closer to the mainline view. Both must 'be in the *Right or Initiative Method*; otherwise [studies] will lead [undergraduates] *from* instead of *to* the Truth, into Sophistry instead of Science'.[14] Clearly, then, while 'the times' may require some additions or alterations to what is known, there are right and wrong ways of learning, *a fortiori*, there is truth. A university exists to sort this out.

Many years later another Oxford don, on this occasion Newman's contemporary and sometime associate in the Oxford Movement, Edward Pusey, was less equivocal in announcing what should be taught:

> The object of Universities is . . . not how to advance science, not how to make discoveries, not to form new schools of mental philosophy, nor to invent new modes of analysis, not to produce works in Medicine, Jurisprudence or even Theology, but to form minds religiously, morally, intellectually, which shall discharge aright whatever duties God, in his Providence, shall appoint to them.

And to drive the point home, Pusey answered those who believed that a university ought to develop 'acute and subtle intellects'. They are not needed 'for most offices in the body politic . . . It would be a perversion of our institutions to turn the University into a forcing-house for intellect.'[15]

When Newman spoke about the idea of a university being a place where the teaching of universal knowledge took place, he was not talking about what the Germans would call *Lehrfreiheit*, the right to teach one's competence, or *Lernfreiheit,* the right of students to have open access to knowledge. Since teaching was the function of a university, it was important to teach the right things. Why should this even be an issue in a free society? Why not allow young adults the privilege – in America, with its natural rights traditions, one is almost always tempted to say 'right' – of reading and studying virtually whatever stimulates curiosity? Isn't the best kind of undergraduate education that which one chooses for oneself?

This is the rationale of today. It is the natural justification for mass education where the vast majority of undergraduates cannot enjoy the luxury of tutorial or small class instruction in the company of senior members of the university. It is the rationale required of research and public service universities where undergraduates are not the only community being served. Newman did not experience this kind of education at first hand, although he anticipated its future. His university had long existed for members of an elite whose lives were to be spent as public leaders in Church and State, in the military and at the bar. A handful of undergraduates were socialised to their future roles by exposure to those ideas and values that contributed to the maintenance of political stability. In the later eighteenth century the schoolmaster Vicesimus Knox, whose writings went through many editions, put the issue this way: 'Men of the world, who follow the opinions of Machiavel and Mandeville, laugh at all schemes of reformation, palliate vice, and justify folly; but it was the design of *universities* to counteract the prevalence of such principles.'[16] How Knox knew what the 'design' of universities was is undiscoverable. The basis is uncertain, but the context is clear. There are times in the life of a nation when the existence of a marketplace of competing ideas is unwise, and from an educational perspective, unsettling.

Newman was aware of the fact that English society was dynamic and changing, but at the top, at least, where the State was to offer guidance, it was essential that educated leaders be loyal. He agreed that ideas could be right or wrong, or, as he was to argue in the *Idea*, incomplete. Young people must not be led astray, particularly in times when values are in contention, religion competes with freethinking, and no consensus exists on moral questions. It should be said in Newman's defence (if it is a defence) that he was less authoritarian than his Roman Catholic superiors, but he did not hesitate to place limits on what ought to be exchanged in classrooms. He was by no means a nineteenth-century liberal individualist. In the famous passages of his remarkable autobiography, *Apologia pro Vita Sua,* he denounced the 'liberal heresy' of the age, its bland toleration and intellectual relativism, and his characterisation of Victorian liberalism is sufficiently vivid to remain a possible way of viewing nineteenth-century transformations. He had been driven from Oxford because of it, as explained in the autobiography. Absolute freedom of thought led to anarchy, to each man doing as he liked, as Matthew Arnold, another Coleridgean, was to state it.

When Newman prepared his discourses, the view that a university was more than a place for teaching universal knowledge, that it was also a place for professional education and primarily a place for the 'endowment of learning' or research, was prevalent enough for him to reassert the older Oxford position. He was aware of the pressure being exerted on Oxford and Cambridge to provide greater opportunities for teaching that was related to investigation and not to character formation. For centuries scholars and scientists had sought openings within universities for work that was not necessarily directly related to the teaching of young persons, or at least teaching dominated by literary, theological and mathematical subjects. There were some successes, and new histories of Oxford and Cambridge universities are uncovering more.[17] Even within the collegiate system, where teaching tutors rather than research professors predominated, research was never altogether out of the question for universities. A life spent in teaching will at some point shade over into research, or perhaps it is better to say 'study', since research is systematic study in a given area of knowledge and its subsequent dissemination, although not necessarily through the medium of the lecture hall. But although university professors wrote books, some of them original treatises and not texts, and learned papers were produced by classicists, philosophers and scientists, the overall intellectual environment was as Newman wished, whether in England or Scotland. The research function had not been raised to the level of an ideology. There was no strong culture of research that put a premium on originality and stressed the importance of discovery and a division of intellectual labour. It was not an era of Ph.D. candidates and graduate schools, extra-mural grants and contract research. University appointments were not made because potential fellows and chairholders were evaluated for their original contributions to knowledge or could be praised for being on the cutting edge of intellectual life. Learned, yes; but that most often meant an impressive command of existing knowledge with no expectation that scholarly work of seminal importance to a particular field of inquiry was some day likely to emerge and – most importantly – be systematically diffused. The principal institutional victories of Victorian researchers and their predecessors lay elsewhere, in the creation of learned societies, botanical gardens, museums, libraries and specialised institutions.

If the 'object' of a university 'was ... scientific and philosophical discovery, I do not see why a university should have students', wrote Newman.[18] The teaching of students had assumed new importance during Newman's lifetime. In arguing for the traditional view that research, while a possible function for universities, should always be secondary, Newman was reflecting important internal transformations that had occurred in his youth. The new examinations culture introduced at Oxford by the reforms of 1800 and developed earlier at Cambridge had reinforced teaching and strengthened the hold of colleges on the university's pedagogical mission, and a new generation of students, of which Newman was one, had in effect demanded more attention from dons and stimulated many of the changes that improved the intellectual standing of the ancient universities of England.

But pressure from the advocates of original inquiry was not limited to England. Influences were arriving from Germany. The model for the scholar and scientist was the German professor. Shortly after Newman delivered his discourses in Ireland, Yale, a university in another corner of the English-speaking world, instituted the first Ph.D. degree in North America, a half century before a similar degree was introduced into the United Kingdom (although the 'research student' appeared in the 1890s).

There is, admittedly, a serious difficulty in understanding Newman on the question of research and teaching. He often reads as if he is supporting pure investigation. His statements about freedom of inquiry and knowledge its own reward are so compelling that virtually all subsequent commentators stress the intellectual argument to the exclusion of all others and use the authority of Newman's name to justify the importance of university based research. Giving testimony before the Royal Commission on the University of London before the First World War, a professor of medicine at University College Hospital distinguished between a university medical school and 'trade school' medicine. The 'main ideal' of a university is 'the acquisition and making of knowledge for its own sake and not for the sake of the money which may be gained by knowing how to do certain things'.[19] Alfred North Whitehead, Trinity College, Cambridge and Harvard University, repeats the grand sentiments in 'Universities and Their Functions' while adding the strong, appealing and dangerous word 'imaginative': 'Thus the proper function of a university is the imaginative acquisition of knowledge ... A university is imaginative or it is nothing – at least nothing useful ... Imagination is a contagious disease.'[20] Indeed, which is why one form of it, 'genius', was so long considered to be tantamount to madness.

But we cannot confuse Newman with German influences, nor with the sort of Victorian liberalism of mind that prompted John Stuart Mill to assert the promiscuous obligation of an educated man to follow the argument withersoever it goes. Newman's own discourses run to some 560 pages in a recent edition, and they are precisely that, discursive and sometimes wandering statements about the relative merits of various disciplines, interspersed with lapidary remarks about knowledge and culture that are suitable for framing and are often lifted from context to adorn American college catalogues and university bulletins. Every apparently straightforward statement in Newman about open investigation is followed by hard, complicated phrasing and unfamiliar diction, so that his mode of reasoning resembles that of Pusey's acute and subtle intellect. For examples we need only turn to the lecture he wrote on 'Christianity and Scientific Investigations'. In it he observes that,

> it is a matter of primary importance in the cultivation of those sciences, in which truth is discoverable by the human intellect, that the investigator should be free, independent, unshackled in his movements; that he should be allowed and enabled, without impediment, to fix his mind intently, nay exclusively, on his special project, without the risk of being distracted ... by charges of temerariousness, or by warnings against extravagance or scandal.

This seems clear enough except for the qualifiers 'those sciences' and the clause 'in which truth is discoverable by the human intellect'. Presumably there are other kinds of sciences in which truth is not discovered by human intellect. The mitigated word 'distracted' also gives pause. Another paragraph is puzzling. While discussing 'what are called the *dogmas* of faith', Newman announces that 'we, none of us, should say that it is any shackle at all upon the intellect to maintain these inviolate'. Further on he rejects the position that university based scientists should be allowed to contradict [religious] dogma, and relatedly, he announces that the 'independence of philosophical thought' does not apply to *formal teaching* but to 'investigations, speculations, and discussions'. And finally he explains why this must be so, because 'there must be great care taken to avoid scandal, or shocking the popular mind, or unsettling the weak'. So having once told his auditors and readers that the inquiring mind should not be distracted by scandal, he concludes with scandal as a constraint.[21] One hears the cranky voice of Edward Tatham and Oxford's past.

The teaching function of universities is the controlling force in all of Newman's argument. After all, he announced this at the outset. Thus while the 'idea' is that of a university, the teaching emphasis implied the importance of colleges. Newman said very little about colleges in the *Idea*. Because he appears only to be talking about knowledge, its different forms and rankings, with theology at the top, it is easy to see why discussions of a university that take the *Idea* as starting point fail to notice how much Newman takes for granted.[22] The intellectual life is only one kind of life led in universities. Equally important is the human dimension in which personal relationships matter, friendships count, and success is measured not by examinations, however necessary these may be for determining a certain level of competence, but by growth and maturation, by what, in a memorable passage on the qualities of a gentleman, Newman described as civilised behaviour. The pursuit of knowledge, in and for itself, by and for itself, cannot produce similar results. The pursuit of knowledge begets egotism. It is asocial, removing scholars from the world, and it is servile not liberating because it encourages concentration and specialisation.

Newman's emphasis on the college recalls the Greek idea of a liberal education wherein specialisation is illiberal because the skill or proficiency is rated above wholeness or completeness. An additional danger is the governing passion. One's character is subordinated to some task or achievement. The idea of a university is that it must ultimately produce emotionally whole and balanced people, no single part of the personality disproportionate to another.[23]

The English idea of a university was created by thinkers such as Newman associated with literary and philosophical traditions of learning, trained in classical languages, aesthetic in disposition and nurtured within the structure of an Established Church. Romantics all, they valued the personal and regarded universities as places to make friends. To use a difficult word, they were 'humanists', meaning that they favoured knowledge directed towards explicating personal and moral relationships. Hence although the English idea of a university broadened in time to include science, its primary association was with subjects that can be described as literary. It should not therefore be surprising that literary critics like F. R. Leavis have carried the tradition forward into our own century.[24] For a number of reasons – German and Scottish influences among them – the American version of the English idea of a university is less restricted, but the bias is nonetheless present in the writings of recent critics.

The humanistic and aesthetic preconceptions of Newman are discernible in an essay he wrote when the University of London was founded. The new institution in Gower street, renamed University College in 1836, did not embody the idea of a university. How could it? Among its founders were the leading Utilitarians of the day, still pushing the mechanistic philosophy of the eighteenth century. Liberal Anglicans, Dissenting Protestants, Unitarians and Jews were also important players in the foundation of the new institution. To be sure, London was founded to be a teaching institution, but its pride and glory soon became the medical school not the undergraduate college. Newman was not absolutely opposed to university affiliated professional schools. His Irish university included preparation for the professions. In view of the pressures exerted upon him by his Irish Roman Catholic sponsors, he had little choice, but professional education was not his primary concern. The difficulty Newman encountered with London was that it was not an English, that is to say, an Oxford university. It was formed on existing Scottish models. The professorial lecture not the collegiate tutorial was the primary means of instruction, and the student as consumer exercised decisive influence over time-tabling and course provisions, just as in Scotland. The new university was also non-denominational, as well as secular, and for Newman the notion that a university could support a programme of studies where religion was not central was apostasy. One of London's 'spiritual' founders – the Scot Thomas Campbell – had visited the new city-state universities of Bonn and Berlin, and other supporters had taken an interest in Thomas Jefferson's new University of Virginia, another 'godless university', just opening its doors. Low fees, flexible scheduling, professorial lecturing, a certain amount of student choice in what to study, implying the relative worth of knowledge, no compulsory chapel or even instruction in religion – where were the principles of authority, beauty and steadiness of purpose essential to the idea of a university? Furthermore, London was 'Minerva under gaslights', an urban institution, set among streets, some of them dangerous or full of temptations. Students lived at home or in lodgings, and the institution did not concern itself with nurturing and did not worry whether friends were made. The unity of knowledge, as one commentator remarked, was abandoned as a university ideal.[25] In London only the intellectual life mattered, and any wider objective was the responsibility of the urban not the university environment. The lines between university and city were confused, and because of that very confusion and absence of internal cohesion, the 'idea' of a university began to fade.

If the *Idea of a University* was meant to be more than a series of discussions about a Roman Catholic university for Ireland (the bishops sensed that it was an apology for Anglican Oxford), Newman's grand plan was a failure. All the new universities and university colleges of Ireland and the civic universities of England as well as the new University of Wales were like London, inspired by Scottish rather than English examples. Durham was the only exception, and Durham was wrongly conceived for the north of England. All the other new institutions were cost-conscious establishments. They were, to begin with, market-driven, fee-sensitive, vulnerable to changes in demand and willing to take students with weaker preparation than mid-Victorian Oxford and Cambridge. They had no choice. The civics possessed neither the independence nor the teaching resources of Oxford and Cambridge and could not, while they were young, adopt an elitist or meritocratic mission.

I have been describing the beginnings of a new way of looking at institutions by defining their essence, or rather, by claiming in the first instance that they possessed an essence. I have mentioned the philosophical difficulties in defining an idea encountered by Coleridge, and the intellectual problems facing Newman when he tried to turn the idea of a university into a clear statement of goals. Contradictions and semantic confusion arose with every attempt to clarify the question of just what made universities special. Now it should be stressed that what is truly significant about their efforts is not any particular idea of a university, however interesting it may appear, but the very idea of an idea of a university. The genius of Coleridge and Newman lies not in their efforts to isolate the precise functions of a university. It lies in their desire to elevate the university to the moral centre of modern culture and to do so by freeing the university from the grip of utilitarian and hedonistic schools of thought so influential in their own day.

The emotional appeal of thinking of universities as embodying an idea cannot be overestimated in the age of the multiversity, continually bombarded by wide and contradictory demands and commitments. The multiversity is the university of the Benthamites. Its utility is established on the basis of the calculus of pleasure, its capacity to satisfy the greatest number, to provide the greatest number of positional goods for the greatest number of people. However elusive the idea of a university, the conception of a basic thrust or mission is a relief, an attractive alternative to the accurate perhaps but also shapeless, relativistic and uninspiring descriptions of the contemporary university as one-stop shopping.

Nineteenth-century German ideas of a university

In countries influenced by German philosophy, which means in one way or another most of northern, central and eastern Europe but also modern countries like Israel, the idea of the idea of a university has a different history, if a similar purpose. In these nations, universities were regarded as the home of the highest and best form of scholarship and science, so rare and even spiritual that they required vigilant protection from the commercial and vulgar tendencies of modern culture. The line of argument runs back through many thinkers, from the Von Humboldt brothers to Kant and Moses Mendelssohn.[26] In time, a reasonably short time, this special claim, known under various headings such as *Bildung* in German or *bildning* in Swedish, broadened to encompass a research mission. It is consequently often ambiguously referred to as 'Humboldtianism'. In time too the research mission broadened to include a very high level of technological application, so that in Germany (and in Copenhagen, Stockholm, Vienna and Zurich) *technische universitäten* and institutes of technology, excluded from the English idea of a university, entered the lawful penumbra. Nevertheless, the disciplinary crown of the German idea of a university was philosophy (and philology), as incorporated into the faculty organisational structure of the Continental university. Philosophy was the means for unifying the disciplines. The search for a single discipline capable of achieving such an end has never actually ceased. Mathematics, for example, has been suggested as one possibility in discussions over curricular reform in Dutch universities today.[27]

German influence spread outward in several forms. First, it was disseminated as *Bildung*, often translated as self-formation or self-realisation, a conception of education possibly originating in German pietism and having less to do with institutions than with individuals. However, individualism *per se*, at least initially, was not the aim. Rather *Bildung* was the process, the methods, the continual reflection, self-examination and study through which individuals reached and internalised the highest values of national culture. Second, German influence was disseminated as science or *Wissenschaft* (knowledge), but both conceptions shared a common purpose. Such German ideas of the proper aim of a university could be contrasted with the pastoral conception of teaching at Oxford and Cambridge, student-related, centred on the transmission of received values from teacher to disciple and embodied in such forms as college and tutorial.

German conceptions of *Bildung* did not penetrate very deeply into British universities until the end of the nineteenth century with the appearance of a neo-Hellenic aestheticism such as we find in writers like Walter Pater at Oxford and Goldsworthy Lowes Dickinson at Cambridge. The reasons were fundamentally political. In Britain, with its long history of civic humanism as embodied in aristocratic leadership, students were initiated into a world of institutional politics. This had not come easily, it must be admitted. During the period of the French Revolution, Oxbridge dons attempted to suppress student debating societies, driving some of them underground (as indeed also happened in America).[28] Yet the basic point remains. In Britain, undergraduates, few in number in proportion to the relevant age group, were expected to one day participate in public affairs as responsible citizens, exercising a self-discipline learned at home, in chapel or Church, in school and in university. The price of good citizenship was prolonged adolescence. Foreign visitors were alternately attracted to and repelled by what in their view was the schoolboyish quality of the British and American undergraduate.[29] There is a paradox. German universities were hardly 'free' in any absolute sense. They were far more closely attached to the State than were English institutions, although Scottish universities had long received subsidies from the Crown. The professoriate was annexed to the civil service, as was and remains common in Continental countries. English visitors to mid-nineteenth-century Germany remarked on the generally apolitical character of the professors and their detachment from worldly life. Yet students, unlike their British counterparts, were political activists. The Left Hegelians of the universites were the inspiration of Karl Marx, who was driven out of Germany into exile in Britain. The difference between countries is that in Germany undergraduates were allowed to drift into confrontational politics. There was no institutional tradition of *in loco parentis*, no or little concern with the private or personal lives of undergraduates, no need or desire or opportunity, certainly, to develop in young people that sense of wider civic responsibility, aristocratic in the English case, republican in the American, that are such conspicuous features of the inner academic life of nineteenth-century English-speaking universities. It was therefore possible to allow to German students the kind of intellectual (and spatial) freedom which on the whole dons were reluctant to furnish their own students or colleagues and to leave to the State the task of coping with the political consequences of open speculation.

There is some disagreement in the scholarly literature on the extent to which early proponents of *Bildung*, such as Wilhelm von Humboldt, were also interested in western traditions of civic humanism and attempted to unite German Enlightenment considerations of service to the State or possibly nation with self-formation, but the general outcome of this particular educational mission is not in doubt.[30] *Bildung* developed as an essentially apolitical educational theory, centring on the individual's efforts to achieve intellectual or spiritual perfection through *Wissenschaft*. Such conceptions, writes Fritz Ringer, protected (psychologically) the German professoriate from pressures for immediately applicable knowledge. At the turn of the twentieth century, *Wissenschaft* as well as *Bildung* had become deeply emplaced justifications for withdrawal from the actual world of affairs. The desire to avoid contaminating the intellect through contact with everyday life did not, however, spare the German universities from paternalistic control by the State and its bureaucracy.[31] Still, wherever individualism exists, either as a strong feature of culture, as in nineteenth-century America, or as an expression of artistic revolt, *Bildung* is likely to have appeal.[32]

The intellectual ideals of *Bildung, Wissenschaft, Lehrfreiheit* and *Lernfreiheit* were hothouse attractions for British and American scholars more accustomed to colleges than to universities, that is to say, to dealing with under-graduates who still behaved, and were treated, as if they were at school and whose moral superintendence was a critical aspect of the university's inherited functions. They were bored and resented the schoolboy atmosphere of American and British institutions, the poor preparation of students (especially in the United States and the new English civic universities) and the necessity to teach subjects at routine or introductory levels. While *in loco parentis* made sense in earlier centuries when undergraduates were actually of secondary school age, the increase in age of entry in England throughout the eighteenth century, and in Scotland in the nineteenth century, lessened its universal appeal. Academic career-building was possible in nineteenth-century Germany, to a greater degree than in England, where the professor was still for the most part a clergyman usually bent on a clerical career and where research played only a limited part, so that the best place to be intellectually creative was outside rather than inside the universities. The appeal of the German idea of a university consequently grew. British and American scholars visiting or studying in Germany were impressed by the intellectual ethos of Leipzig, Frankfurt and Berlin, and the dons began to divide into two broad categories: the good college man, devoted to the welfare of his (and after 1860 her) charges; and the scholar and scientist who took Germany as an example. 'I only hope you will not copy Oxford and Cambridge too closely,' wrote the new type of post-1860s Cambridge don, John Robert Seeley, to Emily Davies, Mistress of Girton College. 'The German Universities seem to me to be the right model, not the English ones.'[33]

Many consequences follow from the research idea, amongst them the gradual subordination of the past to the future, of old knowledge to new knowledge, of tradition and the accumulation of knowledge in a form known as 'wisdom' to the excitement of making daringly new formulations. But the new German idea of a university did not replace the older Anglo-American idea of a university. Rather, in different ways in the different countries, the two ideas coexisted; and whereas theoretically they are difficult to reconcile if we attempt to draw out the ramifications of each, in practice accommodations between the ideas have of necessity occurred.

Bildung, because it was primarily an intellectual, or in a special sense a 'spiritual' educational ideal, placed teaching in tight proximity to scholarship and especially to the methods for acquiring knowledge, the *wissenschaftliche Methoden* that gave German science its particular eminence.[34] The sober German professor in his seminar or institute expounding his theories and methods could be contrasted to the walk in the park, the socratic tutorial, the personal bonding, however strained or peculiar, between English tutor and undergraduate. Despite the importance of the seminar room with its specialised library, or the carefully arranged scientific laboratory, *Bildung* did not depend upon communal living, or the famous staircase of Oxford and Cambridge. Once the methods had been acquired, they could almost be developed away from the world at large. The literally disembodied discourses of Thomas Mann's novel *The Magic Mountain* take place in a sanitarium in isolated mountains. In Hermann Hesse's *The Glass Bead Game*, that most extraordinary depiction of a life devoted to the cultivation of mind in and for itself, the pursuit of self-knowledge is centred in an unworldly community. The ideal is neither British nor American. Willa Cather's 1920s novel, *The Professor's House*, specifically contrasts Continental-derived scholarship and the benefits of the lonely life with teaching at a midwestern university full of Yahoos.

Historically the university came to be the favoured environment of academics, at least in a number of western European and certainly American universities, precisely because in time it proved to be the institution most congenial to independent research. Before that could happen, however, the numerous State Churches and religious denominations had to accept the principle of free inquiry,[35] the States and various supporting publics had to recognise the value or utility of research in its different forms, undergraduate teaching was no longer to be considered the sole or primary function of universities, the parietal responsibilites of academics in English-speaking countries were no longer to be insisted upon, and professors had to consent to a social contract,[36] an implicit agreement to place objectivity before advocacy and truth before ideology in the pursuit of knowledge.

These conditions were not reached overnight, nor were they achieved in every country nor in the same degree or permanently, nor do they exist in every university even today. The argument has been made that in Latin America the universities are so intensely politicised that free research can only be undertaken in special institutes without an undergraduate teaching mission.[37] The degree to which research is a protected and open-ended form of intellectual inquiry depends on much wider considerations. These are the nature of the research undertaking, whether it is 'pure', 'applied' or technical, whether it is conducted in secret or forms part of the inheritance of public knowledge, how it is funded, whether peer review is respected in the allocation of resources, whether grants are awarded competitively, and the general value placed by a society on educational activity whose results and consequences are difficult to measure, especially in the short run. Political traditions are the most important of all considerations, for it is not the university that ultimately guarantees freedom of inquiry, but the tolerance of government and publics. Universities themselves, in their long history, have no reason to boast of their freedom from the idols of the mind. Towards ideas, towards groups, towards religions and towards open thought, they have very often opposed rigid orthodoxies. They have also been guilty of racial and ethnic exclusion. Their collective record is, alas, far from pretty, but the universities of some nations have fared better in these regards than those of others.

American departures

The American inheritance from Europe is manifold and continuous, and the American use of it highly adaptive and flexible. What makes the American case so interesting is the strong connection between American colleges and universities and the characteristics of American social life, principally its religious pluralism and ethnic diversity, its immigrant composition, and its preference for market discipline interspersed with governmental efforts, many half-hearted or contradictory or unsystematic, to legislate or regulate.

The history of American higher education is characterised by the growth of multi-purpose institutions which continue to add functions and responsibilities without disregarding older commitments. New constituencies and new tasks are absorbed comparatively readily. American higher education institutions have been expansion-minded since the War for Independence and have generally shown a willingness to stretch existing resources to support new ventures. Market discipline has certainly contributed to the comparative openness and flexibility of American institutions as a condition of survival in the public as well as private sector. Market decisions were also a prominent feature of the deliberations leading up to the establishment of the first English university to be founded since the thirteenth century. Some of the founders of the University of London spoke about enrolling at least 2000 students at a time when neither Oxford nor Cambridge could claim more than about 1200. Market-responsive institutions are usually forced to consider student numbers when setting curricula and allocating resources.

The American idea of a university was, in the earliest colonial period, derived from England's before it was common to speak of universities as incorporating an idea or essence. The original American universities were no more than university colleges for the training of clergy and political leaders, each separate colony regarding its college as a public institution, interfering spasmodically in its internal affairs until an extraordinary legal decision known as the Dartmouth case settled the issue of ownership. The decision came in the early nineteenth century, and henceforth the colonial colleges were regarded as private institutions under non-State management but with continued State aid of some kind.

The presence of many distinguished Scottish educators in the colonies in the eighteenth century brought Scottish and Scots-Irish influence into American higher education, leading to two new developments. First, medical and professional education generally were regarded as appropriate university responsibilities, whereas in England training in the law and medicine had devolved upon separate institutions; and second, the teaching of classical languages, mathematics and theology, the backbone of the English curriculum, was broadened into a Scottish humanistic curriculum which included social science, the new Enlightenment Philosophy of Man, and modern subjects, such as non-classical languages and natural science. Scottish influence also reinforced the democratic conceptions spreading throughout the colonies, stressing the notion that education was a national responsibility to be undertaken in the interests and well-being of the many. Without too much fuss, Americans adopted the philosophical Utilitarianism being advocated by the Benthamites, and utility meant, among other things, that education should, depending upon markets, also be low-cost.

One of the most extraordinary differences between American and British higher education was the care taken in the United States to secure the moral, political and financial support of graduates and their attachment to *alma mater*. Indeed, there is an interesting paradox here. The older universities of England had convocations or senates, legislative houses where MAs were entitled to vote, and as these, at least the interested parties, were largely clergy, one feature in the evolution of a secular university in the United Kingdom was neutralising the constitutional power of the graduates. The change occurred at Oxford and Cambridge in the early twentieth century. The newer civic universities, being small and undercapitalised, never really produced sufficient numbers of graduates to provide strong alumni support organisations. By contrast, the American colleges and universities cultivated their alumni without giving them a major governmental role in the life of the institution, apart from representation on lay boards of trustees. In this strategy American institutions were doubtless assisted by the absence of strong competing centres of loyalty, except religious ones, a class system weaker in its boundaries than in Europe, few forms of derived high status, and the importance therefore of institutional identification in providing some form of recognisable status or distinction. To be a graduate or near-graduate was sufficient and, in a continent-sized country, employment opportunities did not always depend upon where the degree had been obtained. The American university or college could not on the whole 'charter' its graduates by guaranteeing employment or career.[38]

After Independence, the Scottish notion of education for a national citizenry received special American emphasis, as colleges and new state universities, which began to spring up at the end of the eighteenth century, adopted republicanism and neo-republicanism as the special purpose of an undergraduate education. This emphasis, centred on the responsibilities of citizenship, is a perennial concern, especially during periods of heavy immigration (and particularly with regard to the flow from eastern or south-eastern Europe and the Far East or Latin America) or when social issues split the nation. These are not the sole reasons, however, for the recurrent interest in national morality and patriotism. The religious divisions of the country, family values, the condition of public schooling, military and political involvement abroad and the national preference for private behaviour and self-aggrandisement are contributing causes.

In 1963 Clark Kerr, then president of the University of California, delivered the Godkin lectures at Harvard. Published in book form, his remarkable analysis is now in a fourth edition and is a landmark contribution to the tradition discussed in this chapter. One of his principal conclusions was that American universities could not be said to be animated by a single idea, that is, by an inherited referent serving as a touchstone or guide, a reminder of the university's true purposes and historical destiny, and as a means of sorting out and deciding between competing missions and rival claims. In place of an idea, there was in time a multiversity containing many ideas and very little unity, except whatever might be imposed upon it from above by a central administrative system and board of trustees, or outside in the form of public opinion or legislative pressure. In historical perspective it is certain that Americans abandoned or failed to adopt the Coleridge–Newman premise that institutions embodied an essential idea in the late nineteenth century, at least, after some initial attempts on the part of a number of institutions – I mentioned the New Haven scholars at Yale – to consider universities as centres of culture, regional but also national, from which the best or the highest or the most noteworthy ideas would be disseminated. The most senior institutions flirted with English ideas, but Harvard, the oldest of them, actually resisted the temptation. Instead, Harvard did the opposite and lent its prestige toward a movement that led away from the idea of a university. It was also Harvard, however, that issued a famous report on general education in 1946 attempting to define something approaching a common curriculum, one of many such on-going efforts in the history of American colleges and universities and one destined to continue – with only limited results the sceptic might conclude.

Harvard's contribution to institutional pluralism was the adoption of the elective system of course-taking which supplemented and later replaced the common degree programme wherein students remained in cohorts throughout their residence. Electives were the forerunner of teaching modules (there is actually no American name for this system) which, by the end of the nineteenth century or the beginning of the twentieth, had become standard educational practice.

In the American version, a degree curriculum was divided into modules that were nearly all self-contained, each taught by a single instructor who also examined and assigned a final mark or grade. A degree was awarded on the basis of a certain number of modules distributed among a large number of different subject areas, customarily with concentration in one subject in the last two years of the undergraduate curriculum. This remains the basic situation, although there are and have been any number of variations on the theme, at the University of Chicago for example, or in the core western civilisation programme at Columbia. In nearly every case, however, some element of student course choice is recognised.

The precise origins of modules and credits may be obscure but not in any way that need detain us. As noted, they first appeared as subject electives at Harvard – or the University of Virginia earlier. Some writers attribute their genesis to German conceptions of freedom of teaching and freedom of learning brought to the United States by an early generation of Americans studying overseas. Others, with pardonable loyalty, find elective modules homegrown and attribute their birth to Thomas Jefferson's belief in the ability of the common man to determine his own educational needs. The University of Virginia experiments broke down because of the poor preparation of entering students. Another version unconvincingly attributes electives to eighteenth-century Scottish sources.[39] Whatever the ultimate derivation, the course structure embodying it is distinctly American. In its earliest American guise, that is, in the middle of the nineteenth century, modularity was mainly an 'elective system'. It represented a complete and decisive break with the old-time college curriculum of classical languages and mathematics, or with the newer Scottish Enlightenment import of moral philosophy in its several forms. Virtually all specified requirements were thrown out in favour of free choice. To begin with the movement went furthest at Harvard under the leadership of President Eliot. Other institutions followed but slowly, waiting upon events. A partial reaction set in towards the end of the century when it was discovered that undergradutes were poorly prepared for university work (which the University of Virginia discovered at the outset), let alone equipped to make choices between competing fields of knowledge. The result was the quadripartite undergraduate curriculum of the present, composed of proficiency requirements, breadth requirements, electives and majors. However, a vast amount of choice still remains within each category, with the independent module as the central feature. The modular system can be contrasted with the historic English honours degree which evolved at Cambridge sometime in the later eighteenth century and at Oxford after 1800. High specialisation was a feature of English undergraduate education while in Scotland greater scope was allowed. In both cases, a final examination occurred at the end of a three- or four-year period of study, but teaching and examining were separated. Exceptions could be found from time to time, as in the somewhat more general undergraduate curriculum of Keele after 1945. But American-style modules were not typical of British higher education until the second half of the present century when numerous versions started to appear at British polytechnics and some universities. Integration through the European Union and the development of mass-access institutions, with a need for greater flexibility in admissions and time-tabling, were causes of an increased interest throughout the 1980s and 1990s.[40]

Several important traits of the present American course structure were added in the late nineteenth or early twentieth centuries. The first was the assignment of unit credits to each module in order to increase flexibility in the curriculum. There could now be half and partial modules. This supported another trend, student transfer from one institution to another without loss of credit. A new national currency had been created capable of being traded almost anywhere in the American higher education system. A third trait of the system led in a wholly different direction, more European one might say and less American, an effort at classroom quality control through the assignment of marks or grades per unit. This began in the last decades of the nineteenth century but seems to have been the subject of more widespread debate in the Progressive Era, a period of concern about national efficiency and common standards, whether of weights and measures or of student achievement.

Modularity addressed and solved an ancient educational problem: how to alter the undergraduate curriculum and admit new subjects into it. Modularity made this relatively simple, since there was virtually no limit to the number of modules that could be added to a curriculum provided resources were available. Resources were stretched through the wide adoption of the lecture method of teaching, replacing the more labour-intensive tutorial or small group instruction. Changes could be introduced merely by having a single instructor alter the methods, scope and content of a course. This was more difficult to achieve in systems where terminal examinations and the separation of teaching and examining existed, if for no other reason than that these curricula were based on syllabi requiring committee approval, or because curricula and examination were set and administered from the outside by State agencies, as on the Continent.

Yet modules had their own drawbacks. Since academic standards varied from teacher to teacher, uniform quality control was awkward, requiring other regulatory devices: hearsay, student evaluations, peer review. The most effective quality control occurred in advance, as it were, in the hiring of faculty, followed by periodic review of the professional record at regular intervals. A further drawback was the vulnerability of the hybrid classroom instructor, both teacher and examiner, to student pressure or outside pressure for higher marks or lenient treatment. There was also an embarrassment of riches. The number of course choices in American institutions multiplied and continued to multiply; and even movements for the reform of the curriculum, for example, the introduction of core courses or interdisciplinary programmes, added to rather than subtracted from the existing body of options.

Despite such departures from European conceptions of proper teaching structure, modularity was perfectly suited to the changing characteristics of American culture. American federalism and localism produced many experiments in higher education, not all of them illustrious when measured by developments abroad. The American belief in market discipline made universities and colleges extremely vulnerable to fluctuations in educational opinion and taste. Wherever possible, American universities and colleges tried to ameliorate or mitigate pressure from outside by attempting to multiply the sources of income and especially to attract unrestricted endowment income, for the mark of a great institution became its ability to resist external demands. For the same reason, a national and even international constituency was preferable to one more purely local and parochial.

Therefore, while in Europe the 'problem' of adapting the university structure to an urban, technological, professional civilisation was often viewed intellectually as finding the correct 'idea' of a university, in the United States a single 'idea' of a university was increasingly impossible. Even the idea of a university having an idea, real but elusive, was doubted. To be sure, many American scholars, scientists, writers and artists found the plural environment of the United States unappealing. They were attracted to the privileges, the State subsidies, the intellectual and artistic culture of settled European capitals. They preferred to live and work abroad, or favoured European standards of artistic and literary taste at home. The most Euro-centred academics were invariably attracted to essentialism either in English or German form, but the German one was easier to assimilate since it was not based on the expensive institutional arrangements of Oxford and Cambridge. Abraham Flexner for one favoured German models as holding out the promise of a higher calling that would insulate universities from the vulgarities and commonplaces of a rather free-wheeling, expansive and aggressive participatory democracy, often populist and certainly individualist. But such partisans of the idea of a university were in the minority among academics for whom the modular teaching system was a liberation from the tedium of undergraduate teaching. Furthermore, the advocates of essentialism did not control American colleges and universities like the faculties of the Continental university, the self-governing societies of Oxford and Cambridge or the senates and courts of other British universities. In America lay boards of trustees delegated authority to presidents. From time to time some academic malcontents took refuge in wholly new institutions, backed by eccentric financiers. Black Mountain College situated in the foothills of North Carolina and lasting only from 1933 to 1956 was one such sanctuary from the world's dross. There, far from the madding crowd, professors could embrace their conception of the good, the true and the beautiful.[41] But these experiments customarily lasted only as long as charismatic leaders were active. They were campuses under one-man rule, unable to develop a constitution assuring longevity in the volatile American educational market.

The modular system, that great antithesis to the very idea of a university having an idea, did not come upon Americans overnight. It took a long time to develop. It proceeded by fits and starts, a response to the decentralised character of American political life and culture, a distant and constantly expanding geographical frontier, and the continual renewal of population through emigration from abroad. Each institution watched the other, borrowing ideas from the market leaders, adjusting them to find a particular niche of its own in order to secure even a tiny competitive advantage, while continuing to dream of an upward drift along a remarkable continuum of educational status hierarchies.

Competition and emulation drove old and new institutions to continued exertion in a search for success or distinction as measured in every possible manner, by income, by wider influence, by status and numbers, by size of plant and extent of acreage, by location and pulling power, even by 'mission'. It is difficult, however, for Americans to use quality as a measure of distinctiveness, although the word springs immediately to the lips of British (or Australian and European) academics. Of course 'quality' is desired, but democratic propensities force Americans to speak in euphemisms. Quality is therefore assessed mainly in relation to an institution's self-declared 'programme' as measured in resources or institutional objectives, language that avoids giving offence to students, faculty, administrators and supporting publics. Six regional educational accrediting agencies exist as voluntary associations of universities and colleges, with some public representatives. Their function is to assess colleges and universities on the basis of their published objectives. Normally only minimum standards are assessed. The question of a Rolls Royce degree rarely enters into the equation.

Neither competition nor emulation would have succeeded in America had there not existed an extraordinary diversity of population, made even more diverse by the great emigrations of the post-Civil War period and the relative absence of central government constraints. I stress both the diversity of the population and the absence of central direction because it is certainly possible to have a diverse population without plural educational aims and structures. And it is quite clear to an American considering the end-of-century role of the Australian Commonwealth Government in the governance and support of Australian universities that a federal constitution is by itself no guarantee of institutional autonomy. Federalism embraces any number of authority arrangements and combinations of central and local decision-making. Until the 1980s federalism in Australia was more likely to reinforce the English idea of a university. The federal constitution of present-day Germany gives Bonn and the *Länder* far more authority over higher education than Washington can claim, and student examinations are primarily a governmental rather than an institutional responsibility. Swiss higher education, however, resembles the American in several ways, most notably in the different systems sponsored by individual cantons. But languages may be a factor.

Attempts to create central universities at public expense occurred early in the history of the American Republic. Shortly after the War for Independence followers of Alexander Hamilton debated with Jefferson on the issue of whether a national university should be established at Washington. The federated states, fearing a government monopoly over intellectual capital, defeated the Hamiltonian proposal. We can contrast this defeat of centralism with what was happening abroad. In Germany, universities were attached to the State, to the purposes of the State and to the very idea of a State, to the great consternation of Max Weber, who a century later wrote a classic essay on the question of university–state relations. We can find nothing in the American experience that corresponds to the systematic reform of Oxford and Cambridge by successive waves of royal and parliamentary commissions of inquiry in the thirty years from about 1850 to 1882, or the establishment of another kind of central institution, the examining University of London of 1836, created to protect the quality of the degree and in time to regulate the growth of new universities in the Midlands and northern cities of England, in Ireland and the Dominions and empire.

No American university could literally be at the centre or possess a monopoly of the nation's resources, not even Ivy with its historic advantages. The absence of an established set of institutions or favoured intelligentsia gave encouragement to new institutions and stimulated rivalries, so that even the oldest and most distinguished universities had to meet the continual competition of upstarts and innovations emanating from elsewhere. Remaining atop the prestige hierarchy required energy and resourcefulness, on-going appeals to donors and a watchful eye for potential growth opportunities. Harvard constantly redefined itself in an effort to stay current. It was overtaken as a birthplace of initiative at certain times by new universities like Chicago, or the Germanophile Johns Hopkins or Cornell or Clark. The next oldest American institution, William and Mary in Virginia, was hardly in the running at all. For a time Columbia University, the colonial King's College, led the pack. New state universities, Michigan or California, the latter enjoying generous gifts of land from the federal government, became instant universities, mixing Latin and the mechanical arts without bothering too much about their compatibility with an historic idea of a university. As Walter Metzger puts it:

> Military science was taught by all land-grant colleges, where it was legally required, and also by Baylor, Georgetown, Brown, and Yale, where it was not; domestic science was offered by state universities known for their 'low' utilitarianism, and also by Clark and Chicago, reputed to seek the most exalted knowledge the fortunes of their founders could buy.[42]

Whatever the fortunes of Oxford and Cambridge in the seminal nineteenth century, they never lost their traditional advantages, their ties to the governing elite, their ability to attract new talent, their close assocation with Church and State. New institutions arose: the London university colleges, Durham, the Federal University of Victoria. The Scottish universities were reformed and flourished; indeed, their intellectual distinction earlier could not be denied. Yet no university ever succeeded in posing a permanent challenge to the prestige of the ancient universities, which itself was an effective means of meeting such competition as from time to time appeared.

Many different ideas of a university contested for supremacy in America, and each institution contained all of these ideas at once, just as the modular system itself incorporated and permitted all forms of teaching at all levels of instruction. But if an historic justification for modules was needed, it could certainly be found in nineteenth-century German ideas of *Lehrfreiheit* and *Lernfreiheit*. Modularity permitted the teacher to teach what he liked, and allowed specialisation an easy entry into the curriculum. Electives permitted the student to choose from among a great array of educational goods. Over decades the principle of *Lernfreiheit* was extended still further with the appearance of student-initiated (and student-funded) courses in the 1960s.

Modules and electives are essential for mass-access institutions in a plural society and perhaps also a justification after the fact for the type of institution that American universities became. In order to make room for knowledge and for the process of specialisation and sub-specialisation and professionalism characteristic of urban societies, there must exist a high degree of curricular flexibility. In order to accommodate a multiplicity of interests, which is both a cause and an effect of the proliferation of course modules, resources must be concentrated on certain functions to the relative exclusion of others. Thus certain standbys of the Newman idea of a university, such as collegiate education and the tutorial system, the 'close action of the . . . matured character on the unformed', as another Oxford don said in the last century,[43] are luxuries barely possible. Students, particularly undergraduates, are presumed to know their own interests and to care for themselves. This assumption is necessary to legitimise poor staffing ratios and the weakening of the faculty role in advising and counselling. Yet American institutions are not altogether comfortable with the assumption that students are sufficiently mature to design their own educational programme. Proof of unease lies in the enormous investment in advising, counselling, psychological testing and health services. The complexity of the modular and unit credit systems requires employment of non-academic administrative staffs, interpenetrated by part-time deans drawn from the faculty. Altogether student services comprise a substantial addition to the costs of running a contemporary university. While long, idyllic walks, leisured conversation between students and teachers in protected islands of discourse are not unheard of in liberal arts colleges and in even the most populous state universities, they are an exception or anomaly and not really a part of the idea of an American university.

Is there really no single idea of an American university? 'Knowledge' comes closest, but knowledge in every conceivable form and application, knowledge abstract and knowledge applied, from simple vocationalism to the most abstruse kind of inquiry. Knowledge as a thing in itself, as its own reward, is for the most part an abstract and impersonal conception, now assuredly, but can we claim that it was ever the dominant conception of a university? Despite the fact that many of Newman's most famous statements are about knowledge, it is all too easy to forget that as a teacher motivated by a pastoral conception of pedagogy, as a theologian concerned with sin and redemption, as a moralist bothered by the dissolution of authority in Liberal England, and as an educational thinker still operating within older notions of the possibility of ranking the arts, he is not talking about a universe of education similar to what obtains in most western universities today. That an undergraduate would attend the university and take away from it a list of courses certified by a degree or credential was exactly what horrified him about the new University of London. Had Newman's idea of a university prevailed, there would have been no London granting huge numbers of external degrees to undergraduates in remote colonial territories, no Manchester or Liverpool where the interests of manufacturers and shipowners had to be considered, no Keele or Sussex experimenting with different styles of curricula, no Cal Tech in Pasadena, no Oregon University of the Health Sciences, no Wirtschafts Universität in Vienna. The educational world would have been easier to define. Perhaps, possessing a beguiling clarity, it might have been more satisfying than what exists today, but it is not for the scientific historian to entertain such careless thoughts.

Multiversity not university

In any case, we must be cautious in how we apply the idea of a university to contemporary or even nineteenth-century American higher education. To say that the governing conception of the American university is the pursuit of knowledge is to falsely suggest that Americans adopted German ideas of a university in more or less pure form. American university teachers did not control their universities through a system of professorial chairs grouped into 'faculties' that could effectively restrict curricular innovation, nor could they adopt and disseminate a conception of education resting on *Bildung* or self-mastery according to the highest aesthetic models. At best a few of them could advocate *Bildung*, which could then be absorbed by a handful of undergraduates of individualist or aesthetic temper. This rarely happened precisely because American universities and colleges, however they might at times resent the intrusion of the market, were forced to respond to it simply to exist. I am not speaking about passive responses, as in certain Marxist theories of social conflict, but about active and creative responses, about efforts to mitigate or mediate or persuade, to deflect and to play off one set of pressures against another, to summon up new worlds to redress the balance of the old, or old worlds to redress the balance of the new. Such strategies necessitated the creation of full-time university administrators and managers, leaders and staff who would negotiate on behalf of the faculty. The result was the rise of the multi-purpose university, incorporating in single institutions and later in systems all of the ideas of a university that had appeared in the nineteenth century, carrying out on a single campus the functions of a polytechnic, a normal school, a college of arts and crafts, a technological college, law and medical schools, a business school, research institutes and departments, an American community college (even an American upper secondary school) and a sprawling catch-all for undergraduates known variously as a College of Letters and Science or a College of Arts and Sciences, that is, the attenuated descendant of university colleges. Tucked away in the interstices of departments and laboratories were honours programmes for those who qualified by the test of merit. Even whole honours colleges within universities were created here and there, notably at Michigan, performing classic elite-training functions. Nevertheless, programmes for the meritorious coexisted with instruction that in Europe would surely be disdained as remedial and outside the definition of a true university.

The blurring of the boundaries between types of institutions, programmes and categories, the intermixture of liberal, vocational, professional and graduate research functions is perfectly captured in the way Americans confuse the words 'school', 'college', and 'university'. Originally, confusion between 'college' and 'university' was Scottish; but the addition of 'school' to mean higher education without a reference to 'schools of study' (as in the 'Old Schools' at Oxford) is, I believe, purely American. 'It would help', wrote one exasperated critic in 1911 of the American propensity to avoid careful distinctions,

> For the states to adopt a fairly uniform and severe restriction on the use of the terms 'university' and 'college' . . . it would eliminate some weaklings; though it is true that 'the college that is least worthy of the name, that is in every way inferior to such academies as Exeter and Andover, is the very one which would cling most desperately to the title, would be most reluctant to relinquish its right to confer worthless degrees.'[44]

Universities that are simultaneously regarded as a school, a college or a university envelope structures and traditions that are contradictory, confusing and ambiguous. At one moment in a typical academic senate debate we are told that a university exists to promote knowledge, while at another we are informed that it is a place for self-cultivation. Some speakers denounce the 'worldly university', yet others have contempt for the ivory tower. Other speakers note that the cardinal object of an undergraduate education is citizenship, only to be answered that it is the higher learning that defines a university 'in the true sense of the word'. But the higher learning can also be described as professional education, the oldest of all university functions, and that too is a debate with a nineteenth-century history. Newman himself recognised the validity of professional education but more as a necessity than a priority. Still other voices inform us that a university in a democracy must place itself utterly at the service of society, as if there existed a single voice speaking for 'society'. And once again, in language filled with passion and disarming conviction, we are told that 'liberal education' is the ultimate reason for the existence of universities even though the American definition of a liberal education bears almost no resemblance to that sophistic-Italic humanist tradition that created the notion in the first place. Contradictions can be sustained at the level of ideas because the several disciplines speak from the standpoint of different inheritances and functions, and they can be sustained organisationally because of the many divisions of universities into autonomous or semi-autonomous schools, colleges, departments, programmes, research institutes and centres; student services, public relations, legal staffs and planning offices.

Meanwhile, reports and books are produced from inside the academy by presidents and professors, or from the outside by expatriates now with philanthropic foundations or academic associations, urging the great American university flamingo, its legs, neck and head already sprawling in every conceivable direction, to reconsider past options or new assignments. A sensitively written report from the Association of American Colleges takes up the vexed theme of a common core of undergraduate learning, as does Ernest Boyer of the Carnegie Foundation for the Advancement of Teaching, whose report is also a review of what he called 'best practice' in the existing curriculum. One former Secretary of Education, William Bennett, returns to the Battle of the Books, recommending that all students be exposed to authors and works that put them in the company of 'great souls' (he includes sceptical or cynical Machiavelli and Hobbes). Allan Bloom, who once looked out upon the world from the cosy corner of the tiny Committee on Social Thought of the private University of Chicago, tells us that only certain subjects and certain authors are genuinely worth studying. The former president of Harvard, Derek Bok, examines the service role of American universities in relation to traditional considerations like academic freedom, the pursuit of intellect and high standards of teaching. He questions whether great research universities ought to provide research and consulting facilities to city officials, or establish schools of hotel management, doctoral programmes in physical studies, radio and television communications 'and other doubtful enterprises' – all of which are in existence somewhere, including leading places. Yet he is solidly in favour of a service function for private research universities, which, after all, as he says, receive one-fifth to two-thirds of their income from a combination of government grants for research and student aid, as well as relief from taxes and other assessments. For such institutions, social problems cannot be off-limits. Yet other authors emphasise the importance of moral education (but whose set of morals?). Individual professors may dissent from, but university presidents ordinarily assent to, the multiversity conception, since it is their task to connect universities to the rest of American society in response to consumer demand and political pressure and in the understandable interests of longevity.[45] No idea of a university, past or present, escapes discussion at some level, but can a single university contain every one?

From the standpoint of the idea of an idea of a university, American forms of higher education represent a development that Newman and his successors in spirit could only deplore. Newman called the new London University a 'pantechnicon', and also a 'bazaar', and since then descriptions like 'supermarket', 'smorgasbord' and other references to education as a commodity or item of consumption have been common.

For those familiar with this line of criticism, Allan Bloom's best-seller, *The Closing of the American Mind*, is not a departure but yet another restatement of the position that a university ought to stand for the highest and the best, that a university education ought to be exclusive, that it should not be vulgarly utilitarian, or utilitarian *tout court*, that it should deal with great and proven works, and that it should pose an alternative to whatever is popular, trendy or currently in vogue. It should nourish imagination and creativity and a love for knowledge as a thing in itself. The idea of a university demands that a true university should never succumb to the dictum that more is better and should fight vigorously against any crude market measure of success, such as classroom headcounts or value-added accountability or citation indices or productivity standards of research or any other attempt to apply cost-benefit analysis to universities as if they were banks and manufacturing firms. What makes Bloom's position somewhat different from the typical complaint is that, paradoxically, he attached a commercial title to his surprising best-seller, so that the very market that was the cause of his irritation was simultaneously the source of his success.

It is hardly evident that higher education has failed democracy in the United States, although definition of the word 'democracy' is critical to the argument. But if we take the historical perspective I have offered and consider the demographic and political pressures brought to bear on American higher education during and since the nineteenth century, we may well conclude that far from failing American democracy, American colleges and universities have served it well, providing widespread access, diversity and flexibility. One criticism that can be made is that they have served a particular conception of democracy all too well. Such criticism, however, must ultimately apply to the American political tradition and American consumerism which created higher education, and that is a completely different kind of critique.

Ironically, it is not the grand tradition of criticising American higher education from the standpoint of an idea of a university that produces consternation in the American academic environment. What makes American university administrators wince and orders public relations staffs into the field is the criticism that American higher education does not do enough of what in fact, comparatively speaking, it does extremely well. The persistent complaint is that it does not provide *enough* access, diversity and flexibility. Open admissions, a policy adopted in the City University of New York in the 1970s, a cry for greater breadth and choice in a curriculum already disconnected and incoherent, more part-time degrees in institutions as yet committed to some notion of the full-time student, credit for employment in certain occupations – these have been the louder and stronger demands, the demands which politicians heed. Even private institutions, great as well as small, are not immune from these pressures to make educational opportunity widespread and virtually universal. Meritocracy, an idea implicit in the English idea of a university, is difficult to defend in a society where young people do not begin life with the same social or natural advantages. While such may be true of all societies, not all societies have been politically committed to equality of opportunity. But the desire to expand access to universities (or other higher education institutions) is spreading rapidly everywhere at the end of the twentieth century.

Lesser ideas

The idea of an idea of a university is important. Without it, a university is utterly shapeless and possesses no means of distinguishing itself from any other kind of educational institution, the corporate classrooms, for example, appearing in giant firms. Even the promoters of corporate classrooms have seized upon the understanding that a university has a special history and appeal. Writing in 1990 about the lack of literacy and numeracy at the giant telecommunications firm, Motorola, its corporate vice-president for training and education and president of 'Motorola University' explained that the word 'university' seemed to reconcile 'public educators' to the $120 million investment in in-house education. 'The word university is undeniably ambitious . . . but will raise the expectations of the work force.' Who would have been 'electrified' by the term 'educational resource facility'?[46] Indeed! And the author knows his Newman, 'which, after 150 years, is still the cornerstone of liberal education'.

> But what *was* a university. And more to the point, what was a Motorola University? What kind of model should we work from? Newman's ideal university had no place for vocational training, so in that sense he and we part ways. But in another sense, we're in complete agreement. Newman wanted his university to mold the kind of individual who can 'fill any post with credit' and 'master any subject with facility' – an excellent description of what we wanted Motorola University to do.[47]

What's in a name? Or idea? The idea of the idea of a university is talismanic. Yet Newman had little or nothing to say about the issues agitating university communities at the end of the twentieth century: affirmative action, competition, the transfer function, retention rates, binary systems, the role of planning, State–university relations, peer-review in the awarding of grants and contracts, flexibility and diversity, formula-funding, academic self-government, tenure, the ratio of professorial chairs to total faculty appointments, value-added learning, the use of Scholastic Aptitude Test scores in admissions (US) and 'useful knowledge'. For some of these, useful knowledge, for example, we can deduce his possible response. On others, student support and housing, he had fixed views, since he was founding a new university and had to involve himself in such matters. But we are rarely interested in what Newman thought about these 'lesser' issues.

Nevertheless, it is precisely the lesser issues that determine how an idea is to be carried out and that in time supplant any discernible idea of a university. As current American debates indicate, and the present strained central government–university relations in Britain and Australia prove, it is not so much the primary idea of a university that is producing controversy as the secondary ideas, the subsidiary ideas of a university, or rather, the other defining characteristics listed at the outset of this chapter.

Thus in the context of present-day tensions, the English idea of a university means a certain expensive staffing ratio, a high degree of self-government (so that even the lay councils of new universities like Essex include faculty),[48] students largely in residence, tutorials or small classes, a 'national' in preference to a 'local' mission,[49] the single honours degree or a linked 'curriculum' (in the spirit of 'Greats' or 'Modern Greats') with few options or modules. Students, wrote the first vice-chancellor of Essex, may have *table d'hôte* courses, but no *à la carte*.[50] The English idea of a university has meant devising machinery for the maintenance of a more or less common standard of excellence across different universities and 'places' for undergraduates gaining admission by competitive entry, with tuition payments and maintenance grants supplied as needed by local and central government.[51] It means, again in the interests of common standards and equity, a degree of supervision from Westminster, by no means as systematically severe or Cartesian as in the French higher education system; but the presence of the centre, whether of Crown, Privy Council, Parliament or Whitehall, was always noticeable. In the building of the new University of Essex more than thirty years ago, the University Grants Committee specified the amount of square footage per lecture hall per student, the maximum price of an office chair, required prior approval for the expenditure of public money on buildings and set salary scales and ranges. The vice-chancellor, while expressing a wish for greater flexibility, nevertheless remarked upon the freedom he enjoyed to plan a new university![52]

American academics have had to live without an idea of a university for at least a century. Its relative absence has also been an advantage. It means that there is very little prior restraint on experiment. It means that Americans have not created a privileged academic class that arrogates to itself the right to speak on behalf of the higher culture (the distinguished Oxonian historian-civil servant G. M. Young of another generation once spoke of the 'terrorists of the higher culture' whom he contrasted with proponents of Liberal Curiosity).[53] It means, in the words of a 1930s president of a land grant university, that the 'state universities hold that there is no intellectual service too undignified for them to perform'.[54] It means that if the academic community cannot reach a consensus on the idea of a university, then neither can the State, the general public, alumni and benefactors. And in view of the attacks on Australian universities as represented in the Dawkins Green Paper and Mrs Thatcher's attack on British universities in the 1980s, this may well be a relief. It also means that the terms of debate are fuzzy and indistinct, and potentially divisive issues concerning academic matters are transformed into side issues and details.[55] It means that a 'binary policy' such as arose in post-Robbins Britain and a similar policy in Australia, equal but separate segments of higher education, is only acceptable if student mobility across the dividing lines is guaranteed. In the United States the segments have been separate and unequal but also, in educational jargon, 'articulated', interconnected through modularity and the transfer function. Movement from one segment to another is possible, indeed, is essential to the maintenance of the legitimacy of higher education institutions in the eyes of the public and its legislative representatives.

I have stated the American problem as one of survival, but I hardly think the situation has been that desperate. The interconnections of an institution with society and culture through market discipline are complex and intricate. At any one time numerous markets are in existence, some soft and some stable, and there never can be a perfect fit between supply and demand. Markets are not always rigid. Some of them create slack, which provides openings for inspired selling and innovation, as well as opportunities to protect less popular but valued teaching. Historically, supply in higher education has often led demand, especially in providing for curricula, and we may even notice developments that seem to bear no direct relationship to market pressures at all, subjects that are taught because the faculty believes it is fitting they should be taught even if only the few are interested.

Market response is not passive, since the market is an arena for negotiation. American universities have been active participants in the elaborate and creative process of accommodation that enables Plato and courses in film-making to exist side by side, that provides a half-unit credit for classes in handball and four units for working in the laboratory of an internationally famous scientist and credit towards graduation for courses taken by advanced placement examinations while in high school, in the United States Army, in a community college over the summer, in extramural courses and by correspondence or during a year abroad learning the maxims of La Rochefoucauld in Grenoble. Historically, American universities and colleges, their presidents and deans and their faculties have reached out to the society, actively seeking the entanglements and compromises that are so fully captured in the modular system. The search for patrons, markets, supporters and funding has gone on for 200 years. Far from continually resenting the participation of the outside world, colleges and universities have often sought it, reacting adversely, of course, whenever that participation seemed to be restrictive rather than collaborative, or whenever the professorial guild was in danger of losing control.

Nevertheless, there are deep cultural and institutional problems associated with markets. The subject has its share of inherent tensions, paradoxes and ironies.[56] No university can survive without a high degree of external support, but the question is the nature and terms of that support. One of the more interesting findings of the first three volumes of the new Oxford *History of Oxford University* is the degree to which medieval Oxford willingly connected itself to the Crown in an effort to detach itself from the control of bishops, using its graduates to reach the ears and purse of the royal court, and ultimately enabling the Renaissance State to bludgeon and bribe the university into compliance with its goals of religious and ideological uniformity. The successful efforts of the aristocracy to control the instruments of monarchy allowed the universities a high measure of autonomy by the eighteenth century, yet it was nineteenth-century liberalism – the same liberalism against which Newman railed – that established the principle that universities must be independent of State authority. Until the early twentieth century the British State was reluctant to assist the universities old and new to any great extent. State reluctance was eventually overcome by pressure from the universities themselves, which, having lost the capacity to mobilise large amounts of private giving, found their income insufficient to undertake research in science and applied science.[57]

The search for patrons is common to all university systems in all ages and countries. The difference between Britain and Progressive Era America is that in Britain the academics (once) preferred the State to the public, the centre to the periphery, the metropolis to the province. For the State, like the Church and the universities, was staffed by the same sort of person, the product of the same kind of elite schooling and conceptions of liberal education, holder of the same belief in the idea of the idea of a university. But in the United States, the State was one source among many, one patron among several, one alternative among a number of them, sometimes a welcome partner in the grand exercise of higher education, on other occasions a necessary evil. And since Americans, because of their federal constitution, did not establish a Ministry of Higher Education or a Department of Education and Science with authority to control the destinies of the higher education community, income for higher education was remarkably diverse and uncoordinated, divided between feepayers and scholarship donors, private and public, state and national sources. Government support itself was distributed through a number of different civil service departments and national research institutes, each with separate policy-making authority, each exposed to a great number of educational lobbying organisations, the famous acronyms clustered for warmth in the vicinity of One Dupont Circle in Washington, DC.

The antithesis of the idea of a university

If the American university is so fractured that it cannot organise itself around a distinct idea, it nevertheless exists in a recognisable container. Shared decision-making between trustees, administrators and professors creates bondings of sorts, as does the organisation of the institution around disciplines, which escape their perimeters and join allied fields and projects.[58] The allocation of resources is mainly a home affair, although multicampus systems impose a mega-university level of administration on top of the subordinate structures.

The American university attempts to incorporate all ideas of a university, so that the long shadow of the idea of the idea of a university is still discernible, however faint. It is not in the United States but in France that the anti- or non-essentialist idea of a university has in fact received its greatest expression. The most highly centralised of all western European systems, in theory as well as practice, French higher education institutions are virtually disembodied. Different government ministries, external councils, agencies and disciplinary boards, regional as well as national, prescribe and regulate teaching, research, curricula, examinations and degrees. Budgets are handled discretely. Research and teaching are separated and placed in separate institutional structures, with a few crossovers. Individual universities tend towards high specialisation. The university as a distinct institution, as a living organism, to use a biological metaphor, has disintegrated into many independent lines of bureaucratic management.[59]

Such a conception of a university can never inspire a masterpiece of literature capable of competing with Newman. Even the far more integrated American university has the same difficulty according to Clark Kerr:

> The Idea of a Multiversity has no bard to sing its praises; no prophet to proclaim its vision; no guardian to protect its sanctity. It has its critics, its detractors, its transgressors. It also has its reality rooted in the logic of history. It is an imperative rather than a reasoned choice among elegant alternatives.[60]

A university whose borders are so penetrable will have Romans and barbarians mixing freely on campus streets. The American Puritans wanted to establish a city on the hill, an outpost of spiritual dedication and devotion, but the American university of today is more like a city of the plain, culturally and ethnically heterogenous, full of milling crowds, jugglers and tumblers. It has suburbs and subcultures, separate neighbourhoods, even local government, and sometimes the campus is so dispersed that a transport system is required to convey inhabitants to one location or another. Of course it has a parking problem. The division of labour prevails – one of the defining characteristics of a city. Elite functions jostle with popular ones, and a huge service organisation of counselling, housing and financial services coexists with an academic sector. The large American university is properly an urban conception, in fact a functional substitute for cities in areas of the continent where metropolises do not exist, providing galleries, concert halls and museums for the local population, not to mention highly commercial sporting events. It is a creation that has grown up in time and adjusted to its culture, not smoothly but inevitably. Like the city, it is forever pushing at its boundaries, always pointing beyond itself, inviting inhabitants to consider a long list of available opportunities and choices without guaranteeing that they will be experienced or used by everyone.

In asking what binds such an institution and keeps its parts together, we might well ask what holds a city together. For some the bonding is an 'idea'. For others it is a conception. Still others accept the challenge of the campus-city, focusing on the more immediate task of getting on, of coping with the exigencies of daily life and finding a niche for themselves. Therefore we can say that while it is often impossible to live in a city, so is it also impossible to live elsewhere.

Notes

1 E.g., *The Role of the University: a Global Perspective*, ed. Torsten Husén (The United Nations University and UNESCO, Tokyo, 1994).
2 On this note, see the lectures by Mary Douglas, *How Institutions Think* (Syracuse, 1986).
3 Louise Stevenson, *Scholarly Means to Evangelical Ends: The New Haven Scholars and the Transformation of Higher Learning in America, 1830–1890* (Baltimore, 1986).
4 Samuel Taylor Coleridge, *Lay Sermons*, ed. R. J. White, VI (Princeton, 1972), 100n, 101n, 43; *Collected Letters of Samuel Taylor Coleridge*, ed. Earl Leslie Briggs, II (Oxford, 1956), 677–704, 708–10.
5 John Henry Newman, *The Letters and Diaries*, ed. Charles Stephen Dessain, XV (London, 1964), 90.
6 Samuel Taylor Coleridge, *On the Constitution of the Church and State*, ed. John Colmer (Princeton, 1976), 12; John Stuart Mill, *On Bentham and Coleridge*, intro. F. R. Leavis (New York, 1962), 110–12.
7 Coleridge, *Constitution*, 20.
8 Mill, *Bentham and Coleridge*.
9 Jacques Dreze and Jean Debelle, *Conceptions de l'université* (Paris, 1968).
10 John Henry Newman, *Historical Sketches*, III (London, 1881).
11 See John Thelin, *The Cultivation of Ivy: a Saga of the College in America* (Cambridge, MA, 1976).

12 John Henry Newman, 'The Tamworth Reading Room', in *The Evangelical and Oxford Movements*, ed. Elisabeth Jay (Cambridge, 1983).

13 John Henry Newman, *The Idea of a University*, ed. I. T. Ker (Oxford, 1976), 5.

14 Edward Tatham (Rector of Lincoln College, Oxford), *An Address to the Members of Convocation at Large, on the Proposed New Statutes Respecting Public Examination in the University of Oxford*, 2nd ed. (London, 1807), 1.

15 E. B. Pusey, *Collegiate and Professorial Teaching and Discipline* (Oxford and London, 1854), 215–16.

16 Vicesimus Knox, *Liberal Education; or, a Practical Treatise on the Methods of Acquiring Useful and Polite Learning*, 11th ed., II (London, 1795), 113n.

17 E.g., *The History of the University of Oxford*, V, *The Eighteenth Century*, ed. L. S. Sutherland and L. G. Mitchell (Oxford, 1986), Chapters 15–25.

18 *Idea*, 5.

19 Royal Commission on London 1912–1913. Cd. 6312 xxii, 793. Evidence of Professor Starling.

20 Alfred North Whitehead, 'Universities and Their Functions', in *The Aims of Education and Other Essays* (New York, 1957), 145.

21 Newman, *Idea*, 379–80.

22 E.g., in Jaroslav Pelikan's inspiring book, *The Idea of the University, A Reexamination* (New Haven and London, 1992), 181, research and publication are given central importance, and other passages suggest that Newman would approve. But perhaps in light of the fact that Pelikan's book is a 'reexamination', my point is too finicky.

23 See Sheldon Rothblatt, 'The Limbs of Osiris', in *The European and American University since 1800, Historical and Sociological Essays*, ed. Sheldon Rothblatt and Björn Wittrock (Cambridge, 1993), 19–73.

24 An unflattering but interesting account of how Oxbridge 'humanism' has dominated fiction to the detriment of viewpoints arising from non-literary perspectives appears in Ian Carter, *Ancient Cultures of Conceit, British University Fiction in the Post-War Years* (London and New York, 1990).

25 George B. Jeffery, *The Unity of Knowledge: Some Reflections on the Universities of Cambridge and London* (Cambridge, 1950).

26 Sven-Eric Liedman, 'In Search of Isis: General Education in Germany and Sweden', in Rothblatt and Wittrock, 74–106.

27 Information communicated to me by Louis Vos of Leuven University in connection with the Standing Conference of European Rectors' project on the history of the university in Europe.

28 See Chapters 3, 5 and 6.

29 Jacques Bardoux, *Memories of Oxford* (London, 1899), 9, 12, 13, 34–5, 40.

30 See David Sorkin, 'Wilhelm von Humboldt: The Theory and Practice of Self-Formation (*Bildung*), 1791–1810', *Journal of the History of Ideas*, 44 (January–March 1983), 55–74.

31 Fritz Ringer, 'Comparing Two Academic Cultures: The University in Germany and France around 1900', in *History of Education*, 16 (September 1987), 181–5. Knowledge as the process by which the mind comes to understand itself also contains the notion of wholeness, the personality as a totality. Therefore at another level *Wissenschaft* and *Bildung* are part of the larger western tradition of liberal education, which in highly attenuated form resurfaces in American concerns for undergraduate general education. It is also as general education that *Bildung* has recently re-emerged in Sweden – in Swedish as *bildning* and *allmänbildning*. My source is Sven-Eric Liedman and Lennart Olausson, 'General Education, Culture, and Specialization', *Studies of Higher Education and Research* (1987), 6.

32 The Yale scholars, however, believed they could attach German ideas of self-development to a wider sense of public responsibility, thus, evidently, pursuing a goal that seems to have eluded Humboldt. See Stevenson, *Scholarly Means*, Chapter 4.

33 Barbara Stephen, *Emily Davies and Girton College* (London, 1927), 155.

34 Lorraine Daston, 'Wissenschaft, Research and the Institute', in *Universities and the Sciences*, ed. Guiliano Pancaldi (Bologna, 1993), 76.

35 A serious problem, however, from the standpoint of maintaining the integrity and cohesion of a religious vision. Nor did the abolition of one form of dogmatism prevent the arrival of another.

36 Sheldon Rothblatt, 'The Last Thing Said in Germany', *The London Review of Books* (19 May 1988), 12–18.

37 See Simon Schwartzman, 'The Focus on Scientific Activity', in *Perspectives on Higher Education, Eight Disciplinary and Comparative Views*, ed. Burton R. Clark (Berkeley and Los Angeles, 1984), 199–232.

38 John W. Meyer, 'The Charter: Conditions of Diffuse Socialization in Schools', in *Social Process and Social Structures: an Introduction to Sociology*, ed. W. R. Scott (New York, 1970), 564–78.

39 Sheldon Rothblatt, 'The American Modular System', in *Quality and Access in Higher Education, Comparing Britain and the United States*, ed. Robert O. Berdahl, Graeme C. Moodie and Irving J. Spitzberg, Jr. (Ballmoor, Buckingham, 1991), 130–2.

40 Oliver Fulton, 'Modular Systems in Britain', in *Quality and Access in Higher Education, Comparing Britain and the United States*, ed. Robert O. Berdahl, Graeme C. Moodie and Irving J. Spitzberg, Jr. (Ballmoor, Buckingham, 1991), 142–51. By 1995 modular schemes had spread throughout the United Kingdom and Northern Ireland, taking several main forms. A summary appears in *The Times Higher Education Supplement* (29 September 1995), in the section called 'Synthesis'. British modules are more complex than American versions, since many of them are linked or shared between departments and programmes, do not allow for student choice in every instance and often feature centrally managed assessment.

41 See Martin Duberman, *Black Mountain, An Exploration in Community* (Garden City, New York, 1973). For other experiments, see Gerald Grant and David Riesman, *The Perpetual Dream* (Chicago, 1978).

42 Walter P. Metzger. 'Academic Profession in the United States', in *The Academic Profession*, ed. Burton R. Clark (Berkeley and Los Angeles, 1987), 132.

43 Sheldon Rothblatt, *The Revolution of the Dons: Cambridge and Society in Victorian England* (London and New York, 1968, reissued Cambridge, 1981), 194–5.

44 William T. Foster, *Administration of the College Curriculum* (New York, 1911), 316. The odd punctuation appears in the original.

45 *A New Vitality in General Education* (Association of American Colleges, 1988); William Bennett, *To Reclaim a Legacy* (November, 1984), 11; Allan Bloom, *The Closing of the American Mind: How Higher Education has Failed Democracy and Impoverished the Souls of Today's Students* (New York, 1987); Ernest L. Boyer, *College, The Undergraduate Experience in America* (New York, 1987); Derek Bok, *Beyond the Ivory Tower, Social Responsibilites of the Modern University* (Cambridge, MA, 1982), 62, 64, 77, 88. See also *The Future of State Universities*, ed. Leslie W. Koepplin and David Wilson (New Brunswick, NJ, 1985); Frank Newman, *Choosing Quality, Reducing the Conflict between the State and the University* (Education Commission of the States, September, 1987); and *Higher*

Education and the American Resurgence (Carnegie Foundation for the Advancement of Teaching, 1985).

46 William Wiggenhorn, 'Motorola U: When Training Becomes an Education', *Harvard Business Review* (July–August 1990), 83.

47 *Ibid.*, 81.

48 Albert E. Sloman, *A University in the Making* (1964), 80, the BBC Reith Lectures for 1963.

49 I noticed with interest that some participants in the 1980s Australian debate over the federal government's Green Paper reconsidered the advantages of local over central control with respect to academic freedom.

50 Sloman, *University*, 41–2.

51 Loan schemes, however, have become important in the 1990s as higher education expenses increase more rapidly than government expenditure.

52 Sloman, *University*, 12–15.

53 George Malcolm Young, 'The New Cortegiano', in *Victorian Essays* (London, 1962), 210.

54 Quoted in Bok, *A New Vitality*, 62.

55 There are major exceptions to this general observation. Controversial issues arising from larger American conflicts inevitably force their way into universities. This is especially damaging wherever no strong consensual 'idea' exists to provide guidance. McCarthy era restrictions on academic freedom are one example, affirmative action hiring and admission policies are another. These continue to divide the academy.

56 For a start, Sheldon Rothblatt, ' "Standing Antagonisms": the Relationship of Undergraduate to Graduate Education', in Koepplin and Wilson, 39–66.

57 For this story see Sheldon Rothblatt and Martin Trow, 'Government Policies and Higher Education: a Comparison of Britain and the United States from about 1630 to 1860', in *Social Research and Social Reform: Essays in Honour of A. H. Halsey*, ed. Colin Crouch and Anthony Heath (Oxford, 1992), 173–216.

58 As explained by Burton R. Clark, 'The Problem of Complexity in Modern Higher Education', in Rothblatt and Wittrock, 263–79. But 'Shared decision-making' may be a cliche. It certainly begs the question of how much or just what is shared: admissions, curricula, research, appointments, grantsmanship? An analysis would require a separate chapter.

59 Christine Musselin, 'Steering Higher Education in France: 1981–1991', *Higher Education in Europe*, 17 (1992), 70; Guy Neave, 'Séparation de Corps: The Training of Advanced Students and the Organization of Research in France', in *The Research Foundations of Graduate Education, Germany, Britain, France, the United States, Japan*, ed. Burton R. Clark (Berkeley and Los Angeles, 1993), 159–91, and Guy Neave and Richard Edelstein, 'The Research Training System in France: Microstudy of Three Academic Disciplines', in Clark, *ibid.*, 192–220.

60 Clark Kerr, *The Uses of the University* (Cambridge, MA, 1963), 6.

42

THE CHANGING FUNCTIONS
OF UNIVERSITIES

A. H. Halsey and M. A. Trow

Source: A. H. Halsey and M. A. Trow, *The British Academics*, London: Faber and Faber, 1971, pp. 31–7.

Some kind of intellectual life goes on in all societies. There are always processes of cultural transmission to each new generation. There is, in other words, always teaching and hence the possibility of 'men of knowledge'. Where there are specialised guardians of highly prized elements in the culture we have the prototype of the academic man. Societies also change and where intellectual discovery is the agent of change there is the possibility of 'men of new knowledge'. In the modern world the discovery of new knowledge has been institutionalised as research and thereby, over a wide range of scientific enquiry, has acquired a cumulative character. The implications for economic growth and social change of this recent development are vast and probably as yet largely unrealised. Academic men were not especially prominent in the beginning of this revolution in the creation of knowledge, but have become so since the middle of the nineteenth century. Thus higher education has become one of the means of creating a new form of society, economically rich, organised in larger economic and political units, connected by increasingly elaborate networks of communications and above all containing large investments of skill and resources in further economic and social change through the extending applications of science to human activity.

The Unbound Prometheus is David Landes' apt title for a description of the inter-related set of changes which began with the Industrial Revolution in eighteenth-century England, i.e. 'the first historical instance of the breakthrough from an agrarian handicraft economy to one dominated by industry and machine manufacture'.[1]

The historical primacy of Britain in the early revolution of industrial technique has had special consequences for the subsequent development of organised science and education in general and universities in particular. It meant, among other things, that an industrial middle class developed before the system of modern or reformed universities, and thus outside the university system. On one side this middle class developed attitudes that were by no means favourable to the universities either for their sons or for their managerial and technical employees. On the other side there was little interest in this new middle class within the ancient foundations of Oxford and Cambridge, which functioned mainly to serve the needs of the upper classes and those intending to enter the Anglican ministry.

More generally, this historical background suggests part of the explanation for the distinctive position of academic men in contemporary Britain. But as well as national peculiarities the academic role has common elements which derive basically from the intrinsic social and cultural imperialism of the new form of society. Landes' summary of the character of the relevant societies is as follows.

Industrialisation in turn is at the heart of a larger, more complex process often designated as *modernisation*. This is that combination of changes – in the mode of production and government, in the social and institutional order, in the corpus of knowledge and in attitudes and values – that make it possible for a society to hold its own in the twentieth century; that is, to compete on even terms in the generation of material and cultural wealth, to sustain its independence, and to promote and accommodate to further change. Modernisation comprises such developments as urbanisation (a concentration of the population in cities that serve as nodes of industrial production, administration, and intellectual and artistic activity); a sharp reduction in both death-rates and birth-rates from traditional levels (the so-called demographic transition); the establishment of an effective, fairly centralised bureaucratic government; the creation of an educational system capable of training and socialising the children of a society to a level compatible with their capacities and best contemporary knowledge; and of course, the acquisition of the ability and means to use an up-to-date technology.[2]

Advanced industrial societies everywhere have developed institutions of higher education which, through technological innovation by research and through educating and training recruits for the professions, form an essential part of the economy. Universities, in which teaching and research are combined, form a more or less important part of these structures of higher education – more important in the U.S.A.[3] and Great Britain, less in France and the U.S.S.R. where specialised training institutions have a large place. In general, however, academic men have come to occupy a position at the apex of teaching and research mainly through the development of universities. The university is only one of the possible forms of organisation for transmitting and creating knowledge: it is the combination of teaching and research which, while permitting wide variation between its elements and emphases, defines the distinctive character of the university as a social institution. The place of this institution in the British version of an emerging system of higher education is our main concern in Chapter 2.[4]

The characteristics of the British as of all modern systems of education are products of adaptation to a changing society. Changes in social structure create changes in the structure and functions of universities which in turn promote or impede further changes in society. This kind of interaction dates at least from medieval Europe. Thus explanation of the character of universities and the role of academic men within them requires in principle an examination of the history of every aspect of social structure. Society sets changing supply and demand conditions for universities and thereby closely constrains the choice of functions open to them. For example, there have been changes in the employment opportunities for graduates over the course of industrialisation and in the demand for the intellectual output of university teachers and research workers. The internal life of universities has accordingly changed, and the explanation of these changes lies in changes in the religious, economic and political structure of society.

The main trends in the development of the general relation between the universities and society are clear enough. In the nineteenth and twentieth centuries there has been a transformation in the functions of universities for the economy, an increase in state control, and a widening of social class connection both in the recruitment of students and in the training of professional people.

The European universities were, in the middle ages, an organic part of religious rather than economic life and the subsequent growth of economic functions for them with the rise of industrialism is part of a broader process of secularisation of learning which can be traced at least as far back as the fourteenth century. In the fifteenth century the European universities – some seventy in all – 'constituted an intellectual commonwealth embodying the same ideal'[5] and they were based on a common religion, language and culture. The schismatic effects of the Reformation and the rise of nationalisms undermined the foundations of university life in the following centuries, but when the universities began to respond to the scientific revolution and its effects in industry and government during the nineteenth century, a new period of expansion and prestige opened for them which led to the diversified modern secular systems of higher education. Thus, in the nineteenth and twentieth centuries, pressure from economic development evoked response from the universities or the setting up of other institutions of higher education which gradually linked the universities to the economy through the market for professional manpower, through research activities in the applied sciences and through a slowly widening consumption of 'high culture'. A new commonwealth of educated men has emerged in the form of international coteries of experts involved in science and scholarship, the management of economic enterprise and economic growth and intellectual and cultural activities of every kind.

This fundamental change in their functions has brought the universities increasingly into, the political arena, financed and managed more and more by national governments. In responding to the manpower and research needs of modernisation universities have outstripped the capacity or willingness of the private purse. In any case, in recent decades, a conscious attempt to plan and manage economic growth and military efficiency has become more or less universal among the governments of industrial and industrialising countries and has led to the development of a new sphere of science policy which relates the polity to the scientific community. Consequently, universities everywhere attract increasing governmental interest and control, no matter what the political constitution of the country in which they are placed.

The political significance of the modern university, moreover, does not stem solely from new relations to the productive system. It is also a result of class and status struggles over the distribution of opportunity afforded by a university education. The trend is towards more democratic entry into an expanded and diversified system of higher education which offers chances for mobility through professional qualifications and a generally superior life style for those in possession of the culture of the educated.[6] Over a period of emerging industrialism in Europe and America the universities have served as an avenue of recruiting and educating political, industrial and social élites which have become larger and more diversified during the course of industrialisation and which have had to absorb some men from the lower social strata to secure their development and maintenance.

Thus, the secularisation of higher learning, and especially the incorporation of science into research and teaching, has increased the potential of the universities as sources of technological, and therefore of social, change until now they form part of the economic foundations of a new type of society. In this new technological society educational institutions have expanded, not only to exercise research functions, but also to play a central role in the economy and system of stratification as agencies for the selection, training and placement of individuals in an ever-widening range of professional and quasi-professional occupations and in a corresponding hierarchy of life styles.

Movement towards these conditions has been uneven among the Western industrial countries and university systems have accordingly diversified.[7] But the direction of movement is common despite political and social differences. Democratisation and expansion have been more or less successful and accompanied by a greater or lesser degree of differentiation within higher education systems. At one end of the spectrum, large numbers and a wide range of vocational studies are gathered under the university umbrella in the United States and, at the other end, a system of specialised institutions in which the university as such constitutes a relatively minor part has developed in Russia. The American and Russian systems of higher education represent the two dominating and contrasting forms at the present time just as university development in the middle of the nineteenth century was dominated by the German idea of the university.

British conceptions of the university still exercise considerable sway over the ex-colonial territories in Africa and the Caribbean and British intellectual traditions retain extraordinary dominance over the educated Indian,[8] but the U.S.A. and the Soviet Union now receive rather than send the would-be planner of new universities. A Royal Commission on Oxford and Cambridge in 1922 could say that 'the two senior Universities of the Empire have also now the chance of becoming to a much greater extent than formerly centres of research, and of graduate study for the whole Empire and for American and foreign guests'.[9] A generation later David Riesman, surveying the American universities, asserted that 'we can no longer look abroad for our models of cultural and educational advance, Europeans and Japanese, West Africans and Burmese now come here to look for models or invite American professors to visit and bring with them the "American Way" in higher education'.[10] Western Europe was becoming a cultural province of North America.

The American system was dominated by the German idea of a university in the early nineteenth century. But in the second half of the century, after the Civil War, it expanded more rapidly than any other as a heterogeneous, large-scale and internally differentiated set of competitive educational enterprises serving the needs of a rapidly growing economy and unhampered by a restrictive class hierarchy or undue dominance from a metropolitan élite centre. The expansion of the Russian system dates from the Revolution of 1917 and owes a great deal to central political control which has directed the supply of graduates to the needs of planned economic growth and has regulated the number of places accordingly, giving special emphasis to the supply of professional engineers.

In his comparative analysis of the changing functions of modern universities over the course of the last hundred years, Joseph Ben-David has shown that the willingness and capacity of universities 'to recognise and develop innovations into new disciplines depended on the existence of a decentralised competitive market for academic achievements . . . and on their direct, or government-mediated relationship to the different classes of society'.[11] A highly differentiated organisation is needed to carry out the greatly increased and increasingly varied functions of higher education and research. 'Such complex academic organisation has arisen in the United States and the Soviet Union. In spite of the vast difference in the formal organisation of their higher education and research, both countries have developed clearly differentiated functions of pure as well as applied research and purely scientific and scholarly education alongside highly practical professional training. And both countries managed to create a much greater variety of academic roles than the European countries.'[12]

Our main concern in this book is with Britain, which was the first country to be influenced by the development of the German universities in the nineteenth century. Influence, however, did not mean repetition. As Ben-David has put it 'what emerged was something rather baffling to observers accustomed to use the German "idea of the university" as a yardstick of measuring academic accomplishment. . . . They admired English universities for the quality of their graduates; criticised them for their mediocre performance in many fields and their seeming indifference towards the active promotion of research; and were mystified by the nevertheless brilliant work of some English scientists.'[13] We turn to an exploration of the particular form of British university development in the next chapter.

Notes

1 David S. Landes, *The Unbound Prometheus: technological change and industrial development in Western Europe from 1750 to the present*, Cambridge University Press, 1969.
2 *Ibid.*, p. 6.
3 Cf. T. Parsons and G. M. Platt, 'Considerations on the American Academic System', *Minerva*, Vol. 6, No. 4, Summer 1968.
4 By the word 'system' we refer to the web of social relationships and the institutional division of labour which are involved in advanced teaching and research and which in turn form part of the wider process of formal education in schools, colleges and institutes. Such a system is a sociological abstraction. It may be more or less consciously organised, controlled and standardised in the forms and procedures of its constituent units. There was no popular conception of a British system of higher education before the Robbins Report. Far less was there an administrative entity. Indeed, a centralised direction for higher education remains a contentious issue of policy with all its attendant problems of defining the legitimate degree of autonomy of academic institutions and the division of powers between central and local government, governing bodies and the numerous professional, business, academic and civic interests.
5 Eric Ashby, *Universities: British, Indian, African*, Weidenfeld and Nicolson, 1966, p. 4.
6 The extension of university opportunities to women is a subsidiary element in political movements aimed to 'universalise' access to higher education. See Annie Rogers, *Degree by Degrees*, Oxford University Press, 1938, and Vera Brittain, *The Women of Oxford*, George G. Harrap, 1960.
7 See Ashby, *op. cit.*, for a more extended discussion and an analysis of the transplantation of the Western university to India and Africa.
8 Cf. Edward Shils, 'The Intellectual Between Tradition and Modernity: The Indian Situation', *Comparative Studies in Society and History*, Supplement I, 1961, pp. 81–7. 'India was, and remains, an intellectual province of London, Oxford and Cambridge.'
9 Report of the Royal Commission on Oxford and Cambridge, 1922, Cmd. 1588, para. 33.

10 David Riesman in A. H. Halsey *et al.* (eds.), *Education, Economy and Society*, The Free Press, 1961, p. 481.
11 Joseph Ben-David and Awraham Zloczower, 'Universities and Academic Systems in Modern Societies', *European Journal of Sociology*, Vol. 1, 1962.
12 *Ibid.*, p. 82.
13 *Ibid.*, p. 62.

43

THE UNIVERSITY IN THE MODERN WORLD

An address delivered to the Conference of
European Rectors and Vice-Chancellors at
Göttingen on September 2nd, 1964

Lionel Robbins

Source: Lord Robbins, *The University in the Modern World*, London: Macmillan, 1966, pp. 1–16.

I

In rising to play my part in inaugurating this very important Conference, I should be doing less than justice to the occasion did I not pay tribute to the felicity of its location. For those of us who have the solidarity of international learning at heart, your famous University of Göttingen must always occupy a special place in our admiration and respect. From the days of its foundation — when, incidentally, Mr. Rector, your predecessors and mine lived under a common monarch — it has been one of the main centres of thought and scholarship in the civilization of the West; and the protest of the *Göttingen Sieben* is notable as an outstanding gesture in defence of freedom. We are grateful, Mr. Rector, for your hospitality; and as, under your auspices, we consider the problems of the future, we shall be conscious of the achievements of your glorious past.

Rectors and Vice-Chancellors, you are met here to discuss in all its different aspects a very important problem, the appropriate size of universities: and the very fact of your meeting in this way is itself indicative of an important change which has taken place in our time — the change in the social position and the social function of our universities. Since the days of their foundation, the universities have played an important part in the life of western societies: they have provided education for talented (or gilded) youth and they have fostered scholarship and the advancement of learning. But on the whole, while this rôle has been self-conscious enough, its

relationship to the general purposes of society has been more or less unconscious: in the past it was the exception rather than the rule to ask whether
the universities provided enough places and what their relation should be to
other sections of the community as a whole. But today the position is changed.
We are continually asking where we stand and where we are going. It is safe
to say that never before in history was there such an incessant process of
self-examination as ours. I should like to devote this inaugural address to
commenting on the causes of this situation and on some of the problems
to which it gives rise.

II

To begin then with causes. I detect two main groups of influences.

First, comes the pressure of numbers. This derives, partly, of course, from
the mere pressure of population. The population explosion has left hardly
any western community unaffected, though its more frightening effects are
to be seen elsewhere; and the mere increase of the relevant age groups,
regardless of social policy, brings about a situation in which, if standards of
admission are not to be continually raised, more places must be provided.

But partly it comes from a change in social attitudes. For, regardless
of the increase in numbers, I would say that in most western communities
there has come about a radical and far-reaching change in conceptions
of eligibility for higher education: the maxim *la carrière ouverte aux talents*
has become a dominating principle of policy. So that, whereas, in the
past the university population consisted largely of those whose parents had
the private means to finance them *plus* the exceptionally gifted who had the
capacity to win the comparatively few scholarships available, in the future
provision is likely to be made for all those who are capable of passing tests
of what is judged to be the requisite intellectual standard and who wish to
take advantage of the opportunity. From a world in which numbers were
largely a function of family resources, we have moved into a world in which
the state, whether by loans or direct subventions, has to a very large extent
taken over responsibility.

So much is common knowledge. What I do not think is as yet fully
appreciated in many quarters is the extent to which the application of this
principle is likely to increase the pressure of numbers. We have been too apt
to assume — at any rate, in my country — that the existing scholarship
system already provided for the greater number of those likely to profit from
higher education. But unless we restrict this criterion to capacity to emerge
with the highest first-class honours — or, as we should put it at home, to
fellowship quality — this is not so. A great variety of statistical tests, which
it would be perverse to question, go to demonstrate that the so-called pool
of ability is much more extensive than has been commonly realized and
that, given adequate financial support, the supply of those who are able, on

present admission standards, to achieve good university qualifications, is likely to be an increasing proportion of the relevant age groups for very many years to come. We may, or may not, have creamed off the larger proportion of young people of fellowship quality. But the reserve of these with qualities which, among the moneyed and professional classes, would automatically be regarded as deserving higher education, is still very extensive indeed.

In this connection, perhaps I might inflict on you a few figures emerging from a public inquiry which has recently been made in my own country; they illustrate better than any amount of qualitative asseveration, the orders of magnitude involved in the tendencies I have been mentioning. Our inquiry revealed that, of the children born in 1940–41, those whose fathers' occupation was non-manual had five times as many chances of entering degree level higher education as the children of manual workers. We found that those whose fathers' own education was prolonged at least to 18, had sixteen times the chance of those whose fathers left school under 16. It might, perhaps, be argued that there were biological differences operative here: and, of course, on a matter so obscure, categorical denial of all such influence would be unjustified. But against major explanation of the disparities in these terms must be set the significant fact that, *whatever the education of the parent*, a child who is one of a family of two is more than twice as likely to reach higher education as a child from a family of four and about four times as likely as a child from a family of five or more. Whatever the ultimate influence of biological factors, I see no reason to suppose any near limit of the reserves of latent ability in the relevant age groups of modern western populations.

So much for the pressure of numbers. But, in addition to this, and in a sense perhaps rival to it, comes a second group of influences springing from an enhanced valuation of what universities and such-like institutions have to give. I am not thinking here of the various skills which are conferred by higher education; the enhanced value which we set upon these nowadays is yet another of the influences which make for the pressure of numbers. I am thinking rather of the contribution to the progress and texture of civilization which our universities have to make, not only as centres of training, but also as centres of thought and learning.

Let me make my thought more explicit on this point. It is, of course, a commonplace that our civilization depends in its material aspects on the achievements of science and technology and that the hope of further progress rests on the expectation of further advances in these fields. It is no less true — though not so generally recognized — that, in a complex society such as ours, the hope of order and freedom in social conditions must rest in considerable measure upon the advancement of systematic knowledge in social studies. Gone are the days — if ever they existed — when statesmanship could hope to muddle through on the strength of ancient custom and intuition. We do not commit the heresy of regarding society as pure artifact, if we recognize that only on the basis of understanding and measurement can the persistent spontaneous elements in social relationships be harmonized and controlled. There may be reasons deep in the nature of things why the knowledge yielded by social studies can never have the certainty or predictive value of the knowledge yielded by the natural sciences. But that is no reason for believing that now, or at any time in the foreseeable future, we can afford to dispense with their aid. And here, as with the natural sciences, the universities have a fundamental contribution to make.

But their contribution is not limited to these essentially practical functions — important though these may be. In some sense which it is difficult exactly to define, but which it is easy enough to recognize, the activities which they foster are activities which most of us would regard as good in themselves. To attempt to understand the world, to contemplate and to analyse its values — these are activities which, even if they were never associated with practical advantage, would still lend meaning and dignity to life on this planet. And in our day, with the visible crumbling of the ascendancy of so many of the more dogmatic creeds, it is perhaps in such activities, in such *milieux*, that the life of the spirit seems to flourish with least inhibition and with most intensity. And it is realization of this, equally with realization of their more utilitarian functions, which has led to that elevation of the expectations of what the university has to give of which I have just been speaking.

III

Here then are the influences which have brought about the increased self-consciousness which was the occasion of these observations: the pressure of numbers and the enhanced valuation of universities as the fountain of ideas and spiritual leadership. At once we are faced with the question, to what extent can these needs be met simultaneously? The tradition of our universities in these respects is essentially a tradition of what we economists call *joint supply*: they have been at once institutions for training the young and fostering the advancement of learning. Can this tradition be maintained? The question is not superfluous; in various quarters recently there have been voices declaring that this historical conjunction is now obsolete; and that henceforward the responsibility for the performance of these two functions should be divided between institutions specialized on training and institutions specialized on research. At one time at least, there were significant moves in this direction in the Soviet Union.

I hope very much that these views will be rejected: their acceptance, I am convinced, would involve the abandonment of something which is intrinsically valuable. I say nothing against the existence of research institutes as such: who can doubt that in many connections, the development of special techniques and the nature of the problems to be solved render them not only desirable, but even essential? Nor would I deny that, at the undergraduate level in universities, it may happen, may indeed be very desirable, that some of the staff will be almost wholly specialized on teaching; I am inclined to think that this kind of talent not infrequently receives less recognition and has lets value set upon it than is its due. But I do not believe in an institutional separation of the functions — at any rate as a principle of policy. I am sure that, at this stage, teaching itself tends to be impoverished if it is not carried on in the neighbourhood of research: it is *morally* important for the young people to live in an atmosphere in which everything is subject to criticism and new ideas keep breaking through. And I think too, that there is apt to be some impoverishment — and probably some waste of latent teaching capacity — if research institutes are not situated in close juxtaposition to a university — there is less danger of inbreeding in such surroundings; moreover, the best intuitions frequently come when one is seeking to make one's thoughts intelligible to learners. I submit that the habit which in the past has associated teaching and research is on the whole a healthy one: and I am inclined to suspect that where it is departed from on a large scale, the results are not at all satisfactory. I think it is worth making a great effort to ensure that this habit persists: and I see nothing in the nature of things which prevents its persistence. It is all a matter of appropriate organization.

It is sometimes suggested — it is in a way a variant of the proposal I have just been examining — that the teaching function *at the lower end* should be segregated. The advocates of this suggestion do not deny that, in the more advanced stages of university education, there is benefit from the intermixture of teaching and research. But at the beginning, it is urged, immediately after leaving school, there is a stage when the desirability of being in proximity to research activities is minimal, and when concentration on instruction as such is even advantageous. There is scope therefore for the creation of a system of sub-universities, or junior colleges, at which the earlier stages of training may be carried out and where there may take place a process of selection of students yet to proceed to more advanced studies.

Proposals of this sort seem to me much more persuasive than those which I examined earlier. I do not think it can be denied that the research atmosphere is much less essential in the first year or two of an undergraduate's training than it is later on; and I can see arguments deriving from the possible specialization of staff and equipment which can also be invoked in this connection. Whether such a system is actually desirable seems to me to depend, at least in part, upon the nature and the structure of instruction at the earlier stage in the schools. I am convinced that it would not be well suited to our local structure in England, where, for good or for bad, the sixth form in fact performs many of the functions postulated for the junior colleges; but I can conceive other educational systems, such as the Californian, to which it may be well suited. In general, however, I confess to some bias against the multiplication of hierarchical distinctions which this sort of organization involves: if there are to be junior colleges, I should prefer that they should be *within* the university ambit, rather than *outside*. I know very well that the process of higher education must eventually involve hierarchy and the selection of an *élite*. But the question is, *at what stage is the selection to take place*? And, on the whole, I am inclined to believe that, given present admission standards — at least the sort of admission standards which we have at home — it best takes place at the end of a three- or four-year period of undergraduate training, rather than earlier. I should not wish to be dogmatic about what is best in other conditions. But on the whole, I should be against such differentiation at the undergraduate stage. I do not think it is morally good for very clever young people to be marked out as an *élite* and segregated as such in these early years; it is better that they should mix with more ordinary people and learn that there are qualities of character and sensibility, other than the purely intellectual, which are also deserving of respect.

IV

Whatever is done in this respect, the university institution of the future is likely to be large — large, that is to say, in comparison with standards of the past. There are many reasons for this. Conspicuous, of course, are considerations of economy — of economy of equipment, economy of expensive apparatus, economy of libraries and buildings. Equally important, although not so generally realized, are considerations of division of labour: in many subjects in our time, the advancement of knowledge has been so considerable, that only by the employment of a large staff, each member specializing in particular sectors, is it at all possible to cover the field at the requisite level. I think, for instance, of my own subject, Economics. Forty years ago it was still possible for a single professor with two or three assistants to keep in effective touch with what was going on in the main language areas. Today it would be quite out of the question: only a department of at least ten, and better considerably more, is really adequate to the task — quite apart from teaching responsibilities. All this has made for increasing size of university institutions as a whole and, in greater or less degree according to the subjects involved, it is likely to continue to do so as we go forward into the future.

What under such conditions is the optimal size is a question which is to be considered at length at this Conference; and I will not presume to anticipate the deliberations of experts. But I will permit myself two observations of a very general nature.

First, as regards coverage. I have argued that in my judgment the university institution of the future is bound to be *large*. But I would not argue that it must necessarily be *comprehensive* in the old meaning of the term university. Needless to say, I say nothing in criticism of that conception and that tradition; it has given us institutions which are among the glories of western civilization. But I do not think that, at the present day, it is necessary to have that comprehensive coverage in order to achieve the standards or the *ethos* of a university. The contention that it is necessary to embrace the whole range of knowledge in order that there shall be sufficient cross-fertilization of minds, either at the student or the senior level, does not seem to me to stand up to the test of experience. It is quite impossible for any single individual to be cross-fertilized to that extent. I have myself taught in a full university — Oxford — and in a more specialized institution — the London School of Economics: and I am bound to say that I get as much cross-fertilization as I can take in the latter as I did in the former. Provided that there is some range, some variety, it does not seem to be necessary that *everything* should be covered.

Hence, in the world of the future I should expect to see more and more university institutions with limited areas of activity, although each seeking sufficient diversity to provide an adequate range of studies. This is what has happened already on the side of science and technology. The great technological institutions have reached out to pure science and then to relevant liberal studies and, in so doing, have in effect created a new type of university, although with a different centre of gravity. It may, or may not, have been sensible in the old days to differentiate, on some ground or other, between the intellectual and moral status of the so-called technical high school and the university proper. But who would have the temerity nowadays to make such judgments in regard, let us say, to the great technological high school of Zürich or the Massachusetts Institute of Technology. I can conceive other such variants with centres of gravity other than technology — Applied Arts or Social Studies, for example. And to the extent that such institutions do not attempt to cover the entire field of knowledge, there to that extent, their optimal size will be smaller.

My second point relates to atmosphere and human relations. I do not doubt that, as an institution grows, there are certain intimacies that it loses. One of my first recollections of the London School of Economics in 1920 is of the small common room which we students shared with the staff: I retain a vivid picture of Edwin Cannan, at that time one of the senior and most famous English economists, playing chess in a corner with a student, while a rather pretty young woman is drying a pair of red stockings by an open fire. Alas, there are no such scenes to be witnessed nowadays at L.S.E. You cannot arrange widespread spontaneous intimacy with the eminent in institutions of even two or three thousand — let alone larger numbers. But I do not share the view that expansion necessarily involves the sacrifice of all human contacts, with the individual student lost in an atomistic Sahara. It may happen, but it need not happen. It is a matter of will and organization. It is possible in large universities to have groupings and subgroupings — colleges or houses or departments — which provide some at least of the intimacies and opportunities of contact between staff and students which, in smaller institutions, arise simply in virtue of smallness. I count it highly significant that with us, at any rate, the institutions where relationships of this sort are still the most frequent and the most characteristic, the two senior universities of Oxford and Cambridge, are also (apart from London, which in all sorts of ways is *sui generis*) the largest of their kind. It is a direct by-product of the collegiate system prevailing there. This doubtless is something which would not be suitable nowadays to reproduce in its entirety. But it is easy to conceive of variants more appropriate to the modern age; and recent experience in various quarters suggests that they are quite practicable.

V

All this relates to the structure of modern university institutions. Equally important problems arise concerning the content and nature of what they teach. We are contemplating a state of affairs in which, for reasons I have already touched upon, in the next twenty years the population of our universities is likely to be something like doubled; and the proportion of the relevant age groups receiving university instruction is likely to be very considerably greater. Are we certain that the existing pattern of courses is satisfactory for these larger numbers? Is it not possible that courses designed mainly for the training of teachers and specialists may be very much less appropriate for the training of those who will have less differentiated tasks to perform later on?

To such questions it is impossible to give short answers: conditions vary so greatly in different parts. One has only to think, for instance, of the contrast between England and Scotland in this respect, to see how impossible it would be to deliver any general verdict on the facts. But I think that certain generalizations of principle are possible.

First, I submit that the mere fact of the increase of knowledge obliges us to recognize more and more the distinction between graduate and undergraduate studies and the importance of the graduate school. In very many fields, in the time available for First degrees, it is now literally impossible to train specialists adequately, even if such a degree of concentration is otherwise deemed desirable. The graduate school has thus become the appropriate *milieu* for the more intensive kinds of training. Once this is realized, and once provision is made whereby students who are likely to benefit are enabled to stay on at this stage, it should be easier to plan courses for First degrees with wider considerations in mind; it should be easier for teachers to avoid overloading the curricula; and it should be possible to ensure an adequate infusion of liberal studies.

There still remains, however, a real problem of the First degree course. Should it be wide, embracing a number of subjects, or deep, confining itself to the various aspects of one, or perhaps one main and one auxiliary subject? The question can be put too sharply: for, as we know, in practice all sorts of intermediate positions are possible and in fact exist on an extensive scale. But there is nevertheless a distinction between the two halves of the spectrum; and there are real problems of policy in which direction to move.

As we know, different choices have been made in different university systems. In England, for the greater part of this century although perhaps not now, the tendency has been to greater and greater specialization. In the United States, at any rate for a very long period — although there has been some change recently — the typical First degree course has encouraged much greater width. Perhaps each of these tendencies can be explained in terms of different local history and different social objectives. But, as I conceive matters, at the present stage in history, at any rate in the western world, it is desirable that *both* types of training should be generally available. In my judgment at least, experience tends to show that, among the members of the relevant age group who possess the capacity in one way or another to profit by training at the university level, there are both those who benefit more from courses in depth and those who benefit more from courses which are more widely spread. Moreover, in so far as we regard university courses as being in part preparation for various careers — and we cannot ignore this aspect — there is the same diversity of requirement: there are some careers, preparation for which, even at this stage demands specialization; there are others which definitely require a broader background.

It is in this area, the provision of broader courses for First degrees, that I perceive the greatest opportunity for experiment, at any rate in the systems with which I have intimate acquaintance. I am not in favour of experimentation *at this stage* with completely new subjects. The place for radically new subjects, in my opinion, is the graduate school, where perpetual reformulation and restatement are necessarily the order of the day; and I am sufficient of an academic conservative to believe that it is not a good thing for beginners to have to work in fields where there is no background of standard literature or oral tradition and where, in consequence, everything tends to depend on the *ipse dixit* of the individual teacher. But I do believe strongly in the desirability of novel *combinations* of subjects. By this I do not mean what our American friends call the elective system — the system under which the student can gain his degree in what subjects he pleases, provided that he obtains credits in a sufficient number of them. I find it difficult to believe that such complete freedom necessarily results in well-integrated intellectual habits; and I fancy that this is coming more and more to be the verdict in many American universities. But I do believe that there is much more scope than exists at present in many quarters, for joint or combined courses in which different subjects, having in some way either organic connection or complementary utility, may be taken in conjunction for the final qualification. An obvious example is the conjunction of Philosophy and Mathematics, or Philosophy and some Natural Science. Social Studies — Economics, Politics, History and so on — also furnish many opportunities for alternative combinations. But there are plenty of others and experiment will doubtless reveal more.

VI

If the diagnosis of the earlier part of these observations is correct, the conception of what may be expected of university education in the modern world is not limited to instruction in particular subjects. As university teachers, we are naturally expected to provide acquaintance with particular branches of knowledge and training in the exercise of various intellectual skills. But we are expected to do more than that: we are expected to inculcate general capacities for thought and contemplation; and, what is more, we are expected, as a complement to what is done in the family, to cultivate intellectual and moral habits suitable for adult membership of a civilized society.

It is this last duty which raises problems. So far as the more general requirements of the individual *as individual* are concerned, we may hope that his studies of particular subjects and combinations of subjects will bring with them habits of thought which transcend the particular content of their subject matter. But the inculcation of attitudes appropriate to full membership of the community is more difficult. We are the universities of free societies; and nothing could be more alien to the spirit of such societies than that we should again become the instruments for the inculcation of particular dogmas or creeds.

There is, however, an exception to this rule. There is one creed which the free society cannot repudiate without decreeing its own abdication — the creed of freedom itself. And this, I submit, is the answer to our problem. For the life of a free society is not a spontaneous phenomenon: it is the product of institutions and customs of great complexity and sophistication. Rousseau said that men are born free. Nothing could be more ridiculous: they become free only by adaptation and education. The habits of self-restraint and toleration, which alone make possible a free society, are not to be seen in the cradle or the nursery: they come only as a result of a process of learning and discipline, often very painful and difficult. And it is to the formation of these habits that we may legitimately be expected to contribute — not addiction to this or that dogmatic *Weltanschauung*, but education for membership of a free society.

I do not think that this is to be done mainly by direct instruction: we shall not sufficiently train the young in the habits of freedom by requiring the reading of Humboldt, or J. S. Mill on Liberty — valuable though that experience may be. The performance of this function must be chiefly indirect through the example of attitudes and behaviour which permeate our instruction as a whole — not so much by specific exhortation, but rather by teaching which is inspired throughout by intellectual habits and moral assumptions appropriate to the ethos of freedom.

Such habits and assumptions are many; and the emphasis which we lay on each will doubtless vary with circumstances of time and place. But I would venture to single out three whose importance I regard as invariant. If you will bear with me, I would like to conclude my address by stating them very shortly. They are not *directly* concerned with freedom. But, in my judgment, they are indispensable to its achievement and preservation.

First, comes what I would call the habit of critical objectivity. We must acknowledge, in our teaching and in our own speculative thought, that all statements of fact are subject to the criteria of logical consistency and conformity with observation. We must recognize that the essence of intellectual progress is critical discussion and willingness to submit our propositions to whatever objective tests are available. And, even in the sphere of valuations where scientific verification is impossible, we must insist that positions are to be established by pointing and persuasion, rather than by dogmatic assertion.

Secondly, comes the habit of social judgment in terms of consequences rather than categories. We must assess the value of actions, not in terms of pre-established classification according to this or that *a priori* ethic, but rather in terms of their effect on human happiness. We must teach that the maxim, *let justice be done if the skies fall*, comes from the childhood of the race; and that, on any civilized assessment, the falling of the skies is one of the consequences which have to be taken into account before we can say whether a certain course of action is, or is not, just. In a grown-up community the Faustian moment comes, not in the *Heldenleben* or in ritualistic exercises, but in contemplation of the happiness of contented men and women.

Thirdly, we must emphasize the common element in civilizations, rather than the minor variations. We must teach at all times the impersonality of knowledge and the transcendence of values. We must dwell always on the universal element in the human spirit. Above all, we should set our forces against the intrusion into science and learning of the anti-social forces of nationalism. Under the influence of a misguided historicism, our universities have not been guiltless of fostering such fissiparous tendencies. We need — Britons, Frenchmen, Germans, all of us — to return to the outlook and values of the *Aufklärungzeit*, to that Enlightenment which stressed the unity of humanity, rather than its differences. Without weakening the sense of duty to their local societies, we must seek to make our young men and women citizens of that republic of the mind which knows no frontiers.

If we are to have peace on this earth — and if there is no peace, there is no freedom — if the youth that we train are not to be slaughtered at intervals in what is essentially civil war, we need more than this: we need a political structure which shall bring it about that relations between nations are subject to the same rule of law as relations within nations. And if we cannot as yet hope for world government, at least we should hope for a more limited but non-exclusive political structure which produces order and solidarity among the peoples who love freedom and which provides a sure shield for a civilization of hope and progress. Agreed, that to do this will need much more than can be done by the universities alone. But if the universities, in their common life of education and thought, can produce an intellectual atmosphere conducive to such developments, they will have rendered what, in our age at least, is the greatest service they can render to humanity. Rectors and Vice-Chancellors, you have a grave responsibility: the future is very much in your hands.

44

IDEA OF A UNIVERSITY

Eric Ashby

Source: E. Ashby, *Adapting Universities to a Technological Society*, San Francisco, Washington and London: Jossey-Bass, 1974, pp. 1–15.

The German academic tradition has deeply influenced universities in the United States, Britain, the Soviet Union, and elsewhere. But in each of these countries social forces have acted to adapt the tradition to national needs. Universities therefore have to strike a balance between an adaptation which is too pliable and an adherence to tradition which is too inflexible. To achieve this balance universities need to initiate and control their adaptation to society, not to allow it to be imposed on them from outside.

The university is a mechanism for the inheritance of the Western style of civilization. It preserves, transmits, and enriches learning; and it evolves as animals and plants do. Therefore one can say that the pattern of any particular university is a result of heredity and environment.

Let us carry this biological analogy one step further. Among communities of organisms, and among communities of universities, there are episodes of innovation and hybridisation when new forms appear. For universities one of these episodes occurred in the nineteenth century. It was due largely to Wilhelm von Humboldt. The two hundredth anniversary of his birth fell on 22 June 1967. Not only Germany, but the whole world of learning, is in his debt.

There had already been a reawakening of universities in Germany during the eighteenth century; but the moment of destiny for German higher education was 1810, when Humboldt founded a university in Berlin dedicated to a fresh concept of humanism. In the following generations there were, of course, tensions in ideology: a severe intellectualism displaced the humanism of Humboldt and the idealism of Johann Gottlieb Fichte. From time to time the autonomy of the German universities was infringed upon, but nevertheless they became the envy of the Western world. Scholars returned to England and America from Berlin and Göttingen enchanted and eager to reform their own institutions of higher education. To pursue learning was to embark upon an adventure. In Justus Liebig's laboratory in Giessen, for example, students came to work from all over Europe. Every student had to find his own way for himself. Liebig and his disciples were in the laboratory from dawn until far into the night. There were no recreations or pleasures outside the institute. The only complaints came from the attendant who could not get the workers out of the laboratory in the evenings so that he could clean. This would be a familiar experience today, but it was an exciting innovation in 1839.

In that year a student from Britain, Lyon Playfair, came to work at Giessen. Although Liebig welcomed him, he pitted him against one of his own assistants to make an analysis of an unknown substance. The results of the two analyses were identical to the first decimal place. Playfair was accepted as a coworker. It was he, more than any other man at that time, who brought the German style of academic life to England. Many similar stories can be told about American students in Germany. Henry P. Tappan, who laid the foundation of the University of Michigan, Charles W. Eliot of Harvard, Andrew Dickson White of Cornell, Daniel Coit Gilman of Johns Hopkins: all these men drank from the springs of German academic life.

From the 1860s until 1914 thousands of young men from England and America made the pilgrimage to German universities. An estimated nine thousand Americans studied in Germany during the nineteenth century, and the number of Englishmen there must have been at least as large. I recollect my own professor in London telling us proudly that he had been a pupil of the famous botanist Julian von Sachs in Würzburg. We felt the continuity of a line of descent, almost spiritual: an apostolic succession of learning. In the German tradition this loyalty of discipleship corresponds to loyalty to a college in Cambridge and to *alma mater* in Yale. It is no accident that the *Festschrift* is a German invention.

A new thread of inheritance was woven into the higher education of England and America during the second half of the nineteenth century. It was the thread of education through training in science and scholarship (*Erziehung durch Wissenschaft*). Its first impact was on newly created institutions: University College London, Owens College in Manchester, the University of Michigan in Ann Arbor, and Johns Hopkins University, which at its foundation in 1876 had so many German-trained professors it was nicknamed "Göttingen in Baltimore."

When a gene enters a new environment the manifestation of that gene may change. This is what happened to German concepts of a university when they crossed the Channel. Confronted with a different academic tradition in a different society, the German concepts were assimilated but transformed.

There were many reasons for the transformation. One important reason was that there was no effective competition among British universities, such as existed among the universities in the German states. In Germany rivalry stimulated universities to adopt new ideas. In England higher education was dominated by the influence of Oxford and Cambridge; prestige was concentrated in these two centres in a way it has never been in the universities of Germany. Although the new institutions of higher education in England were in part a protest against the exclusiveness of Oxford and Cambridge, they nevertheless had to live under the hegemony of these ancient universities. They acquired by a process of social mimicry some of the prevailing assumptions about higher education. Prominent among these assumptions in Oxford and Cambridge was a conviction that the university exists to produce servants for church and state,—cultivated men but not intellectuals. It was more important for university graduates to be civilised than learned; they were to be doers not thinkers, bishops not theologians, statesmen not philosophers, schoolmasters not scholars. Liberal education (*Bildung*) rather than vocational training (*Ausbildung*) was the responsibility of the university. This then was the pattern of teaching through the first half of the nineteenth century in an Oxford college: a single tutor nurtured a select group of pupils for three years, and he taught them the whole range of the curriculum. His personality and outlook on life were as much a part of the curriculum as were the Latin texts and Greek philosophy.

It is not surprising that the universities which set the fashion for British higher education stubbornly resisted the idea of research as an instrument of education. As some witnesses told a Royal Commission in 1852, research would propagate infidelity and scepticism. Stimulated by their own reformers Oxford and Cambridge finally accepted the idea (already adopted in the newer universities of London and Manchester) that teaching should be in the hands of professors rather than tutors. However, the underlying purpose of the German university—no longer Humboldt's humanism, but the empiricism of Hermann von Helmholtz—was never fully accepted by British universities. The implicit purpose of British universities was still to make men cultivated, not learned. As Mark Pattison, one of the Oxford reformers, said: the fruit of learning is "not a book, but a man."

To this day the heart of teaching in Oxford and Cambridge (and among many other British universities) is personal confrontation with a tutor; values and style of thinking still count more than facts. The German philosopher and educational reformer Max Scheler (1925) echoed this attitude when he wrote about general education *(Bildungswissen)*.

The matter as well as the manner of teaching is prescribed. Courses must be studied in a strict sequence, and in most universities examinations must be passed in one course before a student is permitted to proceed to the next. This introduces another element in the German idea of a university which failed to take root in Britain: the freedom of the research worker or student to learn what and how he wishes *(Lernfreiheit)*. The colleges of Oxford and Cambridge regarded themselves as parent substitutes. To be parent substitutes is to restrict freedom of learning. First, a student who has the equivalent of an *Abitur* does not have any right to a place in a university. The university can select and reject whom it likes. Second, an English student finds that once he has chosen the subject he will study, the curriculum he follows, the number of years he takes to complete the course, the intervals at which he is obliged to sit for examinations are all prescribed for him, and he has very little freedom to vary them. Humboldt's vision of solitude and freedom *(Einsamkeit und Freiheit)* for students has never been accepted in the English university.

The freedom of teaching *(Lehrfreiheit)* was eagerly accepted in Britain. It was not only accepted but extended beyond the classroom to cover the "right" of a university teacher to make public assertions beyond his expertise without fear of reprisal. British professors can and do criticise public policy with a degree of freedom which would certainly be denied British civil servants. The reason for this is simple: British universities were never organs of the state. They were and still are autonomous corporations, and university teachers are not civil servants. Freedom of teaching covers the operations of the entire institution and not just the operations of teaching and writing. This expansion of freedom of teaching gives birth to several interesting conventions. For example, 80 percent of the income of British universities is derived from central or local government; yet a convention long ago established that university expenditure was exempt from scrutiny by parliament (although this is now eroded) or by local government.

While all this was happening the German idea of a university crossed the Atlantic. It entered a different environment and underwent different modifications. The most powerful environmental factor in America was not the hegemony of established universities; it was the utilitarian attitude toward higher education. This attitude could be expected from a pioneer and frontier population. It was a reaction against the conservative curriculum which most of the older colleges had inherited from Europe. Even as recently as 1875 the only fulltime studies offered in the first four semesters at Yale University were Greek, Latin, and mathematics. It is no wonder that the German enthusiasm for science in the curriculum and the scholar's dedication to science and scholarship *(Wissenschaft)* were eagerly accepted. But the exuberant interpreters of *Wissenschaft* extended it to subjects of study which no German university would have tolerated. There arose a bewildering variety of offerings. Cornell University, for example, offers about 12,500 courses of study ranging from hotel management to symbolic logic. Students have a wide freedom of choice among these courses. They are awarded degrees after they have accumulated so many credits for attending courses and passing examinations; and within limits the credits can be transferred from one university to another. Clearly some features of the German concept of freedom of learning took root in America although not in Britain. In America, however, there remains a tyranny of frequent examinations which no German university would tolerate.

The German influence worked deeply into American higher education, but it did not produce facsimiles of German universities. Under the influence of American society it produced a new species of university. There is an obvious family likeness. There is a considerable degree of freedom of learning and (apart from some deplorable lapses) as much freedom of teaching as is found in Germany or in Britain. American graduate schools correspond to German institutes. The German prescriptions of unity of research and teaching (*Einheit von Forschung und Lehre*) and education through scholarship receive in the graduate schools an almost ritualistic devotion. But there are two fundamental differences between the American and the German university. First, higher education is a consumer commodity in America, and in an egalitarian society there must be enough of it available for all who want it. Second, there is no minimum common level of achievement for degrees among American universities, such as is guaranteed by the *Staatsexamen* in Germany, the *licence* in France, and the degree examinations conducted by external examiners in Britain. Nor can standards be controlled by a severe selection of students. Consequently there is in America something unfamiliar in the university systems of Europe: a great diversity in quality of education and in the standards of achievement required for a bachelor degree. At first this seems to be a weakness in the system, but in the long run it turns out to be a valuable adaptation to the American environment. Not all qualifications are on the gold standard of learning, but there is a legitimate market for cheap diplomas, as there is for cheap automobiles. This market does not in any way debase the quality of the good institution. Indeed, by siphoning off students with modest aspirations into universities with modest standards, this system protects high standards in the universities which do have international standing. In the bloodstream of American and British universities there is a precious inheritance from the German university, adapted by each country to fit its own academic traditions and style of society.

Turning now from reflection about the past and some of the forces which have determined the pattern of the modern university in America, Britain, and Germany, let us conjecture regarding the future. It is a dangerous future. Today universities everywhere face a common peril: the peril of success. Formerly each was a detached organism, assimilating and growing in accordance with its own internal laws. Now universities have become absolutely essential to the economy and to the very survival of nations. Under the patronage of princes or bishops they were cultivated as garden flowers of no more significance to the economy than the court musician. Under the patronage of modern governments they are cultivated as intensive crops, heavily manured and expected to give a high yield essential to the nourishment of the state. Universities are, then, mechanisms for the inheritance of culture, and like other genetic systems they have great inertia. They are living through one of the classical dilemmas of systems in evolution: they must adapt themselves to the consequence of success or they will be discarded by society: they must do so without shattering their integrity or they will fail in duty to society.

What is the consequence of the success of the universities? Simply, forces from outside the university, which formerly had only a marginal effect upon the evolution of the university, are now likely to exert a powerful influence on this evolution. Governments which hitherto have been content to leave universities alone are now tempted to exert more and more control. Querulous protestations about this are useless. Universities are now very expensive to run. None of them can hope to survive without patrons. Between universities and patrons there have always been buffers of convention. The patron is now the man in the street; universities must negotiate with him and establish new conventions to safeguard what they have inherited. Conventions differ from one nation to another, but the topics of confrontation between universities and society are similar everywhere. Two of these topics are: How large should university systems be? What should universities teach?

The size and shape of a university system are determined by three major forces: the most prominent force in the United States is pressure from students to enter the system; the most prominent force in the Soviet Union is the "suction" (or manpower needs) drawing graduates out of the system; the most prominent force in Germany, and until recently in Britain, is the inner logic of the system itself. In all advanced countries it is now clear that systems of higher education will break down unless there is a balance between these three forces. One thing is certain about the future: the force which I call the inner logic of the university, the heredity of the university, will have to adapt itself to increases in the other two forces coming from the social environment.

In every country there is pressure to increase the size of university systems. The reasons are obvious. If governments finance universities, the children of voters must have a reasonable chance to be placed in them; and since the operations of commerce, industry, and government now depend on technology, the institutions which transmit technology must be expanded to meet national needs.

The patterns of response to this pressure differ considerably from country to country. In Britain the policy is to maintain very good conditions for university education by rigorously restricting the number of students who enjoy these conditions, not by erecting a financial barrier (nine out of ten students in British universities receive financial help) but by a severe number quota based on merit as measured by examinations. One consequence of the British system is that the ratio of output to input is very high. Of every hundred students who enter British universities about eighty-seven earn bachelor degrees; furthermore they do so in the minimum time or at most one year over the minimum time. Those who are not expected to be able to run the course at the prescribed speed are not permitted to enter the race, but they do have the opportunity to continue their training through polytechnics and other colleges of further education. There is a vigorous argument in Britain about how much of this vocational training should carry the promise of a degree, which has (unfortunately) become in Britain a ticket for social mobility. Until this argument is settled the British universities will not adapt themselves to the social forces which are enlarging the university system. The disequilibrium lies not in the treatment of those who are accepted in the universities and who have good conditions for study; rather it is in the treatment of those who are qualified technically to enter universities but who are nevertheless excluded.

In the United States the policy is quite different. There is an open door to higher education. The university course is an obstacle race open to all competitors who care to enter it; but—and this is the significant feature—owing to the diversity of standards among universities, the competitors can choose whether to enter difficult races by going to institutions of international standing or to enter easy races by going to institutions of more modest pretensions. America responds to pressures for expansion by expanding freely, but the expanded system is separated into different levels of quality. There are opportunities for fulltime higher education at some level to four out of ten children, but the American system, like the British, is not yet adapted to the contemporary environment. About half the students who enter American universities fail to complete their courses of study; and in the huge state universities there are two unresolved problems. One is how to provide for the coexistence of mediocrity and excellence within one academic society. The other is how to maintain on a campus of thirty thousand students any contact between teachers and students. If the Americans can solve these problems (and they are making great efforts to do so), it will be a valuable contribution to the security of all universities everywhere since these problems are common to the intellectual life of all egalitarian societies.

The Soviet Union responds to pressure upon the capacity of universities in a different way. The policy is to provide a specialized education on a narrow front in a great variety of technical colleges—there are about 650 of them—for 90 percent of the students. Only 10 percent of the students in the Soviet Union go to universities (this is reminiscent of the Flugge Plan put forward in Germany in 1960). There is, therefore, in the Soviet Union a diversity of institutions stratified according to subject, not as in America according to quality. There too, adaptation has a long way to go before it meets the aspirations of the people. One symptom is that only about half the students in the Soviet Union study fulltime; the others must be content with parttime or correspondence courses.

In Germany every qualified student has a right to enrol for higher education; and the *Honnefer Modell* (a scheme which subsidises university education for gifted students) at least lowers the financial barrier which would otherwise exclude some capable students. The problem of adaptation seems to lie inside the universities rather than outside them. On one hand some students take far too long to complete their studies; on the other hand lecture halls and seminars are crowded. There is great difficulty in preserving the tradition of *Wissenschaft* with the present ratio of teachers to students. The seminar class is often as large as a lecture audience. German professors must envy their predecessors in Marburg ninety years ago, when there were sixty-two professors and lecturers for 430 students. The new environment challenges old practices. For centuries students hung around universities for years, putting off the day of examinations; but irreversible changes in society have transformed what used to be a harmless indulgence into what is now a grave problem. The controversial report of the Council for Higher Education (Wissenschaftsrat, 1966) proposes a prescribed four-year programme and an interim examination in an attempt to resolve this problem. Some of the problems discussed in the report have close parallels to those in large American universities. There is a remarkable convergence of opinion between some passages in the report of the Council for Higher Education and the Muscatine Report on the University of California, Berkeley (1966). These two documents were published within a few weeks of each other. It is interesting that the Council for Higher Education in an earlier report (Wissenschaftsrat, 1960) opposed restricted entry to German universities and opposed even entrance examinations. Instead the report favours one element in the American philosophy: expanding the system until it is large enough to take all qualified candidates. Events are moving too fast for this policy, however. Already in medical faculties, and even in the philosophical faculty at Heidelberg, a number quota is imposed.

The pressure from society to enlarge university systems is a comparatively simple phenomenon. Much more controversial are pressures from society upon courses of study in universities. For one thing, society does not know what it wants. Predictions of the numbers of medical doctors, mathematicians, economists, and so on, which the state will require five years ahead, are notoriously unreliable. Even if they were reliable, it is questionable whether anything but propaganda can be used to persuade students to follow one kind of course rather than another. In Britain, for example, we have tried to plan university development on the assumption that two-thirds of the students would study natural science and technology, and one-third would study humanities and the social sciences. In fact, the present ratio is not two to one but one to one.

But to discuss what universities ought to teach in terms of manpower needs is to touch only the fringe of the problem. The core of the problem is the antithesis (although some would deny that it *is* an antithesis) between education (*Bildung*) and vocational training (*Ausbildung*). No doubt society needs citizens with education even more than with vocational training; and there is no doubt that in America and Britain and Germany the universities admit that they are not supplying this need. The spirit of Wilhelm von Humboldt troubles the consciences of us all.

Let us glance at the problem as it occurs in America, Britain, and Germany. The Muscatine Report on the University of California makes an interesting point: America accepted Humboldt's pattern of a university without introducing his pattern for the intermediate school and this is the cause of much discontent with American higher education. There is something to be learnt from American efforts to dispel this discontent. The theme of the famous Harvard University report on general education (1945) was that all Harvard students, whatever their field of specialisation, should become familiar, through formal, examined courses, with a body of knowledge, ideas, and values which constitute the "heritage of Western civilisation." At the time this report was regarded as the beginning of a new era in American higher education. It turns out to have marked the end of an old era. When Harvard came to review the general education programme twenty years later, it was clear that this particular technique had failed. Attempts to impart a common core of culture led to the shallow swamps of superficiality. A similar fate seems to have befallen the general education which German universities established in the 1950s. The original general education programme at Harvard has now been abandoned and replaced by a pattern of education which obliges the student to spend some of his formal learning time in courses outside his specialism. A really satisfactory way to do this has not yet been discovered. At the worst it can become an intellectual tourism. Just as we are all adopting package products in our domestic life ("instant" coffee, canned pies, inclusive coach tours to Italy), so are we being pressed to adopt "instant knowledge." The campus bookstore of any American university has shelves of "quick-learn" summaries of everything from world history to English literature. Occasionally (as, for example, in the humanities course at Columbia University) the formal curriculum for general education does give scientists and technologists an understanding of a world of values. But American opinion is now moving away from the survey course as an instrument of general education toward an attitude which has its origin in Germany. It was a German belief that contact with research was itself a liberal education; by watching a professor working on the frontiers of knowledge, a student understood new techniques of thinking. The most recent American approach (and it is similar to the approach in some of the new British universities) is based on two assumptions. The first assumption is that the best way to enlist the enthusiasm of a student is through the specialism he has chosen. If a student wants to be a physicist, he may well be impatient if he is required to spend part of his time on the heritage of Western civilisation. But if physics is made the core of his discipline, he will respond to courses which discuss the impact of physics on history, its social consequences, and its implications for ethics. If a student is convinced that his nonspecialist studies are relevant to his specialist studies, then he will pursue them with enthusiasm. The second assumption is that what a physicist needs to know about history and what a philologist needs to know about biology is a style of thinking, not a repertoire of facts. This style of thinking can be acquired better from a detailed exposition of one fragment of the subject, given by an active research worker, than from a broad survey.

In Britain we are less interested in curriculum reform than the Americans are. There are many reasons for this, but one reason is outstanding: reverence for science never overcame the influence of such Oxford humanists as John Henry Newman, Benjamin Jowett, and Mark Pattison in the nineteenth century. For them the touchstone of a university education was not to teach great truths, but to teach truth in a great way. What was taught, therefore, was less important than how it was taught. As the English philosopher Samuel Alexander put it: "Liberality is a spirit of pursuit, not a choice of subject."

In present-day German universities the tide of influence, which a century ago flowed so strongly across the Channel and the Atlantic, may now be flowing back to Germany. It would indeed be gratifying if American and British universities could repay some of the debt they owe to Humboldt. Several passages in reports of the Council for Higher Education indicate that Germany may be interested in proposals which we have considerable experience with in Britain. For example, the Council has proposed a diminution of freedom of learning, coupled with an increase in the amount of "pastoral" help offered to students in their studies and even in building character (*Persönlichkeitsbildung*). If the proposals are agreed to, freedom would be restricted by a prescribed sequence of courses, a limited time to complete courses, and an obligation to take an interim examination; though the German student would still have more freedom of learning than his British counterpart. I see from press reports, (*Die Welt,* September 19, 1966) that a sample of students, at any rate, approves these proposals. It has long been a cardinal belief in British universities that the most effective instrument for education was the residential college, where students and faculty members meet together in order to cultivate the intellect. That similar ideas are now being discussed in Germany is evident from the memoranda of suggestions from the Council for Higher Education on college residences (Wissenschaftsrat, 1962). The prime function of these proposed residences is educational: to initiate the new student into the adult life of an intellectual; and it is interesting (as an example of academic influences crossing the Channel from west to east) that the suggestions are strongly influenced by English practice. For example, it is suggested that there should be a mixing of senior and junior members, with wardens (*Kollegienleiter*) assisted by subwardens (*Protektoren*) and tutors (research students), living in the houses and having charge of twenty students each. The Council for Higher Education suggests that some teaching through pro-seminars and colloquia to supplement the university lectures, should go on in the college residences. This proposal is close to the traditional system in the Colleges of Oxford and Cambridge, which the German "invasion" of professorial teaching failed to displace a century ago!

The nineteenth-century idea of a university is a hybrid, with a heredity from Germany, Britain, and America. It is a German trait—of course any summary greatly oversimplifies the matter—to put emphasis on the *subject* rather than the *student*. As Humboldt wrote in 1810: (reprinted 1964): "The relationship between teacher and student ... is changing. The former does not exist for the sake of the latter. They are both at the university for the sake of science and scholarship." So arose the idea of education through training in scientific and scholarly research; so, too, the idea that teaching and research are inseparable. It is an English trait (I am still oversimplifying) to put emphasis on the cultivation of the student's intellectual health. "To discover and to teach," wrote Newman (1915), "are distinct functions"—and he recommended a division of intellectual labour between academies (for research) and universities (for teaching). In Britain we no longer fully agree with Newman, but some of his influence remains: we still regard ourselves as parent substitutes regarding our students' minds, if not regarding their morals. It is an American trait to emphasize that there is no wall separating scholar from citizen or academic knowledge from useful knowledge. The great seal of Cornell University has inscribed upon it these words: "I would found an institution where any person can find instruction in any study."

Many elements in this heredity are now being challenged by the environment. Universities are at a phase of self-examination. American universities confess that they have been weakened through admitting too many students and teaching too many subjects. British universities are finding themselves obliged to review their traditional paternal attitude toward students. In Germany the Council for Higher Education (Wissenschaftsrat, 1962) has written: "The universities can no longer disregard the question whether education through training in scientific and scholarly research is still possible and adequate." The inner logic of universities is under pressure from governments, the public, and students themselves. Yet one thing is certain: at the end of this century society will still need universities. They will not be needed merely to train professional manpower; they will be needed to serve the intellectual needs of our grandchildren. Something, therefore, of the nineteenth-century inheritance must be preserved. Now is the time to assert what must be preserved.

Universities still need freedom, detachment, and opportunity for solitude, adapted to a new age. But they also need something not so necessary in

Humboldt's time because now the wave-length of change is shorter than the lifespan of man. They need one reform which, if it could be achieved, would subsume all other reforms: the ability to initiate their own adaptations to society. They are already capable of some self-change, but the resistances are very great. It is a melancholy fact that universities have not devised efficient built-in mechanisms for change. There are, of course, some virtues in inertia, but not if the inertia is so great that change has to be imposed from outside. Such changes are often so violent that they endanger the heredity of the university. Anyone with experience of universities knows that academic evolution, like organic evolution, is accomplished in small continuous changes. Major mutations are generally lethal. Change must be based upon what is already inherited. Through a study of the descent of universities from their medieval ancestors and their effects upon one another in the contemporary world, we might learn how to control their evolution through the rest of this century. No one can predict what Europe will be like at the dawn of the twenty-first century; yet we do know one thing: the men and women who will be in posts of responsibility then are already university students. The future of the nineteenth-century idea of a university is in their hands.

45

MASS HIGHER EDUCATION

Eric Ashby

Source: E. Ashby, *Adapting Universities to a Technological Society*, San Francisco, Washington and London: Jossey-Bass, 1974, pp. 134–44.

Three major environmental forces are pushing higher education towards vocationalism while the internal heredity of universities retains its non-vocational aim. Mass systems of higher education can offer excellence in both vocational and non-vocational programs if universities do not permit their non-vocational programs to be used by employers as screening devices for jobs, if they maintain opportunities for intellectual talent and avoid the inappropriate use of cost-benefit analysis, and if they develop mission-oriented studies as well as discipline-oriented programs.

Before one considers the implications of mass higher education, a semantic distinction is necessary. This distinction is best introduced by an analogy: everyone ought to have as much food as he needs, but not everyone needs or wants to be fed on caviare. Or, everyone in a society which can afford mass education is entitled to as much education (primary, secondary, postsecondary) as he needs, but not everyone needs or wants what we in Britian call higher—as contrasted with further—education.

Another semantic distinction concerns the term "higher education," which generally includes all postsecondary education, but which in Britain is restricted to mean university study. So I have to distinguish between vocational higher education and nonvocational higher education. Notice that this distinction cuts across some familiar boundaries. It puts into the same category the education provided by the faculty of medicine at Cambridge and by the department of catering at Colchester Technical College; and it puts into the same category Oxford Greats and Workers' Educational Association courses on archaeology. The boundaries between vocational and nonvocational higher education are blurred, but by and large vocational

253

higher education qualifies a person to pursue a specific vocation or profession; nonvocational higher education does not. It may seem a perverse distinction, but I hope to show that it does make sense.

Higher education, defined in this way, is certain to become more than a minority interest. It has already, in two generations, increased by an order of magnitude, and it will do so again before the end of this century. That is why several countries have carried out sophisticated exercises such as the Robbins report in Great Britain (*Higher Education*, 1963), the reports of the Council for Higher Education in Germany (Wissenschaftsrat, 1960), and the colossal encyclopedia, already in some thirty volumes, of the Carnegie Commission on Higher Education in the United States. Yet in all these thousands of pages there is something missing. They go into great detail about increase in size of the system, about how the enlarged system shall be financed, about the way to make the system accessible to all who need to enter it, about the cost effectiveness and efficiency of the system. But they have comparatively little to say about whether the system should change and the function it should fulfill in the society of tomorrow.

To me it is clear that the system will have to change in all countries which undertake mass higher education. "More" does not mean "worse," but undoubtedly "more means different." Already our plans for expansion may fail to meet the needs of the majority for whom the expansion is planned. What are the educational implications of "more means different" in mass higher education?

Let me offer a conceptual framework into which facts and arguments can be conveniently fitted. It is characteristic of higher education systems that they are strongly influenced by tradition. They display what a biologist calls phylogenetic inertia. This is not surprising, for one of their functions is to conserve and transmit the cultural inheritance. It is characteristic of them, too, that from time to time they adjust themselves—sometimes painfully —to the social environment which surrounds them. There is an analogy, therefore, between these systems and biological systems: they are the resultant of hereditary and environmental forces, of nature and nurture. So universities, for instance, have everywhere a generic similarity, and yet they differ greatly from one nation to another.

There are, therefore, internal and external forces acting on higher education systems and when all is well there is an unstable equilibrium between these forces. At present there is a worldwide instability in higher education systems, and these systems are shifting, one hopes toward fresh equilibria which will be different for different societies. But while the movement is going on there are strains and anxieties; none of us know where the new equilibrium will lie. That is why it is disappointing that so much emphasis, by governments, by the press, and indeed within the systems themselves, is on how to expand, how to pay for expansion, and not on how to change.

254

There are three main environmental forces acting on systems of higher education. One is *customer demand*: the pressure of students to get into colleges and universities and to pursue the curricula they want when they get in. A second force is *manpower needs*: the "suction" drawing graduates into employment, and therefore influencing curricula and certification. The third force is the *patron's influence:* higher education systems are not (they never have been) supported by customers or employers; they are nowadays under the patronage, that is, the ultimate financial control, of the state.

When forces in the social environment press for change in a higher education system they are likely to encounter two kinds of hereditary resistance. One is the inertia of the system to any change; and this is a virtue (though often an infuriating one), for systems do need some stability and the influence can be capricious. The other resistance is not a negative one and it is much more important; it is the belief in the purpose of the system which is held by those who are engaged in it. A higher education system has its articles of faith by which its practioners live, and these are not always consistent with the demands which society makes on the system. These hereditary forces constitute what I call the "inner logic" of the system. It may show itself as the determination of a technological university to foster sandwich courses, or the determination of a faculty of arts to resist noncognitive material in its curriculum, or the determination of a physics department to refuse a research contract. The inner logic does for higher education systems what genes do for biological systems: it preserves identity; it is a built-in gyroscope.

The balance between these forces differs in different countries. In the Soviet Union manpower needs and the patron's influence play a predominant part, and inner logic is muted. But in the Academy of Sciences, to which the more distinguished scholars belong, inner logic plays a great part. In the United States customer demand has had a predominant influence, both on the size of the system and on its astonishing diversity; but the graduate schools are guided by inner logic. In Germany, and until recently in Britain, inner logic has played a predominant part in the universities, but in Britain the influence of the social environment (customer demand and manpower needs) has operated most noticeably on colleges in the public sector; in Germany on the schools of technology. In all these systems—even in the Soviet Union—there have been healthy checks and balances between the forces. When there are no healthy checks and balances (as, for instance in some of the universities of India and Latin America, where the influence of inner logic is very weak) the systems fail to serve their societies well.

We are at a moment of history when the balance of forces in systems of higher education all over the world is upset by social changes, and fascinating realignments of forces are taking place. The central motive of Robbins was to give priority in education to customer demand; a place in fulltime higher education for every qualified candidate. This is already diminishing the influence of inner logic, and at the same time the influence of the

255

patron—the State—is increasing. There is a backlash in the United States against the unmotivated student: the customers (estimated at 30 percent) who really do not want to be there; and a backlash too against one manifestation of inner logic: the determined efforts of many universities to devise freshman and sophomore years of general education. In Germany the supremacy of inner logic, cherished by the professoriate, has been shattered by the recent legislation for university governance, which prescribes that membership of all the main university committees should include one third professors, one third junior staff, and one third students—the so-called *Drittelparität*. The shifts in equilibrium are complex and very diverse; many of them seem to be strengthening the influence of the social environment at the expense of the cultural heredity of the systems.

Forces from the social environment are capricious. It is therefore essential that those engaged in higher education should decide what each sector in the system stands for, that is, their inner logic; and (in this context I am in favor of the "university militant") defend it against erosion from the currents of society. But the dilemma is that there is no consensus, even within one sector of the system in one country, about what higher education systems do stand for. In Britain, for instance, should polytechnics offer a liberal education; should they promote research? Should universities offer a choice of easy and hard bachelor degrees? We are assuming (on both sides of the Atlantic) that growth, diversification of curriculum (such as area studies and interdisciplinary mixes), and changes in mode of government (such as student participation) will solve our problems. They will not. Our problems centre round a definition, for each sector of higher education, of its inner logic; which is another way of putting my question: what are the implications, for the inner logic of educational systems, of "more means different"?

Higher education systems offer both vocational and nonvocational curricula. A common controversy is whether these two kinds of curricula should be in one kind of institution (the multiversity) or in separate, different kinds. I think this controversy is fruitless and futile. Whether higher education is organised in a binary or unitary system is merely a matter of logistics; the boundaries of our binary system are dissolving before our eyes, and a good thing too. Universities have always mixed vocational and nonvocational studies, and polytechnics are already doing the same. It is important to reflect on the changes which may be necessary in these two kinds of education, wherever they occur in the higher education system.

Vocational higher education ends in certification of recruits as fit to enter vocations and professions. In many fields this education is obsolete in a decade or so, but the certification remains valid. It is a serious indictment of the higher education system in Britain (and indeed of most of those elsewhere) that there is no provision except at Birkbeck College and in the Open University for the easy readmission of adult students for *extended* postexperience courses, to accord with the pace of technological and social change. But if higher education systems are to take on this burden, there will need to be a corresponding economy in the vocational courses given to young students. The Carnegie Commission has already proposed ways to do this for medical education, by cutting a four-year course to three years and offering honourable exits to higher education at two-year intervals; and Brian Pippard has proposed ways to do it in Britain for the education of scientists, by restricting professional training to those who will become professionals. As more and more people aspire to postsecondary vocational education, the reasonable response would seem to be to offer it in modules in such a way that engineers, doctors, accountants, even lawyers, renew their certification by returning to take modules in their expertise every decade or so throughout their careers. There is at present a built-in discrimination against the adult student. One realises how powerful it is when one immediately thinks of eighteen to twenty-one year olds at the mention of "the undergraduate age group," or "people of college age," or "the student culture." At the mention of the "museum" or "library" age group, the impression is not the same. This discrimination must be dispelled if we are to have successful mass higher education.

It is right and proper that employers, professional associations, and the state should influence vocational higher education; but the authority for nonvocational higher education must be inherent in the inner logic of the system itself. This means that those of us who are engaged in nonvocational higher education must reach some consensus about why we are engaged in it. There is no problem in justifying to the public why they should pay for mass higher education for vocations and professions. But a great deal of mass higher education is going to be nonvocational, whether in universities or polytechnics or other further education colleges. Why should the public pay for mass nonvocational education?

The difficulty is that nonvocational education is pursued for a variety of motives. One motive which must be resisted is the pursuit of nonvocational higher education solely in order to get certification for a job. The employers must be reformed first in this regard. They are doing a great disservice to higher education by using degrees and diplomas, which are quite irrelevant for the jobs they are filling, as filters for selecting candidates. As more and more young people go to college, employers raise the educational standards they require, yet the educational credentials essential for getting a job often have little to do with how well an individual performs that job. I suggest that if nonvocational higher education is to serve its real purpose (which is to civilise people) it ought not to attract people who only want to be certified, not civilised. I can see only one way in which higher education systems can promote this, and it would be an unpopular way: *not* to certify nonvocational education, but simply to do what was common in Scottish universities in the nineteenth century—issue class certificates to those who have attended courses and done the required written work.

In universities particularly we have, I believe, been diverted from the true goal of education (only in some subjects) to the false goal of certification. Perhaps one of the uncovenanted benefits of mass higher education will be that a certificate which almost everyone possesses will no longer be coveted by anyone. We can in any case expect that as a greater proportion of the age group acquires certificates of higher education, the salary differential between certified and uncertified will diminish. But, in my view, we who are engaged in higher education should do all we can to hasten this process. The way to get rid of elitism is not to lower standards but to offer a wide range of standards (which the whole system but not the university sector is trying to do), and to do nothing which accentuates the status gap between those with different education (the gap is maintained, for instance, by degrees, gowns, classification—or at any rate the publication—of examination results). Our responsibility is to rid ourselves of the idea that an educated person is socially superior.

My claim that the purpose of nonvocational education is to civilise people is an example of a motive for higher education which must be encouraged. It is a caricature with that core of truth which caricature contains that vocational education is concerned primarily with means and nonvocational education with ends. The primary aspiration which a good teacher has when he is teaching any nonvocational subject in higher education (history or German or physics, for example, to students who are not going to become historians or linguists or physicists) is to carry the student from the uncritical acceptance of orthodoxy to creative dissent over the values and standards of society. Polanyi (1962) puts this clearly: the professional standard of science (and it could be said of all knowledge at the level of higher education) must "impose a framework and at the same time encourage rebellion against it." The beneficial effect of nonvocational higher education is to lift the student from a level of conventional moral reasoning, to what Keniston (1972) describes as the postconventional level, where students are deliberately challenged "to reexamine assumptions, convictions, and world views they previously took for granted." In pluralistic society it is essential that as many people as possible are lifted from the conventional to the postconventional level. I can do better to illustrate this argument than to paraphrase two arguments made by Keniston: It is well known that the half-life of some technologies is less than the life span of an ordinary man or woman. We now realise that one consequence of this is that the half-life of some social institutions and cultural and moral values is just as brief. People may not only become uneducated for the job: they may become uneducated for living. Therefore individuals have to reorient themselves during their lifetimes to new cultural and moral values as well as to new technologies: "If ... technologies, definitions of truth, and conceptions of morality change within the individual's lifetime, ironclad adherence to one set of skills, to one view of the truth, or to the present moral standards of one subculture will leave the individual stranded, isolated, and displaced before he reaches middle age" (Keniston, 1972).

We see the menace of obsolete, even atavistic, value judgements all around us. The prime aspiration in nonvocational higher education is to keep our society pluralistic, humane, tolerant, open to alternative truths, and able to distinguish prejudice from error.

Most of nonvocational higher education falls short of this aspiration. But there is evidence that enlightenment has changed for the better the values of the "common man." We no longer tolerate slavery, child labour, or the worst forms of pollution. It is likely that education has greatly contributed to these value changes. This is the justification for asking the public to support nonvocational higher education on a mass scale. "Seen in this light," writes Keniston (1972), "the question is not whether we can afford universal higher education, but whether we can afford to be without it."

Many controversial implications arise from this theme. One is that mass higher education, like mass production, is a different thing from "handmade" education or production. A lot of it is impersonal, even using techniques of videotape, TV, and correspondence courses. The experience of the London external degree and the promise of the Open University show that this can be done successfully. But there are still two kinds of education which demand a personal teacher-student relationship, for which there is no substitute. One is vocational, the education of master craftsmen and artists. To become an engraver on glass, or a silversmith, or a solo violinist, there is only one recipe: to be apprenticed to a master and to submit to his regime of discipline. The other is nonvocational, the education of the innovators in intellectual life and the pacesetters in cultural and moral standards. For this, too, there is only one recipe: the sustained dialectic with a master whose own intellectual and cultural achievements are distinguished. So, within the system of mass higher education, there must be opportunities for the intellect to be stretched to its capacity (the critical faculty sharpened to the point where it can change ideas), by close contact with men who are intellectual masters. Not many students are fit for this austere discipline or are willing to submit to it but those who are must be able to find it, or the thin clear stream of excellence on which society depends for innovation and for statesmanship will dry up. Personally I am not in favour of herding such talented students into special institutions. Talent and mediocrity can share the same central heating plant and cafeteria, and they should, for talent has to learn to operate in a world of mediocrity. Talented people should not be considered socially superior.

A second provocative implication arises from the first one. Cost-benefit analysis can be applied to vocational education; a vocational qualification probably puts up the earnings of the person who possesses it and possibly benefits the economy. But cost-benefit analysis applied to nonvocational education is nonsense; indeed such education may be counterproductive, producing men and women who not only eschew high-income careers for themselves but even reject and oppose the commonly accepted norms of Western society, such as the necessity for an ever-increasing Gross National Product. Cost-benefit analysis can doubtless suggest ways in which mass higher education can be more efficiently conducted; but it would be positively inefficient to try to increase the efficiency of that sector devoted to minority "handmade" education. We still cannot teach or learn at this level any faster than did our ancestors in medieval Oxford. An illuminating comment I heard recently in a discussion of the arts is equally applicable to this level of higher education: despite all our advances in technology it still takes three manhours to play a forty-five-minute quartet. Technology enables more people to hear the quartet; but technology never will improve the productivity of the performers.

Finally there is another and different conceptual framework which is helpful in some discussions of higher education. A person's capacity to contribute to society can be broken down into three different kinds of skill: skill in working with ideas, skill in working with things, skill in working with people. Traditionally in Britain the first skill and the third are learnt if at all "on the job." Everyone needs a mixture of all three skills, though in different proportions. What we are now experiencing is pressure from the young to put more emphasis in higher education on the skill of working with people. I believe the young are right. And if they are, mass higher education must take account of this.

How is this to be done? Not by discussing noncognitive, affective approaches to experience. These approaches are an essential ingredient of living, and institutions of higher education should provide opportunities for them as they do for physical recreation and for catering. But they should be part of the social environment of a college, not its narrow social purpose; that (I believe) ought to be confined to the cognitive, rational approach to experience, simply because that is what the teachers are competent to teach.

46

FEDERAL UNIVERSITIES AND MULTI-CAMPUS SYSTEMS

Britain and the United States since the nineteenth century

Sheldon Rothblatt

Source: J. J. Carter and D. J. Withrington (eds) *Scottish Universities: Distinctiveness and Diversity*, Edinburgh: John Donald, 1992, pp. 164–87.

In Presbyterian Scotland references to the Old Testament are assuredly in order. Moses's father-in-law, Jethro, finding the prophet weary from days of adjudicating disputes among the tribes, suggested that a system of courts be instituted to spread the juridical burden, 'for the thing is too heavy for you; you will not be able to perform it yourself alone.' We must conclude that Jethro did not believe that his system of judgeships would necessarily dispense justice more equitably than the great but harried statesman — indeed, how could he? — but presumably he anticipated gains in productivity and scheduling.

From that episode it is perhaps only a step to the truism that the appearance of new social problems requires new organisational models for coping with altered or strange circumstances, and those models reflect a rationalising mentality or outlook characteristic of all societies at virtually any time. This tempting conclusion — to find the systematising human intellect at work at particularly interesting moments in the organisational history of institutions — is, from an historian's perspective, greatly oversimplified. One obvious objection is that the existence of a rationalising mentality does not in itself predict the exact form a particular organisational change might take. For that we would have to look elsewhere, possibly within the host culture or in its pre-existing institutional disposition. Another caveat is that organisational innovation or complexity can rarely be attributed to a single motive or source. One generation's rationalising is not always another's. Because present-day societies appear to be interested in some form of 'efficiency,' or in productivity gains or 'coordination' or 'accountability' — the terms which we use to explain and justify the bureaucratic introductions of modern societies — hardly proves that the same impulse was at work in the past. Innovation may be the result of ideology, or problem-solving, or accident or a conjunction of events.[1] It may arise from certain identifiable cultural inclinations on the part of a society, or it may well be a combination of more than one variable, which is the more likely explanation, especially as we move forward in time to societies with many political actors and numerous decision-making centres. The value of an historical view of the origins and rise of complex institutions lies in emphasising circumstances specific to time and context; and this in turn leads to wider conclusions about the nature and meaning of innovation.

These opening remarks have their own historical context. As we close the twentieth century there exists an unusual amount of international interest in devising and expanding the organisational forms of higher education. Indeed, this interest is already embodied in a great number of experiments and revisions, some of which result from the internal differentiation of higher education institutions in response to changing external circumstances and some from less evolutionary and more dirigiste or ideological causes, as in the university reforms undergone in Sweden in the late 1960s and now in the process of radical revision once again.[2] The prospect of a forthcoming united Europe has understandably awakened considerable thought about how nations based on different linguistic and cultural inheritances might combine their resources, encouraging an easier movement of students, researchers and teachers across the boundaries of national sovereignties. Experiments along such lines are already well advanced, most notably in programs like ERASMUS, and both market and étatist possibilities, as well as partnerships between public and private sectors, are actively discussed.

But also within nations there exist new interest and energy in breaking down or in challenging historic conceptions of institutional autonomy and academic frontiers hitherto zealously guarded. Some of these fall into the category of programmes affording greater academic mobility to student populations, and they do not exactly directly affect the overall administration or control of separate participating institutions. The Polylink arrangements within the polytechnic sector as centred at Newcastle in England is one example. There is, especially in countries like Australia, a policy of central government-mandated amalgamations, usually between technical colleges or teacher-training institutions, and these mergers could take many forms, from simple combinations leading to the disappearance of smaller and more vulnerable institutions to new organisations with expanded hierarchies. At the University of New England in Armidale, a local educational college has been combined with the university's school of education, increasing the size of the teaching staff and producing (so I understand) a tension between teaching and research and the value assigned to each.[3] At Brisbane, a number of city colleges have been joined with the local technological institute — an MIT or Imperial College — to produce a new system. The resulting organisational difficulties, compounded by geography, are a headache for the vice-chancellors.

Experiments with organisational groupings and inter-institutional cooperation have characterised American higher education, both public and private, since the nineteenth century. These have taken a number of primary forms, of which just a few will be mentioned here. Since the Progressive Era of the first decades of the present century, when modern theories of scientific management and time and motion studies were first popular, Americans rationalised the propensity of students to move at will from institution to institution into what today amounts to a national system of student exchanges. Called 'articulation' (the word also appeared in the Progressive Era) or transferring, the habit of students to wander doubtless originated long before. Articulation consisted of voluntary agreements between institutions freely entered into — although, since no action is truly 'free,' market discipline can certainly be listed as a form of coercion. That articulation was not to every institution's liking is evidenced by the fact that the higher education institutions in the United States which participated least in these exchanges of students are the highly-endowed, elite prestige colleges and universities, those most resistant to consumer pressure.

Transfer students have a direct affect on the administration and even the organisation of American universities. They require special administrative and record-keeping units, special admissions policies and the adjustment of academic standards, insofar as no national standard of achievement exists. And transfer students affect the control that American universities have over their curriculum and degree qualifications, for in accepting articulating students, American colleges and universities agree to accept course work done elsewhere, as well as months or years invested in that work, thus effectively reducing the time to complete the degree at their own institutions for twentieth-century scholar gypsies. Such considerations will arise, or have already arisen, with ERASMUS and similar intra-European exchanges.

But whereas articulation may directly affect the curricular autonomy or admissions policies of individual institutions, it does not directly affect governance. Nevertheless, other forms of inter-institutional cooperation may well do so — federations for example. In an article published in 1987, I defined multi-campus or multi-institutional clusters as parts relating to a centre, with the centre responsible for some major function.[4] I noted that the centre could be strong or weak. I cited the collegiate structure of Cambridge University as the oldest example in the English-speaking world, Cambridge rather than Oxford because at an early date — somewhere around the middle of the eighteenth century — the introduction of the tripos gave the university, as distinct from the colleges, a new role in education. As a modified version of the Cambridge model, I cited the creation of the examining University of London in 1836, with its metropolitan jurisdiction broadening fairly rapidly to include national and imperial responsibilities; and then, on the London model, again with modifications, federal universities in other parts of England, Ireland and Wales. Scotland did not have a federal system, having five universities of a unitary kind until a merger reduced the universities to four in 1860; but Scots had long debated among themselves the creation of some form of national higher education system incorporating the considerable sophistication of their school feeder system. It is true that some collegiate differentiation did exist within the Scottish universities, principally, I understand, as a device for supplementing the incomes of the teaching staff before about 1820.[5] However, undergraduates at new Scottish colleges founded later in the nineteenth century, like that at Dundee, read for the London degree. In my article I traced recent arrangements for degree-taking in the polytechnics through centralised bureaucracies like the Council for National Academic Awards back to Victorian innovations. One could also cite the local examinations of the last century as conceived in the same spirit, the top (or a perceived top such as Oxford or Cambridge) pressing down upon, and setting standards for, the developing sectors of state and private schooling. The first unitary university to be created in England was Birmingham less than a century ago. The University of Durham, founded in the 1830s, was devised on the collegiate model.

The precise origins of the Royal University of London of 1836 are obscure. Daylight and champagne discover not more. The historiographical literature dealing with its beginning generally accepts London University's organisation as a given, simply a fact of history or a happenstance. While it is true that the origins of the first University of London of the 1820s, subsequently called University College, London, makes sense in a familiar English context — the rise in numbers, wealth and influence of the Dissenting community, the growth of London to metropolitan stature and its bursting demography, the expansion of the professions, especially medicine — the origins of the Royal University of London 1836 makes almost no sense in the context of the 1830s; for to term it a compromise, which it unquestionably was, does not at all explain why it was that particular kind of compromise, or who thought of it, or where exactly its philosophical origins lay.

Consequently, the historian must and should remain surprised and puzzled, but also delighted, by the creation of the examining University of London, by its sudden or apparently sudden fabrication, by the minds who created it and the reasoning behind it. The delight derives from encountering an institution which appears wholly or nearly wholly new, thus representing an historical and intellectual conundrum in need of solving. The story of the founding and history of the examining university of 1836 may also be one of those instances in which the offshore observer can be useful — that is, the observer whose own national educational institutions do not include the conception of an examining university; for although nineteenth-century Americans certainly knew of London's existence, and here and there founding bodies of new institutions remarked upon the idea, and were here and there attracted to it, no such institution was created or evolved south of the Canadian border. And the reasons are not difficult to adduce. No national conception of university education existed in the United States once the followers of Alexander Hamilton in the Early Republic were defeated in their scheme to establish a federal university in the District of Columbia. The states of the Union feared the influence that a concentration of intellectual resources might have on American pluralism. The federal constitution prevailed, and the separate states retained their monopoly over public-sector higher education. But in England — and one might add Scotland, where the state as well as the idea of the state appears to have been less feared in the nineteenth century than in England (or so Robert Anderson has cogently argued) — a national conception of higher education was entertained by intellectual and governing elites and put into practice in the mild form, the only form which would have been acceptable in the 1830s, of a degree-granting monopoly whose authority, nevertheless, could not touch the established institutions of Oxford and Cambridge but did, for the briefest imaginable time, a year or less, touch the Anglican, collegiate university of Durham.

Unable to locate the deliberations of the Privy Council that may have cast light on the origins of 1836, I have tried to consider the foundation of the University of London in the more general historical context of the changing religious and political configuration of the 1820s and 1830s and to view the outcome as the result of a series of trade-offs rooted in England's culture. Broadly, the creation of the London federal university was an attempt to cope with several important emerging problems or questions, foremost among them being the definition of a university. It should not exactly surprise us to learn, but in some fashion it may well do so, that it was precisely the controversies over the meaning of a university engendered by the first London University that excited and angered John Henry Newman and led in a direct line to the writing of those discourses, some thirty years later, that remain the most stimulating attempt to define a university in the English language.

Discussion over the definition of a university had actually been going on ever since the newly-founded quality periodical, the *Edinburgh Review*, pitched Scotland against England in the earliest part of the nineteenth century by questioning the value and nature of the education acquired at Oxford.[6] The debate effectively forced argument along three lines:

— What is a university? How does it differ from a college? What are its distinguishing features? What is its purpose? Is there a legal definition of a university? These questions involve the critical dimensions of curriculum, access, financing and the organisation of teaching.

— Is there a distinction between a private educational institution and a public one?

— In what body or authority should control of a university be invested? in the Church? in the state? in a legal trust, and if so, are the trustees to be drawn from laymen or from the academy? in the professions? or, effectively if not legally, in the operations of a free market, implying the sovereignty of the consumer?

The context in which these questions must be understood has to be the 1820s and 1830s. In these two decades — actually the crucial answers are given in less than one decade, from 1828 to 1836 — the context was being altered. Quite suddenly the legal status of Dissenters and Roman Catholics was transformed. Their disabilities were removed, at least respecting public life, and they became citizens at last. This in turn implied a change in the future social and class composition of Parliament, the Cabinet, the departments of state and the Privy Council, although the change was delayed far longer than anyone initially expected, Parliament changing before the Cabinet and the various departments at differential rates into the twentieth century.[7] Also, in educational matters, market discipline was instrumental. As Margaret Bryant has shown with respect to the London area before about 1860, consumer demand had resulted in the creation of a substantial number of varied secondary schools, from private to proprietary,[8] and both of the new London university colleges represented the play of market forces, unlike, I believe, Durham, which appears to have been a defensive operation to stave off an attack by political radicals on the surpluses generated by Durham Cathedral's ownership of coal mines.[9]

Very generally, the 1830s was a period in which the division of national feeling was acute. The reform of parliament encouraged the Dissenting community and all those who were anxious for radical reform. Radical reform there was, in municipal government, the poor laws, the law of tithes, and perhaps less radical, in the provision for popular education. Reform parties had been forming at Oxford since the 1820s. Newman excoriated the Noetics at Oriel and other academic liberals in his *Apologia;* but, if one examines the history of academic and curricular innovation at both senior universities, it is apparent that reform could come from either end of the political spectrum. In the 1820s and 1830s entrenched and vested interests — the older liberal professions, especially the London-based physicians, the Church, and sections of the aristocracy — were eager to hold on to some historical advantages.[10] The creation of the University of London was a comprise between these contending forces, a trade-off between a metropolitan or centre culture which we can in cultural terms call 'aristocratic,' and a provincial or peripheral culture which we can term 'liberal'.[11] The former embodied the idea of taste, or a standard imposed from above, excellence by consensus on high. The latter embodied the principles of diversity, variety, plurality, or excellence through individual competition. The former realised its idea in the formation of an examining university which alone could award degrees. The latter realised its aims through the establishment of colleges. Some of these were secular, some religious, some interdenominational, some devoted to the liberal arts, others (for example, Mason College, Manchester, as yet to come) to the sciences. The definition of a college could also be revised to mean institutions that could be non-residential rather than upscale boarding establishments or professorial rather than tutorial — drawing, therefore, from the substantial Scottish inheritance which had such a great impact on the curricular and organisational structure of University College, London, as well as on the entire range of systems of American colleges and universities developing from colonial times onwards.

As I have stated the situation, the cardinal principle of the metropolitan culture appears to have been the idea of measuring academic achievement by using a separate central authority. The specific model or forerunner of this notion was the Cambridge Senate House examinations which had appeared sometime in the middle of the eighteenth century.[12] The exact origins of these are as vague to us as the exact origins of the Burlington House, University of London examinations, but the evidence suggests that the tripos and Honours schools at Oxford (established first in 1800) had what may be broadly called political origins and were thought of as instruments for maintaining discipline.[13] What made the tripos distinctive — different, let us say, from the scholastic or public disputations which still existed when the new mathematical honours examination evolved in the later eighteenth century — was its written nature, the first such examination in England, and the order of merit. Written examinations were regarded or came to be regarded with considerable justification (given the historical context) as more rigorous, more demanding, more accurate and consequently of a higher level than oral examinations, where candidates could be led or coaxed into acceptable answers. When speed and endurance were added to the examination formula, many Victorians believed that they had created the perfect instrument for choosing the leaders of an evolving liberal democracy and imperial kingdom. The order of merit in mathematics at Cambridge was a further refinement. Candidates were ranked twice: once according to category — first-class, second-class, etc — and again according to absolute rank: senior wrangler downwards.

Yet to describe examinations as a metropolitan/aristocratic principle presents certain difficulties, most conspicuously because aristocracies do not enjoy competing for distinction, especially with outsiders, and a governing class does not like to be publicly humiliated. Yet it was not only members of landed elites who disliked competitive assessments. Resistance to the coming and the spread of examination-fever at Oxford and Cambridge in the early nineteenth century was widespread, taking the form of an elaborate counter-culture celebration of failure and a repudiation of success as measured by examinations. Matthew Arnold and other humanists who associated themselves with the metropolitan culture continued to question the value of examinations, although from a less apologetic perspective, finding them narrowing, denaturing and mechanical, and a positive hindrance to creating a higher type of national character. Yet other, equally serious members of the reformed and reforming university culture, both students and junior dons, embraced the new definition of success as measured by competitive examinations, and played a major part in transforming the internal academic culture of the senior universities of England long before direct state intervention commenced in the middle decades of the nineteenth century.[14] A bifurcation of academic culture was already in place in the first half of the nineteenth century, taking the form of the serious 'reading man' and the old-fashioned Regency 'buck' or 'pickle,' but this division certainly became even more pronounced in the second half of the Victorian era, after the numerous reforms conferred greater legitimacy on the schemes and proposals of the reforming party.

While I believe that the London University idea of an examination has a strong connection to the metropolitan culture, I also accept the usual assumption that it was related to the liberal individualist culture of the periphery and endorse the less common assumption that it was connected to the liberal professional culture of the capital. It was a combination of ideals, a fusion of different value systems, not unlike the other cultural and institutional combinations giving us Victorian culture which was both retrospective and forward-looking at the same time. The very idea of measuring worth by competitive examination represents yet another area of Victorian or proto-Victorian compromise, or a special amalgamation of metropolitan ideas of the importance of a centre with a standard and a liberal idea of the significance of competition in achieving that standard. One can, after all, have competition without a standard, winner take all, but winning against a standard provides an independent measure and a more lasting basis of comparison, and reduces the market and the idea of the market, where competition prevails, to a subsidiary position.

What gave these ideas of competition and a standard both substance and influence was their adoption, and therefore sanctioning, by the elite institutions of England, by the ancient universities and the public schools, and by the civil service, all of which underwent significant reform by the middle decades of Victoria's century.

The Royal University of London, then, as well as the other federations that sprang from its inspiration, were mechanisms for achieving what Cambridge and Oxford had achieved, or were claiming they had achieved, for by 1836 reading for Honours examinations was an activity still only favoured by a few. Federations had the further advantage of being inexpensive, for their sole function was to set and mark examinations and award first degrees, and frugality was also a principle of the periphery in mid-Victorian England.

But I would like to suggest that federations were widely acceptable, at least to begin with, not so much because they embodied the contradictory principles of merit selection and the idea of a metropolitan standard and culture but because the burden of sitting examinations was regarded as essentially optional, a matter of choice and hence uncoercive, and therefore well in keeping with nineteenth-century liberal conceptions of freedom and initiative.

Degrees were for those who wanted them. Dissenters might want degrees because they had some value in medicine or, more broadly, because they were indicative of citizenship status and were the symbolic counterparts of the vote. But apart from this special consideration, degrees were not important in the 1830s. The aristocracy and gentry at Oxford and Cambridge had not necessarily taken degrees. Intending clergy took degrees because bishops required them for ordination, and Oxbridge colleges usually required them for fellowships. Even in medicine as practised in England, entry into the profession lay through the teaching hospitals and medical societies, not through universities, although a first degree cleared the way for election to a fellowship in the Royal College of Physicians. Being called to the bar also did not require a university degree, and practice as a solicitor certainly not. From the standpoint of King's College and University College in London, federation through the form of an examining university may have severely compromised their curricular autonomy and educational flexibility, but only if degrees were sought. And federation, at least to begin with, did not really threaten existing professional monopolies.

In Scotland by contrast, efforts to tighten standards and raise the level of the degree had met with keen resistance, for many undergraduates considered the Scottish universities to be a form of extra-mural teaching, rather than a total way of life. Intending clergy and ministers took degrees. The few who would become professors or college and public school teachers took degrees; but in general the degree had not risen to the position it holds today. Federations, whatever principles of merit selection they may have embodied, were directly proportional in value to the degrees that were sought. And degrees were sought when aristocratic patronage and other forms of sponsorship waned, and when an urban professional culture began to challenge an entrepreneurial one, as Harold Perkin has discussed at great length in his studies of the coming of a service culture to Britain.[15]

Not to draw the contrasts too sharply, but to allow for other slow developments contributing to the enhanced respect for selection by merit, I would point out that in a modest way the career open to talent had been evolving in government since the eighteenth century. The relatively weak character of Cabinet government contributed to the evolution. In the absence of strong political parties, ministers of the crown were sufficiently independent to exercise their own judgment and patronage, and in certain departments of state, notably the Victorian ministry concerned with education, some staff were being hired on meritocratic criteria.[16] Indeed, it was this existing

practice which undoubtedly led to the Northcote-Trevelyan recommendations, not so much as a wholly new idea as the wholesale advocacy of a new
practice and its elevation into principle.

At present the usual reasons offered for the creation of federal systems of
higher education involve the rationalization of resources in the interests
of some form of efficiency or productivity, involving lower costs in the
unit of resource or coordination or accountability, with accountability
leading to outside or ministerial control of systems and budgets in countries
like present-day Australia. I hardly struggle with myself to include in such a
list of reasons, knowing full well that it is frivolous, the pleasure taken by
some in the creation of organisational charts and management models and
what is thought to be a superior way of handling complexity. By complexity, the sociologists of higher education mean social and cultural pluralism
as represented by demands for access, curriculum reform, affirmative action,
articulation, and accountability. A standard and important work on multi-
campus systems in the United States refers to 'the promotion of "intentional
change" through academic planning', budgeting and programme review as
'the heart of system activity.'[17] But none of these contemporary management ideas helps us fully to understand the origins of Victorian federations.
They were not created to rationalise a system in terms of expenditures,
growth, admissions, and planning, nor to advance productivity targets and
improve efficiency, nor yet to stimulate creativity. They also were not created
to manage complexity or introduce diversity — objectives which appear in
today's American multiversities. Such objectives were in Victorian times
relegated to market forces, which many Victorians respected but hardly all,
especially those who identified with the metropolitan culture. The Victorian
federations were established as forms of quality control, as mechanisms for
guaranteeing the value of the degree against its expected debasement in the
marketplace. What is even more special about this development is the means
chosen to support the degree, namely a system of examining that featured
written examinations, blind marking and the total separation of the act
of teaching from the act of examining, leading to the development of the
system of external examiners, a system barely recognised in the United States.
In this last respect, the divorce between teaching and examining, London
even went beyond Cambridge, Burlington House beyond the Senate House,
for on the Cam there were indeed written examinations and blind marking,
but teachers also examined.

The metropolitan ideal was also embodied in another Oxbridge innovation, perhaps not so thorough-going if we consider the hybrid curriculum
called *literae humaniores* installed at Oxford in the early nineteenth century,
but thorough-going enough; and that was the elevation of the single-subject
examination above the more general examination (with a modified version
in Scotland) on the grounds that specialisation also promotes rigour. Here
too, as in so many other instances, Americans and British parted company.

The American undergraduate university curriculum, truer perhaps to its Scottish roots, continued to broaden in the course of the nineteenth and twentieth centuries. The safeguarding of quality became less important than providing for options and electives, and when Americans did discuss quality — which of course they had to do — the public discussion was and is normally centred on programmes of study, the curricular 'canon,' and the availability of resources. So the history of federation in Victorian Britain is also the history of the triumph of a particular kind of examining system and equally the triumph of faith in that kind of examining, in its accuracy and as the best means for both producing and recognising a 'first-class' mind.

The question of the standard of academic achievement in Scotland was really at the heart of the inquiries conducted by the Royal Commission on the Scottish Universities of 1826–30, the very first royal commission on universities to be appointed in the nineteenth century. The commission proposed the introduction of an Honours degree, amongst other considerations, as a means of encouraging rigour and competition. The opposing sides took shape immediately. There were those who agreed with the commissioners and were willing to be guided by 'English' sentiment. And then there were the Scottish nationals who adhered to older (shall we call them 'democratic'?) policies and who were willing to trade off high student drop-out rates for relatively open admissions. At mid century a proposal was circulated for a single board of degree examiners for all of Scotland, but this was beaten back.

Let me take this analysis one step further. The history of federation in Victorian Britain is also the history of faith in science, by which I mean that the reaction to the older, that is to say, aristocratic forms of networking was so strong that the search commenced for a means of objectively assessing worth, a means independent of the widespread belief in the value of 'character' summed up in the eighteenth-century tag, 'men and manners.'[18] The federal principle challenged this older conception of worth, which was closely related to style, to the ability to present oneself publicly, or to what may also be called 'acting.'

The aristocratic culture of the eighteenth century was strongly influenced by Italian models of civic conduct. It was openly social and as such heavily theatrical. Aristocratic leaders were public figures and continually on view, and Georgian principles of town planning, derived from Italian models, featured the open square which encouraged visibility and display. The square was supported and reinforced by the promenade and the 'parade,' which likewise encouraged strolling but also the new habit of window shopping. The novelist Henry Fielding described the great wen of London in 1749 as a place in which style and street commingled.[19] The extravagant dress of London men and women of fashion derived from the same spirit of openness. The theatre itself was immensely popular in the Georgian period, partly, as we know, in reaction to puritan dislike of the stage. It had moved out of the court into the new London playhouses, where high and low mixed, if literally not on the same levels. The Georgian theatre attempted to become yet more popular by becoming respectable. Playwrights displayed a great variety of virtuous as well as fatuous types on the stage as examples to be emulated or avoided. Nevertheless, the anti-theatrical bias which Jonas Barish has traced back to Plato was sufficiently strong, especially during the evangelical revival of the early nineteenth century, to call spectacle and performance into question and to continue the bias against acting as no more than a form of deceit and dissimulation, as likely to fool the performer as it was the audience.[20]

The federal principle was therefore a profound attack on a hallowed theory of liberal education which equated manner with education. At the older universities of England the theory did not immediately disappear. There the division between college and university allowed for the simultaneous existence of the older conception that style makes the man[21] and the newer one emphasising more cerebral or intellectual qualities. (Something of the former still lingers in the noted American liberal arts colleges, where student-oriented learning and 'moral' education remain ideals.) The conflict between the two conceptions was sharp, if mitigated in practice. For example, in the older version of liberal education, failure was a moral or personal failing, the result of not working sufficiently hard. The stigma of failure could therefore be eradicated by applying oneself in some recognisable way, either through reading hard or rowing hard. But insofar as the examination system emphasised qualities of mind, the results of Judgement Day could not be easily eradicated. Once posted on the noticeboards outside the Senate House, the tripos results became a fact of history. Furthermore, re-trial was made difficult or even impossible. Undergraduates who missed examinations, or performed badly because of illness or circumstances beyond their control, lost the chance to become first-class men. Examinations were the Victorian side of Dr Johnson's belief in the utility of caning. He accepted caning because it settled an issue at once. (Hanging, he might have noticed, accomplished the same end.) Examinations, too, were final and decisive. They erased any lingering doubt as to intellectual worth. It is hardly an accident that eugenics, the measurement of cranial capacity, and the efforts to define 'intelligence' all appear at approximately the same time as examination fever takes hold in Britain.

The federal principle represented the separation of mind from style or personality, and the latter were to be replaced by a less flexible conception of character, which Lionel Trilling calls 'authenticity' or 'sincerity'. Trilling notices national differences in expressing individual sincerity or authenticity. Thus in France sincerity consisted in revealing oneself truthfully, but in Britain (or England) a national reticence required a veil to be drawn over matters intimate, leaving sincerity to mean deeds, actions or forthright communication. In either case, the relationship between individuals and social institutions shifted; for once it was accepted that the members of a particular culture act sincerely or authentically as a matter of course, break-downs in moral behaviour have to be attributed to less personal causes. They become the fault of institutions and social systems.[22] Not to exaggerate the point, the logic of the argument suggests that if examinations do in fact reveal one's 'true' intellectual qualities (and perhaps moral ones as well — for example, self-discipline, responsibility, diligence, a capacity to plan), the only way in which a 'second-class mind' can improve is for an examination system to be changed or its results de-emphasised. This was the strategy adopted by Victorian humanists and critics — a strategy that failed.

Interestingly enough, the distinction between college and university in the federal systems did not produce a partition between character-formation and mind-training. In fact, federated colleges were not so much Oxbridge colleges as "university colleges," smaller versions of universities without degree-giving powers. Possibly the reason lay in the fact that professional even more than liberal education was the raison d'etre behind University College, London. It was King's College, London, which actually had the honour of introducing the first school or department of engineering into English university education, although the first chair was established at the rival college in 1841.[23] One of the continual complaints of undergraduates at London but especially at the redbricks founded later — complaints that go well into the twentieth century — was the relative absence of style with its glittering past associations.

The examining university derived its authority and legitimacy from three sources. The first was the slowly-growing prestige of the degree as a valida-tion of competence. The second was simplicity in coping with complexity. Almost no bureaucracy was necessary, expenses were customarily met out of fees — at worst, only a tiny state subsidy was necessary. Throughout the Victorian period, government resisted pressure from below to bail out or finance federal systems, except on a one-time basis, but that was before the incorporation of big science into the universities. The dominant Victorian belief was that teaching, which also included professional teaching, could be met out of a combination of endowments, gifts and fees.

The third source of legitimacy for the federal universities was their royal origins. That is, they were agencies of the state. This might appear to us ludicrous, since the London University of 1836 consisted of a miniscule staff, technically a committee of the Treasury. The premises were main-tained by the Office of Works. But, however odd this first bureaucratic system might appear to us today, it held two contradictory principles in easy tension. Both have been mentioned. The first was the metropolitan or centre culture, here represented by the prestige of the state, and the second was the principle of liberty. The state was present, if just barely; but a precedent had been laid down, to be used if ever necessary.

The comparative case, referred to thus far only in passing, can now be examined in more detail and perspective. Federalism in the form of multi-campus academic systems has been called 'one of the most extensive and significant developments in university organisation in the past quarter century' in the United States.[24] It is mainly a twentieth-century phenomenon. Adumbrations existed as early as the Federal period following Independence, however, and are probably traceable to the rising competition for resources and market shares by institutions as varied as schools, academies, colleges and universities. Concern over the rampant proliferation of teaching institutions is the origin of the famous Yale Report of 1828 bemoaning the cheapening of education through the creation of fly-by-night opportunists.[25] In other words, in America as in England, the existing elite sectors of what we today might call 'higher education' but then less specific and layered, were concerned about the rise of new institutions without standards; but federal systems were not created to promote a standard of culture as expressed through a particular kind of examining system. The centre of a federal system did not and does not 'examine.' It does not embody an 'idea' in the European sense, Humboldtian or Newmanesque, although such ideas flowed into American universities in the course of the nineteenth century, and have never departed. But, however much lofty ideas or special conceptions of a university may have influenced and inspired individual teachers or presidents, they never succeeded in fastening upon universities a single conception of their role in society, their duties or their historical legacy.[26]

Nor did the multi-campus system come into being to protect the word 'university' as properly belonging only to a particular type of superior higher education institution. 'University' had come into use in the late eighteenth century at Harvard to describe a single institution with more than one college or 'school' attached to it — in this case, a medical school or department — but no reference was made to degrees or examinations. A university was a form of organisation.

Yet there are exceptions even if they prove the rule, the rule being the inability of American universities or university elites or the centre to monopolise a particular conception of a university by denying use of the word to other and usually newer institutions, or to those regarded as inferior in status or quality. Thus alongside state universities there arose in the United States a second tier of state-supported institutions, usually or often normal schools in origin, which in time, particularly during the extraordinary higher education expansion following the Second World War, grew into large-scale bodies with high aspirations. Among those aspirations was access to the name 'university,' which implied 'higher' tasks such as educating future members of the liberal professions and the granting of doctorates of philosophy. Insofar as these educational missions had acquired prestige in American society, the title of university was coveted. The older or original state universities wanted to hold the line at both title and mission, but lobbying efforts with legislatures usually came to nought. Losing title, the older institutions usually retained mission, but the word university was degraded even further, acquiring a wholly neutral and almost meaningless connotation in the American context. The contrast with London University could not be greater.

A multi-campus, federal system became the basic type of university for state-supported higher education in the United States. The word university, with its European echoes and ancient legacies, symbols and rituals, was asked to accept as partner a neologism which disturbed all those who recoiled at the vulgarities of modern, mass higher education culture, a neologism which carried none of the antique meanings but suggested a bureaucratic or technocratic or managerial culture. That neologism was of course the 'multiversity' (or 'pluriversity' as it was sometimes known in the Britain of the 1960s), which implied a certain size and complexity. (Although writers sometimes distinguish between multiversities and multi-campus systems, for present purposes the two will be conflated.) From that followed a classificatory lexicon of a technical character. Consequently present-day authorities on the subject of American academic federalism distinguish between two types: the first is called 'segmental,' a grouping of campuses with similar functions, as in the case of the nine-campus University of California under a president (although the San Francisco campus is exclusively a medical school). Another Californian segment is the California State University and College system — about half a dozen campuses with four- and five-year degree programmes similar in function to British polytechnics; and a third public segment is composed of some hundred, two-year community colleges, whose chancellor sits in the state capital, Sacramento. Occasionally the private colleges and universities are loosely termed a 'segment,' but only as a semantic convenience. The Claremont colleges in Southern California are an example of a private federation consisting of colleges and graduate schools of independent origins retaining some of their former identifying characteristics.

The second kind of federal system in existence in the United States is often called 'comprehensive.' American comprehensives come in all shapes and sizes, but are characterised by the great variety of institutional forms which they encompass. The constituent institutions range from community colleges to research and professional schools. Examples are the City University of New York (CUNY) and the State University of New York (SUNY). The London University, with its present collection of schools, colleges and hospitals, is of this nature, but with a weak centre and with legally independent colleges and schools which have their own governing boards. It is, therefore, rather a confederation than a federation. California supports a tripartite federated system surmounted by no single authority. Illinois has another version of this. Texas supports no fewer than thirty-seven public senior universities under fifteen different governing boards, six of which govern systems. About one third of the states have created single systems with a single state governing board.[27]

Although I cannot speak for all the state systems of higher education, I can hypothesise that many of the systems, at least the earlier, famous ones, were built from the inside out rather than from the outside in, being created, as at the University of California, by innovative academic leaders winning the support of key government officials. But other systems were undoubtedly created at the initiative of government officials themselves, as Burton Clark has noted, in order to simplify the difficulty of choosing between a large number of public institutions clamoring for funding and attention, lobbying and in other ways attempting to seek favors and privileges.[28]

For what reason or purpose? I doubt very much if we could say that Californians or Americans generally have an in-built liking for systems. Certainly the American professoriate is either mildly hostile or indifferent, but more the latter because the teachers find in general that the 'system' does not really impose upon them all that much — although I am sure that this generalisation would have to be highly qualified according to types of systems. Boards of trustees and regents may well impose upon teaching staff, but that is a different point. The ostensible or manifest function of American higher education federations lies in the familiar bureaucratic notions that I mentioned at the outset: overall planning, to include resource allocation and priorities, something called efficiency, the avoidance of duplication, accountability, 'coordination' — another wonderfully confusing word — and, a contrast this with the Victorian British federations, quality control, which in the American context usually means minimal not optimal standards.[29] Even more so, as I mentioned in passing, it usually means programme evaluation, which is a far less invidious method of assessment than measuring the intellectual quality of teaching by some external yardstick. When such a yardstick is applied, Americans prefer that it be done through peer review or by 'voluntary' accrediting agencies which lack the authority to implement findings and recommendations. It is difficult to find in the United States the kind of central assessment of disciplines and departments introduced by the University Grants Committee in its final years, and indeed American institutions would fear the ramifications of such an assessment by a powerful arm of the government, whether in the nation's Capitol or in the state houses. With their national ideology of opportunity for individuals, their commitment to social mobility and their perennial optimism, not to mention the populism that is generally available for use, Americans do not like to embarrass institutions by pointing to defects that may not be correctable if subjected to an elite standard.

But the latent function or hidden agenda of American federations, which has just now been hinted at, is far more interesting as a comparison to British university history than their apparent or manifest functions. The hidden agenda of federated systems in the United States is to minimise the intrusion of government into everyday decision-making and to reduce externally-mandated policy decisions to the broadest and most innocuous level of generalisation, so that the business of research, teaching, consultation and public service may continue with a high level of de facto independence. Federalism is also a means for encouraging a tolerance for ambiguity — ambiguity in the relations of heads of systems to heads of constituent campuses or indeed throughout the system's functionings.[30] So strongly is this the American — or Californian? — position that I note with some satisfaction that the American rationale for federation is provided in a March 1989 report on London University commissioned by the vice-chancellor and prepared by two Californians. Among the statements about the virtues of federation we find the need for an enhanced central administration in order to facilitate planning in an era of growing demands and complexity (these demands and complexities being manifest in school-based or decentralised degree-giving and an increasing number of modular courses. Indeed, the Murray Committee of 1972 had mentioned something of the same sort). Another statement quietly suggests that greater attention to the federal organisation of the London University would better prepare the institutes, university colleges, medical and other specialised components to meet the challenge of Westminster, Whitehall and the Universities Funding Council — in other words, provide London with a greater capacity for fighting back, anticipating outside reform, mediating and negotiating.[31]

Segmental federal systems have another, not quite so latent, function which at first glance appears un-American. It is to prevent the dilution of mission that occurs or can occur in the comprehensive systems or that exists or can exist under conditions of unfettered institutional competition. Market discipline either forces competition along the same route or leads to wholly new directions as institutions attempt to find a special niche for themselves, a place in the consumption structure that provides unique opportunities. Segments try to prevent 'mission creep' by formalising boundaries and having them recognised by state legislatures, and by being vigilant in protecting monopoly functions, for example, research or medical education. Or the 'mother' campuses of federal systems may object to the establishment of new sites on a variety of grounds, snobbery or financial fears, as the campus at Berkeley and Northern Californians generally objected to the creation of a southern branch, now the University of California at Los Angeles, in the 1920s.[32]

Throughout the 1980s the University of California system fought off the claims of the California State University system, which through its chancellor tried to leverage its component campuses into the high-status research market and attract the substantial resources that accompany 'upward academic drift'. Here and there such inroads have in fact been made at the disciplinary level; but on the whole, the intrusions have been resisted, and the formal boundaries have held, probably because the process of upward academic drift brings different funding formulae into play and immensely increases the cost of higher education. American state governments, then, in the name of diversity and access, have resisted applying the Robbins principle to new or ambitious higher education institutions and have instead adhered to the practice of differential segmental financing.

Establishing bulwarks against intruders from 'below,' and appealing to the authority and assistance of government in doing so, appear to resemble the British desire to preserve the standards and definition of a university, and it would be foolish to deny the imputation. American universities and colleges belong to a reputational or status system. Prestige drives many of the hiring and admissions policies of higher education institutions in the United States.[33] It may in particular be argued that prestige is all the more important as a regulator of American colleges and universities precisely because few outside high-status institutions exist with which higher education institutions can associate, deriving their prestige from a halo effect. The United States never had a national church, a landed aristocracy, a governing elite (after about 1820), a highly-regarded civil service, or a 'state' representing the nation in its 'noblest' and most idealised guise, as in France, Sweden, or Germany. The liberal professions in America come closest to possessing a traditional status. Perhaps that, as well as the antiquity of the association, is why the ties between universities and the professions are close. Otherwise, it is the colleges and universities of the United States that help to create status distinctions in the United States, rather than merely reproducing such distinctions as European universities are sometimes charged with doing.[34]

But it is still the case that prestige cannot rest upon the authority of state governments to establish mission boundaries and funding differentials between public-sector institutions. A prestigious private sector stands outside state higher education legislation; and furthermore, the public legitimacy of all higher education depends upon its accessibility to students. This especially applies to the public elite sector, which must pay attention to the transfer process, even at the cost of lessening institutional control over the degree. Consequently, however much federal systems may attempt to protect the characteristics of their satellite campuses, the essential point is that they do compete against one another for talent, resources and status advantages in their own and against other states, and against the private sector, in a bewildering array of leagues, circles and other groupings. That competition includes what to Europeans must and does appear a baffling amount of fuss over intercollegiate athletics in a highly commercialised form, and other activities not historically associated with universities. Furthermore, since the centre of the federal system in many state multi-campus arrangements does not even supply the bulk of the total operating and research budget to its constitutents, corporate raiding can and does occur within systems, and lures are dangled before undergraduates and postgraduates. Ultimately, no federal system can claim the loyalty of its colonial dependencies and academic faculties, which remain wholly attached to their outlying disciplinary fiefs and tribal territories, a fact of life made famous in different words by the chief architect of one of the celebrated multi-campus systems.[35] Whether or not individual universities (wherever they are) will lose their 'soul' in the future service of multiple clients, as one recent writer suggests,[36] it is certain that the federal university in America never had one.

In a sense then — and to repeat — the Royal University of London, the Victoria University, the University of Wales and so on, and the American segmented systems, have had a common objective in the preservation of a particular kind of monopoly through constraint of market competition. In the British case, the monopoly was the degree. In the American one, it was the mission, to which degrees may be attached (for example, the Ph D). The similarities are always interesting, but the differences are what really matter. In England, the task of preserving or establishing a monopoly was a task that fell to central government at precisely the moment when the higher education system in England began to expand and the market began to play an important role in the provision for post-secondary instruction.

A further essential point is that government in Britain could exercise its authority over both the public and the private sector because fundamentally there was no conception of 'society' such as had developed in the United States, by which I mean no legitimate source of authority to appeal to beyond the prerogative state, beyond the crown in parliament. In America an inherent distrust of political authority made itself felt at the time of the Revolution and just afterwards, as manifested in the intense dispute between Jeffersonians and Hamiltonians. The result was a weakening of central power, an increase in states' rights and, more importantly, a conception of 'society' or 'public opinion' as being above and beyond government, both morally and legitimately. One can see this very clearly in the debates over the privileges to be accorded the University of California at the time of the Second Constitutional Convention in 1878. Efforts by the highly organised populist farmers' and urban workers' movements to use government to force the university into a heavily utilitarian and vocational curriculum were defeated by a widespread distrust of state power in the regulation of educational matters, and the result was the relatively autonomous position which the university enjoys in the Californian Constitution today.[37]

The ability of American universities and colleges to appeal over the heads of politicians to a conception like 'society' has, over time, produced a special definition of American freedom. Customarily — and Max Weber's famous essay warning about the intrusions of the German Imperial State fed American fears — academic freedom in the United States is defined as being outside political interference, both in the running of universities and in attempts to influence the subject matter of teaching. In earlier periods, as American colleges and universities were breaking away from religious ties and affiliations important in their founding, academic freedom was also described in the language of religious freedom. 'Society,' regarded as antithetical to government possibly because it was plural and hence divided, was looked upon more as an ally than a threat; and to this day university presidents in the public sector will campaign against impending legislation considered inimical to university interests. It is only recently that threats to academic freedom have been seen as emanating from sources internal to the universities themselves, sources representing radical student movements or teaching staff with specific ideologies.

By contrast with an American concern for the independence of universities and colleges as expressed in conceptions of academic freedom, there is very little literature on the subject in writings on the history of British universities, and no single comprehensive work such as Richard Hofstadter and Walter Metzger have produced for the United States.[38] State or religious interference in the running of British universities is a well-established historical fact, and the revolt against religious orthodoxy at Oxford and Cambridge that marked the middle decades of the nineteenth century is not an exception to that remark but a confirmation of it. The dons who advocated religious toleration in undergraduate admissions, the receipt of degrees and the appointment of fellows did not really mind if the state replaced the Church as the primary influence on the ancient universities. Indeed, it was the academic Tories, the clerical dons, who worried most about the intrusion of state power and who resisted the demands and initially refused to answer the questions of royal commissioners appointed to inquire into the running of their colleges.

But I have stated the problem incorrectly. Where Church and state are one, embodied in the person of the crown, and where the crown's prerogative, as expressed through the Privy Council, remains legitimate, and where universities identify completely with the state and Church establishments, the word 'interference' is misleading. The polarities which Americans take for granted as an essential part of their institutional history, leading to shifts from consensus one day to litigation the next, do not exist to the same degree in Britain. A fortiori, when Victorian dons wanted to protest against the intrusion of outside influence into university affairs, they frequently spoke of standing up to 'public opinion'. What they feared was the unfettered consumerism of Victorian liberal society. An historian like Edward Gibbon might well write in his autobiography a propos the successful sale and reception of his *Decline and Fall of the Roman Empire* that 'the public is seldom wrong'.[39] But that is because he was an Augustan who felt liberated from patronage by his success in the market place. The situation was perceived differently in the different value system of the nineteenth century.

Do these sketchy remarks account for the comparatively weak responses by British universities to government policy in the 1980s, or are we also to attribute the relative calm or sense of defeat to the absence of effective institutions for channelling protest, such as law courts, constitutional rights with regard to tenure, an independent or private sector of higher education, a conception of society as distinct from government? Perhaps so — if the Charter 88 movement is to be taken seriously.

Whether public or private, American institutions of higher education attempt to preserve their independence by acting as if they were private, by automatically, as it were, conducting their affairs as if they possessed natural rights. Although today only the University of Buckingham is considered to be a private university in Britain, not answerable to the Universities Funding Council, the conception of a private higher education was actually very prevalent in the 1830s. The private sector in Britain consisted of the new London colleges of King's and University, and as the century progressed other private colleges were formed. But actually, the private sector also included the ancient colleges of Oxford and Cambridge, for the definition of a college had been greatly clarified by the decisions of 1836 to invest the word 'university' with a special definition. It was the academic Tories who took the lead in defining a college as a private body owing its origins 'not to Kings or Parliaments, but . . . to the piety and benevolence, and enlarged and far-seeing liberality of private individuals'.[40] While a 'college' could be a university college or a type of school — the College at Eton, Bedford College for Women, or in our time, Carmel College — it could also have a private identity allowing it to decide upon its own curriculum, admissions policies and religious affiliation or leanings. Colleges could be non-denominational, even secular, even in some respects atheistic, or, as in the case of King's College, they could be Anglican. At Durham, the colleges were regarded as private — hence religious subscription could be required of matriculands.

However, the University of Durham (as distinct from its colleges) was public, and its lectures were consequently open to all comers. By contrast, the word 'university' belonged to the public sphere of higher education. Because of the London compromise of 1836, a university was a public entity, beholden to the state, since the state had declared its interest in upholding qualifications as represented by the degree. The university was public, its lectures consequently open to all comers. The private/public distinction in the United States had nothing to do with the type of institution or mission or degree-granting capability. The distinction existed because in the early nineteenth century the State of New Hampshire was prevented by the courts from taking over Dartmouth College, one of the seven colonial colleges which the state had hitherto supported as a kind of state-supported college. But if one of the states was prevented from exercising control over a college for which it had once had some degree of fiscal responsibility, in a deeper sense the distinction between private and public in the United States is misleading. Both sectors emulate one another because they are competitive. Both appeal to the same sources for financial support (the private sector has access to all kinds of federal dollars), and both are beholden to 'society' and claim to be serving the general public.

Victorian Britain, as a liberal society albeit with a prerogative state, had a number of features in common with the world of twentieth-century America, but the differences are always more striking. The metropolitan culture

captured the degree examinations and made them into an effective instrument for imposing curricular control from above, waiting patiently for degree
demand to build up. Federal university systems in the United States did
not attempt to impose quality control, beyond some minimal regulation,
because federal systems in the United States looked outward as much as
inward, generally alert to the enemies lurking beneath the walls. Even within
segments, serious differences have existed and continue to exist on the constituent campuses with respect to admissions, curriculum and the recruitment
of academic staff and students, not to mention athletic programmes and
solicitations for private funding. In fact, as I have noted, it is precisely the
preservation of differences that public segments desire, differences which
define their identities and independence but do not restrict their ability
to compete against other similar segments or the independents outside the
federal system.

To be sure, it is not always easy to notice the differences. One might
be just as much astonished by the homogeneity of American universities,
and wonder whether their claims to being unique are rhetorical rather than
actual market hype rather than reality, a part of the recruiting game and
self-advertisement that is especially conspicuous at the moment as higher
education costs mount furiously. All American universities or colleges, beyond a handful, are divided into teaching departments based on disciplines.
All feature modular course structures, offer credits or units, and combine
teaching with examining. All claim to be 'diverse' — a word rapidly becoming
a cliche. The differences are quite probably not so much differences of aim
and organisation, but differences in intangibles, depending upon geographic
location, urban or small-town settings, the composition of the student body,
their prior schooling or family culture or ethnicity, the early history and
prestige of the institution, or the national and international reputation of
the academic staff.

But whether the differences are actual or only a matter of emphasis, or
whether they are created as marketing strategies, many American university
teachers and administrators think they need to be preserved and legitimated
against the homogenising tendencies of a populist culture which every now
and then arouses itself against the suggestion of elitism in any form — this
is perhaps easiest to resist in some of its political forms than in its social
forms. Segments and systems have large bureaucracies. Martin Trow has
pointed out that the answer to big government is an equally big university-
based bureaucracy, which speaks the same language as the civil servants
in the state capitals and the 'pols' in the state houses and keeps them
well supplied with a himalayan quantity of facts, figures, phone calls and
legislative appearances.[41] Burton Clark has suggested that a similar stand-
off is produced through voluntarism, pre-emptive strikes taken with the
assistance of a network of interlinked self-help associations of universities,
colleges, graduate schools, governing boards and other Washington-based

organisations acting as a kind of larger federal centre. These associations 'nationalise' the higher education system, lobby for it and keep it in touch with a very broad range of public opinion. Clark has also noted that it would be a mistake to think that the creation of numerous public or quasi-public coordinating agencies and councils at governmental levels really means coordination. In the American context it means rather the protection of diversity and differentiation within a segment. As he says, it is essential to divide power, support variety and legitimate disorder.[42]

These examples, historical as well as more recent, establish, I believe, that there exist and have existed a great many different federated academic communities, certainly in Britain and the United States, serving quite different and often enough quite contrasting purposes. Those purposes also probably underwent periodic changes of emphasis or possibly transformations which a more detailed examination might reveal. In any case, the different uses of federation are undoubtedly worth bearing in mind as in the 1990s the nations of Europe set about creating a federated system of sometime sovereign states and experience inter-institutional arrangements well below both political initiative and political control. Even where bureaucratic agencies appear to resemble one another, they are not necessarily driven by the same mental laws (as a Victorian philosopher might say). Civil servants abound in the United States, but they are not necessarily dirigiste in outlook. While they 'coordinate' and recommend, their decisions also reflect the intricate system of checks and balances, of trade-offs and conceptions of spheres of autonomy and independence that pervade American legal and political life in a nation that has remained peculiarly loyal to its special Enlightenment roots.

Notes

1 See the famous debate of the 1960s over the origins of public intervention in England as started by Oliver MacDonagh, *A Pattern of Government Growth, 1880–1860* (London, 1961).

2 An account of recent events is provided by Peter Scott, *Higher Education in Sweden — a Look from the Outside* (London and Lund, 1991). I am also greatly indebted to forthcoming work by Aant Elzinga of the University of Gothenburg.

3 See Grant Harman and V. Lynn Meek (eds), *Institutional Amalgamations in Higher Education, Process and Outcome in Five Countries* (Armidale, New South Wales, 1988). Also by the same editors, *Australian Higher Education Reconstructed? Analysis of the Proposals and Assumptions of the Dawkins Green Paper* (Armidale, N.S.W., 1988).

4 Sheldon Rothblatt, 'Historical and comparative remarks on the federal principle in higher education,' in *History of Education*, 16 (1987), 151–80; also 'London: a metropolitan university,' in Thomas Bender (ed.), *The City and the University* (Oxford and New York, 1988), 119–149.

5 For these facts and others about Scotland, I am indebted to conversations with Donald Withrington and to Robert Anderson, *Education and Opportunity in Victorian Scotland* (Oxford, 1983).

6 See the *Edinburgh Review* articles by John Playfair, (xi, Jan. 1808, 249–284); Richard Payne Knight (xiv, July 1809, 429–441); and Sydney Smith (xv, Oct. 1809, 40–53, and xvii, Nov. 1810, 122–135). These essays were published anonymously. The famous Oxford rebuttal is by Edward Copleston of Oriel, *A Reply to the Calumnies of the Edinburgh Review against Oxford Containing an Account of the Studies Pursued in the University* (Oxford, 1810).

7 The best source for this is W. L. Guttsman, *The British Political Elite* (London, 1963).

8 Margaret Bryant, *The London Experience of Secondary Education* (London, 1986).

9 Alan Heeson, *The Founding of the University of Durham* (Durham, 1982); C. E. Whiting, *The University of Durham, 1832–1932* (London, 1932).

10 The early controversies surrounding the first London university are detailed in H. Hale Bellot, *University College London 1826–1926* (London, 1929).

11 My use of words like 'metropolitan' or 'peripheral' is obviously indebted to Edward Shils's well-known essays appearing in *Center and Periphery: Essays in Macrosociology* (Chicago, 1975), but also to the writings of Lawrence Cremin on the history of American education.

12 Negley Harte, *The University of London, 1836–1986* (London, 1986), 73.

13 John Gascoigne, 'Mathematics and meritocracy: the emergence of the Cambridge mathematical tripos,' in *Social Studies of Science*, 14 (1984), 547–584; Sheldon Rothblatt, 'The student sub-culture and the examination system in early nineteenth-century Oxbridge,' in Lawrence Stone (ed.), *The University in Society* (Princeton, 1974), i, 247–304.

14 Sheldon Rothblatt, *The Revolution of the Dons, Cambridge and Society in Victorian England* (Cambridge, 1981).

15 Harold Perkin, *The Origins of Modern English Society, 1780–1880* (London, 1969, repr. 1972); and *The Rise of Professional Society, England since 1880* (London, 1989).

16 See, for example, George Kitson Clark, 'Statesmen in disguise: reflections on the history of the neutrality of the civil service,' reprinted in Peter Stansky, *The Victorian Revolution: Government and Society in Victorian Britain* (New York, 1973); and Franklin B. Wickwire, 'King's friends, civil servants, or politicians,' *American Historical Review*, 71 (Oct. 1965), 18–42.

17 Eugene C. Lee and Frank M. Bowen, *The Multicampus University: a Study of Academic Governance* (Berkeley, 1971), 215.

18 Stefan Collini takes education for character formation into the Victorian era in 'The idea of "character" in Victorian political thought,' *Transactions of the Royal Historical Society*, 5th ser., 35 (London, 1985), 29–50.

19 Mentioned by Richard Sennet, *The Fall of Public Man* (Cambridge, 1977), 64.

20 Jonas Barish, *The Antitheatrical Prejudice* (Berkeley, 1981).

21 Does this apply to women? Insofar as character formation was thought to be the peculiar virtue of a collegiate education, the answer may be no. Many late Victorian dons thought that collegiate life was especially suited to men students and not to women, because only men by their nature and their public destinations were able to profit from the kind of interpersonal communication characterised by residence in a college. I am indebted to conversations with my student Monica Rico for these thoughts.

22 Lionel Trilling, *Sincerity and Authenticity* (Cambridge, 1973), 10, 14, 58.

23 F. G. Brook, 'The early years of London University — its influence on higher education and the professions,' *Universities Review*, 33 (1960), 12.

24 Lee and Bowen, *Multicampus University*, 1.

25 'Original papers in relation to a course of liberal education', *The American Journal of Science and Arts*, 15 (Jan. 1829), 297–351.

26 Sheldon Rothblatt, 'The idea of the idea of a university and its antithesis', in *Conversazione* (La Trobe University, Australia, 1989).

27 Information on the variety of federal systems is taken from a draft article by Eugene Lee on the subject of multicampus universities, prepared for the forthcoming *Encyclopaedia of Higher Education*; see also Lee and Bowen, *Multicampus University*, chaps 2 and 3.

28 I am referring specifically to the recollections of Clark Kerr, President Emeritus of the University of California, as contained in an unpublished paper entitled 'The California master plan of 1960 for higher education: an ex ante view', written in 990–91; see also the draft article by Eugene Lee, where Clark is cited.

29 Eugene C. Lee and Frank M. Bowen, *The University of London: an American Perspective* (Working Paper 89–3, Institute of Governmental Studies, University of California, Berkeley, March 1989), list 'quality control' among the general missions of multi-campus universities, but they almost immediately temper this object with another, 'the promotion of differential dimensions of quality' — a very different purpose.

30 *Ibid.*, 14.

31 *Ibid.*, 10.

32 Remarks made by Julie Robinson during discussion at the University History Seminar, Center for Studies in Higher Education, University of California, May 14, 1991.

33 Martin Trow, 'Analysis of status', in Burton Clark (ed.), *Perspectives on Higher Education: Eight Disciplinary and Comparative Views* (Berkeley and Los Angeles, 1984), 132–164.

34 As in Detlef K. Muller, Fritz Ringer and Brian Simon (eds), *The Rise of the Modern Educational System: Structural Change and Social Reproduction, 1870–1920* (Cambridge and Paris, 1987). The editors have included critiques of reproduction theory, but see also Sheldon Rothblatt, 'Supply and demand: the "two histories" of English education', *History of Education Quarterly*, 28 (1988), 627–644.

35 Clark Kerr, *The Uses of the University* (Cambridge, Ma, 1963). For disciplinary and professional attachments, Tony Becher, *Academic Tribes and Territories, Intellectual Enquiry and the Cultures of Disciplines* (Milton Keynes, 1989).

36 Scott, *Higher Education in Sweden*, 21.

37 Peter Van Houten, 'The Development of the Constitutional Provisions Pertaining to the University of California in the California Constitutional Convention of 1878–79' (unpublished Ph D dissertation, University of California, 1973).

38 Richard Hofstadter and Walter Metzger, *Academic Freedom in the United States* (New York, 1955).

39 Edward Gibbon, *Memories of My Life* (Harmondsworth, 1984), 163.

40 Sir Robert Inglis, *The Universities* (London, 1850), 54.

41 In conversation with Martin Trow.

42 Remarks made at a *Conversazione* held at the University of California at Berkeley, 21 and 22 May 1990 on the report, *A Review of Higher Education Policy in California* commissioned and released by the Organisation for Economic Co-Operation and Development, Paris, in 1989. The word conversazione to describe the Berkeley meetings was inspired by the Conversazione that Claudio Veliz has held for many years at La Trobe University, Australia, and which he has now expanded to include Boston University and Oxford University.

47

FUNCTIONS—THE PLURALISTIC UNIVERSITY IN THE PLURALISTIC SOCIETY*

Clark Kerr

Source: C. Kerr, *The Great Transformation in Higher Education, 1960–1980*, Albany: State University of New York Press, 1991, pp. 47–67.

The occasion for this essay was the *Great Ideas Today* series of the *Encyclopaedia Brittanica*, which in 1969 concentrated on *The University Today*. Robert M. Hutchins, the great sponsor of the *Encyclopaedia*, later in life chaired the Center for the Study of Democratic Institutions, to which he invited me as a regular participant. I was a member of his committee of consultants throughout the period of his leadership, and I admired him greatly as a personality. At a Center meeting, he once said that my ideas on pluralism placed me down in the Agora doing the "bumps and grinds" while he preferred to live up on the top of the Acropolis thinking philosophical thoughts. His thoughts, he believed, were a continuation of the great dialogue that began in Greece at the time of Socrates, Plato, and Aristotle. Hutchins's vision, from my point of view, is fine, but there is more to education than that alone.

The battle over functions has been and will continue to be fought at many times and in many places. The monists glory in their rectitude and their rhetoric; and the pluralists struggle in the mud of reality.

The functions of the university have always been more or less complex and never as simple as some have supposed. The historical tendency has been for university functions to become more complex, and to leave simplicity ever farther behind. Yet there are still those who cry for the simple life, the homogeneous institution.

The university, through its expanding functions, is also ever more central to the life of society; more involved in more of the affairs of more individuals and institutions. Yet there are still those who say the university should stand outside society, or should stand within but serve only one social force—and that social force the one they favor.

The functions of the university have often been controversial and not fully accepted by everyone. Currently the controversy is more intense than in earlier periods. Yet there are those who think that controversy should be foreign to the university.

Complexity, centrality to society, and controversy mark the American university of today. Is this inevitable? Is it to some extent undesirable? And, to the extent it is deemed undesirable, what should be done?

The American university is now one hundred years of age. The first true university was Johns Hopkins in 1876; Harvard transformed itself from a college into a university during the immediately subsequent period. There were other new beginnings, such as at Chicago and Stanford, and many additional transformations by the time of World War I.

Two points should be made clear in advance of discussing the problems of the American university today.

One point is that the problems of the university assume different but related forms in Rome, Berlin, Paris, London, Tokyo, Calcutta, Madrid, Warsaw, Prague, Moscow, Peking, Buenos Aires; they are found wherever great universities with their concentrations of intellectuals come into contact with the surrounding industrial society, and, of almost equal importance, with their own myriad selves.

The other point is that this is not the first time in history that the functions of the university have been under intense discussion. In England, for example, there were violent discussions when Henry VIII separated Oxford and Cambridge from the Church, when Cromwell separated them from the Crown, when Parliament in the middle of the last century separated them from the Anglican aristocracy; in Germany, at the time of the Thirty Years' War, with the battle over the Reformation that also tore the universities apart, and again when Humboldt started the University of Berlin at the beginning of the nineteenth century; in France, when Napoleon took moribund institutions and sought to turn them into servants of the new state; in the United States, when the newly created modern university began taking over from the classical college a century ago, and later when Lowell and then Hutchins attempted a counterrevolution.

The university in the toils of intense controversy is not limited to this one place—the United States—and this one time—the second half of the twentieth century. The university in many places and at many times has been torn by internal and external conflict; the ivory tower of fond but forgetful memory has often been a bloody battlefield. And the university has always survived, though often changed. It, and the church, are the two most persistent institutions society has known. This has been true in the past. It is true now. It will be true in the future.

Returning to a golden age

There are those who would like the university to return to a Golden Age of purity and harmony. They see in the past their hopes for the future. But which golden age? At least three golden ages now seem attractive to one or another of those concerned with a better vision for higher education. Each of these golden ages is quite distinctive; each is essentially incompatible with the others; each has its merits.

1. The "Golden Age of Research" hearkens back to the Johns Hopkins of 1876, and the Humboldt of Berlin in 1809. The emphasis is upon pure research, upon the autonomous scholar, upon "isolation and freedom" and the "pure idea of learning," to quote Humboldt.[1] "It is a further characteristic of higher institutions of learning that they treat all knowledge as a not yet wholly solved problem and are therefore never done with investigation and research." Discovery of truth is the great challenge, the highest aspiration of the academic.

Abraham Flexner,[2] in particular, but many before and since, lamented the fall from grace that came with desertion of the single-minded pursuit of the Holy Grail of Truth. The path down from Humboldt's "summit" led to applied research, to service (the "service station"), to the new professions like business administration, to football stadia, to correspondence courses. This was the "false path" that was followed by all American universities, even Harvard and John Hopkins. Rockefeller University alone would have been seen as staying at the "summit."

Many in the modern university support this emphasis on pure research, on truth, on new knowledge. They and their precursors have made enormous contributions to knowledge and, through knowledge, to society, and, in the course of doing so, to the growth and prestige of the university. We know more about physiology, and the health of the people has been improved; about agriculture, and there is more food and fiber; about sources of energy, and there are more material goods; and much else. The pursuit of truth has carried society and the university a very long way forward.

But this golden age had its seamy side. It led to the dominance of the full professor in the German university and of the science "star" in the American. It led to ultraspecializaton in the curriculum and rigidity in course sequences, as against the broader point of view sought by many students. It led to heavy dependence on the state as the source of research funds in the older Germany and the newer United States alike. It led to a single-minded pursuit of truth in narrow field after narrow field with little or no concern for the broader consequences of the application of piecemeal truth. It led to heavy emphasis on the areas of science where new discoveries could most easily be made, to the neglect of other areas, especially the humanities.

Nor was the purity of the approach easy to defend. How pure is "pure" research? The tendency was always for some scholars to move down the seamless web from the very pure to the wholly applied, with no clear place to draw the line and call a halt. Moreover, it turned out that contact with actual problems to be solved enhanced even the purest of research. World War II was an enormous stimulus to pure research in science, just as the Great Depression was to pure theory in economics. Also, know-ledge and service tend to merge. The people with knowledge often have a passion to make it available, and those who can use it want access to it. The transition from knowledge to service, from the laboratory to the "service station," drew inspiration from both the producers and consumers of the new knowledge. The path to this version of sin was downhill all the way; the fall from the "summit" was both inevitable and irreversible. Yet indi-vidual summits of pure research have dominant positions in all the great universities.

2. The "Golden Age of the Classics" is a vision that looks back to Cardi-nal Newman's[3] "idea of a university," to John Stuart Mill's[4] "accumulated treasure of the thoughts of mankind," to Thomas Aquinas, to the Lyceum of Aristotle and the Academy of Plato. The best historical model would perhaps be Oxford as seen by Newman a little over a century ago, before it was changed by Parliament and the scientists. The search was for wisdom as found in the classics, in the "Great Books"; and as refined and applied through dialogue and "free speculation." The "intellectual" and the "moral" were intertwined, as Mill noted in his *Inaugural Address* at St. Andrews in 1867; "knowledge" and "conscience" supported each other. The university should make students "more effective combatants in the great fight which never ceases to rage between Good and Evil." The emphasis was not on the new truth but the old wisdom, on the "liberal knowledge" that Newman thought prepared a man "to fill any post with credit, and to master any subject with facility." The university was for the generalist, not the scientific specialist; it was "a place of teaching universal knowledge"; it was a beauti-ful ivory tower.

Hutchins and Barzun have led the current laments of those who regret the fading of this great ideal; and Hutchins sought with great courage and some modest effect to resurrect it at Chicago. To Hutchins[5] the university has become a "nationalized industry" as a result of the "rise of the nation-state and the beginning of the Industrial Revolution." Hutchins saw as evil influ-ences both the "service" that Flexner hated, and the "research" that Flexner loved, for research leads to specialization and a degradation of the teaching function. The purpose of a university is to have people "think together so that everybody may think better than he would alone," and not to have each go off in his own direction in pursuit of new knowledge or added skills.

"Many large American universities appear to be devoted to three unrelated activities: vocational certification, child care, and scientific research." This is a long way from the "ancient ideal" of the "autonomous intellectual community" where "unity and clarity of purpose are fundamental."

To Barzun,[6] "the fabric of the former single-minded, easily defined American university" has been torn apart. Where Hutchins looks all the way back to Aristotle in Athens, Barzun looks back only to Nicholas Murray Butler's rule at Columbia; for the decay Barzun sees has taken place since Butler's retirement at the end of World War II. The university has become "bankrupt in mind and purse" now that it is no longer a "sheltered spot for study only," now that it has entered "the marketplace." The Manhattan Project, the GI Bill of Rights, the legacy of faculty participation in the New Deal and of academic advice to a world power are markers on the road to ruin; and the university has come to cater to "proletarian culture"— even Chicago and Columbia. Only St. John's College, Annapolis, which draws much of its inspiration from Hutchins, remains true to the classics. Barzun is critical of "service," such for example, as helping to meet the needs of urban life. Yet all institutions have rendered service to some segment of society. The service that Barzun favors is service best fitted to the interests of an aristocracy and of the "liberal professions" that draw their members from an aristocracy and cater to it.

This ideal of a perpetual discourse about general ideas today holds the allegiance of many students and a few teachers. It gets resurrected on a grand scale, not as a continuing pursuit but as an *ad hoc* inspiration, when great issues such as civil rights and the war in Vietnam rend the nation. And the university does remain as one of the few places in modern society where fundamental discussions of basic issues can and do take place. In a world of specialists, the university is one of the last hunting grounds for the generalist; and society can be as much aided by better general views as by better specialized research.

Oxford and Cambridge before 1850 and Yale College in 1828 (at the time of the famous faculty report defending the classical curriculum) did not appear so golden to their own contemporaries, except to the guilds that ran them. The classical approach looked more to the past than to the present or the future, and thus had a conservative cast. As a result, the campus seemed isolated from the contemporary reality. General discussions lacked the sharpness that comes from attention to actual and specific cases, and often became ideological and sectarian in their nature—it was no accident that many of the teachers were trained in theology. The whole approach either led to or was at least compatible with an *in loco parentis* approach to the students, an insistent concern with a rigid curriculum and the development of "character." Moreover, the approach had greater appeal to the children of an hereditary aristocracy and of a comfortable upper-middle class than to those of workers and farmers; it made a greater contribution to the would-be gentlemen than to the ex-artisans. It was sometimes hostile to science—one of the great and growing streams of human thought. And the contest of Good against Evil came to be fought at least as much by the middle class and the working class, without benefit of a classical education, as by the members of the aristocracy, who were supposed to be the "more effective combatants" by virtue of their education.

The Classical College did not and indeed could not survive as *the* model of the university, nor could it be restored. The spread of democracy meant that opportunity had to be made available to new elements of the population to whom a classical education did not prove so attractive. Industrialization demanded new skills beyond those of a merchant class or a colonial service or the historic professions; it demanded engineers and architects and administrative specialists. No longer could the professions of real value be limited to those that had served the upper classes: the doctors, the lawyers, and the ministers. New professions arose and the university came to train for them also. The welfare state brought new demands for teachers, public administrators, and public health personnel. And science could not be ignored. The new culture might be called "proletarian." It was also more democractic, more technological, more oriented toward the general welfare, more scientific. And any university that limited itself to the classics for the aristocracy would have condemned itself to oblivion in the new age—but none chose to do so.

Yet elements of the old Classical College grace any system of higher education, and merit preservation as well as encouragement. In fact, the new leisure class of affluent students is bringing a resurrection, a renewed attention, to "knowledge" and to "conscience."

3. The "Golden Age of the Scholarly Community" looks back to the Middle Ages when small bands of scholars met in face-to-face discussions in a legendary "community of scholars"—with more emphasis on "community" and less on "scholars." One modern version is that of Paul Goodman,[7] who favors educational communities of a couple of hundred students (150 is suggested as ideal) meeting in free discussion with a few senior persons drawn from practical pursuits in the surrounding society. The historical model cannot be that of the early Bologna, for the students ruled the rebellious professors there; nor of the early Paris, which was under the domination of the church. It may be the early Oxford and Cambridge, before they became highly organized and subject to traditions; or perhaps the religious discussion groups around the monks that congregated at Glendalough in Ireland. In any event, the model, past or proposed, assumes small communities of scholars voluntarily formed, in which everyone participates as equals, but with some having more experience than others. One such community, although rather large in size from this ideal point of view, is the new student-run Rochdale College on the edge of the University of Toronto; another, the early Kresge College of the University of California at Santa Cruz.

The tutorial and the seminar and the "bull session" may be taken as modern counterparts of the ancient communities of scholars and each has made and does make a substantial contribution to personal and intellectual development.

The "scholarly community" would seem to fit best those aspects of education which benefit from the oral tradition, the personal example, and the experimental doing of things, like an apprenticeship. It relies less on books and not at all on laboratories—the library is at the center of the Classical College, and the laboratory of the Research University; the small discussion group takes their places in the Scholarly Community. Tests and degrees and formal curricula are not an inherent part of it; in fact, they are rather anathema to it. This approach is better at effecting sensitivity and understanding than at imparting high skills and deep knowledge, or discovering new and complicated relationships.

In a world that also calls for high skills and deep knowledge and new discoveries, the "community of scholars" can at best be an aspect of or an appendage to higher education. It could be the totality of higher learning only when knowledge was more limited and consisted more of beliefs and observations than of intricate theory and complicated facts—only when the world was a simpler place.

And yet this personalized kind of education about the general nature of the world and the individual's place within it holds great and valid attraction for many students in the fragmented and mechanized world of today.

The "golden age" of the Community of Scholars goes back to the days before the printing press, when the oral tradition was supreme; that of the Classical College to an era before the laboratory, when the classical texts were the greatest source of knowledge; and that of the Research University, to an epoch before egalitarianism and the welfare state became such central features of society and when science was viewed as the great and even the only key to progress. Each "golden age" relates to its own layer of history; each has its great contributions; each has left an important legacy within the higher education of today. Yet no one of these models was as "golden" when it existed as hindsight makes it appear; and none could serve as the sole model for the university of modern times. The earliest of these golden ages fitted the religious orders of a more religious era; the next, the aristocracy of a less democratic society; and the last, the scientific elite in a period of rapid industrialization. Why were these earlier models abandoned, and why can they not be recreated readily? Basically the reason is that each one, in turn, became increasingly incompatible with the changed conditions of its society.

Flying the flag of dissent

Others view the functions of the university from the perspective not of past models but rather of future possibilities. They emphasize the function of evaluation criticism dissent as a central purpose of the university. This function of dissent was a possible activity of each of the "golden age" universities, but it was not a main function. Social change might be a consequence of scientific research; it might be accepted and accommodated effectively by leaders trained in the classical tradition; it might flow from the little communities of scholars. But social change was not the avowed *raison d'être* of any of them as they actually existed.

Those who see dissent as a central function of the university may be divided into three general groups, with many variations and refinements within each grouping.

1. First, there are those who emphasize the "dissenting professor" and his or her protection—the professor who individually and of his or her own free will decides to criticize some aspect of society or society in its totality. The rules governing academic freedom and tenure grow out of the concept of the "dissenting professor." Some believe that the professor, out of his or her knowledge, has an obligation to provide a free and independent criticism of the surrounding society in his area of specialty. Others view the professor as having a more generalized obligation, as an educated man or woman and a free agent, to comment upon the affairs of society outside as well as inside his or her specialty. They argue that few other persons are so well stationed and so well equipped to perform this essential service to society. Many of the policies of the American Association of University Professors are aimed at guarantees of his right to dissent. The *Lehrfreiheit* of the German universities was to protect this function. Acceptance of this role, as *a* role of the professor, is almost universal among the best of the American universities.

2. A more recent development is the call for the "dissenting academy," to use the phrase of Roszak.[8] Here the responsibility of providing dissent is collective, rather than individual: the "central business of the academy is the public examination of man's life with respect to its moral quality"; universities should "cease functioning as the handmaidens of whatever political, military, paramilitary, or economic elite happens to be financing their operations." Galbraith[9] sees this responsibility (or possibility) as extending beyond the universities to the wider circle of the "educational and scientific estate," which, with its increasing numbers and new positions of power, can become a major force for social change. "The responsibility of intellectuals," says Chomsky,[10] is "the creation and analysis of ideology," not just the creation of experts to run society.

The supporters of the "dissenting academy" see the academy, as a collectivity, helping to change society. They seek to have faculties and professional associations as a whole, such as the sociologists, take positions on public issues. Some even seek to have "the University" as a corporate body take positions on the great issues of the day, for "a university that will not speak for man . . . has ceased to be a human enterprise."[11] They do not support violence in these efforts of the academy, on the grounds that violence has no moral validity in an intellectual community and, in any event, is ineffective against the armed power of the state. The reliance is on persuasion and also, perhaps, on passive disobedience. To perform this dissenting function effectively, the academy requires corporate autonomy and freedom from external obligations for its individual members. The campus becomes, in the words of Tussman,[12] "the most crucial of battlefields" where "the essential vitality of society is tested."

3. Beyond the "dissenting academy" lies what may be called the concept of the "partisan camp," the university which serves as a base for guerrilla activity against the surrounding society. This was the successful strategy of Mao in China and of Castro in Cuba, and the unsuccessful effort in 1968 of the student rebels in France and of some faculty members and students of Berkeley in the late 1960s to "reconstitute" the university into a mechanism intent on reconstituting society. The universities were also one base for violent activity as Hitler conquered Germany. It is argued that the trustees and administrators of the traditional university must be viewed as "occupying powers" and that "terror reigns,"[13] and that the occupying powers should be thrown out and the terror ended. A university, to become "partisan," must have autonomy from control by the police, and internal authority must rest largely in the hands of the students.

Individual dissent is now well accepted within the modern university; the basic battles have been won. It is protected by the rules of the campus and the efforts of the administration. Its costs in public support are generally accepted. It is part of the reality of the pluralistic university as it now exists.

The "dissenting academy" is not accepted. The proponents seek rules or informal actions that discourage or prohibit service and research involving actual or implied commitments to the established order (particularly the "military-industrial complex"), that reward individuals for their contributions to dissenting activities or punish them for "improper" service to the established order, and also, perhaps, that favor the appointment to the faculty of persons with a record of dissent or potentialities for dissent. They may also seek actions by the collective faculty or the collective profession or both attacking policies of the established order, and appropriate policy statements from the university as a corporate body. For these tasks it is essential to have faculty control of university governance, or at least substantial influence over it, perhaps with student allies. Efforts at such results lead to great internal strains within a faculty, or, if successful, to the development of a faculty or segments of a faculty with a single point of view; to major battles over governing authority with trustees and public bodies; and to public distrust of an institution that is inclined to constant and unified dissent rather than to more or less balanced comments. Some German universities during the Reformation were captured by the Protestants, and others remained under the Catholics, as German society divided. The "dissenting academy" was a divided academy; and this may be the natural tendency at all times and in all places.

The "partisan camp" either helps destroy society or is destroyed by society.

These three dissenting views reflect the essential natures of the liberal, the radical, and the revolutionary university. Dissent for the first is an important product; for the second, the main product; and for the last, the sole product.

Dissent, in any of these three forms, has never (with a few temporary exceptions) been the sole or even the central function of actual universities; it has never been the basic organizing principle in the long run. Yet dissent is one function of an academic institution, and a particularly important one if handled effectively, especially now that so many other sources of independent comment, such as the church, the trade union, the independent newspaper editor, have become muted. Even the "partisan university" may have its occasional and temporary place in acting against a clearly oppressive regime (as Harvard and Columbia did before and during the American Revolution, and as Charles University in Prague did in a restrained fashion in the face of the Russian invasion in 1968). The appropriateness of the nature of dissent is related to time and to place.

Criticisms of the modern university made from the side of dissent sound like many of those from the several versions of the "golden age." Proponents of each view quote one another in condemnation of the actual university. None, for example, like the "service station" aspect of the modern university; all speak for "free speculation"; and all prefer a simplification of present functions. They vary greatly among themselves, however, in what they would put in place of the university today—the Research University with its laboratories, the traditional College with its classics, the small community of participating scholars and practitioners, the academy dissenting as a collectivity, or the partisan camp. The critics seem united against the modern university, but they stand divided as architects of the new institution that is to take its place. They are comrades in arms as they attack the status quo, but enemies when it comes to putting something new in place.

Serving the special interests

Criticism comes also from sources other than from the philosophical positions we have been discussing. It flows from a sense that the university is not providing adequate service for some point of view or some group. These special interests either accept the modern university in general but criticize it specifically, or they are unconcerned with the totality and concentrate only on their own claim for service. The philosophical positions set forth above are more eternal and global in their approach; these special interest positions, more current and particular.

The special interest criticisms spring from many groups:

From the conservatives, including many parents, who feel that the university is not properly socializing the students in the manners and beliefs of the surrounding community, that the campus is not politically quiet and culturally orthodox, that the campus neglects its duties *in loco parentis*.

From the organized alumni, often conservatives and often parents, who believe that the old campus traditions are not being maintained.

From the employers of the graduates, the consumers of the research, the users of the services, who complain that the work of the university is not practical enough, not useful enough, that industry or agriculture or the trade unions or the elementary and secondary schools or the government are not getting the immediately effective services they want; from all those who say that the graduates should have better vocational skills, research more geared to their immediate needs, services more responsive to their requests.

From students in general, who say that teaching is neglected, that the curriculum is too rigid and too irrelevant, that the routine "grind" goes on endlessly, that even their own parents can no longer perform the *parentis* role; from black students, in particular, who say the academic life of the white culture is repugnant to them and must be changed.

From neglected areas of the campus such as the humanities, the lesser professions, and the creative arts, which claim more of a place in the sun.

From historically neglected areas in society, such as religious institutions and the newer professions (like real estate), or newly neglected areas, such as the American Legion with its interest in ROTC, which claim their share of attention.

The first four groups want "better" service; the latter two, more service or even some service.

These views about functions demonstrate the variety of expectations that have come to converge on the modern university: that it conserve the past; that it give useful service to the currently powerful forces in society; that it not neglect any group that feels a claim upon its attention. These concerns indicate the myraid groups that feel related to the university, and the extent to which the university is many different things to many different people. A full view of the university requires an appreciation of the claims of these special interests on its functions, an understanding of how potentially useful it has become to how many people.

The intricate web of functions

It is customary to say that the university has three functions: teaching, research, and service. Actually, as the above discussion has indicated, the pattern of functions is more complicated, and any effort to understand the problem must include a comprehension of the complexities. Neither the actual criticisms of functions nor the possible solutions can be evaluated with the simplified threefold system of categorization.

Higher education may be said to perform a series of services related to production, to consumption, and to citizenship.

1. The functions related to production are all those that potentially add to the output of goods and services in society:

> *The talent hunt.*—The selection, guidance, rating, and placement of students for productive occupations. Higher education acts as a great sorting machine. It rejects as well as selects and grades.

> *The training in vocational, technical, preprofessional, and professional skills.*—This is carried on at three levels: terminal vocational work often included in the junior college program leading to a certificate or an Associate in Arts degree, introductory technical training leading to the Bachelor's and Master's degree, and advanced professional training leading to the Doctor's degree. Related to this is postgraduate retraining.

> *Research.*

> *Service.*—Through formal and informal advice and consultation.

All of these functions are best carried out by specialists and through highly organized programs that proceed in sequence, step by step. They draw support from industry, government, the professions, and the academic world itself. The test of performance is technical competence. The line of authority is from the expert to the novice.

2. The consumption functions are those that relate to current consumption of goods and services by the students or by others in the campus community, or to "durable" consumption through changed tastes, sensitivities, skills, and opportunities that lead to a fuller life for the individual:

> *General education.*—This gives students a better understanding of their cultural heritages and perhaps of other cultures as well, and assists them to understand more deeply themselves and their relationships with others. The classics, with their emphasis on personal character, were once the single chosen instrument for general education. Now there are several approaches available. General education for cultural and recreational purposes is increasingly demanded and is available also at the older adult level.

> *Provision of community life on campus.*—Once this life was highly moral and religious; later it came to be predominantly collegiate—athletics, journalistic activities, fraternities, sororities, and so forth. Currently the emphasis is more on external political activity, on service projects to aid others, on experimental cultures of dress and conduct,

on artistic affairs; and increasingly there is the tendency to consider people other than strictly defined members of the campus as part of the "community"—the walls fall down. In the early American colleges, community life was determined by the college itself. Beginning with the movement for student control of extra-curricular activities a century ago, the nature of the community life has been more responsive to the changing interests of the students, to the wishes of the peer group.

Custodial.—Students, somehow, must be housed and fed, given medical care and personal counseling, and preferably kept out of trouble during the period between the time they leave the homes of their parents and start their own families.

Holding operation.—Many students, particularly at the lower division, but also at the M.A. level, are uncertain about what they want to do—get a job, get married, get more education, choose a new field of emphasis. The college provides a place for them to be and an excuse for being while they survey their opportunities and make up their minds. The high dropout rate at these levels can also be viewed as a high "drop-in" rate to other activities. The college, by providing a holding pattern for many students, extends their practical range of choices and the time to make these choices, and thus may improve the quality of the choices.

These several functions are best assisted by persons oriented not so much toward subject matter as toward students as individual human beings and through programs that are flexible and diversified in response to the changing and varied interests of the students. These functions consider the student—not industry, government, the professions, or the academic world—as their main source of orientation. The test of performance is less in technical competence and more in student acceptance. The line of authority is more from the consumer (the student) and less from the teacher and the administrator. Influence over the student relies more on guidance than on control of a technical program. This is the realm for the generalist, not the specialist.

3. The citizenship functions of higher education are those that relate to the performance of students, alumni, and faculty members in relation to their civic responsibilities:

Socialization.—This involves giving the student a basic understanding of the nature of and the rules governing political, economic, and community life. Some would add: indoctrination.

Evaluation.—This calls for critical analysis of the purposes and conduct of established society, and for opportunities to voice objections and make proposals. Some would add: direct social action.

298

Remedial.—Students drawn from many types of homes, many different communities, many diverse school systems come to the campus with quite different qualities of preparation. Once there, the concept of equality of opportunity requires that provision be made so that deficiencies can be made up and subsequent competition put on a more equal footing.

Returning for a moment to our earlier discussion, the Research University approach ties in most closely to the talent hunt, high-level training, and research; the Classical College, to general education; the Community of Scholars, to community life; and the several approaches to dissent, to the function of evaluation.

Higher education over the past few years has seen an enormous shift in the concern attached to these several functions. During and after World War II, with the emphasis upon military and material strength, and going back a century to the rapid industrialization of the United States, the emphasis was upon the functions tied to production. Prolonged prosperity and personal affluence are shifting the emphasis toward the functions tied to consumption, and internal and external political controversies of great intensity, toward functions tied to citizenship. Jobs are more taken for granted, and public policy is less accepted. Higher education is now caught in the turmoil of these historical shifts. The shift is from domination by production considerations toward consumer sovereignty and citizenship participation. Russia, by contrast, still conducts higher education under the domination of production considerations and "socialization" of its own sort. In England, the trends are more mixed, partly because the functions related to production were never so heavily emphasized. Other shifts are taking place around the globe in the comparative emphasis upon one function or another. As the emphasis from function to function shifts, the institution is, of course, changed—also the roles and the lives of individuals within it, and they are not passive about these shifts.

The functioning of the functions

Toynbee has noted that "there seems to be a worldwide consensus that the traditional system of higher education does not meet, any longer, the educational needs of a more and more rapidly changing society."[14] I should now like to examine how the present functions of higher education relate to a changing society, how adequately they are being performed when viewed one at a time, and how they may best be related to each other in different types of institutions.

1. Higher education is a part of society, not apart from it. It is a partially autonomous subsystem of society. It draws on the material resources of society, and may add to them in the long run as much as or more than

it draws out. It reflects the political arrangements of the surrounding society and seldom has much more freedom than is generally provided other institutions and their members, and it almost never has much less freedom. It draws on the accumulated cultural resources of its society and, beyond that, of the world, but it can never be far in front of the cultural resources of the world. Thus higher education benefits from rich material resources, a favorable political climate, and cultural growth, and, generally, the more it adds to each, the more in turn it will benefit from each.

Society is changing, and the functions of higher education are changing. The university, like all other human institutions, has always survived by changing, and change always starts from where you are.

The changes now needed in the functions of American higher education related to production, reflecting changes in society, would seem to be these:

A search for talent from more elements of society, particularly from low-income groups and disadvantaged minorities

The extension of training into advanced adult levels and newly arising professions and occupations

The development of research into the general consequences of specific research, now that research is increasingly viewed as a potential enemy of humanity rather than only as a constant friend

Service to urban life such as the land-grant university has previously provided to rural life

In the functions related to consumption, the changes encouraged by changes in society include these:

A great new emphasis on general education, perhaps reoriented around social problems and field service, reflecting the interests of the new generation of affluent students facing a life of greater opportunity beyond work and thus more like the aristocratic clientele of the older Classical College, a new general education that may also include place for more such subjects as the creative arts and religious philosophy

Much greater stress on the intensity and diversity of community life, reflecting the new vitality and sense of freedom of students, the attraction to them of the view that life is drama, their craving for a variety of personal experiences, their emphasis on peer-group culture

The rejection of custodial functions by the campus, reflecting the greater maturity of students and the more permissive environments from which they have come—the campus can no longer be a "company town"

More realization of the importance of the holding-pattern function of some campuses, as access to higher education becomes more nearly universal and is made available to many who may not be fully committed to it

The first of these directions of change in the functions related to consumption will please Hutchins; the second, Goodman; the third, nearly all students; the fourth, the half of the students who do not go straight through.

The major changes in the functions related to citizenship may well be these:

A tendency to count more on the high school for the socialization function

An inevitable increase, at least temporarily, in remedial work

A new attention to the function of evaluation, both because society is undergoing such great change and because elements on campus are taking such great interest in the direction of these changes

2. Higher education has fulfilled its individual functions with varying degrees of success.

Generally, the production functions have been well performed. Skilled personnel has been supplied at a high level of skill for an expanding economy, and research has moved well in advance of technology to assist ever higher levels of productivity. However, there are inadequacies aside from lack of full adaptation to the changing nature of the external society as noted already. The talent hunt, according to the best available evidence, has often eliminated some of the most creative, experimentally minded students. Secret research is anathema to the open nature of a campus in that it places students and professors in untenable categories of the "cleared" and the "not cleared"; yet it has been accepted on many campuses.

The consumption functions have been poorly performed. The undergraduate curriculum for the student wanting a liberal education, rather than a vocational preparation, is often a disaster area. It has come under the dictatorship of the graduate program, as Riesman[15] has noted, with its emphasis upon specialization and its downgrading of undergraduate instruction. It serves the research interests of the faculty more than the educational concerns of the students. The guild has been dominant over the interests of the consumers. William Rainey Harper, when founding the University of Chicago, was one of the few who realized how the graduate emphasis of the university might overwhelm the undergraduate concerns of the college, and how they might be incompatible. The development of attractive and inspiring communities for undergraduates has been sadly neglected, with little realization of what a major aspect of their lives is determined by the quality of the communities in which they live. Too little attention has been paid to the possibilities of placing auxiliary enterprises, like residence halls and cafeteria, in the hands of private entrepreneurs or student cooperatives so that consumer tastes and preferences can be reflected more readily than through institutional policies and rules. Additionally, the holding function calls for an affirmative attitude toward the experimental dropout, and not one of condemnation and retribution.

The citizenship functions are always more delicate in a society in turmoil than in a society more content with itself. Generally the function of social-ization has been handled with balanced description and comment, not with the rigid indoctrination of communist nations. The remedial function has been neglected; it has too often been assumed that all students enter on an equal footing; and too little has been done in working with high schools to improve their performances. The function of evaluation, as noted earlier, is subject to great internal and external debate. To be effective it must be carried out with a reasonable sense of balance so that no important point of view dominates unfairly or is excluded—this approach is in keeping with the morality of academic life that all voices should be heard, and with the need to preserve the credibility of the academic community before the sur-rounding society; with an emphasis on constructive proposals rather than destructive criticisms alone, for the sake of drawing society toward better solutions; and with reliance on persuasion, since resort to violence is anti-thetical to devotion to reason and can readily lead to reactions that endanger the essential freedoms of the academic community and even of society. In a volatile political climate tending toward polarization, the academic com-munity should be one of the strongholds of reflection and reason and the arts of persuasion. Generally this has been the approach of the "liberal university" now under such aggressive attack from the more extreme sup-porters of the "dissenting academy" and all of the supporters of the "partisan camp." The academic community needs to give the most careful consider-ation to the performance of its evaluative function so that it abides by its own highest principles and helps to meet the needs of the society for better solutions to urgent problems.

Overall, the individual functions more poorly performed are general education and the creation of exciting communities; and the function most in need of clarification is the function of evaluation.

3. Higher education must live with itself as well as with society. Not all functions are equally well performed when combined with others, since some are inherently contradictory. Not all institutions of higher education need be alike; some can specialize in one set of functions and others in another. How best may the several functions be combined?

The two-year community college and the four-year urban college can best serve in the areas of technical training (including related adult education); performance of the holding function (including providing options for advanc-ing into general education and preprofessional work); and remedial work.

The liberal arts college, either as an independent institution, or as a largely independent entity with its own budget and its own curriculum but attached as a "cluster college" to a university, can best perform the functions of general education and the provision of an effective community life, and can help provide general evaluation of society. To perform these functions well, these colleges should glory in their diversity and their flexibility. The university best supplies advanced technical and professional training (along with the specialized technical school, the state college, and the independent professional school—each in its area of competence and at the appropriate level), research, and service; and its particular contribution to evaluation is in the more technical and specialized areas. General education is less well performed in the monolithic university because of its inherent nature; it is carried on better in a different environment from that of the university, where it has been a notable failure.

It might be said that the community colleges and the urban colleges best serve certain of the citizenship functions; the liberal arts colleges, certain of the consumer functions; and the universities, certain of the production functions. Since the production functions are now particularly well performed, it is the other functions that require the intensified attention that over the past century has been paid to the production functions almost alone.

Each campus must live with itself. Perkins[16] has suggested the goal of "internal coherence": Each activity on the campus should "strengthen the others." The more modest goal suggested above is that the activities be able to coexist effectively with each other, each drawing strength from, and hopefully also adding strength to, the common campus environment; and, thus, that essentially incompatible functions be eliminated—ones that are weakened by others or weaken others. Beyond the compatibility of functions lie the questions of whether they are worthwhile in and of themselves, whether they are suitable to the campus or are more suitably performed elsewhere, and whether they are of a level of quality that matches the general quality that matches the general quality of the overall endeavor. The campus does not have a residual function that requires it to fulfill all the otherwise unmet needs of society. It must pick and choose. Internal consistency is one important principle of choice.

It deserves a passing note that functions affect other aspects of the university. One is scale. The liberal arts college performs best when small, when it is a community; the junior college when it is moderate in size, when locally oriented; and the university when it is large enough to warrant adequate library and other research facilities, when nationally and internationally oriented. Another aspect is governance. The liberal arts college needs to be particularly responsive to its students, the junior college to its community, and the university to its faculty. A third aspect is financing. The production and citizenship functions have more of a claim on public funds, and the consumption functions on private money.

In summary, five competing views about the proper nature of higher education in the United States now confront the reality of the existing system: the Research University serving the specialized pursuit of knowledge, the Classical College serving the generalist, the Community of Scholars serving the changing and diverse interests of students, the Dissenting Academy serving the reform of society, and the Partisan Camp serving revolutionary change in society. The reality is a pluralistic system in a pluralistic society serving many functions including constant evaluation of society. The single-purpose campus is as unlikely as the single-purpose wife or husband; the nature of both is to serve more than one function. Nor can there easily be a single model for the multipurpose campus, since some functions combine better than others and there are a number of functions in totality to be performed by higher education.

It is relatively easy to attack the current reality from the perspective of a Golden Past that is no longer totally relevant or from that of a Utopian Future that may never be totally realized. It is more difficult to assist higher education as it actually exists, to change as society changes, to improve its individual functions, to preserve its own integrity. This is the greater challenge.

Notes

* From *The Great Ideas Today 1969* (Chicago: Encyclopaedia Brittanica, 1969), 6–29. Reprinted by permission of the publisher.

1 Wilhelm von Humboldt, *Humanist Without Portfolio: An Anthology of the Writings of Wilhelm von Humboldt*, trans. and intro. by Marianne Cowan (Detroit: Wayne State University Press, 1963).

2 Abraham Flexner, *Universities: American, English, German* (New York: Oxford University Press, 1930).

3 John Henry Cardinal Newman, *The Idea of a University Defined and Illustrated* (London, 1873). Originally *Discourses on the Scope and Nature of University Education, Addressed to the Catholics of Dublin* (Dublin, 1852).

4 John Stuart Mill, "Inaugural Address," delivered to St. Andrews University, February 1, 1867, *Dissertations and Discussions: Political, Philosophical, and Historical*, vol. 4 (Boston, 1867).

5 Robert M. Hutchins, *The Learning Society* (New York: Frederick A. Praeger, Inc., 1968; originally "Education: The Learning Society," in *Britannica Perspectives*, ed. Harry S. Ashmore [Chicago: Encyclopaedia Britannica, Inc., 1968], vol. 2).

6 Jacques M. Barzun, *The American University: How It Runs, Where It Is Going* (New York: Harper & Row, 1968).

7 Paul Goodman, *The Community of Scholars* (New York: Random House, 1962).

8 Theodore Roszak, ed., *The Dissenting Academy* (New York: Random House, 1968).

9 John Kenneth Galbraith, *The New Industrial State* (Boston: Houghton Mifflin, 1967).

10 Noam Chomsky, "The Responsibility of Intellectuals," in Roszak, *The Dissenting Academy*.

11 Richard Lichtman, "The University: Mask for Privilege?" *The Center Magazine*, January 1968.

12 Joseph Tussman, "The Collegiate Rite of Passage," *Experiment and Innovation*, July 1968.

13 John R. Seeley, "The Fateful Trumpet, II" (unpublished manuscript, April 1966).

14 Arnold J. Toynbee, "Higher Education in a Time of Accelerating Change," Academy for Educational Development, paper no. 3, 1968.
15 Christopher Jencks and David Riesman, *The Academic Revolution* (New York: Doubleday, 1968).
16 James A. Perkins, *The University in Transition* (Princeton, NJ: Princeton University Press, 1966).

48

THE IDEA OF A MULTIVERSITY

Clark Kerr

Source: C. Kerr, *The Uses of the University*, Cambridge, Mass.: Harvard University Press, 1995, pp. 1–34.

The university started as a single community—a community of masters and students. It may even be said to have had a soul in the sense of a central animating principle. Today the large American university is, rather, a whole series of communities and activities held together by a common name, a common governing board, and related purposes. This great transformation is regretted by some, accepted by many, gloried in, as yet, by few. But it should be understood by all.

The university of today can perhaps be understood, in part, by comparing it with what it once was—with the academic cloister of Cardinal Newman, with the research organism of Abraham Flexner. Those are the ideal types from which it has derived, ideal types which still constitute the illusions of some of its inhabitants. The modern American university, however, is not Oxford nor is it Berlin; it is a new type of institution in the world. As a new type of institution, it is not really private and it is not really public; it is neither entirely of the world nor entirely apart from it. It is unique.

"The Idea of a University" was, perhaps, never so well expressed as by Cardinal Newman when engaged in founding the University of Dublin a little over a century ago.[1] His views reflected the Oxford of his day whence he had come. A university, wrote Cardinal Newman, is "the high protecting power of all knowledge and science, of fact and principle, of inquiry and discovery, of experiment and speculation; it maps out the territory of the intellect, and sees that . . . there is neither encroachment nor surrender on any side." He favored "liberal knowledge," and said that "useful knowledge" was a "deal of trash."

Newman was particularly fighting the ghost of Bacon who some 250 years before had condemned "a kind of adoration of the mind . . . by means whereof men have withdrawn themselves too much from the contemplation of nature, and the observations of experience, and have tumbled up and down in their own reason and conceits." Bacon believed that knowledge should be for the benefit and use of men, that it should "not be as a courtesan, for pleasure and vanity only, or as a bond-woman, to acquire and gain to her master's use; but as a spouse, for generation, fruit and comfort."[2]

To this Newman replied that "Knowledge is capable of being its own end. Such is the constitution of the human mind, that any kind of knowledge, if it really be such, is its own reward." And in a sharp jab at Bacon he said: "The Philosophy of Utility, you will say, Gentlemen, has at least done its work; and I grant it—it aimed low, but it has fulfilled its aim." Newman felt that other institutions should carry on research, for "If its object were scientific and philosophical discovery, I do not see why a University should have any students"—an observation sardonically echoed by today's students who often think their professors are not interested in them at all but only in research. A University training, said Newman, "aims at raising the intellectual tone of society, at cultivating the public mind, at purifying the national taste, at supplying true principles to popular enthusiasm and fixed aims to popular aspirations, at giving enlargement and sobriety to the ideas of the age, at facilitating the exercise of political powers, and refining the intercourse of private life." It prepares a man "to fill any post with credit, and to master any subject with facility."

This beautiful world was being shattered forever even as it was being so beautifully portrayed. By 1852, when Newman wrote, the German universities were becoming the new model. The democratic and industrial and scientific revolutions were all well underway in the western world. The gentleman "at home in any society" was soon to be at home in none. Science was beginning to take the place of moral philosophy, research the place of teaching.

"The Idea of a Modern University," to use Flexner's phrase,[3] was already being born. "A University," said Flexner in 1930, "is not outside, but inside the general social fabric of a given era. . . . It is not something apart, something historic, something that yields as little as possible to forces and influences that are more or less new. It is on the contrary . . . an expression of the age, as well as an influence operating upon both present and future."

It was clear by 1930 that "Universities have changed profoundly—and commonly in the direction of the social evolution of which they are part." This evolution had brought departments into universities, and still new departments; institutes and ever more institutes; created vast research libraries; turned the philosopher on his log into a researcher in his laboratory or the library stacks; taken medicine out of the hands of the profession and put it into the hands of the scientists; and much more. Instead of the individual student, there were the needs of society; instead of Newman's eternal "truths in the natural order," there was discovery of the new; instead of the generalist, there was the specialist. The university became, in the words of Flexner, "an institution consciously devoted to the pursuit of knowledge, the solution of problems, the critical appreciation of achievement and the training of men at a really high level." No longer could a single individual "master any subject"—Newman's universal liberal man was gone forever.

But as Flexner was writing of the "Modern University," it, in turn, was ceasing to exist. The Berlin of Humboldt was being violated just as Berlin had violated the soul of Oxford. The universities were becoming too many things. Flexner himself complained that they were "secondary schools, vocational schools, teacher-training schools, research centers, 'uplift' agencies, businesses—these and other things simultaneously." They engaged in "incredible absurdities," "a host of inconsequential things." They "needlessly cheapened, vulgarized and mechanized themselves." Worst of all, they became " 'service stations' for the general public."

Even Harvard. "It is clear," calculated Flexner, "that of Harvard's total expenditures not more than one-eighth is devoted to the *central* university disciplines at the level at which a university ought to be conducted." He wondered: "Who has forced Harvard into this false path? No one. It does as it pleases; and this sort of thing pleases." It obviously did not please Flexner. He wanted Harvard to disown the Graduate School of Business and let it become, if it had to survive at all, the "Boston School of Business." He would also have banished all Schools of Journalism and Home Economics, football, correspondence courses, and much else.

It was not only Harvard and other American universities, but also London. Flexner asked "in what sense the University of London is a university at all." It was only "a federation."

By 1930, American universities had moved a long way from Flexner's "Modern University" where "The heart of a university is a graduate school of arts and sciences, the solidly professional schools (mainly, in America, medicine and law) and certain research institutes." They were becoming less and less like a "genuine university," by which Flexner meant "an organism, characterized by highness and definiteness of aim, unity of spirit and purpose." The "Modern University" was as nearly dead in 1930 when Flexner wrote about it as the old Oxford was in 1852 when Newman idealized it. History moves faster than the observer's pen. Neither the ancient classics and theology nor the German philosophers and scientists could set the tone for the really modern university—the multiversity.

"The Idea of a Multiversity" has no bard to sing its praises; no prophet to proclaim its vision; no guardian to protect its sanctity. It has its critics, its detractors, its transgressors. It also has its barkers selling its wares to all who will listen—and many do. But it also has its reality rooted in the logic of history. It is an imperative rather than a reasoned choice among elegant alternatives.

President Nathan Pusey wrote in his latest annual report to the members of the Harvard Board of Overseers that the average date of graduation of the present Board members was 1924; and much has happened to Harvard since 1924. Half of the buildings are new. The faculty has grown five-fold, the budget nearly fifteen-fold. "One can find almost anywhere one looks similar examples of the effect wrought in the curriculum and in the nature of the contemporary university by widening international awareness, advancing knowledge, and increasingly sophisticated methods of research. . . . Asia and Africa, radio telescopes, masers and lasers and devices for interplanetary exploration unimagined in 1924—these and other developments have effected such enormous changes in the intellectual orientation and aspiration of the contemporary university as to have made the university we knew as students now seem a strangely underdeveloped, indeed a very simple and an almost unconcerned kind of institution. And the pace of change continues."[4]

Not only at Harvard. The University of California last year had operating expenditures from all sources of nearly half a billion dollars, with almost another 100 million for construction; a total employment of over 40,000 people, more than IBM and in a far greater variety of endeavors; operations in over a hundred locations, counting campuses, experiment stations, agricultural and urban extension centers, and projects abroad involving more than fifty countries; nearly 10,000 courses in its catalogues; some form of contact with nearly every industry, nearly every level of government, nearly every person in its region. Vast amounts of expensive equipment were serviced and maintained. Over 4,000 babies were born in its hospitals. It is the world's largest purveyor of white mice. It will soon have the world's largest primate colony. It will soon also have 100,000 students—30,000 of them at the graduate level; yet much less than one third of its expenditures are directly related to teaching. It already has nearly 200,000 students in extension courses—including one out of every three lawyers and one out of every six doctors in the state. And Harvard and California are illustrative of many more.

Newman's "Idea of a University" still has its devotees—chiefly the humanists and the generalists and the undergraduates. Flexner's "Idea of a Modern University" still has its supporters—chiefly the scientists and the specialists and the graduate students. "The Idea of a Multiversity" has its practitioners—chiefly the administrators, who now number many of the faculty among them, and the leadership groups in society at large. The controversies are still around in the faculty clubs and the student coffee houses; and the models of Oxford and Berlin and modern Harvard all animate segments of what was once a "community of masters and students" with a single vision of its nature and purpose. These several competing visions of true purpose, each relating to a different layer of history, a different web of forces, cause much of the malaise in the university communities of today. The university is so many things to so many different people that it must, of necessity, be partially at war with itself.

How did the multiversity happen? No man created it; in fact, no man visualized it. It has been a long time coming about and it has a long way to go. What is its history? How is it governed? What is life like within it? What is its justification? Does it have a future?

The strands of history

The multiversity draws on many strands of history. To the extent that its origins can be identified, they can be traced to the Greeks. But there were several traditions even then. Plato had his Academy devoted to truth largely for its own sake, but also truth for the philosophers who were to be kings. The Sophists, whom Plato detested so much that he gave them an evil aura persisting to this day, had their schools too. These schools taught rhetoric and other useful skills—they were more interested in attainable success in life than they were in the unattainable truth. The Pythagoreans were concerned, among other things, with mathematics and astronomy. The modern academician likes to trace his intellectual forebears to the groves of Academe; but the modern university with its professional schools and scientific institutes might look equally to the Sophists and the Pythagoreans. The humanists, the professionals, and the scientists all have their roots in ancient times. The "Two Cultures" or the "Three Cultures" are almost as old as culture itself.

Despite its Greek precursors, however, the university is, as Hastings Rashdall wrote, "a distinctly medieval institution."[5] In the Middle Ages it developed many of the features that prevail today—a name and a central location, masters with a degree of autonomy, students, a system of lectures, a procedure for examinations and degrees, and even an administrative structure with its "faculties." Salerno in medicine, Bologna in law, and Paris in theology and philosophy were the great pacesetters. The university came to be a center for the professions, for the study of the classics, for theological and philosophical disputes. Oxford and Cambridge, growing out of Paris, developed in their distinctive ways with their particular emphasis on the residential college instead of the separate faculties as the primary unit.

By the end of the eighteenth century the European universities had long since become oligarchies, rigid in their subject matter, centers of reaction in their societies—opposed, in large part, to the Reformation, unsympathetic to the spirit of creativity of the Renaissance, antagonistic to the new science. There was something almost splendid in their disdain for contemporary events. They stood like castles without windows, profoundly introverted. But the tides of change can cut very deep. In France the universities were swept away by the Revolution, as they almost had been in England at the time of Cromwell.

It was in Germany that the rebirth of the university took place. Halle had dropped teaching exclusively in Latin in 1693; Göttingen had started the teaching of history in 1736; but it was the establishment of Berlin by Wilhelm von Humboldt in 1809 from his vantage point in the Prussian Ministry that was the dramatic event. The emphasis was on philosophy and science, on research, on graduate instruction, on the freedom of professors and students (*Lehrfreiheit* and *Lernfreiheit*). The department was created, and the institute. The professor was established as a great figure within and without the university. The Berlin plan spread rapidly throughout Germany, which was then entering a period of industrialization and intense nationalism following the shock of the defeat at the hands of Napoleon. The university carried with it two great new forces: science and nationalism. It is true that the German university system later bogged down through its uncritical reliance on the great professional figure who ruled for life over his department and institute, and that it could be subverted by Hitler because of its total dependence on the state. But this does not vitiate the fact that the German university in the nineteenth century was one of the vigorous new institutions in the world.

In 1809 when Berlin was founded, the United States already had a number of colleges developed on the model of the colleges at Oxford and Cambridge. They concentrated on Calvinism for the would-be preacher and classics for the young gentleman. Benjamin Franklin had had other ideas for the University of Pennsylvania, then the College of Philadelphia, in the 1750's.[6] Reflecting Locke, he wanted "a *more useful* culture of young minds." He was interested in training people for agriculture and commerce; in exploring science. Education should "serve mankind." These ideas were not to take root for another century. Drawing on the French Enlightenment, Jefferson started the University of Virginia with a broad curriculum including mathematics and science, and with the electives that Eliot was to make so famous at Harvard half a century later. He put great emphasis on a library—an almost revolutionary idea at the time. Again the application of the ideas was to be long delayed.

The real line of development for the modern American university began with Professor George Ticknor at Harvard in 1825. He tried to reform Harvard on the model of Göttingen where he had studied, and found that reforming Harvard must wait for an Eliot with forty years and the powers of the presidency at his disposal. Yale at the time was the great center of reaction—its famous faculty report of 1828 was a ringing proclamation to do nothing, or at least nothing that had not always been done at Yale or by God.[7] Francis Wayland at Brown in the 1850's made a great fight for the German system, including a program of electives, as did Henry Tappan at Michigan—both without success.

Then the breakthrough came. Daniel Coit Gilman, disenchanted with the then grim prospects at California, became the first president of the new university of Johns Hopkins in 1876. The institution began as a graduate school with an emphasis on research. For Flexner, Gilman was the great hero-figure—and Johns Hopkins "the most stimulating influence that higher education in America had ever known." Charles W. Eliot at Harvard followed the Gilman breakthrough and Harvard during his period (1869 to 1909) placed great emphasis on the graduate school, the professional school, and research—it became a university. But Eliot made his own particular contribution by establishing the elective system permitting students to choose their own courses of study. Others quickly followed—Andrew Dickson White at Cornell, James B. Angell at Michigan, Frederick Barnard at Columbia, William W. Folwell at Minnesota, David Starr Jordan at Stanford, William Rainey Harper at Chicago, Charles K. Adams at Wisconsin, Benjamin Ide Wheeler at California. The state universities, just then expanding, followed the Hopkins idea. Yale and Princeton trailed behind.

The Hopkins idea brought with it the graduate school with exceptionally high academic standards in what was still a rather new and raw civilization; the renovation of professional education, particularly in medicine; the establishment of the preeminent influence of the department; the creation of research institutes and centers, of university presses and learned journals and the "academic ladder"; and also the great proliferation of courses. If students were to be free to choose their courses (one aspect of the *Lernfreiheit* of the early nineteenth-century German university), then professors were free to offer their wares (as *Lehrfreiheit*, the other great slogan of the developing German universities of a century and a half ago, essentially assured). The elective system, however, came more to serve the professors than the students for whom it was first intended, for it meant that the curriculum was no longer controlled by educational policy as the Yale faculty in 1828 had insisted that it should be. Each professor had his own interests, each professor wanted the status of having his own special course, each professor got his own course—and university catalogues came to include 3,000 or more of them. There was, of course, as a result of the new research, more knowledge to spread over the 3,000 courses; otherwise the situation would have been impossible. In any event, freedom for the student to choose became freedom for the professor to invent; and the professor's love of specialization has become the student's hate of fragmentation. A kind of bizarre version of academic laissez-faire has emerged. The student, unlike Adam Smith's idealized buyer, *must* consume—usually at the rate of fifteen hours a week. The modern university was born.

Along with the Hopkins experiment came the land grant movement—and these two influences turned out to be more compatible than might at first appear. The one was Prussian, the other American; one elitist, the other democratic; one academically pure, the other sullied by contact with the soil and the machine. The one looked to Kant and Hegel, the other to Franklin, Jefferson, and Lincoln. But they both served an industrializing nation and they both did it through research and the training of technical competence. Two strands of history were woven together in the modern American university. Michigan became a German-style university and Harvard a land grant type of institution, without the land.

The land grant movement brought schools of agriculture and engineering (in Germany relegated to the *Technische Hochschulen*), of home economics and business administration; opened the doors of universities to the children of farmers and workers, as well as of the middle and upper classes; introduced agricultural experiment stations and service bureaus. Allan Nevins in commenting on the Morrill Act of 1862 said: "The law annexed wide neglected areas to the domain of instruction. Widening the gates of opportunity, it made democracy freer, more adaptable and more kinetic."[8]

A major new departure in the land grant movement came before World War I when the land grant universities extended their activities beyond their campus boundaries. "The Wisconsin Idea" came to flower under the progressivism of the first Roosevelt and the first La Follette. The University of Wisconsin, particularly during the presidency of Charles Van Hise (1903 to 1918), entered the legislative halls in Madison with reform programs, supported the trade union movement through John R. Commons, developed agricultural and urban extension as never before. The university served the whole state. Other state universities did likewise. Even private universities, like Chicago and Columbia, developed important extension programs.

New contacts with the community were created. University athletics became, particularly in the 1920's, a form of public entertainment, which is not unknown even in the 1960's, even in the Ivy League. Once started, university spectator sports could not be killed even by the worst of teams or the best of deemphasis; and few universities seriously sought after either.

A counterrevolution against these developments was occasionally waged. A. Lawrence Lowell at Harvard (1909 to 1934) emphasized the undergraduate houses and concentration of course work, as against the graduate work and electives of Eliot. It is a commentary not just on Harvard but also on the modern American university that Eliot and Lowell could look in opposite directions and the same institution could follow them both and glory in it. Universities have a unique capacity for riding off in all directions and still staying in the same place, as Harvard has so decisively demonstrated. At Chicago, long after Lowell, Robert M. Hutchins tried to take the university back to Cardinal Newman, to Thomas Aquinas, and to Plato and Aristotle. He succeeded in reviving the philosophic dialogue he loves so well and practices so expertly; but Chicago went on being a modern American university.

Out of the counterreformation, however, came a great new emphasis on student life—particularly undergraduate. Earnest attempts were made to create American counterparts of Oxford and Cambridge; residence halls, student unions, intramural playfields, undergraduate libraries, counseling centers sprang up in many places during the thirties, forties, and fifties. This was a long way from the pure German model, which had provided the student with only the professor and the classroom, and which had led Tappan to abolish dormitories at Michigan. British influence was back, as it was also with the introduction of honors programs, tutorials, independent study.

Out of all these fragments, experiments, and conflicts a kind of unlikely consensus has been reached. Undergraduate life seeks to follow the British, who have done the best with it, and an historical line that goes back to Plato; the humanists often find their sympathies here. Graduate life and research follow the Germans, who once did best with them, and an historical line that goes back to Pythagoras; the scientists lend their support to all this. The "lesser" professions (lesser than law and medicine) and the service activities follow the American pattern, since the Americans have been best at them, and an historical line that goes back to the Sophists; the social scientists are most likely to be sympathetic. Lowell found his greatest interest in the first, Eliot in the second, and James Bryant Conant (1934 to 1954) in the third line of development and in the synthesis. The resulting combination does not seem plausible but it has given America a remarkably effective educational institution. A university anywhere can aim no higher than to be as British as possible for the sake of the undergraduates, as German as possible for the sake of the graduates and the research personnel, as American as possible for the sake of the public at large—and as confused as possible for the sake of the preservation of the whole uneasy balance.

The governance of the multiversity

The multiversity is an inconsistent institution. It is not one community but several—the community of the undergraduate and the community of the graduate; the community of the humanist, the community of the social scientist, and the community of the scientist; the communities of the professional schools; the community of all the nonacademic personnel; the community of the administrators. Its edges are fuzzy—it reaches out to alumni, legislators, farmers, businessmen, who are all related to one or more of these internal communities. As an institution, it looks far into the past and far into the future, and is often at odds with the present. It serves society almost slavishly—a society it also criticizes, sometimes unmercifully. Devoted to equality of opportunity, it is itself a class society. A community, like the medieval communities of masters and students, should have common interests; in the multiversity, they are quite varied, even conflicting. A community should have a soul, a single animating principle; the multiversity has several—some of them quite good, although there is much debate on which souls really deserve salvation.

The multiversity is a name. This means a great deal more than it sounds as though it might. The name of the institution stands for a certain standard of performance, a certain degree of respect, a certain historical legacy, a characteristic quality of spirit. This is of the utmost importance to faculty and to students, to the government agencies and the industries with which

314

the institution deals. Protection and enhancement of the prestige of the name are central to the multiversity. How good is its reputation, what John J. Corson calls its "institutional character"?[9]

Flexner thought of a university as an "organism." In an organism, the parts and the whole are inextricably bound together. Not so the multiversity—many parts can be added and subtracted with little effect on the whole or even little notice taken or any blood spilled. It is more a mechanism—a series of processes producing a series of results—a mechanism held together by administrative rules and powered by money.

Hutchins once described the modern university as a series of separate schools and departments held together by a central heating system. In an area where heating is less important and the automobile more, I have sometimes thought of it as a series of individual faculty entrepreneurs held together by a common grievance over parking.

It is, also, a system of government like a city, or a city state: the city state of the multiversity. It may be inconsistent but it must be governed—not as the guild it once was, but as a complex entity with greatly fractionalized power. There are several competitors for this power.

The students

The students had all the power once; that was in Bologna. Their guilds ran the university and dominated the masters. And the students were tougher on the masters than the masters have ever been on the students. The Bologna pattern had an impact on Salamanca and Spain generally and then in Latin America, where students to this day are usually found in the top governing councils. Their impact is generally more to lower than to raise academic standards although there are exceptions such as Buenos Aires after Peron under the leadership of Risieri Frondizi. Students also involve the university as an institution in the national political controversies of the moment.

Jefferson tried a system of student self-government in the 1820's but quickly abandoned it when all the professors tendered their resignations. He favored self-government by both students and faculty, but never discovered how both could have it at the same time—nor has anybody else. Although José Ortega y Gasset, in addressing the student federation at the University of Madrid, was willing to turn over the entire "mission of the university" to the students, he neglected to comment on faculty reaction.[10]

As part of the "Wisconsin idea" before World War I, there was quite a wave of creation of student governments. They found their power in the area of extracurricular activities, where it has remained. Their extracurricular programs helped broaden student life in such diverse fields as debating, theatrical productions, literary magazines.

Students do have considerable strictly academic influence, however, quite beyond that with which they are usually credited. The system of electives gives them a chance to help determine in which areas and disciplines a university will grow. Their choices, as consumers, guide university expansion and contraction, and this process is far superior to a more rigid guild system of producer determination as in medicine where quotas are traditional. Also students, by their patronage, designate the university teachers. The faculty may, in fact, appoint the faculty, but within this faculty group the students choose the real teachers. In a large university a quarter of the faculty may be selected by the students to do half or more of the actual teaching; the students also "select" ten percent or more to do almost none at all.

The faculty

The guilds of masters organized and ran the University of Paris, and later they did the same at Oxford and Cambridge. Faculty control at Oxford and Cambridge, through the colleges, has remained stronger than anywhere else over the centuries, but even there it has been greatly diminished in recent times.

In the United States, the first great grant of power to the faculty of a major university was at Yale when Jeremiah Day was president (1817 to 1846). It was during the Day regime that the Yale faculty report of 1828 was issued. Harvard has had, by contrast, as McGeorge Bundy has said in his inimitable style, "a tradition of quite high-handed and centralized executive behavior—and it has not suffered, in balance, as a consequence."[11]

Faculties generally in the United States and the British Commonwealth, some earlier and some later, have achieved authority over admissions, approval of courses, examinations, and granting of degrees—all handled in a rather routine fashion from the point of view of the faculty as a whole. They have also achieved considerable influence over faculty appointments and academic freedom, which are not handled routinely. Faculty control and influence in these areas are essential to the proper conduct of academic life. Once the elective system was established, educational policy became less important to the faculty, although, as at Harvard under Lowell, the elective system was modified to call for general rules on concentration and distribution of work. Since Harvard adopted its program for general education in 1945[12] and Hutchins left Chicago, there has been remarkably little faculty discussion of general educational policy. By contrast, there has been a great deal in England, particularly in the "new universities," where faculty discussion of educational policy has been very lively, and faculty influence, as a consequence, substantial.

Organized faculty control or influence over the general direction of growth of the American multiversity has been quite small, as illustrated by the development of the federal grant university. Individual faculty influence, however, has been quite substantial, even determinative, in the expanding areas of institutes and research grants. Still it is a long way from Paris at the time of Abelard.

Public authority

"Public" authority is a very mixed entity of emperors and popes, ministers of education, grants committees, trustees, and Royal Commissions. But almost everywhere, regardless of the origin of the system, there has come to be a public authority. Even in the Middle Ages, emperors and popes, dukes, cardinals, and city councils came to authorize or establish the universities to make them legitimate—the guild alone was not enough. When Henry VIII had trouble about a wife it shook Oxford and Cambridge to the core.

In modern times, Napoleon was the first to seize control of a university system. He completely reorganized it and made it part of the nationally administered educational system of France, as it remains to this day. He separated off research activities and special training institutions for teachers, engineers, and so forth. The universities became a series of loosely related professional schools. Not until the 1890's were the universities brought back together as meaningful entities and a measure of faculty control restored. Soviet Russia has followed the French pattern with even greater state control.

In Germany, the state governments traditionally have controlled the universities in great detail. So also has the government in Italy. In Latin America a degree of formal autonomy from the government has either been retained or attained, although informal reality usually contradicts the theory.

Even in Great Britain, the "public" has moved in on the faculties. Royal Commissions have helped modernize Oxford and Cambridge. The Redbrick and Scottish universities and London either have had from the beginning or acquired governing boards of a mixed nature, including lay members representative of public authority. Since 1919, and particularly since World War II, the University Grants Committee has made its influence felt in a less and less gentle and more and more effective way.

The lay board has been the distinctive American device for "public" authority in connection with universities, although the device was used in Holland in the late sixteenth century. Beyond the lay board in the state universities are the state department of finance and the governor and the legislature with a tendency toward increasingly detailed review.

Richard Hofstadter has made the interesting observation that the first lay board and the first effective concept of academic freedom developed in Holland at the same time; and that academic freedom has never been inherited from some Golden Age of the past but has instead been imported from the institutions of the surrounding society.[13]

Through all these devices, public influences have been asserted in university affairs. Public influence has increased as much in Paris as student influence has declined in Bologna. Everywhere, with the decreasing exception of Oxford and Cambridge, the ultimate authority lies in the "public" domain; everywhere, with a few exceptions, it is fortunately not exercised in an ultimate fashion. We have, however, come a long way from the guilds of masters, the guilds of students, the guilds of masters and students. The location of power has generally moved from inside to outside the original community of masters and students. The nature of the multiversity makes it inevitable that this historical transfer will not be reversed in any significant fashion, although the multiversity does permit the growth of subcultures which can be relatively autonomous and can have an impact on the totality.

The distribution of power is of great importance. In Germany it came to be lodged too completely in the figure of the full professor at one end and the minister of education at the other; in Oxford and Cambridge, at one time, in an oligarchy of professors; in the United States, during a substantial period, almost exclusively in the president; in Latin America, too often, in the students within and the politicians without.

Influences—external and semi-external

Beyond the formal structure of power, as lodged in students, faculty, administration, or "public" instrumentalities, lie the sources of informal influence. The American system is particularly sensitive to the pressures of its many particular publics. Continental and British universities are less intertwined with their surrounding societies than the American and thus more inward-looking and self-contained. When "the borders of the campus are the boundaries of our state," the lines dividing what is internal from what is external become quite blurred; taking the campus to the state brings the state to the campus. In the so-called "private" universities, alumni, donors, foundations, the federal agencies, the professional and business communities bulk large among the semi-external influences; and in the so-called "public" universities, the agricultural, trade union, and public school communities are likely to be added to the list, and also a more searching press. The multiversity has many "publics" with many interests; and by the very nature of the multiversity many of these interests are quite legitimate and others are quite frivolous.

The administration

The original medieval universities had at the start nothing that could be identified as a separate administration, but one quickly developed. The guild of masters or students selected a rector; and later there were deans of the faculties. At Oxford and Cambridge, there came to be the masters of the colleges. In more modern times in France, Germany, and Italy, the rector has come to stand between the faculty and the minister of education, closer to the minister of education in France and closer to the faculty in Germany; internally he has served principally as chairman of the council of deans

318

where deans still retain substantial authority as in France and Italy. In Germany the full professor, chairman of his department, director of his institute, is a figure of commanding authority.

Even in England, even in Oxford and Cambridge, the central administration is attaining more influence—the vice chancellorship can no longer be rotated casually among the masters. The vice chancellor now must deal with the university grants committee and the vice chancellors of the other universities. The university itself is a much more important unit with its research laboratories, central library, its lecturers in specialized subjects; the college is much less self-contained than it was. All of this has created something of a crisis in the administration of Oxford and Cambridge where administrators once were not to be seen or heard and the work was accomplished by a handful of clerks working in a Dickensian office. Oxbridge is becoming more like the Redbricks. London is *sui generis*.

The general rule is that the administration everywhere becomes, by force of circumstances if not by choice, a more prominent feature of the university. As the institution becomes larger, administration becomes more formalized and separated as a distinct function; as the institution becomes more complex, the role of administration becomes more central in integrating it; as it becomes more related to the once external world, the administration assumes the burdens of these relationships. The managerial revolution has been going on also in the university.

Multiversity president, giant or mediator-initiator?

It is sometimes said that the American multiversity president is a two-faced character. This is not so. If he were, he could not survive. He is a many-faced character, in the sense that he must face in many directions at once while contriving to turn his back on no important group. In this he is different in degree from his counterparts of rectors and vice chancellors, since they face in fewer directions because their institutions have fewer doors and windows to the outside world. The difference, however, is not one of kind. And intensities of relationships vary greatly; the rector of a Latin American university, from this point of view, may well have the most trying task of all, though he is less intertwined in a range of relationships than the North American university president.

The university president in the United States is expected to be a friend of the students, a colleague of the faculty, a good fellow with the alumni, a sound administrator with the trustees, a good speaker with the public, an astute bargainer with the foundations and the federal agencies, a politician with the state legislature, a friend of industry, labor, and agriculture, a persuasive diplomat with donors, a champion of education generally, a supporter of the professions (particularly law and medicine), a spokesman to the press, a scholar in his own right, a public servant at the state and national levels, a devotee of opera and football equally, a decent human being, a good husband and father, an active member of a church. Above all he must enjoy traveling in airplanes, eating his meals in public, and attending public ceremonies. No one can be all of these things. Some succeed at being none.

He should be firm, yet gentle; sensitive to others, insensitive to himself; look to the past and the future, yet be firmly planted in the present; both visionary and sound; affable, yet reflective; know the value of a dollar and realize that ideas cannot be bought; inspiring in his visions yet cautious in what he does; a man of principle yet able to make a deal; a man with broad perspective who will follow the details conscientiously; a good American but ready to criticize the status quo fearlessly; a seeker of truth where the truth may not hurt too much; a source of public policy pronouncements when they do not reflect on his own institution. He should sound like a mouse at home and look like a lion abroad. He is one of the marginal men in a democratic society—of whom there are many others—on the margin of many groups, many ideas, many endeavors, many characteristics. He is a marginal man but at the very center of the total process.

Who is he really?

To Flexner, he was a hero-figure, "a daring pioneer" who filled an "impossible post" yet some of his accomplishments were "little short of miraculous"; thus the "forceful president"—the Gilman, the Eliot, the Harper. The necessary revolutions came from on high. There should be Giants in the Groves. To Thorstein Veblen he was a "Captain of Erudition,"[14] and Veblen did not think well of captains. To Upton Sinclair, the university president was "the most universal faker and most variegated prevaricator that has yet appeared in the civilized world."[15]

To the faculty, he is usually not a hero-figure. Hutchins observed that the faculty really "prefer anarchy to any form of government"[16]—particularly the presidential form.

The issue is whether the president should be "leader" or "officeholder," as Hutchins phrased it; "educator" or "caretaker," as Harold W. Dodds[17] stated it; "creator" or "inheritor," as Frederick Rudolph[18] saw it; "initiator" as viewed by James L. Morrill[19] or consensus-seeker as viewed by John D. Millett;[20] the wielder of power or the persuader, as visualized by Henry M. Wriston;[21] "pump" or "bottleneck" as categorized by Eric Ashby.[22]

The case for leadership has been strongly put by Hutchins. A university needs a purpose, "a vision of the end." If it is to have a "vision," the president must identify it; and, without vision, there is "aimlessness" and the "vast chaos of the American university." "The administrator must accept a special responsibility for the discussion, clarification, definition and proclamation of this end." He must be a "troublemaker, for every change in education is a change in the habits of some members of the faculty." For all this he needs the great "moral virtues" of "courage," "fortitude," "justice,"

320

and "prudence." In looking for administrators who really thought and wrote about the "end" of their institution, Hutchins particularly identified Marcus Aurelius as the great prototype.[23] Lowell, too, believed a president should have a "plan" and that although the faculty was "entitled to propose changes," the plan should not basically be subject to interference. He also had the rather quaint idea that the president should "never feel hurried" or "work . . . under pressure."[24]

There were such leaders in higher education. Hutchins was one. Lowell was another; and so was Eliot. When Eliot was asked by a faculty member of the medical school how it could be after eighty years of managing its own affairs the faculty had to accommodate to so many changes, he could answer, "There is a new president."[25] Even in Oxford, of all places, as it belatedly adapted to the new world of scholarship, Benjamin Jowett as Master of Balliol could set as his rule: "Never retract, never explain. Get it done and let them howl."[26] Lord Bryce could comment in his *American Commonwealth* on the great authority of the president in the American university, on his "almost monarchical position."[27]

But the day of the monarchs has passed—the day when Benjamin Ide Wheeler could ride his white horse across the Berkeley campus or Nicholas Murray Butler rule from Morningside Heights. Flexner rather sadly recorded that "the day of the excessively autocratic president is . . . over. He has done a great service . . ." Paul Lazarsfeld could observe the "academic power vacuum" that resulted—leadership no longer taken by the president nor assumed by the faculty, with the result of little "institutional development."[28] Hutchins was the last of the giants in the sense that he was the last of the university presidents who really tried to change his institution and higher education in any fundamental way. Instead of the not always so agreeable autocracy, there is now the usually benevolent bureaucracy, as in so much of the rest of the world. Instead of the Captain of Erudition or even David Riesman's "staff sergeant," there is the Captain of the Bureaucracy who is sometimes a galley slave on his own ship; and "no great revolutionary figure is likely to appear."[29]

The role of giant was never a happy one. Hutchins concluded that the administrator has many ways to lose, and no way to win, and came to acknowledge that patience, which he once called a "delusion and a snare," was also a virtue. "It is one thing to get things done. It is another to make them last." The experience of Tappan at Michigan was typical of many, as Angell later saw it: "Tappan was the largest figure of a man that ever appeared on the Michigan campus. And he was stung to death by gnats."[30]

The giant was seldom popular with the faculty and was often bitterly opposed, as in the "revolution" against Wheeler at California. And faculty government gained strength as faculties gained distinction. The experiences of Tappan, Wheeler, Hutchins, even Thomas Jefferson, are part of the lore of the university presidency. So are those of Wayland, who resigned from

Brown in frustration after vainly trying something new, Woodrow Wilson with all his battles over innovations at Princeton, and many others.

Moreover, the university has changed; it has become bigger and more complex, more tensed with checks and balances. As Rudolph saw it, there came to be "a delicate balance of interests, a polite tug of war, a blending of emphases." The presidency was "an office fraught with so many perils, shot through with so many ambiguities, an office that was many things to many men."[31] There are more elements to conciliate, fewer in a position to be led. The university has become the multiversity and the nature of the presidency has followed this change.

Also, the times have changed. The giants were innovators during a wave of innovation, to use the terms of Joseph Schumpeter drawn from another context. The American university required vast renovation to meet the needs of the changing and growing nation. As Eliot said in his inaugural address, "The University must accommodate itself promptly to significant changes in the character of the people for whom it exists." The title of Wilson's inaugural address was, "Princeton for the Nation's Service." They and others helped take what had been denominational colleges and turn them into modern national universities. They were not inventors—the Germans did the inventing—but they came along at a stage in history when massive innovation was the order of the day. The giants today, when found at all, are more likely to be in a few of the old Latin American universities undergoing modernization or the new British universities in the midst of an intense discussion of educational policy.

The giants had performed "a great service," but gentler hands were needed. University administration reverted to the more standard British model of "government by consent and after consultation."[32] There is a "kind of lawlessness"[33] in any large university with many separate sources of initiative and power; and the task is to keep this lawlessness within reasonable bounds. The president must seek "consensus" in a situation where there is a "struggle for power" among groups that share it.[34] "The president must use power economically, and persuasion to the fullest extent."[35] As Allan Nevins sees it, "The sharpest strain on growth lies not in finding the teachers, but expert administrators," and the new type of president required by the large universities "will be a coordinator rather than a creative leader . . . an expert executive, a tactful moderator. . . ."[36]

Academic government has taken the form of the Guild, as in the colleges of Oxford and Cambridge until recent times; of the Manor, as in Columbia under Butler; and of the United Nations, as in the modern multiversity. There are several "nations" of students, of faculty, of alumni, of trustees, of public groups. Each has its territory, its jurisdiction, its form of government. Each can declare war on the others; some have the power of veto. Each can settle its own problems by a majority vote, but altogether they form no single constituency. It is a pluralistic society with multiple cultures.

Coexistence is more likely than unity. Peace is one priority item, progress another.

The president in the multiversity is leader, educator, creator, initiator, wielder of power, pump; he is *also* officeholder, caretaker, inheritor, consensus-seeker, persuader, bottleneck. But he is mostly a mediator.

The first task of the mediator is peace—how he may "the Two-and-Seventy jarring Sects confute." Peace within the student body, the faculty, the trustees; and peace between and among them. Peace between the "Two Cultures" and the "Three Cultures" and their subcultures; among all the ideas competing for support. Peace between the internal environment of the academic community and the external society that surrounds and sometimes times almost engulfs it. But peace has its attributes. There is the "workable compromise" of the day that resolves the current problem. Beyond this lies the effective solution that enhances the long-run distinction and character of the institution. In seeking it, there are some things that should not be compromised, like freedom and quality—then the mediator needs to become the gladiator. The dividing lines between these two roles may not be as clear as crystal, but they are at least as fragile.

The second task is progress; institutional and personal survival are not enough. A multiversity is inherently a conservative institution but with radical functions. There are so many groups with a legitimate interest in the status quo, so many veto groups; yet the university must serve a knowledge explosion and a population explosion simultaneously. The president becomes the central mediator among the values of the past, the prospects for the future, and the realities of the present. He is the mediator among groups and institutions moving at different rates of speed and sometimes in different directions; a carrier of change—as infectious and sometimes as feared as a "Typhoid Mary." He is not an innovator for the sake of innovation, but he must be sensitive to the fruitful innovation. He has no new and bold "vision of the end." He is driven more by necessity than by voices in the air. "Innovation" may be the historical "measurement of success," the great characterizing feature of the "giants of the past";[37] but innovations sometimes succeed best when they have no obvious author. Lowell once observed that a president "cannot both do things and get credit for them"—that he should not "cackle like a hen that laid an egg."

The ends are already given—the preservation of the eternal truths, the creation of new knowledge, the improvement of service wherever truth and knowledge of high order may serve the needs of man. The ends are there; the means must be ever improved in a competitive dynamic environment. There is no single "end" to be discovered; there are several ends and many groups to be served.

The quality of the mediation is subject to judgment on two grounds, the keeping of the peace and the furthering of progress—the resolution of inter-personal and inter-group warfare, and the reconciliation of the tug of the anchor to the past with the pull of the Holy Grail of the future. Unfortunately peace and progress are more frequently enemies than friends; and since, in the long run, progress is more important than peace to a university, the effective mediator must, at times, sacrifice peace to progress. The ultimate test is whether the mediation permits progress to be made fast enough and in the right directions, whether the needed innovations take precedence over the conservatism of the institution. Mediators, though less dramatic than giants, are not a homogenized group; they only look that way.

They also appear to some people to be doing very little of consequence. Yet their role is absolutely essential if carried out constructively. They serve something of the function of the clerk of the meeting for the Quakers—the person who keeps the business moving, draws forth ideas, seeks the "sense of the meeting." David Riesman has suggested the term "evocator." The techniques must be those of the mediator; but to the techniques may also be added the goals of the innovator. The essence of the role, when adequately performed, is perhaps best conveyed by the term "mediator-initiator."

Power is not necessary to the task, though there must be a consciousness of power. The president must police its use by the constituent groups, so that none will have too much or too little or use it too unwisely. To make the multiversity work really effectively, the moderates need to be in control of each power center and there needs to be an attitude of tolerance between and among the power centers, with few territorial ambitions. When the extremists get in control of the students, the faculty, or the trustees with class warfare concepts, then the "delicate balance of interests" becomes an actual war.

The usual axiom is that power should be commensurate with responsibility, but, for the president, the *opportunity to persuade* should be commensurate with the responsibility. He must have ready access to each center of power, a fair chance in each forum of opinion, a chance to paint reality in place of illusion and to argue the cause of reason as he sees it.

Not all presidents seek to be constructive mediators amid their complexities. One famous president of a New York university succeeded in being at home only five months in five years. Some find it more pleasant to attend meetings, visit projects abroad, even give lectures at other universities; and at home they attend ceremonial functions, go to the local clubs, and allow the winds of controversy to swirl past them. Others look for "visions." But most presidents are in the control tower helping the real pilots make their landings without crashes, even in the fog.

Hutchins wrote of the four moral virtues for a university president. I should like to suggest a slightly different three—judgment, courage, and fortitude—but the greatest of these is fortitude since others have so little charity. The mediator, whether in government or industry or labor relations or domestic quarrels, is always subject to some abuse. He wins few clear-cut victories; he must aim more at avoiding the worst than seizing the best. He must find satisfaction in being *equally* distasteful to each of his constituencies; he must reconcile himself to the harsh reality that successes are shrouded in silence while failures are spotlighted in notoriety. The president of the multiversity must be content to hold its constituent elements loosely together and to move the whole enterprise another foot ahead in what often seems an unequal race with history.

Life in the multiversity

The "Idea of a University" was a village with its priests. The "Idea of a Modern University" was a town—a one-industry town—with its intellectual oligarchy. "The Idea of a Multiversity" is a city of infinite variety. Some get lost in the city; some rise to the top within it; most fashion their lives within one of its many subcultures. There is less sense of community than in the village but also less sense of confinement. There is less sense of purpose than within the town but there are more ways to excel. There are also more refuges of anonymity—both for the creative person and the drifter. As against the village and the town, the "city" is more like the totality of civilization as it has evolved and more an integral part of it; and movement to and from the surrounding society has been greatly accelerated. As in a city, there are many separate endeavors under a single rule of law.

The students in the "city" are older, more likely to be married, more vocationally oriented, more drawn from all classes and races than the students in the village;[38] and they find themselves in a most intensely competitive atmosphere. They identify less with the total community and more with its subgroups. Burton R. Clark and Martin Trow have a particularly interesting typology of these subcultures: the "collegiate" of the fraternities and sororities and the athletes and activities majors; the "academic" of the serious students; the "vocational" of the students seeking training for specific jobs; and the "nonconformist" of the political activists, the aggressive intellectuals, and the bohemians.[39] These subcultures are not mutually exclusive, and some of the fascinating pageantry of the multiversity is found in their interaction one on another.

The multiversity is a confusing place for the student. He has problems of establishing his identity and sense of security within it. But it offers him a vast range of choices, enough literally to stagger the mind. In this range of choices he encounters the opportunities and the dilemmas of freedom. The casualty rate is high. The walking wounded are many. *Lernfreiheit* —the freedom of the student to pick and choose, to stay or to move on—is triumphant.

Life has changed also for the faculty member. The multiversity is in the main stream of events. To the teacher and the researcher have been added the consultant and the administrator. Teaching is less central than it once was for most faculty members; research has become more important. This has given rise to what has been called the "nonteacher"[40]—"the higher a man's standing, the less he has to do with students"—and to a threefold class structure of what used to be "the faculty": those who only do research, those who only teach (and they are largely in an auxiliary role), and those who still do some of both. In one university I know, the proportions at the Ph.D. level or its equivalent are roughly one researcher to two teachers to four who do both.

Consulting work and other sources of additional income have given rise to what is called the "affluent professor," a category that does include some but by no means all of the faculty. Additionally, many faculty members, with their research assistants and teaching assistants, their departments and institutes, have become administrators. A professor's life has become, it is said, "a rat race of business and activity, managing contracts and projects, guiding teams and assistants, bossing crews of technicians, making numerous trips, sitting on committees for government agencies, and engaging in other distractions necessary to keep the whole frenetic business from collapse."[41]

The intellectual world has been fractionalized as interests have become much more diverse; and there are fewer common topics of conversation at the faculty clubs. Faculty government has become more cumbersome, more the avocation of active minorities; and there are real questions whether it can work effectively on a large scale, whether it can agree on more than preservation of the status quo. Faculty members are less members of the particular university and more colleagues within their national academic discipline groups.

But there are many compensations. "The American professoriate" is no longer, as Flexner once called it, "a proletariat." Salaries and status have risen considerably. The faculty member is more a fully participating member of society, rather than a creature on the periphery; some are at the very center of national and world events. Research opportunities have been enormously increased. The faculty member within the big mechanism and with all his opportunities has a new sense of independence from the domination of the administration or his colleagues; much administration has been effectively decentralized to the level of the individual professor. In particular, he has a choice of roles and mixtures of roles to suit his taste as never before. He need not leave the Groves for the Acropolis unless he wishes; but he can, if he wishes. He may even become, as some have, essentially a professional man with his home office and basic retainer on the campus of the multiversity but with his clients scattered from coast to coast. He can also even remain the professor of old, as many do. There are several patterns of life from which to choose. So the professor too has greater freedom. *Lehrfreiheit*, in the old German sense of the freedom of the professor to do as he pleases, also is triumphant.

What is the justification of the modern American multiversity? History is one answer. Consistency with the surrounding society is another. Beyond that, it has few peers in the preservation and dissemination and examination of the eternal truths; no living peers in the search for new knowledge; and no peers in all history among institutions of higher learning in serving so many of the segments of an advancing civilization. Inconsistent internally as an institution, it is consistently productive. Torn by change, it has the stability of freedom. Though it has not a single soul to call its own, its members pay their devotions to truth.

The multiversity in America is perhaps best seen at work, adapting and growing, as it responded to the massive impact of federal programs beginning with World War II. A vast transformation has taken place without a revolution, for a time almost without notice being taken. The multiversity has demonstrated how adaptive it can be to new opportunities for creativity; how responsive to money; how eagerly it can play a new and useful role; how fast it can change while pretending that nothing has happened at all; how fast it can neglect some of its ancient virtues. What are the current realities of the federal grant university?

Notes

1 John Henry Cardinal Newman, *The Idea of a University* (New York: Longmans Green and Co., 1947). The quotations used here are from pp. 129, 91, xxvii, 157.

2 Francis Bacon, "The Advancement of Learning," *Essays, Advance of Learning, New Atlantis and Other Places* (New York: Odyssey Press, Inc., 1937), pp. 214–215.

3 Abraham Flexner, *Universities: American English German* (New York: Oxford University Press, 1930). The quotations are from pp. 3, 4, 42, 179, 132, 25, 44–45, 197, 193, 231, 235, 197 (again), 178–179.

4 Harvard University, *The President's Report, 1961–62*, p. 3.

5 Hastings Rashdall, *The Universities of Europe in the Middle Ages* (3 vols., 1895, ed. F. M. Powicke and A. B. Emden, Oxford: Clarendon Press, 1936), III, 358.

6 Benjamin Franklin, *Proposals Relating to the Education of Youth in Pensilvania* (Philadelphia, 1749).

7 *Reports of the Course of Instruction in Yale College by a Committee of the Corporation and the Academical Faculty* (New Haven, Conn.: Hezekiah Howe, 1828).

8 Allan Nevins, *The State Universities and Democracy* (Urbana: University of Illinois Press, 1962), p. vi.

9 John J. Corson, *Governance of Colleges and Universities* (New York: McGraw-Hill, 1960), pp. 175–179.

10 José Ortega y Gasset, *The Mission of the University* (London: Kegan Paul, Trench, Trubner and Co., Ltd., 1946), p. 56.

11 McGeorge Bundy, "Of Winds and Windmills: Free Universities and Public Policy," in Charles G. Dobbins, ed., *Higher Education and the Federal Government, Programs and Problems* (Washington, D.C.: American Council on Education, 1963), p. 93.

12 *General Education in a Free Society*, Report of the Harvard Committee with an Introduction by James Bryant Conant (Cambridge, Mass.: Harvard University Press, 1945).

13 Richard Hofstadter and Walter P. Metzger, *The Development of Academic Freedom in the United States* (New York: Columbia University Press, 1955), pp. 71, 61.

14 Thorstein Veblen, *The Higher Learning in America* (Stanford, Calif.: Academic Reprints, 1954), p. 85.
15 Upton Sinclair, *The Goose-Step: A Study of American Education* (Pasadena: John Regan & Co., 1923), pp. 382–384.
16 Robert Maynard Hutchins, *Freedom, Education and The Fund: Essays and Addresses, 1946–1956* (New York: Meridian Books, 1956), pp. 167–196.
17 Harold W. Dodds, *The Academic President—Educator or Caretaker?* (New York: McGraw-Hill, 1962).
18 Frederick Rudolph, *The American College and University: A History* (New York: Alfred A. Knopf, 1962), p. 492.
19 James Lewis Morrill, *The Ongoing State University* (Minneapolis: University of Minnesota Press, 1960), p. 48.
20 John D. Millett, *The Academic Community: An Essay on Organization* (New York: McGraw-Hill, 1962), p. 259.
21 Henry M. Wriston, *Academic Procession: Reflections of a College President* (New York: Columbia University Press, 1959), p. 172.
22 Eric Ashby, "The Administrator: Bottleneck or Pump?" *Daedalus*, Spring 1962, pp. 264–278.
23 Hutchins, pp. 177, 169.
24 A. Lawrence Lowell, *What a University President Has Learned* (New York: Macmillan, 1938), pp. 12, 19.
25 Rudolph, p. 291.
26 James Morris, "Is Oxford Out of This World?" *Horizon*, January 1963, p. 86.
27 James Bryce, *The American Commonwealth*, new edition (New York: Macmillan, 1914), II, 718–719.
28 Paul F. Lazarsfeld, "The Sociology of Empirical Social Research," *American Sociological Review*, December 1962, pp. 751–767.
29 David Riesman, *Constraint and Variety in American Education* (Garden City, N.Y.: Doubleday, 1958), pp. 30–32.
30 Ernest Earnest, *Academic Procession* (Indianapolis: Bobbs-Merrill, 1953), p. 74.
31 Rudolph, p. 423.
32 Eric Ashby, "Self-Government in Modern British Universities," *Science and Freedom*, December 1956, p. 10.
33 Theodore Caplow and Reece J. McGee, *The Academic Marketplace* (New York: Basic Books, 1958), p. 206.
34 Millett, p. 224.
35 Wriston, p. 172.
36 Nevins, pp. 118–119.
37 Dodds, p. 43.
38 W. Max Wise, *They Come For the Best of Reasons—College Students Today* (Washington, D.C.: American Council on Education, 1958).
39 Burton R. Clark and Martin Trow, *Determinants of College Student Subculture*, unpublished manuscript, Center for the Study of Higher Education, University of California, Berkeley, 1963.
40 Robert Bendiner, "The Non-Teacher," *Horizon*, September 1962, p. 14.
41 Merle A. Tuve, "Is Science Too Big for the Scientist?" *Saturday Review*, June 6, 1959, p. 49.

49

IDEAS OF THE UNIVERSITY

A. H. Halsey

Source: A. H. Halsey, *Decline of Donnish Dominion: The British Academic Profession in the Twentieth Century*, Oxford: Clarendon Press, 1995, pp. 23–57.

The modern university, and indeed the polytechnic, began with the Victorians. I have mentioned Weber and Veblen, who published highly relevant essays in 1918. But further back, in 1873, there appeared two views of educational expansion, the one Catholic and clerical, the other Protestant and secular, by John Henry Newman on *The Idea of a University* and Alfred Marshall on 'The Future of the Working Classes' (A. Marshall 1925).

Calendar dates, of course, give false clarity to the ebb and flow of ideas; otherwise, in these two discourses we might identify 1873 as the end of the ecclesiastical and the beginning of the lay conception of education. A truer chronology would note that Marshall stood on the shoulders of John Stuart Mill, modernizing the chapter from the latter's *Principles of Economics* on 'The Futurity of the Labouring Classes'. Newman began his work in 1851, published the first half in 1853 as *Discourses on University Education*, a second volume five years later entitled *Lectures and Essays on University Subjects*, and a combined and revised edition of both in 1873 (Newman 1853–73). Indeed, so slow was the tide on his own view that he saw the office which occasioned the *Discourses*—his Rectorship of the Catholic University of Ireland—as resting on the millenial authority established by St Peter.

Our concern at this point is with the Cardinal, not the Professor. Yet it is right first to couple them, for they both experienced and interpreted the evolving liberalism of nineteenth-century thought—the Oxford divine as traditionalist critic, the Cambridge economist as progressive champion. To point only to their differences would be to distract attention from their common inheritance. Thus Marshall's biblical allusions are no less intrusive than Newman's, and Newman's claim for educational opportunity on behalf of Irish Catholics was not fundamentally different from Marshall's advocacy of the educational cause of the English working class. Moreover, it could have been Marshall just as plausibly as in fact it was Newman who wrote:

> The view taken of the university in these discourses is the following: that it is a place of *teaching* universal *knowledge*. This implies that its object is, on the one hand, intellectual, not moral; and on the other, that it is the diffusion and extension of knowledge rather than the advancement. If its object were scientific and philosophical discovery, I do not see why universities should have students; if religious training, I do not see how it can be the seat of literature and science.
>
> (Newman 1959)

Newman's view of a place for teaching universal knowledge, in other words, was in no way original. Indeed, it was a consensual commonplace. The reason why the term university had originally come into medieval usage is not known. (In Roman law it meant a corporation.) But Newman offered no new definition on behalf of Catholicism. Samuel Johnson in the previous century had entered the university in his Dictionary as 'a school where all arts and faculties are taught'. Even the emphasis on teaching would have commended itself to Marshall, to Cambridge, and to colleges throughout the English and American territories where the German challenge on behalf of research and discovery had as yet made no serious impact.

The crucial difference, however, may be put in a short overstatement. Marshall succeeded and Newman failed to persuade their successors. Marshall's faith in education to bring rising wealth, cultural progress, and narrowing income differentials has since provided the orthodoxy of educational reform for more than a century. His adroit marriage of high-mindedness to material prosperity through educational expansion encouraged state patronage of schools and universities beyond all Victorian dreams. That, *ambulando*, his theory has falsified itself has yet to become fully appreciated. No matter that the original text has gone unread: Robbins rewrote it and more. No matter that the utility of the educational programme is more revered than its egalitarianism: the march towards universal higher education continues and its standard-bearers are Marshallian.

Newman's failure was that he addressed himself not to the abstractions of the *universitas* but to its practicalities. Teaching universal knowledge— 'such is a university in its *essence*, and independently of its relation to the Church. But, practically speaking, it cannot fulfil its object duly, such as I have described it, without the Church's assistance; or, to use the theological term, the Church is necessary for its integrity. Not that its main characters are changed by this incorporation: it still has the office of intellectual education; but the Church steadies it in the performance of that office' (Newman 1959: 7).

There are two arguments here, neither of which have convinced or been resolved by the modern university. The first is an inference from the idea of universal knowledge. If theology is knowledge and the university is what it claims to be, then it must have chairs of theology. Newman elaborates this case at length and with passion, particularly against the pretensions and predications of the first Oxford professor of economics, who, in his introductory lectures, asserted that in the course of a few years political economy would 'rank in public estimation among the first of *moral* sciences in interest and in utility'. Newman's reply was that 'if theology is not allowed to occupy its own territory, adjacent sciences, nay, sciences which are quite foreign to theology, will take possession of it . . . It is a mere unwarranted assumption if . . . the political economist [says] "easy circumstances make man virtuous". These are enunciations, not of science, but of private judgement; and it is a private judgement that infects every science which it touches with a hostility to theology, a hostility which properly attaches to no science in itself whatever' (Newman 1959: 125).

The first argument has had no theoretical solution. In practice it has been resolved by compromise and by that most idle of unintellectual means which expansion affords to institutions—simple neglect. But the second practical thesis advanced by Newman is less easily set aside. It is the problem of how to justify the power and privilege required for the exercise of the academic role. Newman put forward his view in the context of the foundation of a new Catholic university. In its more general form it is the question of the authority and organized purpose which makes a university possible. The liberal tradition has appealed directly to the values of reason and tolerance. Thus, for example, the University of Chicago rests its viability as an institution—i.e. as something more than an aggregate of researchers and teachers—on adherence to these values. It follows that all appointees should possess the requisite 'academic citizenship'. 'Appointive committees . . . must expect that those whom they appoint will enjoy the protection of academic freedom and that they will also be the guardians of that freedom.' These are noble and necessary commitments. But what they lack and what Newman offered is a moral authority on which to base them.

Newman was the Vice-Chancellor of a new Victorian university, who took his authority from the Church. His successors to the vice-chancellorships of the present century are creatures of the State. It is highly improbable that we can return to the one, but no less hazardous to expect that we shall always be sustained by the other.

A legend survives from 1845 that had he not missed the coach from Oxford to Birmingham, Mark Pattison would have accompanied John Henry Newman to Rome. Instead he stayed, first as perhaps the most perfect exemplar of that new model of the inspired working tutor which has served ever since as an alternative to the professional and professorial hierarchy in the English idea of a university, and second to produce an agenda for university reform which embodied a radically different alternative to both the tutorial model and to the purpose of higher education propounded by Newman. His was the prototype of the research university with open entry and exit, and his the most direct English translation of the German idea of a university—translated that is by direct experience and not as imported later to the provincial redbrick universities via Scottish and American example.

Pattison's journey from the first to the second of these two major Victorian positions, which in mutual adaptation evolved as the bases of the distinctive English idea of a university, at least until the Robbins Report, was, on one view, personally idiosyncratic.[1] Pattison can hardly be said to have travelled hopefully. He was privately obsessed with the fear of hereditary insanity. His academic career was a process of embittered frustration, including failure to be elected Rector of Lincoln in 1851 under circumstances and in relation to persons vastly more implausible than those invented by C. P. Snow in *The Masters*. If he finally arrived at the Lincoln Rector's Lodge in 1861 it was to enter a marriage in which love was denied to him by Emilia Strong (who transferred herself to Sir Charles Dilke as soon as Pattison was dead), to look out on an Oxford he thought made worse by the reforms he had advocated to the 1850 Commission, to see his second advocacy rejected by the Salisbury Commission of 1877, and to die in 1881 before publishing the major work on which he had spent most of his life.

Though Pattison wrote one of his last letters to Newman as 'your affectionate son and pupil', the two men were antithetical figures. Pattison's arid pilgrimage had carried him steadily further, first from Canterbury, then from Rome, and finally to a religious scepticism beyond Christianity. Oddly to us, but characteristic of the Victorian definition of appropriate locations and 'media', his *Suggestions on Academical Organisation* (1868) were adumbrated in sermons delivered from the pulpit of the University Church earlier in the 1860s. As John Sparrow puts it, 'he did not advertise his religious scepticism or allow it to affect his everyday life. To renounce Holy Orders would have been ridiculous; besides, it would have meant giving up his position and its emoluments—a crippling sacrifice that would have served no useful purpose. So he continued to the end of his days to officiate, and to administer the Sacrament, in the college chapel' (Sparrow 1967: 57).

Yet it would be utterly misleading to suggest that the Victorian debate was pivoted on the alternative conceptions of two personalities. There were other voices—Matthew Arnold and Benjamin Jowett at Oxford; Sedgwick and Seeley, who have been described as equivalent figures at Cambridge by Sheldon Rothblatt (1968); John Stuart Mill in London; and, indeed, a sizeable proportion of the intellectual aristocracy of the day. Nor was the debate confined to a choice between a teaching and a research conception of the university. No serious contributor, then or now, would settle for either end of this crude dichotomy. It was never, in other words, a simple option between either the don as transmitter of 'universal knowledge' or the professor as creator of new knowledge. The idea of a university has other dimensions and its modernization was seen as a multi-faceted problem of political, religious, and economic as well as educational reform.

The essence of Pattison's ideas was to create conditions for 'the close action of the teacher on the pupil', with its accompanying 'beneficial reaction of the young on the ageing man' resulting in a mutual search for 'mental culture'. He thus implied criteria for the recruitment of dons and students and for the content of higher education which fused what to us now appear as elements from conservative and radical thought. The apparent conservatism was expressed in his evidence to the 1850 Commission as a plea for the college against the professorial system: 'the perfect idea of the Collegiate system proposed to take up the student from quite tender years, and conduct him through his life till death. A college was not divided into tutors and pupils but . . . all were students alike, only differing in being at different stages of their progress . . . The seniors were at once the instructors and example of the juniors, who shared the same food, simple life, narrow economy, looking forward themselves to no other life' (Rothblatt 1968: 194). The apparently radical element could scarcely have a more modern ring. He wanted to do away with both entrance requirements and examinations.

But these are apparent rather than real truths about Pattison's ideal for the organization of higher learning. In fact he held a general view which is radical in a timeless sense. This is that the university ought to be a sanctuary reserved only for those who are so single-minded in their resolve to know the world and themselves to the utmost limit of available knowledge and their capacity to master it that they are willing to give up all the material rewards that otherwise accrue to such a sustained effort of intellectual labour.

In the 1840s this view necessarily expressed itself in antipathy to old Tory Oxford, with its largely exclusive recruitment from the aristocracy and the gentry whose sons had little inclination or encouragement to scholarship, to the corrupted traditions of almost all the colleges with their irresponsible wealth, donnish hierarchy, neglect of the university and of science, and their inefficient teaching. Above all, it meant condemnation of the system of closed fellowships.

By the 1870s Oxford had been transformed by the efforts of the liberal dons among whom Pattison had stood before the 1850 Commission. Honours degrees and strict examinations were becoming central to the undergraduate career. Religious tests were abolished. Science had begun to flourish. There were intercollegiate lectures. The university was governed by a democracy of dons and, most important, fellowships were awarded in open competition on merit. Yet Pattison came to see it all with a jaundiced eye as a system of over-tutoring both the apt and the inept for the degree stakes rather than as a realization of the 'close action of teacher on pupil' for which he had hoped. He retained the original conception but its application was redirected. Rothblatt suggests that his abandonment of the college ideal was connected with 'the improbable circumstances that deprived him of the headship of Lincoln' (Rothblatt 1968: 194). Certainly in the twenty-five years between the two Commissions, he switched his allegiance from college to university, from tutor to professor, from education to learning. The disastrous election of 1851 perhaps precipitated the process. He resigned his college tutorship, took no part in university administration, and spent much time abroad. His wanderings took him to Germany in the 1850s and there he gained crucial experience of a type of university life which was totally different from that of Oxford. An organized professoriate occupied the frontiers of the whole range of knowledge, pushing back its boundaries and instructing willing students through seminars and lectures. The ex-tutor was converted from his Oxford collegiate to a German university ideal.

In consequence, his submission to the Salisbury Commission included a recommendation which might have come from an Oxford student 'sit-in' in the late 1960s—the abolition of the colleges and their fellowships. The corporations were to be dissolved and their endowments transferred to the University. Nine colleges were to become the centres of the nine faculties. The rest were to be halls of residence and, no doubt, the modern radicals could have had one for a central student union. Entrance examinations were to be abolished. The cost of an Oxford education was to be nominal and no one would be forced to take degree examinations. Pattison thus qualified himself for rediscovery as a prophet for the student radicals of the 1970s. Except perhaps that his underlying motive was not to create a power base for social revolution, though he held uncompromising contempt for Oxford and Cambridge as finishing-schools for the upper classes. His passion was to make over the university not to youth, nor to professional training, nor to the social life of the high-born or highly connected, but to those who were consumed with the purest love of learning.

Newman and Pattison were illustrious figures who failed to make either the Catholic University of Ireland or Lincoln College amount to much. Jowett, on the other hand, was the embodiment of Victorian success and Balliol was the leading university institution of Victorian England. There had been worthy predecessors in the Mastership—Parsons (1798–1819) and 'the Old Master' Jenkyns (1813–1854)—but by the time Jowett had reigned for the last quarter of the nineteenth century the college was virtually identified with his name.

Balliol came into prominence with the decline of Oriel which had dominated the Oxford scene after the Napoleonic wars. Newman was an Oriel tutor in the 1820s and Pattison entered as an undergraduate in 1832. Jowett entered Balliol in 1835, was elected a Fellow while still an undergraduate, became one of the three Balliol tutors when he was 25, and stayed there almost to the end of the century, as Regius Professor of Greek from 1855, as Master from 1870, and as Vice-Chancellor of the University from 1882 to 1886. He died in 1893 at the age of 76.

Balliol has never lost the fame which Jowett consolidated for it. Only the direction changed, the college 'becoming concerned for the cure of a sick society rather than the improvement of a healthy social order' (Faber 1957: 32). This apt phrase is Geoffrey Faber's and he was presumably referring to the generation to which Archbishop Temple and R. H. Tawney belonged. Jowett's young men passed and continued to pass with 'effortless superiority' into *Who's Who*. They attained high imperial office at home and abroad, wrested pride of place in the All Souls prize fellowship examinations from Christ Church, colonized other colleges, and occupied the heights of the educational establishment throughout Victorian, Edwardian, and Elizabethan expansion. Charles Morris, for example, was the inter-war doyen of the Vice-Chancellors who carried Balliol to Leeds. John Fulton founded 'Balliol by the Sea' in Sussex.

For an appraisal of Jowett's life the obvious comparison is with Pattison. Nor is comparison here all contrast. They were contemporaries. Both were Oxford classical scholars, both exemplary tutors, both influenced by German experience (Jowett was the first Englishman to read and understand the work of Hegel). Moreover, both were first rejected and later elected to be head of their colleges, and the parallel runs even further here in that both first reacted to electoral disappointment—Pattison in 1851 and Jowett three years later—by withdrawal from the life of their senior common rooms.

Subsequently, however, their lives diverged. Jowett went on with his tutorial devotion to gain reputation and influence among the highest levels of British society through an ascendancy over the younger men and an indefatigable involvement in their graduate careers. His steady, triumphant march through Victoria's monarchy seems somehow, and faithfully, to reflect the confident progress of an imperial nation. Moreover, his personal life was largely free of the miseries endured by Pattison. He remained faithful to that peculiar brand of stern evangelical childhood which, in nineteenth-century England, fitted men for bachelorhood and dedication to work. Unlike Pattison, he entered on no disastrous marriage and, though he too acquired enemies, he developed a genius for friendship, including a platonic and protracted love for Florence Nightingale, which has practically disappeared from middle-class life in our own day.

Post-Freudians have learned to dismiss this type of character as 'homosexual', and to debunk its expression in sustained personal intimacy without carnality as 'sublimation'. Yet it is open to doubt whether this peculiar style of life and personality has ever been fully appreciated in its significance for the idea of a university which made the accomplishments of Oxford and Cambridge in the second half of the nineteenth century such a puzzle to foreign observers. The sexual institutions of Victorian Oxford gave firm if unplanned support to the tutorial idea of a university for recruits to the imperial ruling class. For example, the 'reading party', which, if he did not invent, Jowett developed to the highest level of personal comradeship in learning, was a typical manifestation of the potentiality of 'libidinal energy' to support a distinctive vision of university purposes. The abolition of the celibacy rule signalled the slow death of tutorial relations which set out not merely to instruct the mind but to fashion the character of the undergraduate and to absorb him into a lifelong nostalgia for his college years and a loyal membership of the educated élite. Today the tutor who carries on that tradition is a demographic and psychological oddity, weakly supported by his collegiate traditions and strongly rejected by the heterosexual compulsions of both his colleagues and his students. If Balliol still has devoted tutors it is despite the fact that the spouses and children of North Oxford continually call them away from collegiate commensality. Not so for Jowett. His marriage was to his college. He was undisputed master in his own house and the union spawned half a century and more of Britain's most glitteringly successful children.

As with sex, so too with the institutions of authority. There were multiple reasons in the anthropology and politics of the day which made Jowett a nationalist in an assuredly hierarchical nation. From this point of view the Church of England appears as another social foundation for the English idea of a university. It gave an ideological form to the education of an élite as well as an occupational destination for large, if decreasing, numbers of Oxford and Cambridge graduates. Newman, Pattison, and Jowett, it must be remembered, were all in Orders, and theology was Jowett's primary intellectual concern. The education of undergraduates, both its content and the social organization of its experience, had to be justified in relation to Church doctrine and Church authority.

Jowett never challenged that authority. He remained a believer all his life, though he moved from the characteristically evangelical outlook of his youthful contemporaries to a 'liberalism' which took him on a sharply different course from that of Newman and which, at least for his successors, eventually permitted reason to undermine faith. Today it would be inconceivable for the Head of a House in Oxford or Cambridge to emulate Jowett's autocratic self-confidence without revolution in both the senior and junior common rooms. The modern authority of science and reason has to take more democratic and anarchical form.

It was Jowett's liberalism, expressed in his contribution to *Essays and Reviews* (1860), that constituted the one major blunder of his career. His views on the interpretation of scripture were ahead of his time. Today those few who could bring themselves to be concerned at all over that old doctrinal conflict would, in almost every case, support him. The details are a minor episode in the history of the advancement of scientific authority. But for Jowett it was more a failure to judge the temper of Church authority, and he never afterwards repeated the error. What is interesting for us about the affair is the light it sheds on the utterly different notions of authority which were still current in Victorian Oxford. In 1863 the Vice-Chancellor's

Court issued a 'monition' which 'commanded the Yeoman Bedell of Law to cite the Rev. Benjamin Jowett to appear before our Vice-Chancellor . . . concerning the reformation and correction of his manners and excesses, but more especially for infringing the Statutes and privileges of the University by having published . . . certain erroneous and strange doctrines . . . contrary to and inconsistent with the doctrines of the Church of England . . .' (Faber 1957: 268).

Admittedly, *The Times* referred to the Vice-Chancellor's jurisdiction as 'a rusty engine of intolerance' (Faber 1957: 269) and Jowett was not in the end forced to appear. But what the episode underlines for our understanding of the idea of a university is that scientific authority is a precondition of the research university. Jowett stands as the last champion of an earlier idea, first because of the particular social context of Victorian Oxford and second because for him not science but the Church and the imperial hierarchy were the integrated sources of his theory of higher education.

But what was the fate of democratic access to higher education in all this? Seventy years ago Albert Manbridge described 'a general labourer, and an ardent socialist, (who) could not restrain his tears as, standing upon New College Tower, he gazed on the incomparable beauty of Oxford. "I want my comrades to see this", he said; he really meant that, in season and out of season, he would strive with all his power to make the dingy, gloomy crowded town in which he lived as near to the ideal of beauty as ever it was in his power to do' (Mansbridge 1923: 185). In 1973 a student minority of a minority spoke with a different proletarian voice: having been repulsed by a collection of elderly clerks from an attempt to break and enter the offices of the Indian Institute in Oxford, they described their unwilling hosts as 'hired thugs'.

Two generations separated two opposing views of Oxford, but both claimed to represent working-class interests. This can be put in the context of the evolving conception of a university in which I have described Pattison and Jowett as the radical luminaries of Victorian higher education, though some modern radicals would dismiss this harking back to them, and even more to Newman, as an antiquarian and suspect salutation of élitists.

Thus the French sociologist Alan Touraine, after the May Events, sketched a view of the university as a polarized factory of intellectual production, owned, managed, and controlled in the interests of the ruling class. He saw the modern campus, at Nanterre or Santa Barbara, as Marx saw the industrial town in the nineteenth century with its central factory and its dormitory annexe for the proletariat. Deans and professors were the managers of the new industrial-academic knowledge factories, halls of residence the equivalent of the dormitory annexe, and the products were technology and technologists for the 'military-industrial complex' and the mass media (defined to include the compulsory school as well as all the other organs of press, television, and radio which together make up the formidable modern means of propaganda). Universities maintained a modernized system of class exploitation by their socially selective 'intake' and their 'output' of men and knowledge for the service of the status quo. They reflected the structure of the national and international society in their internal regimes of 'repressive tolerance' and cosmopolitan culture. Student revolutionaries believed that the values of the ruling class permeated down from the top and determined what was to be considered academically permissible in teaching and research. Pattison's or Jowett's idea of a university here finds expression only as a qualification to the description of an institution fundamentally dominated by class interests.

What happened to the idea of a university between 1868 and 1968 or between New College Tower and the Indian Institute? From a study of the century before 'student power', Martin Trow and I distinguished four general views of the university from the denizens of the senior common room. On one dimension academic men and women inclined either towards élitist or towards expansionist views of the functions of the university in society. On a second dimension they were inclined to stress either the function of preserving and transmitting knowledge to the students under their care or the task which was given such powerful impetus in the nineteenth century by the German universities—the search for new knowledge. They tended, in other words, to occupy one of four positions in their conception of the university: they were élitist teachers, élitist researchers, expansionist teachers, or expansionist researchers.

There can be no doubt that Newman, Pattison, and Jowett were élitist teachers. Admittedly, both Pattison and Jowett had expansionist sympathies and both used the expression 'unnational' to describe the Oxford of their day and to refer to its religious, sexual, and class exclusiveness. But the measure of their expansionism has been put into context by John Sparrow, who points out that Pattison's 'ideal of a national university . . .' as . . . 'co-extensive with the nation' meant in practice that he wished to 'draft in five hundred, say three hundred, students (additional) from a class whose education hitherto terminated with the national school, or the commercial academy' (Sparrow 1967: 38), whereas the number of 'additional students' planned to be 'drafted' in the twenty years after Robbins was 350,000.

The expansionist teacher idea of the university none the less has Victorian origins. The reference here is not so much to the London University, Josiah Mason College in Birmingham, or Owens College in Manchester, which were institutions created by and for the sons of a rising bourgeoisie, but to the university extension movement founded by the Cambridge professor James Stewart in 1873, which was a primary influence in the emergence of university colleges like those of Nottingham and Sheffield.

What, in retrospect, is so striking about the expansionist-teacher view is the failure of the national labour colleges (or any equivalent of the German *proletkult*) to offer a successful alternative conception of adult education to

338

working men. The WEA was the monument to working-class acceptance of the traditional idea of the university, and Albert Mansbridge was its chronicler.

Mansbridge published his *The Older Universities of England* in 1923. He saw Oxford and Cambridge as venerable institutions slowly adapting, as would also the institutions of government and industry, to a democratic age. Belief in the power of democratic socialism to bring about peaceful revolution is nowhere more faithfully or more hopefully expressed. He saw the signs in the admission of women and the abolition of Greek as a condition of matriculation. Both innovations, in his judgement, had to be submitted to the test of reinforcing in the ancient universities 'the purity and power of their mind and spirit'. His concern was not to abolish classical education but to extend it. 'The English working man', he wrote, 'is interested in ancient Greece and Rome; left to himself he is attracted by it as by few other things' (Mansbridge 1923: 123). He looked forward not to changes in the definition of what ought to be taught but only to an extension of the definition of to whom it should be taught. 'The whole idea of university education is democratic, in the sense that anyone who has the capacity and the good will, no matter what his previous experience has been, or what his father was before him—shall have full free opportunity to develop his mental faculties. It is clear that the policy of providing university education for working men and women must not be taken as omitting others in the community' (Mansbridge 1923: 177). He then went on to argue that working men themselves wished ardently not to change Oxford but only to join it. And he cited the experience of the WEA (which began in 1903 as an 'association to promote the higher education of working men') and especially of the university tutorial class movement exemplified in Rochdale under R. H. Tawney's tutorship.

'The working man', Mansbridge tells us, 'fresh from his industrial city, was by no means a mere worshipper at the shrine of Oxford or Cambridge; he saw in them the promise of a fuller life which it was his duty to achieve for his comrades of the mine or factory . . . There was never any bitterness in their minds. To look forward with generous enthusiasm to the finer life to be is characteristic of the thoughtful English workman' (Mansbridge 1923: 185–6).

These views serve to remind us of a significant element in the social thought of our fathers and grandfathers. Not, of course, a majority voice, but still an authentic one which once informed the attitude of the labour movement to the British universities, but which has apparently been lost in the thought of the Labour Party since Robbins. A modern aspirant to the post of Secretary of State for Education is unlikely to have read either Mansbridge or the 'student power' literature. The older working-class idealism has no spokesman in a dominantly graduate House of Commons. But the modern proletarian 'realism' has its malign effects among both Labour and Conservative politicians. The modern parliamentary Left seems to have a tacit and diluted feeling of hostility to the élitist and allegedly unresponsive universities. The modern Right seems to offer a mirror reflection—suspicion and resentment that the universities offer an easy sanctuary to revolutionaries and subversives. Between them a noble idea of rational radicalism above the clash of class interests still struggles for life.

Élitism and university expansion

Élitist teachers fashioned the Victorian idea of the university in England. Newman, Pattison, and Jowett propounded more or less worldly and more or less qualified versions of the view which, for all the revolutionary implications of the industrial society in which they lived, did not differ essentially from ancient and medieval traditions. Max Weber in Germany summarized these traditions as a cultivation of young men in the humanistic outlook and style of life of the dominant strata. Charisma apart, he distinguished between two types of social personality as the products of higher education—the *cultivated* man and the *expert*, and the British Victorians had certainly made much of the correlative curricular distinction between *education* and *training*. Behind these distinctions Weber had identified two corresponding forms of power—the *traditional* and the *rational*—and the twentieth-century history of universities may be understood as a struggle between drives to express these underlying forms of authority in the curriculum and organization of the university and its claims to enter its alumni into positions of occupational and social authority.

The sociology of education is essentially a study of these issues. Weber's formulation of them has the merit of neither ignoring nor accepting a mechanical subsumption of cultural and organizational conflict as epiphenomenal to class warfare. In this way he invites us to recognize that what a society defines as knowledge, how that knowledge shall be distributed, in what form, and by what method, are not simply educational questions.

Answers require an appraisal of the political character of society. At the same time, Weber's approach leaves open the possibility of an interactive and indeterminate relation between, on the one hand, education (which is the process whereby knowledge is defined, distributed, and transmitted) and, on the other hand, the power structure of society.

Forms of society in which authority is sanctioned by custom and tradition have varied widely not in their common characteristic of restricting higher education to élites but in the cultural character of élite formations. The commonality and the variations include the education of Chinese mandarins, the minority leisure class of citizens in ancient Greece or Rome, or the gentlemanly strata of eighteenth-century Europe. Thus the aim of the university might have been to turn out a socially distinctive type of knight or courtier as in the case of the Japanese samurai or an educational scribe or intellectual as in the case of a Buddhist priest or a Christian cleric, or it might be the amateur gentlemanly administrator as in Jowett's Balliol.

Systems of education for membership in a cultivated status group have usually been under religious control. This is true of the Christian, Islamic, and Judaic traditions and it was, of course, to the first and third of these that Newman largely owed his idea of the university. But religious control has not been universal in such systems. The Chinese literati and the Hellenic schools of philosophy were important exceptions. Laymen taught laymen in ancient China, and the Hellenic schools were completely secular. Pattison and Jowett, for all that they were in Anglican Orders, felt the pull of Greek tradition.

However, what none of these three English pedagogues ever squarely faced was what Weber saw as the fundamental struggle, in the adaptation of education to industrialism, between the cultivated man and the expert—a fight which he saw as determined by the 'irresistibly expanding bureaucratisation of all public and private relations of authority and by the ever-increasing importance of expert and specialised knowledge' (Weber, in Gerth and Mills 1947: 243).

Thus the outmoded character of the authors I have been discussing consists of their failure to appreciate the reformist strength of the research conception of the university in either its élitist or expansionist forms. Though without benefit of a systematic expositor, the voice of the élitist researcher has probably been the most effective force for change in the twentieth-century English universities, as has been that of the expansionist researcher in the state universities of America.

The research orientation, however, has had a qualitative rather than a quantitative impact. It fostered the single subject honours degree more as a definition of the undergraduate as a potential recruit to the academic succession than as a trainee specialist for the scientific professions. It fostered at the same time a conception of intimate tutorial relations which led the 'provincial' universities to assimilate more to Oxford and Cambridge than to the demands of the industrial centres in which they were located. Consequently, the ideology of the élitist teacher was never seriously challenged. Research institutes never flourished and graduate study, at least in the first sixty years of the century, was never more than a minor appendage to the dominant undergraduate organization of the universities. Writing in the late twenties, the American Abraham Flexner observed that the English were 'curiously averse to recognition of graduate students as a group. They are excessively conscientious teachers: "it is our first business to teach", one hears again and again. Between 1882 and 1928 Manchester conferred 6,473 Bachelor's degrees but only 74 Ph.D's' (Flexner 1930: 222).

Indeed, the concern with 'excellence' on the part of élitist researchers strongly reinforced traditional opposition to expansion of numbers. Sir Eric (later Lord) Ashby entitled his essay for the Carnegie Commission on Higher Education *Any Person, Any Study* (1970), thus characterizing the system of mass higher education in America by reference to Ezra Cornell, whose intention it had been to 'found an institution where any person could find instruction in any study'. This always was and remains the antithesis of the English idea of the university which Flexner, writing in All Souls, could only applaud. At a time when the American universities and colleges had been through an expansion which the British universities were not to match until the late 1960s, he deplored 'a wild, uncontrolled, and uncritical expansion ... the quacks emit publications that travesty research and make a noise that drowns out the still small voice to which America should be listening ...'. And he thought of the ancient English universities as 'seats of higher learning incomparably superior to anything that has yet been created in America' (Flexner 1930: 233–4).

Moreover, the opinion that more means worse maintained itself and even renewed its vigour as the Robbins programme of expansion proceeded; Terence Miller devoted a column in THES (25 Jan. 1974) to demolishing what he believed to be the false vision of mass higher education—'a great many people will, one hopes, remain able to observe that most people, in any nation, are simply not capable of the intellectual effort to take in the stuff of higher education and would therefore be much better off without being dragooned into it.' Thus did the director of a polytechnic in the 1970s echo Flexner, who was telling us in 1930 that 'the English show no signs of being converted to the American theory that college or university education is indiscriminately good for anyone who can make his way through high school. Such is, quite clearly, not the case; hundred of youths, eighteen to twenty-two years of age, can be better employed than in attending a university; and the English, by increasing provision of technical and other schools, try to give this host—the majority—what they need and can assimilate' (Flexner 1930: 227). The expansion of higher education for the working class had thus remained a dream.

Though Pattison in his later years moved towards it, there was no systematic English apology for the research conception of the university. That had to wait for a Professor of Spanish at the University of Liverpool in the 1940s, who wrote under the pseudonym of Bruce Truscot. This was the voice of the dominant English tradition. The research idea of the university was, of course, of German origin and taken up at the turn of the century with enthusiasm by President Gilman at Johns Hopkins and with still more vigorous flair by William Rainey Harper at the University of Chicago.

It was in Chicago in the 1950s that I first learnt to understand this most un-English conception through appreciative acquaintance with that beleaguered academic square mile in which the probability on any given day of an exciting conversation was, and possibly still is, greater than in any other place that I have known. Not surprising, then, that the classic advocacy of this idea of the university should have been written at Chicago by that rare American genius Thorstein Veblen under the title *The Higher Learning in America*: and no less surprising that it was practically unknown in England, at least in the first half of the century. Even Bruce Truscot, when writing *Redbrick University* (Truscot 1943), appears to have been unaware of his distinguished predecessor.

Veblen was the kind of man that legends are made of. 'The last man in the world to have known everything' is one part of his reputation. He was born in 1857 in the obscurity of an immigrant Norwegian farming community in Wisconsin and died, also in obscurity, in 1929 in a cabin in California. In the meantime this alien, gangling, and unfashionable man migrated between several American universities (Hopkins, Yale, Minnesota, Chicago, Stanford, Missouri, and the New School for Social Research in New York). The, perhaps apocryphal, story is told that at one point the President of his university informed Veblen with magisterial reproach that 'the Regents and I are not satisfied, Professor, with your marital arrangements.' 'No, sir,' replied Veblen sadly, 'neither am I.'

Nor was Veblen satisfied, to quote the subtitle of his book, with 'the conduct of universities by business men', whose behaviour he was prone to describe, as Richard Hofstadter remarked, in terms usually reserved for moral delinquents. He saw the ideal milieu for scholarship and science, like the frenetically productive society it reflected, as threatened and corrupted by the predatory ethics of business salesmanship.

For Veblen the possibility of a university was rooted in universal human nature as 'the instinct of workmanship' and the impulse to 'Idle Curiosity'. These impulses, he held, gave rise to esoteric knowledge in all known civilizations and therefore a custodial function for 'a select body of adepts or specialists—scientists, scholars, savants, clerks, priests, shamans, medicine men'. The particular organization of highly valued knowledge varies from one society to another but always makes up the central substance of the civilization in which it is found. In the modern West, social evolution, as he saw it, had brought empirical and scientific knowledge to the highest point of prestige as the ideal aim and method of scholars. 'For good or ill, civilised men have come to hold that this matter-of-fact knowledge of things is the only end in life that indubitably justifies itself' (Veblen 1918: 15).

Here was where Veblen found the basis and justification for the modern university. The single distinguishing function unique to the university was the pursuit of knowledge, not for profit nor indeed for any utilitarian purpose but simply to satisfy idle curiosity. The university of the future, he thought, made this the only unquestioned duty incumbent on the university. He recognized, of course, that the advancement of higher learning involved two lines of work, distinct but closely bound together—scientific enquiry and the instruction of students. But, he argued, 'the former of these is primary and indispensable' (Veblen 1918: 16). The work of teaching properly belonged in the university only in so far as it facilitated the pursuit of new knowledge in science and scholarship. It had an appropriate place only in so far as it trained each rising generation of scholars and scientists for the further pursuit of knowledge. Training for other purposes was necessarily of a different kind and was best done elsewhere.

The university man, for Veblen, was a student, not a schoolmaster. The secondary school, the professional school, the British polytechnic, the American liberal arts college, and indeed pretty well any American university would have been denied the title by his exacting test. Oxford and Cambridge would have been similarly disqualified, for, 'while the lower schools necessarily take over the surveillance of their pupils' everyday life, and exercise a large measure of authority and responsible interference in that behalf, the university assumes (or should assume) no responsibility for its students' fortunes in the moral, religious, pecuniary, domestic or hygienic respect' (Veblen 1918: 201). It was characteristic of his ironical style of thought that he went on to accord the larger and more serious responsibility for preparing citizens and producers, not to the university, but to the lower and professional schools. He was adamant that the university could not be charged 'with extraneous matters that are themselves of such grave consequences as this training for citizenship and practical affairs'. 'These', he argued, 'are too serious a range of duties to be taken care of as a side issue, by a seminary of learning the members of whose faculty, if they are fit for their own special work, are not men of affairs or adepts in worldly wisdom' (Veblen 1918: 21).

The origins of the medieval university in vocational training for ecclesiastical and courtly hierarchies he dismissed as irrelevant evolutionary stages in the evolution of barbarian civilizations. Technologists and medical men could only be corrupted by incorporation. Unless housed in separate establishments, doctors, lawyers, and engineers would be placed in a false position and unavoidably led to court 'a specious appearance of scholarship, and so to invest their technological discipline with a degree of pedantry and sophistication . . .'. 'Doubtless', he added, 'the pursuit of scholarly prestige is commonly successful, to the extent that it produces the desired conviction of awe in the vulgar, who do not know the difference; but all this make-believe scholarship, however successfully staged, is not what these schools are designed for . . . Nor is it what they can do best and most efficiently. It is the quest for knowledge that constitutes the main interest of the university. Utilitarian impulses and applications are alien to that purpose' (Veblen 1918: 31).

Veblen's vision was never realized. The American road was to lead to the 'multiversity'. Perhaps the Princeton Institute for Advanced Studies, post-Franks All Souls College, or the Center for the Study of Behavioural Sciences at Palo Alto were his monuments. But even at those illustrious institutions a visit from Veblen in his customary role as the sardonic cultural anthropologist would have detected the diversion of energies into 'habitual parochialism

. . . and the meticulous manoeuvres of executives seeking each to enhance his own prestige' by men 'picked though they may be with a view to parochialism and blameless futility . . .' and therefore unable 'to forgo their habitual preoccupation with petty intrigue and bombastic publicity' (Veblen 1918: 58). It was always a Utopian dream, naïve, for all the erudition of its author, in the beguiling belief that human organizations can ever be single-mindedly concentrated on a single function: and no less naïve in the unrealistic if flattering Rousseauesque conception that the instinctive virtues of men are perverted only by the institutions of society.

The Victorian and Edwardian legacy of ideas about the nature, purposes, and organization of a university emerged from the struggles of our forebears towards a radical reinterpretation of medieval tradition adequate to the needs of their new industrial society. The redbrick universities early and the polytechnics later in the twentieth century were their major achievements. In the process ecclesiastical was increasingly displaced by secular authority in academic life; and uneasy uncertainty persisted as to what might constitute an appropriate modern curriculum. The writers I have discussed debated the distinction between education and training and anticipated the crisis vulgarized by C. P. Snow in the 1950s as the problem of 'the two cultures'. They discussed these issues as either élitist or expansionist in their view of the place of the university in society and as inclining to emphasize either the teaching or research side of its internal life.

Unhappily, Victorian social inventiveness exhausted itself with the creation of the industrial provincial universities at the turn of the century, and the inter-war years, which gave us Abraham Flexner's commentary, were bleak. Political attention was directed elsewhere, towards economic depression at home and the rise of the new secular religions of communism and fascism abroad. The major current of intellectual thought seemed to bypass the universities, and neither Marxism nor Freudianism had its roots in academic institutions. Looking back, it appears that intellectual activity was heavily and quietly concentrated in the natural sciences, where a few creative men and women with inadequate resources were constructing a body of physical and technological knowledge that was soon to transform the world beyond even their own imagination. The redbrick universities thus went through a generation of unambitious consolidation, completely overshadowed by the 'élitist teaching' conception of the university which gave Oxford and Cambridge their magic and lustre and consigned the civic newcomers to a drab and placeless social obscurity.

It is against this background that Bruce Truscot's *Redbrick University* may be reread. He was an unconscious successor to Veblen. Thus,

> The primary aim of the university must be search for knowledge—
> research as we call it today: not merely actual discovery, not merely
> even the attempt to discover, but the creation and cultivation of the

spirit of discovery. Imagine a group of men, in any age, retiring from the life of the world, forming a society for the pursuit of truth, laying down and voluntarily embracing such discipline as is necessary to that purpose and making provision that whatever they find shall be handed on to others after their deaths. They pool their material resources; build a house; collect books; and plan their corporate studies. This, in its simplest form, is the true idea of a university.

(Truscot 1945: 69)

Veblen would have approved. But later in the book it becomes clear that Truscot would qualify his idea into something much more like the impure practicalities of the university as we know it. He ended by writing of 'two chief aims, research and teaching', which 'blend so frequently and at times so completely, that it is often more accurate to describe them as one single aim which can be regarded from two aspects'. Moreover, he included graduate teaching, having in mind the American type of organization of graduate schools, as part of the research interest.

There had been mild rumbles of complaint and suggestion, particularly from students, along these lines before the war, designed to redefine university courses across the boundaries of the arts and sciences. A new humanistic synthesis had been called for by several writers, including Walter Kotschnig in *The University in a Changing World* (Kotschnig and Prys (eds.) 1932) and Adolf Lôwe in *The Universities in Transformation* (1941). A debate also started in this period as to where, in the disciplinary sense, the new synthesis might lie. Some like Karl Mannheim argued for the social sciences, others like F. R. Leavis at Cambridge in his *Education and the University* (1943) saw a 'humane consciousness' as best nurtured in the schools of English. In the event, when expansion began in earnest in the 1960s, the palm went to the social sciences, and the consequences for the social consciousness of the current generation of educated men can hardly be exaggerated. The dicta of Durkheim, Weber, and C. Wright Mills became part of the common currency of the 'quality newspapers', and Alan Bullock, preparing a dictionary for the *TLS* reader in the 1970s, found it necessary to explain the meanings of the new words from 'anomie' to 'stochastic processes'.

Post-war nostalgia

After Bruce Truscot and the Second World War the first major essay on the idea of a university came from Sir Walter Moberly.

Moberly was Chairman of the UGC in the early post-war years and steered its early movement along an exponential curve of state patronage of higher education which by 1980 appeared to have reached its end. While he was writing *The Crisis in the University* (1949), Treasury finance to the universities

346

was being quadrupled. Yet whether out of confidence or lack of interest in the material future of the universities, Moberly identified the crisis as a spiritual one. We shall never know whether he envisaged the sweep of the curve which was to ascend from about £13 million to over £3 billion now. Nor does it matter. His eyes were turned not to the price of universities but to their value. Since that crisis of aim and purpose remains unresolved we may profit from his description of it.

The war, it may be remembered, had brought a convulsion of social consciousness, not only in the Whitehall corridors, but throughout the nation among both civilians and members of the armed services. Ordinary people had divined that war had brought the opportunity for new beginnings, that it had been fought over the principles and not only the expediencies of human relations, and that a return to civilian life ought to mean also a reconstruction of society on better foundations. Moberly argued that the universities reflected 'the crisis in the world and its pervading sense of insecurity'. Over a large part of Europe and Asia there was a lack of binding conviction and there was confusion, bewilderment, and discord. 'All over the world, indeed, the cake of custom is broken, and old gods are dethroned and none have taken their place' (Moberly 1949: 16). He set out to examine possible plans for a rejuvenation of the universities on the assumption that the essential contribution had to come from Christianity.

It was precisely because Moberly's standpoint was avowedly Christian that his book received scarcely a mention when all the talk turned on crisis at the end of the 1960s. Student movements all over the world phrased their protests, rebellions, and ideological revolutions in secular nostrums. Yet what Moberly had to say remains seriously persuasive, not because of his Christianity, which is subtle and as undogmatic as a religious creed permits, nor because of his thoughtful grasp of previous writings about the idea of a university, but rather because he analysed a problem which refuses to go away. The questions he asked—'What are universities for? What effect should they have on their alumni? What are their responsibilities to the outside world?'—are still with us.

Moberly's view was that, beneath the façade of development and hopefulness of his day, universities all over the world hid a peculiar malaise of impotence. They had little inner self-confidence because they lacked any clear, agreed sense of direction or purpose. As he saw them then, and as observers like Peter Scott continue to see them today, they shared rather than transcended the spiritual confusion of the age. For Moberly the problem had been accentuated by the moral collapse of the German universities under the Nazi regime. The tragedy for his generation was that these universities had occupied a position of the highest intellectual prestige and had been models to the rest of the world. In the next generation a similar disillusionment developed towards the American universities, which had appeared in the 1950s to lead the way towards a democratic amalgam of popular openness and Nobel-prize-winning excellence through the model of the University of California only to be shattered by the 'student troubles' of the following decade.

Already in the 1940s Moberly was setting down an anticipatory description.

> The cultural failure of the universities is seen in the students. In recent years large numbers of these have been apathetic and have had neither wide interests nor compelling convictions. The active-minded minority have often been in revolt. A few years ago a shrewd observer at one of our older universities said that he was struck with the rarity with which undergraduates expressed or felt any deep respect for, or debt to, dons as having opened up for them a whole new attitude to life; though unless all the biographies are untrustworthy, such discipleship was not uncommon in earlier generations. This estrangement between the generations has come about largely because students feel themselves to be living in a different world from their teachers ... If they find prophets at all, it is outside the university ... out there in the street is something new in the making, which will shatter all the syllogisms and formulas of the schools.
>
> (Moberly 1949: 23)

Moberly arrived at his own solution by looking back and identifying three basic ideas of the university—the Christian-Hellenic, the liberal, and the technological-democratic. He saw nineteenth-century Oxford and Cambridge as embodying the Christian and Graeco-Roman tradition. He recognized Newman's *Idea of a University* as a picture of Oxford's characteristic excellences. Basically the same ideal was held by Jowett and had been expounded a few years earlier by Whewell at Cambridge (*On the Principles of English University Education*).

As Moberly put it, 'On this view the chief duty of the university is to produce good citizens. It should train an élite who are to be the future leaders in affairs and in the learned professions.' He appreciated its merits. In it, education is liberal as opposed to servile, general as opposed to specialized, and systematic as opposed to dependent on fashion or individual caprice. He also saw, as did Newman, the expression in nineteenth-century Oxford of the principle that the university, being a community of teachers and learners, has to be regarded as a family. Hence tutorial teaching, essay-writing, disputations, and, above all, 'the relation between the staff and students is regarded as being paternal on the one side and filial on the other. The student is under authority. The office of the teacher is to some extent a pastoral one. He has a responsibility towards his pupils as human beings which extends far beyond his formal obligations as an instructor' (Moberly 1949: 33).

An idealized, Newmanesque Oxford was Moberly's idea of the university for the future. But he recognized that the older medieval conception had already been displaced by liberal ideas in the nineteenth century and foresaw the displacement of the liberal inspired university by what he labelled a technological-democratic movement. His interest and purpose was to understand and thereby to modify both these ideas of the university so as to restore, in modernized and viable form, the Christian principles which had guided the traditional European universities before liberal ideas made the German universities such triumphant leaders in the development of higher learning for advanced industrial societies.

Moberly was at one with Jowett and the Victorian reformist churchmen whose naïve optimism actually welcomed liberalism as a potential emancipation of the Christian university from parochial narrowness and indefensible interference with free enquiry. He was almost as sanguine as his predecessors in taking for granted the capacity of a moral outlook to survive without institutional power. He even echoed the fashionable talk of the early postwar days about Britain's future in the world as a moral force which might be strengthened by loss of empire. At all events, he saw no possible return to direct ecclesiastical control of the life of scholars and sought to incorporate liberalism rather than to defeat it.

Accordingly, he emphasized that the liberal conception of a university stems historically from the Christian-Hellenic traditions but expresses some features of the older ideal rather than others. It was primarily based on the idea that investigation matters more than instruction. Liberalism characterizes the outlook of the élitist researcher. The liberal ideal stresses, second, that learning for learning's sake is the proper business of the university and, third, insists on 'the function of the university as a community of science and learning quite distinct from that of church or state, or commerce and industry, and never to be subservient to them'. It stayed away from current practical controversy in politics or religion. It eschewed partisanship. It was a place for thought rather than action. It followed Max Weber's distinction between science and politics as vocations.

Fourth, following Abraham Flexner, Moberly noted that the university which is liberal assumes a need to be highly selective in the subjects it embraces and the methods it employs. 'It should abhor mediocrity: its business is with an intellectual aristocracy.' And 'the criterion is not the social importance of the proposed faculty or subject but its inherent intellectual value. It is only the learned professions or those that have intellectual content in their own right with which the universities should concern themselves.' And finally, to the doctrine of *Lehrfreiheit* of the teacher corresponds that of the *Lernfreiheit* of the student (Moberly 1949: 42).

For Moberly both Flexner and Bruce Truscot reflected the liberal view which descended from the nineteenth-century prestige of the German universities and had been celebrated by Sir William Hamilton in his attacks on

Oxford in the 1830s, by Mark Pattison in his writing in the 1850s, and by Matthew Arnold in the 1860s. Again, it had found a persuasive missionary in Lord Haldane at the beginning of this century and is probably still the idea of the university to which most senior academic people would subscribe.

But again, as Moberly saw, the twilight of the liberal university was at hand. His third contender was a form of higher education which would be technological and democratic. It was rooted in the rise of applied science and technology, the socially sensitive optimism of the post-war generation, and what he saw as the growing democratic character of the universities. The aim of the university endeavour on this view is predominantly practical and utilitarian; it is the conquest of nature for the satisfaction of human needs. This is the creed of the expansionist researcher. Its discipline is analytic; its political mood is Fabian. In Moberly's words, 'it requires clarity and precision, it steers clear of all that is cloudy, grandiose and emotionally coloured' (Moberly 1949: 45). It discriminates between fields and methods which promise practical results and those which do not. It is activist and optimistic. It gives a rationale to the entry of the university into the modern world of search for new and more efficient solutions to age-old human needs.

The democratic companion to the technological impulse needs no elaboration. These two influences together, as Moberly saw, were producing a new culture, differing sharply from university traditions, condemning liberalism as being aristocratic rather than egalitarian, detached rather than participatory, and 'as exalting a sterile scholarship rather than being frankly occupational and utilitarian' (Moberly 1949: 48).

However, Moberly accepted none of these three views nor the further approach which would emphasize expansion and teaching and which completes the fourfold Trow–Halsey classification. He turned instead to the possibility of a rejuvenated and modernized Christianity for the universities, rid of its ancient guilt over the *odium theologicum* and any attempt to shackle free enquiry with dogmatic orthodoxy. Against the modern hope for progress through pragmatic and positivist science, he argued that the fundamental aim of the university can never be fulfilled by intellectual gadgetry, however sophisticated. It is not enough to know how to apply physics or chemistry or even social science.

Curiously enough, at least some British academics were already ambivalently aware of this model of our educational future from the United States, which had already gone beyond the Robbins targets for 1980, having 3 million college students in 1960 and the expectation of doubling again in the next decade. Ambivalence heavily obscured awareness. Two years before Kerr delivered his lectures at Harvard, I travelled to California with Sir John Cockcroft to survey American educational growth. Cockcroft had formed his idea of a university in the 1930s at the Cavendish Laboratory in Cambridge and fascinated me with the story of his travelling (by train) across America to the Californian Institute of Technology to carry the news of his famous electrical exploits with the atom. We came to La Jolla, where there had been a tiny institute since the 1920s formed by a handful of oceanographers-cum-sailors to map the sea-bed: but now there was to be a new university campus, mounting rapidly on lovely hillsides to house 27,500 students. The Chancellor was appointed, an architect, and a few secretaries. The architect was delighted to see us. 'You people are from Oxbridge?' Sir John blinked a deprecatory nod. 'You have colleges there. We are thinking along the same lines. Tell me, how many guys do you put in these colleges?' Sir John turned nervously to me and I guessed that Christ Church at Oxford or St John's, Cambridge, would be among the biggest, about 500 each. 'Yeah', smiled the architect, 'That'll be the faculty, but how many students?'

Sir John blinked again and retreated towards the oceanographers. The next year, Clark Kerr produced his account of the multiversity. On Kerr's view the idea of a university in medieval traditions was a village with its priests; the idea of a modern university as the Victorians fashioned it was a town—a one-industry town—with its intellectual oligarchy; and the idea of a multiversity 'is a city of infinite variety'. He recognized it as a somewhat amorphous and anarchic place, pluralistic in its base but high at the apex in pursuit of academic excellence. For him, then, it was a city of intellect with a diverse citizenry but held together by a spirit of tolerance and generous conceptions of what was justifiable in the varied realms of teaching, research, service to the community, selectivity, and openness towards student admissions and bargaining for funds with governmental and private patrons.

The Californian vision as described by Kerr was an extravagant dream in Britain on the eve of the Robbins Report. Yet it was, if only a geographically remote reality, a possibly realizable plan for the future of higher education in Britain and Europe, at once germinated and constrained by the ideas of the past which the new social architects had inherited.

Robbins's recommendations had for the most part been accepted wholeheartedly by a Conservative government. But the signposts since 1968 have frequently read doom and crisis, alarm and despondency. Robert Nisbet tells us that 'no one seriously surveying the academic scene today can conclude other than that the American university is in an exceedingly precarious position. The lustre of even the most historic and distinguished universities is fading rapidly. For the first time in the history of this country there is valid reason for wondering whether the university will survive' (Nisbet 1972: 197). In their final report in 1980 (Carnegie Council 1980), summarizing a minor library on American higher education, the Carnegie Commission began with a chapter describing decline from 'Golden Age to Time of Troubles'. They referred to political crises and financial depressions. They noted that the social idealism and social optimism that characterized the New Deal and the period following the Second World War had given way to cynicism and pessimism. 'A lack of confidence now exists in what is being done, in conceptions of what should be done in the processes for making changes ... There has been a basic erosion of affection for and interest in education, including higher education.' This is a recurrent theme of American commentary of which Alan Bloom's best seller of 1987 is a characteristic late example (Bloom 1987).

On the other hand, the Carnegie Commission refused to be daunted. 'We do not believe', they said, 'higher education will decline, and we are convinced that it would be a tragedy for the nation if it did. We end our six years of study of higher education, in the time of its greatest trauma of self-doubt, with faith in its potential continued vitality and with a deepened belief in its essential value to American society.'

The work of the Carnegie Commission on Higher Education invites British comparison with the Robbins Report. The official British inquiry took place in the early 1960s, heralding an unprecedented spurt of expansion. The semi-official American study began in 1967, changed its name in 1974, and presented its final report in 1980, heralding an unprecedented decline. To compare, therefore, is mainly to contrast. In any case the American investigation was larger than the British in rough proportion to the number of students and colleges involved. Under Clark Kerr's indefatigable chairmanship, and supported by such notables as William Bowen, Ernest Boyer, David Reisman, and Martin Trow, a massive and detailed ethnography of American higher education was put together. It documents and analyses the final decades of an expansion of schooling unrivalled in any other country. It gives as complete a picture as any scholar or administrator could hope for of a system of higher education which grew from 1870 to 1970 at a compound annual rate of 5 per cent, taking its share of GNP from 0.1 to 2.1 per cent, and incorporating by 1980 some 8.5 million full-time equivalent students into over 3,000 institutions. As this vast increase of scale and scope appeared to be ending, the Council surveyed and advised on the future (Carnegie Council 1980). What will, and what ought to, happen to these 3,000 universities and colleges in the next twenty years? The answers, which assumed numerical decline, contained interest for European countries facing a similar fate.

American growth in the recent past had not, of course, been free of trouble. The student buffoonery of the sixties shook public confidence in universities, though Americans, by international standards, retained their traditional faith in a college education. The rising production of Ph.D.s had its impact on the labour market in the 1970s, reducing the personal rate of return on high qualifications and forcing down the real incomes of university teachers. The average quality of both entrants and graduates fell as the numbers increased. Financial difficulties multiplied in the later 1970s as the system became dominantly and increasingly one of the large public campuses, funded and increasingly regulated by the State. The aspirations of minority groups for equality of opportunity had not been fully met, the regularizing efforts through 'affirmative action' often clashed with the principle of individual merit on which excellence had traditionally depended. As expansion temporarily tailed off, the average age of university staff rose, defensive unionism grew, and a new generation of students made novel demands. An ageing and relatively impoverished teaching body had to unlearn the established habits of a period of rising budgets, and face students as a market of consumers rather than a guaranteed parade of potential recruits to the academic succession. In short, institutional survival had already come to depend on successful adaptation to an uncertain student market.

The future was dominated by these uncertainties, and the Council accordingly addressed itself first to the prospects for student enrolment. Decline was not inevitable and did not in the event materialize. It was, however, certain that the traditional college-going population of 18–21-year-olds would fall by 25 per cent between 1980 and the end of the century. Some optimists predicted correctly that the falling total would be more than offset by an increasing proportion of college entrants, particularly women and members of ethnic minorities. They argued, too, that as a personal investment in life earnings, the degree would become more rather than less important, and that the return, after falling by one-third between the mid-sixties and the mid-seventies, would rise. So one possible projection was for 25 per cent increase. At the other extreme a decrease of 40 per cent had been forecast. The Carnegie Councillors opted for a mild pessimism in the shape of a fall in undergraduate enrolments of between 5 per cent and 15 per cent between 1980 and 2000. After that, they postulated recovery on the assumption that fertility and/or immigration would increase to keep the total American student population in equilibrium.

What were the solutions? The Carnegie Commission offered nothing spectacular. In effect, they enjoined the universities, the State, the professors, the students, and the public to be their best selves. The federal government should provide ample funds for basic research. The public should be generous, should support tax laws facilitating private gifts, and maintain its enthusiasm. Students should pursue higher education, especially in the humanities, for its own sake as well as for its market advantages. The universities should redouble their efforts to be excellent, to be responsive to social needs, and exemplars of moral probity and devotion to science and scholarship.

These conventional wisdoms, calmly stated, are not to be dismissed. For they reflect the essential and essentially admirable idea of the university. The problem was to deliver them. In reality the staffing of universities is inflexible. Tenure is the prized norm and is tenaciously defended by men and women whose recent material affluence has been somewhat eroded. Academic men and women tend to see themselves as the natural proprietors of their institutions and therefore to be defensive against initiatives from other origins, whether government, unions, presidents, or their own administrators. The challenge was to retain self-government while overcoming its associated conservatism.

Meanwhile the most recent British contribution to discussion of ideas about higher education has been offered by Peter Scott, the editor of the *THES* (P. Scott 1984). It is a notable contribution to the sociology of education and not least because he argues that if there is a crisis, it is of higher education in a liberal-democratic secular society, and not merely of the British universities under a Thatcher administration. Any such argument requires diagnosis of historical trends, not only of the relative simplicities of numbers of students and resources, but also of the complexities of values, purposes, and principles which make up the intellectual culture of a nation. Scott sees the British universities as evolving from traditional through liberal and modern to a post-modern form or alternatively, in the context of post-secondary education as a whole, from élite through mass to universal provision. He refuses to place higher education simplistically into either interpretative framework and so to produce confident and naïve 'waves of the future' in a final chapter. Instead he leaves more questions than answers, more open challenges than closed facts.

He is tempted to declare his own long historical framework irrelevant by awareness that the contemporary British universities were largely created during the 1950s and 1960s, 'the product . . . of the Robbins' Committee blueprint for expansion that was so spectacularly executed during the 1960s and 1970s' (Scott 1984: 118). Had he yielded to that temptation, he would have saved himself the immensely more difficult task of deciphering the eidos and ethos of a tradition reaching back to twelfth-century Paris. He could have dealt with past, present, and future in pragmatic, unmysterious terms, judging achievement more or less numerically from the stated objectives of the UGC and the DES, and the news in the files of the *THES*. But he did not yield to such misleading superficial certainties, though he does include an informative account of the post-Robbins period.

Issue may well be taken with one aspect of his pragmatic interpretation— his flat assertion that 'of course another Robbins is impossible' (Scott 1984: 258). Professor Robin Marris subsequently argued exactly to the contrary (*THES*, 6 Apr. 1984) 'the economic return to the nation from university education is so high, that there is in fact an overwhelming case for a new massive expansion, for, in effect a "new Robbins"'. Marris arrived at his conclusion by strictly economic calculation. Scott, apart from anticipatory criticism of the basis of such arithmetic (for example, that if higher education acts in the labour market mainly as a sieve, its value to individual graduates is bound to decline as the production of graduates increases), devotes much more print to the social and political forces which shape opinion and decision in senior common rooms, boardrooms, and Cabinet offices. To this end he presents a summary recapitulation of the liberal and modern phases of the history of British higher education, attempting to distil their cultural essence as traditions which mould present thought and future possibilities.

This is not to say that his sympathies (or mine) are opposed to the general thrust of Marris's advocacy. It is to say, however, that Scott recognizes the power of inherited ideology; and in this sense the book belongs to the large literature on 'the idea of the university' which I have discussed in this chapter. Scott's interpretation of institutional history is also, in effect, a review and reflection of the ideas of Newman, Pattison, Jowett, Veblen, Mansbridge, Truscot, and (more explicitly) Robbins and Kerr.

From this long lineage of predecessors, Sir Walter Moberly is the most apt for comparison. To select him is at once to throw light on the dubious use of the word crisis: for Moberly's title in 1949 was *The Crisis in the University*. Perhaps the tiny difference of a preposition (from 'in' to 'of') signals a change in the thirty-five years between the two books in the emphasis on the 'public' rather than the 'private' lives of universities. Certainly Scott is more aware than was Moberly of the wider intellectual culture and of the existence of what came to be recognized as the binary line and a system of higher and further education as well as a 'knowledge industry', with which universities have manifold relationships.

But crisis is the conceptual continuity and the definition of it has not changed. Neither author describes crisis in terms of resources. Moberly was Chairman of the UGC in the early post-war years of burgeoning funds. Scott, by contrast, watched and recorded the use of the UGC, the National Advisory Board, and the Research Councils as agents of a governmental drive towards reduced public expenditure on higher education. Yet neither sees the economics of higher learning as crucial.

For Scott as well as Moberly the crisis was spiritual. 'There can be little doubt', he writes, 'that there has been a decisive shift towards pessimism in Britain since the early 1970s and higher education has shared in this mood and been a victim of it.' 'The different branches of knowledge find it increasingly difficult to regard the modern university as in any sense an organic academic society rather than simply as a shared bureaucratic environment' (Scott 1984: 115). Scott could even be held to speak for his pre-Robbins predecessor when he ends his book with the fear that higher education, and the values it embodies, may be condemned to 'marginality and erosion' and the demise of 'that configuration of belief and practice, typical of modern society, and the metaphor of a moral social order that is a guarantee of both freedom and progress' (Scott 1984: 271).

The questions and the crisis are, then, much the same. So, too, are the essential conceptions or 'ideal types' inherited from the past—the traditional (what Moberly calls Graeco-Roman), the liberal, and the modern (Moberly's 'technological-democratic'). Both writers locate the liberal university in the period from the revival led by the eighteenth-century Scottish universities up to the first half of the twentieth century—roughly from Hume to Rutherford. In the three preceding centuries European intellectual life had passed out of the post-medieval university, which slept through the Renaissance, the rise of the Royal Society, and the spread of the Enlightenment. The liberal university was then awakened by the rise of natural and political science. Rationality was, and still is, the value which a university embodies. Reason is the timeless principle of the idea and organization of any university and sets the problem for Scott or any other interpreter of the fate of universities. But universities are also always mirrors of the age. In the case of the age of classical industrialism, Scott argues that there are identifiable social and economic forces which gave the liberal university particular character as the custodian of an intellectual tradition 'derived from the culture of an elite and the codification of scientific principles by a corps of academic experts' (Scott 1984: 31).

These two elements of tradition and pedagogy are our inheritance from the liberal university. They were exemplified in Edwardian Oxford and Cambridge, they modified and contained the 'redbrick' universities which developed in the great provincial cities from the end of the nineteenth century, and they continued to shape the self-conceptions of the new universities of the 1960s. But a new conception—the modern university—is thought of by Scott as based on an emerging redefinition of knowledge as product rather than process. A scientific rather than a cultural definition of knowledge emphasizes research more than teaching, intellect more than sensibility. A reconstruction of intellectual life displaces humanism by academicism; technology replaces education. The university is more fissiparous, less integrated, more eager to respond to external influences, less separate from the mainstream of profane life, and therefore more serviceable as well as more pliant to the power of the State. While central to society for the generation of new scientific knowledge as well as the distribution of occupational chances (at least to the more remunerated, more esteemed, and more powerful echelons of a modern division of labour), the university is also, by the same process, less independent of government and the pressures of industry.

Scott is less sanguine, more sophisticated, and much more forward-looking than was Moberly. He looks for a moral outlook in secular institutions, and the search leads him to a perspicacious discussion of the nature and organization of intellectual enquiry and its disciplines, the differences and similarities of 'cultural' and 'scientific' definitions of knowledge, and the social ethics of access to higher education. If he does not find any simple solution to the threat of academicism and instrumentalism or any guarantee for the preservation of 'cognitive rationality' and social justice in the future organization of higher education, at least he places these problems coherently and practically into the context of contemporary debate. His cautious canvassing of the strategy of a post-binary policy for higher education (including the universities, and designed to balance the need for diversity, efficiency, accountability, and freedom) makes up a short but lucid chapter which deserves and facilitates wide consideration.

Scott's advance on Moberly can also be described by reference to the four basic ideas of the university formed out of the élitist and expansionist teaching and research orientations that we have discussed. Moberly's imagination was confined to two conceptions—those of the élitist teacher and the élitist researcher. Scott's horizons are broader. They encompass the expansionist-teacher and the expansionist-researcher, and accordingly he addresses himself to the whole range of educational institutions beyond school. He wrestles with the problem of finding a place for all four views concerning the development and transmission of knowledge in an integrated system of higher education in Britain. The outcome is his post-binary policy.

For these reasons Scott's contribution is likely to 'stay in the literature' and inform future debate, whereas Moberly's book was but briefly remarked and quickly forgotten. And yet their common 'crisis' remains. A misnomer, perhaps, for a chronic peril, it may never be finally resolvable. For intellectual life, however serviceable to material production or civilized consumption, will always demand its freedoms and its privileges and must therefore remain vulnerable to suspicion from the populace and the powers.

Note

1 The story is well told in John Sparrow's Clark lectures at Cambridge in 1965 (Sparrow 1967) and in V. H. H. Green's *Oxford Common Room*, (1957) which comprises a convincing account of Pattison's college, Lincoln.

References

BLOOM, A. D. (1987), *The Closing of the American Mind: How Higher Education Has Failed Democracy and Impoverished the Souls of Today's Students*, (New York).

Carnegie Council (1980), *Three Thousand Futures: The Next Twenty Years for Higher Education* (San Francisco).

FABER, G. (1957), *Jowett: A Portrait with Background* (London).

FLEXNER, A. (1930), *Universities: American, English, German* (New York).

GERTH, H., and MILLS, C. W. (1947), *Essays from Max Weber* (London).

GREEN, V. H. H. (1957), *Oxford Common Room* (London).

KOTSCHNIG, W. M., and PRYS, E. (eds.) (1932), *The University in a Changing World* (London).

LEAVIS, F. R. (1943), *Education and the University: A Sketch for an 'English School'* (London).

LÔWE, A. (1941), *The Universities in Transformation* (London).

MANSBRIDGE, A. (1923), *The Older Universities of England*, (London).

MARSHALL, A. (1872), 'The Future of the Working Classes', in A. C. Pigou, (ed.), *Memorials of Alfred Marshall* (London 1925).

MOBERLY, W. (1949), *The Crisis of the University* (London).

NEWMAN, J. H. (1959), *The Idea of a University* (London, 1853–73; Image Books edn.).

NISBET, R. (1972), *The Degradation of the Academic Dogma* (London).

ROTHBLATT, S. (1968), *The Revolution of the Dons* (London).

SCOTT, P. (1984), *The Crisis of the University* (London).

SPARROW, J. (1967), *Mark Pattison and the Idea of a University* (Cambridge).

TRUSCOT, B. (1945), *Redbrick University* (London, 1943; Pelican edn.).

VEBLEN, T. (1918), *The Higher Learning in America* (New York).

WHEWELL, W. (1837), *On the Principles of English University Education* (London).

50

PRESSURES AND SILENCES

Harold Silver

Source: H. Silver, *Higher Education and Opinion Making in Twentieth Century England*, London: Woburn Press, 2002, pp. 252–65.

Adaptation

The voices we heard at the beginning of the twentieth century, such as those of Haldane and Webb, considered existing university provision and called for more. By the time of Flexner's intervention in 1930 it was already important to explore and evaluate the different types of university, and the trends. In their separate ways, during and after the Second World War, Truscot and Moberly examined what was wrong in the operation of the university and its failure to position itself amid cyclonic social and international changes. Ashby took Moberly's understanding of the problem further, located the failure in the history of science and technology and confronted the relationship between tradition and adaptation. Robbins and Crosland widened further the understanding of 'higher education' and moved the state into a stronger position to influence and to co-ordinate. Governments increasingly determined directions, planned targets, related higher education to social and economic imperatives. The voices of higher education became concerned largely with response and the short-term. Change in the late-century included the national and institutional machineries for control of and quality in the system, and Dearing raised higher the already growing profile of student learning and the improvement of teaching. The story of twentieth-century higher education therefore includes policies and buildings, students and funds, the organization of the national system and of the curriculum, new institutions and the development of old ones, the community and the Internet, the book and the journal, the conference and the professional network, the parliamentary and the private debate, perplexity and protest, values and purpose, advocates and opinion.

The main focus has been the process of making and transforming a system of higher education, together with attempts to interpret it in massive contextual changes. Moberly most determinedly cleared a way into the territory and Ashby most directly penetrated it. The book that most clearly portrayed its contours in the late century was Ashby's 1974 *Adapting Universities to a Technological Society*, some of the argument having been inaugurated in *Technology and the Academics* and elsewhere. In the later work, considering the nature of a 'mass higher education', he looked carefully at the contemporary features of higher education systems and institutions internationally and placed them, as he had always done, in a conceptual framework derived in large part from biology. There is one passage which serves as an invaluable text for the discussion here:

> It is characteristic of higher education systems that they are strongly influenced by tradition. They display what a biologist calls phylogenetic inertia. This is not surprising, for one of their functions is to conserve and transmit the cultural inheritance. It is characteristic of them, too, that from time to time they adjust themselves – sometimes painfully – to the social environment which surrounds them . . . There are, therefore, internal and external forces acting on higher education systems and when all is well there is an unstable equilibrium between these forces. At present there is a worldwide instability in higher education systems, and these systems are shifting, one hopes toward fresh equilibria which will be different for different societies. But while the movement is going on there are strains and anxieties; none of us know where the new equilibrium will lie. That is why it is disappointing that so much emphasis, by governments, by the press, and indeed within the systems themselves, is on how to expand, how to pay for expansion, and not on how to change.[1]

A good deal of this history has been about the painful 'strains and anxieties' of the changing equilibrium resulting from competing forces. At different times we have witnessed the unstable equilibrium under scrutiny, not necessarily in such a vocabulary, and by advocates who would not have known what 'equilibrium' could be achieved.

The changes of the earlier decades in the scale and variety of university education involved controversy, aspiration and sometimes disappointment. The variety, as Ashby pointed out in 1967, was in part a protest against the exclusiveness of Oxford and Cambridge, but 'by a process of social mimicry' the new institutions acquired some of the prevailing assumptions and characteristics of higher education.[2] In later decades against the backdrop of world war and cold war, social and economic tensions and rapid technological change, the strains became more acute and the universities and their advocates sounded more lost. From the 1970s particularly, critics pointed to the failures of higher education. Niblett declared in 1974 that 'universities are far from realising the extent of the change of outlook that is required of them: changes of assumption, changes of orientation, changes in the content of what they teach'. The expansionist pressures on universities had not yet 'caused them to think in any fundamental way about their new function in society'.[3] Lord Annan, the following year, as we have noted, thought it foolish not to realize 'that if a nation moves from small-scale to mass higher education, it must expect the customs, ideals, organisation and behaviour of its universities and other institutions to change'.[4] Others in these final decades, but also earlier, looked to forms of adaptation, perhaps involving, in Barnett's initial formulations, 'resurrection' or undermined values 'regained'. The book titles underlined conceptions of the processes at work. For Löwe in 1940 it was a case of 'universities in transformation', for Dent in 1961 they were 'in transition', as they were five years later for James Perkins, President of Cornell University. During the 1960s period of American student protest the books told of 'the troubled campus', or the university 'in turmoil' and in the following decades authors wrote of American higher education 'in decline' or the university 'in ruins'.[5] Although Moberly's 1949 *The Crisis in the University* continued to have echoes in some parts of the British literature, the titles were on the whole more measured, reflecting specific aspects of experience and change rather than deeper anxieties or an overall scenario.

Slowly, and under pressure, higher education had to change. In the final decades of the century it did so either by government behest or in anticipation of the consequences of inertia. For some institutions the effort was greater and more traumatic than for others. Although the responses of higher education in different countries were to historically different environments of social, economic, technological or other change, the voices articulating the needs were remarkably similar. Perkins talked in 1966 of the immensely complex task of 'university direction, stability, and growth'. It had to achieve 'not only an internal harmony, but a harmony that is in a state of constant adaptation to the outside world'.[6] Gavin Brown, the new Vice-Chancellor of the University of Sydney, Australia, argued in 1996 that:

> it is only by constant re-appraisal and re-invention that universities can survive to flourish. Moreover, we are driving a vintage model largely designed in late 19th century Germany, with some modifications incorporating the Arcadian vision of Cardinal Newman and more recent body-styling and trim adapted to a down-market reinterpretation of the words 'research' and 'culture'.[7]

The language of change was relatively constant from the Moot to Ashby, from Cornell to Sydney, though the language did not always mean the same thing, and circumstances, emphases and directions differed. Systems of higher education worldwide, and the English system in particular, had spent the late twentieth century in Ashby's 'unstable equilibrium'. In spite of political and ideological certainties, what 'fresh equilibrium' lay ahead at the end of the century – none of us knew.

Which voices?

The advocates of higher education chosen for this discussion were not necessarily 'representative' voices. In some cases they were the only ones speaking aloud – especially in the earlier decades. In others they seemed to be of two kinds, either aiming to encapsulate what was known or needed to be known, or confirming deficiencies and postulating futures. Not surprisingly, the most vocal advocates of system building, the vice-chancellors or the writers of influential tracts or books have been male, since for most of the century women did not have access to the positions of power and influence. From the end of the nineteenth century they did have positions as heads of women's colleges on the margins of Oxford and Cambridge, and as heads of teacher training colleges well beyond the margins of the university system until the second half of the twentieth century. One of the difficulties in the story has been the way threads of public attention have come and gone – including the education of women, advanced technological education, adult education and quality. Others, of course, have been permanently at the surface or not far from it – state funding, privilege, size, student numbers, autonomy. The most important voices for this story have therefore been those that spoke of the present and sketched a future, whether these were individuals, journals or committees. This was the case with the increasingly dominant voice of government, minister, commission or agency.

The advocates we have heard fall into categories. Some came from outside the system – Haldane, Webb, Simon, for example – though these were often participants at the level of university court or government committee. Others were senior insiders, vice-chancellors or others (Moberly, Livingstone, Ashby), who may or may not have continued to participate in teaching or activities other than administration or institutional leadership. Others might be described as 'cross-overs' (Robbins, Crosland, Joseph) who left or temporarily stood outside the academic system and led a committee or a government department. The members of the two rough, basic categories and the occasional cross-overs frequently, of course, strayed into one another's company or behaved untypically. Only at the end of the twentieth century did a third category emerge, one that had a clear public voice – though in different locations and exerting a different kind of influence. They appeared in the story mainly in the last quarter of the century. They were practitioners, trying to understand, implement and adapt pressures for change and opportunities available, the practicalities, potential and limitations of teaching strategies and the ways in which students learn. They wrote articles and books and were consulted about programmes and possibilities, not

362

about purposes and futures. They were course and project leaders, active in their own and others' professional development, researchers, and above all teachers concerned about students and the impact on them and on themselves of policies and funding decisions. They grappled with skills, outcomes, types of assessment, modules, interactive technologies, group projects and other approaches to student learning. The first two categories of 'senior advocates' were heard through the variety of forums and media that we have discussed. This third category tended to speak to one another, in workshops and conferences about teaching strategies and curriculum change, the assessment of prior learning, modular courses – the minutiae of the management of change. Their journal articles, books in series targeted at higher education teachers, conference papers, Internet and intranet papers and materials or reports on their own pedagogical research, represented a changing map of the present. The map reflected what was happening, what was wrong and what was possible, how things worked and might work, and with what ends. The map was constructed of elements generated inside and outside institutions, but elements that became the focus of a new pattern of professional relationships. Not all teachers, of course, took part, but the public voices added to the variety of experience and opinion available in higher education. The other two categories of advocate knew about the *intentions* of changes to the map, but from their distance were aware about the actual changes (when they were aware of them) through the survey, the research, evaluation or other commissioned report. Reports reached steering groups or limited audiences in funding or other bodies, but were mostly forgotten by national organizations or commissions or government departments when the next intentions were formulated.

Since the outcomes of these descriptions and analyses of experience appeared in the professional conference and in publications with defined professional audiences, they reflected the move towards an emphasis on learning and teaching that the Dearing committee confirmed. It would be possible to interpret the history of twentieth-century higher education in terms of teachers' practices, student learning behaviours (including those influenced by gender, class and minority differences), lecture and seminar effectiveness, examination and assessment models – that is, 'internalist' features. Our focus here has been essentially on the phases of growth and change of a higher education 'system' and on attempts to define and amend its purposes. The nature of 'practice' and 'experience' is an essential part of the total landscape of higher education, but to situate it adequately in the story of the relationship between higher education, the state and opinion would also mean considerably extending the story and the discussion to include these and other contingent elements.

One such element is the persistence in all aspects of higher education of the combat between processes of change and attitudes of inertia or conservatism. This was a combat that Flexner found in the emergent system (including some changes that he felt, both in the United States and in Britain, to be profoundly wrong), and which Ashby detected at Belfast and in his later writings as associated with faculty frontiers and professorial oligarchies. It was a combat that Truscot portrayed vividly in *Redbrick* and in the confrontation between old and new in his cameo of 'A redbrick tea-party'. Much of the higher-education literature of the late twentieth century reflected this combat internationally. One image was an American one in 1968: 'the university has been – with the possible exception of the post office – the least inventive (or even adaptive) of our social institutions since the end of World War II'.[8] There is nothing exclusively American about such judgements on university systems, or about the difficulties of organizational change in universities. In the book where this judgement was quoted the possible sources of change were preceded by a list of such difficulties:

> Organizations are inherently passive ... consist of patterns of repetitive and continuing interaction patterns of coordinated and ordered behavior ... organizations are hierarchical ... Organizational activities and procedures tend over time to assume a sacred quality ... these practices – whether they be lecturing or rain dancing – may come to be ritualistically continued without an evaluation of their effectiveness ... most organizations experience some difficulty in adapting to new conditions. Academic institutions, however, appear to have particular problems in addition because of their own distinctive characteristics: their purposes and support are basically conservative ... academic institutions are deliberately structured to resist precipitant change.[9]

There were, of course, commentators who would not have seen most of these as criticisms, but they are footnotes to many of the difficulties perceived at times in the English system. The failure of higher education to recognize the kinds of change to which it needed to respond was the burden of much of the argument we have considered. This provided a 'surface' motive for some of the 1980s and later political intervention in higher education – 'surface' because of the co-existence of deeper political motivation.

None of this suggests that higher education institutions are always incapable of self-directed change. 'Higher education' has been the home of immense variety, including variety of attitude and initiative. The suggestion is that to locate the voices of professional practice in the discussion, it would be necessary to disentangle attitudes to structural, curricular and other aspects of the institutions. It would also be necessary to pursue further the issues surrounding individual, professional initiative and innovation, and the times and conditions in which it has been more or less possible for these to override the 'passive', 'hierarchical' or 'ritualistic' environments in which teaching and other professional activities take place. While it is important to view these aspects of a system, the institutions and their inhabitants in their complexity, it is also useful to be reminded that some of the foundations on which these rest can to a considerable extent be national and international, and the voices that have to be heard speak within institutions and systems, and across national frontiers.

Opinion

In considering advocates and voices it has never been possible accurately to gauge audiences. Who read the book, how interested or responsive the conference was, how widely the messages of the Moot or the Christian Frontier Conference were carried into other circles, what response there was to a leaflet or a speech in Manchester or Bristol or Hull . . . these are other things 'none of us know'. Counting a magazine's or a newspaper's circulation helps little or not at all, and the relationship between advocacy and the laying of the first brick or the appointment of the first professor is a matter for great conjecture. Occasionally there is light. The persistence of local politicians and the Workers Educational Association, the strong support of A.D. Lindsay, Lindsay's friendship with Moberly and the eventual support of the UGC for the creation of what became a University College and then Keele University are clear. So are the Simon campaign for a national review of higher education, his presentation in the House of Lords, responses in the debate and in the press, the views of particular Conservative ministers, the adoption of policies by the Labour Party in opposition, and the establishment of the Robbins committee. Most of the time in this story, however, the focus has had to be on the wishes and intentions of protagonists and what their views and actions reflected, in parallel with demonstrable developments in the emergent and actual system. 'Opinion' cannot be reliably judged in relation to what has been written or proclaimed; nor can the general response and influence of wide constituencies.

Many of the commentators that we have discussed attempted to capture in a sketch or a more detailed portrait the state of public attitudes towards the universities or higher education at different times. Deller, for example, in his 1933 lecture on *Tendencies in Higher Education*, thought that universities were 'increasing in public esteem and respect', though not necessarily praised for what was 'truly praiseworthy'. Praise was accompanied by criticism, and it was said, for example, and 'perhaps not without some justification, that the English universities are too complacent . . . They are accused of being oblivious of the change in the spirit of the age . . . They are remote, unfriendly, melancholy, slow.' Critics from outside, he suggested, do not always know of 'the constant criticism which begins at home, of the continuous process at Boards and Councils and Senates of examination and discussion and debate'.[10] That was a mixed a message about public esteem, and clearer ones only really began to appear in the upsurge of popular interest in education after the Second World War, and particularly in the period leading up to and following the Robbins report. In 1961 Sir Charles Morris reflected that 'for a good many years now the universities have enjoyed a very good press; and public and professional opinion have been hardly less favourable'. Surprising though this was to the hard-pressed universities, 'on balance this period of indulgence and sympathetic friendliness by the public has been a good thing for the universities'.[11] Such press-watching and sensitivity to public mood offer no systematic analysis, but commentary on public opinion and the reputation of higher education was rarely able to do more. In 1963, after the publication of the report, Robbins told a Home Universities Conference that he spoke 'as one who tries to listen in to what is being said in different quarters about universities (particularly now that this subject has become the centre of conversation)'. He identified what he called an 'animus against universities – do not deceive yourselves: there is an animus', that was a result of the complicated ('"unduly complicated", as the outside world sees it') nature of universities' entrance requirements.[12] On this and on other higher education topics, Robbins and his colleagues on the committee had received over 150 memoranda of evidence from organizations and nearly 200 from individuals, and they had interviewed at some length 120 or so individuals and groups of organizational representatives. Most of these were from education or fields closely related to it, but many were from the professions and industry, religious and political organizations. The fact that Robbins had listened to what was being said was no doubt an understatement, but the fact that universities (he was addressing a university conference) had become 'the centre of conversation' was not.

Looking back over the couple of years following the Robbins report, the Vice-Chancellor of the University of Leicester thought that 'in a few months the honeymoon was over', building grants had been cut and a crisis of confidence existed in the universities, partly as a result of 'the ineptitude of the U.G.C.'. The universities were 'getting a bad press', with achievements overlooked and the universities' problems far too complicated for writers about them to understand.[13] The position from this point on was one of what Shils in 1975 called 'public ambivalence' – the universities esteemed for their practical value or ideals, but condemned as elitist or for the behaviour of their students – though there was also some support for students' criticisms of their institutions. Opinion outside the universities was 'complicated and heterogeneous'.[14] The Vice-Chancellor of the University of Durham described the Robbins report as a 'watershed . . . It marked the arrival of an altogether new level of public interest in the universities.'[15] Public interest, however, can be indicative of support, hostility or both in a continuing 'ambivalence'. In fact, from the mid-1960s the reputation of the universities undoubtedly declined. Their 'monastic seclusion' or 'ivory tower' mentality was under attack from government and media, student militancy was pilloried, academics were criticized for joining the 'brain drain' to the United States or taking part in 'unprofessional' strikes and other action.[16] Mistrust and uncertainty (in some quarters including, from the early 1970s, about the status and effectiveness of the polytechnics) went together with other sentiments generated by increased student access and wider family experience of higher education. It is not easy to generalize about public 'opinion' or 'interest' in the complex relationships of higher education with a wide variety of constituencies, but that there had been a considerable change for many people with regard to many issues is evident across these later decades. Sir Frederick Dainton commented in 1981 on a decline in 'public esteem', which universities needed to reclaim: 'there is some public disillusionment with higher education itself', because it did not meet public expectations and did not increase the country's prosperity.[17] A writer in *The Economist* in 1994 assailed what he called 'Towers of babble' (not only in Britain). Universities that 30 years before had been 'arguably the most pampered institutions on earth' and had been seen by Robbins as part of a symbiotic relationship with the economy, enabling both to grow:

> This mood has vanished. Universities are on the defensive everywhere, distrusted by governments, worried about losing income and influence . . . in Britain, the government treats higher education like an inefficient nationalised industry . . . Nothing less than a populist backlash against academia appears to be under way . . . Two complaints are especially prominent: that universities have been hijacked by 1960s radicals, more intent on pandering to minorities than advancing knowledge, and that academics rarely give value for money.[18]

What this picture (and the cartoon of 'Ivory Tower University' accompanying it) represented was one important element in the changed balance of ambivalent attitudes, particularly at the level of government opinion and policy. The 'populist' backlash, however, can easily be misinterpreted as a 'popular' one.

Important in all of this is the distinction between 'opinion' and 'audience'. These fragments of insight into popular or political opinion suggest little or nothing about the relationship between advocate and audience. The 'publics' to whom they addressed their plans or visions were of the many kinds indicated by the medium of their messages – the 'gentlemanly' magazine or the professional conference, book or parliament. Their audiences were potential sponsors, pressure and interest groups, the intellectual elite, academics, university-related constituencies (Court, Council and so forth), the 'public', the interested citizen. The institutions themselves and their collective presence were therefore both audience and advocate, listening and responding, defending, appealing or reaching out. The CVCP and the

CDP, the AUT and to some extent the UGC at various times, spoke for the system and were addressed by Moberly or Simon or the *Universities Quarterly*. The collective presence was always subject to disruption. Truscot spoke from within for the redbrick universities but bluntly attacked important features of them. The replacement of the UGC by new funding arrangements completely changed the pattern of who could speak for the universities. Advocate, audience and system were instruments for shaping opinion, but they were also part of it and its outcomes.

Equilibria

For whom did this whole complex system and set of interactions operate? Four constituencies have presented themselves clearly at different times. First, the institutions of higher education and what developed across the century into a system. The universities and new entrants to the definition of 'higher education' combined their own aims, needs and aspirations with aspects of higher education traditions, and the organizing and representative bodies of the system defended, articulated and promoted its operations and requirements. Second, the state. At the beginning of the century, and particularly from 1919, the state was involved in the financing of the universities and the fledgling university colleges, and from the 'climacteric' of the mid-1940s was a majority paymaster. It was engaged from the early 1960s in extending its co-ordinating role and thereafter in directly influencing and shaping the system, its direction and its values. Third, the participating individuals – students, teaching and support staff, and to a lesser extent external members of university governing bodies. Students and teaching staff were both, particularly in the second half of the century, in the ambiguous position of being independent of the state at the same time as receiving state support (in the case of students) or state-funded salaries. Both operated in environments (buildings, libraries, research and teaching resources) dependent on state funding. Higher education, as many of the voices we have heard have reminded us, existed primarily for the students, though as some others argued, primarily for the purposes of advancing knowledge. Whether as teachers or researchers, however, the system of higher education and its funding mechanisms served them. Fourth, the wider society – employers, the professions, parents, the media, social organizations and processes requiring research and development outcomes, or inputs to community activity. Some of the outside constituencies became increasingly present within the institutions themselves in the later century – not only through governing bodies, but also as members of committees, advisers, involved in projects, supporting sandwich courses and work-based learning. Professional body accreditation and preparation for employment were more part of the polytechnic tradition, but as new curricula developed in the older universities and national pressures for attention to the employment market increased, institutions generally sharpened their employment-directed mission. No one constituency held a monopoly of the answer to the question 'who is higher education for?' though the balance of interpretation changed – most prominently as national economic and ideological considerations came to dictate policies more explicitly, especially from the mid-1980s. Nor was any one of these four constituencies self-contained. Employment affected all of them. Research and scholarship were not a matter solely for staff. Funding and resources were of general concern. Reputation and esteem were the product of interactions amongst them all.

'Who is higher education for?' was replaced as a priority question when the Research Assessment Exercise (RAE) was born in 1986. A focus in higher education, in both sectors, had already been established on issues of quality (often translated into 'excellence', or lack of it) but the RAE was new in offering all the constituencies data on which opinion could be shaped and funding could be allocated. In 1986 and 1989 the RAE was conducted by the UGC and then by its replacement, the UFC, and it therefore covered only the 'old' universities. HEFCE, acting on behalf of all the funding councils, took over the exercise from 1992, therefore also including the 'new' universities and colleges of higher education. The same policy enthusiasm for comparative data and league tables that had penetrated the schools and was to extend to other public bodies had now begun to penetrate the universities. Ashby's 'equilibrium' was being transformed not only between institutions and between them and the funding bodies as state agencies, but also among subjects, within institutions as well as nationally. The outcomes of the RAE and TQA assessments were in fact not just 'data'. They served as impressions, hunches and guidance for parents, students present and potential, schools and employers, as well as academics and institutions in relation to one another. Hierarchies were being reinforced. The long-established but often re-balanced relationships amongst the constituencies were undergoing a different level of transformation.

What we have encountered in the story of these relationships has been a sequence of warnings given about the equilibria at different times:

- There were boundary lines not to be overstepped, mainly regarding the boundaries of state responsibility and intervention (most commentators until the boundaries were removed altogether in the mid-1980s).
- Autonomy was important but not without its own boundaries (for example, Moberly).
- Universities policy and decision making were not just for the professoriate (Truscot and Ashby).
- Universities should not live within frontiers, and should relate to the community in a variety of ways (Haldane, Lindsay, Truscot).
- It was wrong not to address higher technological education, but it was wrong for technology not to be seen as humanist (Ashby).

- The curriculum was not inviolate (Ashby, Robbins).
- There were aspects of the curriculum that had to be safeguarded (Flexner, Livingstone).
- Hierarchy and privilege were unacceptable (Truscot, Simon).
- The system was incomplete (all commentators from Webb and Haldane to Robbins and Crosland).

In stages, the system was steered towards greater spread, scale and complexity. It became a 'good' not for an 'elite' but for a 'mass'. A mass higher education, like higher education itself over the whole century, was also 'for whom?' It was for the population at large – for families, students, the wider society, for lifelong learning, all of which raised questions of access and inequalities. However, it was also for the economy, the professions, jobs, the institutions themselves – not all of the last with unmitigated enthusiasm. A mass higher education was also increasingly 'globalized', notably crossing frontiers electronically and in other ways.

An absence of voices

The kinds of voices that interpreted equilibria and advocated change in the first three-quarters of the twentieth century were absent in the final decades. The silence obviously has to be related to the dominance of the state and confusion in the system, but those references and judgements must not be oversimplified. External pressure is not necessarily to be criticized. At times in the century such pressure was necessary if new institutions were to be created and existing ones to be modified and reformed. The state and higher education's external communities had legitimate concerns about access, institutional direction, effectiveness or outcomes. Institutions and academics are not necessarily conservative or inert, and the abandonment of all aspects of tradition is not a necessary condition even for the most basic forms of adaptation. Perhaps what the century most clearly demonstrates is therefore the possibility of change when there is not just an 'unstable equilibrium' but also a purposeful dialogue about reaching beyond it. The danger is not in pressure but in *unremitting* pressure and beleaguered institutions and individuals. The beleaguered may reform, but they may also remain unrepentantly conservative. From the early 1960s, and most particularly from the mid-1980s, higher education became an instrument to be used explicitly for national economic regeneration, and pressure therefore became unceasing and as fluctuating and unpredictable as economic policy itself. Beleaguerment related to the constant pressure of requirements for expansion, skills, new types of degrees or the kaleidoscopes of market orientation and accountability. The argument is not that these were *wrong*, it is simply that they were frequent, incessant and paralyzing. The conditions of higher education (not only in England and the United Kingdom) in the late twentieth century

– and at the beginning of the twenty-first – were not conducive to the forms of dialogue and advocacy that were central to higher education in the earlier twentieth century.

If individual, institutional, community, state and international interactions are capable of producing creative, unstable equilibria, it is clear at the beginning of the twenty-first century that the growing inequalities amongst the partners have led to what can only be described as an uncreative stable *dis*equilibrium. In these conditions it is difficult within the institutions and the higher education system to see the possibility of influential advocacy or opinion making. The voice, the potential opinion maker, is silent when dominant partners and their publics will not be listening. Decade by decade until the late twentieth century higher education found its advocates, its representatives, its voices (not only its Cassandras and specialists in trench warfare). What became less available to it in the often intrusive, unfamiliar circumstances of the last decades were voices offering messages of new equilibria, of practical vision. Such voices did not appear, to interpret the present as practitioners knew it, to examine the state and its crumbling mansions, to help to create a different kind of ferment, and to persuade – as Ashby and others had done – that there were possibilities of redesign and a new equilibrium.

Notes and references

1 Ashby, E., *Adapting Universities to a Technological Society* (San Francisco, CA: Jossey-Bass, 1974), p. 136.
2 Ashby, E., 'The future of the nineteenth century idea of a university', *Minerva*, vol. 6, 1967, p. 5.
3 Niblett, W. R., *Universities Between Two Worlds* (London: University of London Press, 1974), p. 2.
4 Annan, N., 'The university in Britain', in Stephens, M. D. and Roderick, G. W., *Universities for a Changing World: The Role of the University in the Late Twentieth Century* (London: David & Charles, 1975), p. 25.
5 Löwe, A., *The Universities in Transformation* (London: SCM Press, 1940); Dent, H. C., *Universities in Transition* (London: Cohen & West, 1961); Perkins, J. A., *The University in Transition* (Princeton, NJ: Princeton University Press, 1966); Atlantic *Monthly, The Troubled Campus* (Boston: LittleBrown, 1965); Wallenstein, I., *University in Turmoil: The Politics of Change* (New York: Atheneum, 1969); Ashworth, K. H., *American Higher Education in Decline* (College Station, TX: Texas A&M University Press, 1979); Readings, B., *The University in Ruins* (Cambridge, MA: Harvard University Press, 1996).
6 Perkins, *The University in Transition*, p. 59.
7 Brown, G., 'The University – Past, Present and Future Organisation Structure' (Inaugural address, September 1966), typescript, p. 1. (Cf.www.usyd.edu.au/about/vcinaug.shtml).
8 Kristol, I., 'A different way to restructure the university' (1968), quoted in Hefferlin, Lon, J. B., *Dynamics of Academic Reform* (San Francisco: Jossey-Bass, 1969), p. 6.
9 Hefferling, ibid., pp. 10–15.

10 Deller, E., *Tendencies in University Education* (London: Oxford University Press, 1933), pp. 16–17.

11 Morris, C., 'Some reflections on the conference', *Universities Quarterly*, vol. 15, 1961, p. 189.

12 Lord Robbins, 'Universities and the future pattern of higher education', *Home Universities Conference Proceedings 1963* (London: Association of Universities of the British Commonwealth) pp. 21–2.

13 Noble, T. A. F., in a symposium on 'Who killed Cock Robbins?', *Twentieth Century*, vol. 174, 1966, pp. 47–8.

14 Shils, E., 'The academic ethos under strain', in Seabury, P. (ed.), *Universities in the Western World* (New York: Free Press, 1975), p. 32.

15 Christopherson, D., *The University at Work* (London: SCM Press, 1973), p. 5.

16 Cf. Silver, H., 'From great expectations to bleak house', *Higher Education Quarterly*, vol. 41, 1987, pp. 207–24.

17 Dainton, F., *British Universities: Purposes, Problems and Pressures* (Cambridge: Cambridge University Press, 1981), p. 11.

18 Wooldridge, A., 'Towers of babble', *The Economist*, 25 December 1993–7 January 1994, p. 54.